Modula-2 Programming

Second Edition

B.J.Holmes BSc, MSc, MBCS, Cert Ed.

Principal Lecturer in the School of Computing and Mathematical Sciences,
Oxford Brookes University, Headington, Oxford, OX3 0BP

DP Publications Ltd
Aldine Place, 142/144 Uxbridge Road,
Shepherds Bush Green, London W12 8AW
1994

Acknowledgement

I would like to express my thanks to David Lightfoot in the School of Computing and Mathematical Sciences at Oxford Brookes University and two of the co-authors of the *Draft Standard* - Roger Henry and Mark Woodman, for their advice about the *Draft Standard* for Modula-2. In addition I would like to thank the BSI Standards and the International Standards Organisation for granting me permission to use material from the *Draft Standard*.

Disclaimer

The programs presented in this book have been included for their instructional value. They have been computer-tested with considerable care and are not guaranteed for any particular purpose. The author does not offer any warranties or representations, nor does he accept any liabilities with respect to the programs.

A CIP catalogue record for this book is available from the British Library

First Edition 1989
Second Edition 1994

ISBN 1 85805 081 2

Typeset and illustrated by B.J.Holmes

Printed by The Guernsey Press Company Ltd, Braye Road, Vale, Guernsey, Channel Islands.

Contents

Preface

Audience

This text book should be regarded as essential reading for any student who is studying Computer Studies in either Higher or Further Education, and wants to be fully appraised of the techniques for writing and developing computer programs in a high-level language.

The text may also be used as a suitable conversion course to Modula-2, for those readers who can already program in other high-level languages.

The book is equally suitable as a course text or as a self-instruction text.

Modula-2, designed by Professor Niklaus Wirth, is a successor to Pascal. The language combines many of the features found in Pascal, with additional features for writing large-scale programs and for systems programming. Modula-2 is a general purpose language, that is easy to learn, and can be used over a wide range of applications.

Within a single book there is enough information to provide a foundation for any reader who wishes to develop and implement a wide variety of software systems.

Format

No previous knowledge of computer programming or computer concepts are assumed.

The material is computer-tested and classroom-tested to guarantee its reliability and use as a teaching text.

In addition to an exposition of the Modula-2 language, the text contains a comprehensive appraisal of many important topics found in data structures - arrays, records, linked lists, trees, queues and stacks; in data processing - sorting, searching, merging, report writing and data validation; and in programming - recursion, modularity, data abstraction and concurrency.

The emphasis throughout the book is on the use of carefully chosen examples that highlight the features of the language being studied. Explanation about the language follows from, and is put into context with, the example programs.

The development of the language statements and the programs are taken in manageable steps, to enable the reader to build a firm foundation of knowledge. The type of programming examples used are simple enough to give the reader confidence at each stage of learning to program in Modula-2.

A section on programming questions is found at the end of each chapter. These questions serve to test the reader's understanding of the topics, and reinforce the material of the chapter. The reader is advised to complete the answers to the questions before progressing to the next chapter. The answers to all the questions are given in Appendix I.

Language and computer requirements

Studying Modula-2 can be more effective and enjoyable if a computer is used for running both the demonstration programs and the reader's own answers to the programming questions.

All the programs have been developed and tested on an IBM PC compatible microcomputer under MSDOS.

The author has used *TopSpeed* Modula-2 version 3.0 available from Clarion Software (Europe) Ltd in the preparation of all the programs listed in this book. However, all the programs in the text can also be run using the earlier versions from 1.12 onwards.

In addition to the libraries supplied with *TopSpeed* Modula-2, the author has used a subset of the libraries based on those defined in the *Draft Standard: CD 10514* for Modula-2, published in December 1992. To provide a compatibility between these libraries and *TopSpeed* Modula-2 it was necessary to introduce a new set of library modules that are listed in appendices III and IV and are also supplied in the Lecturers' Supplement.

Notes on the Second Edition

The contents of the new edition has been completely re-ordered. Most of the chapters have been re-written, and in many cases new material has been introduced. Chapters 1 to 8, provide the reader with a gradual introduction to the fundamentals of programming. Chapters 9 to 13 introduce data structures and data processing techniques. Finally chapters 14 to 16 explain programming techniques for data abstraction and concurrent programming.

Lecturers' Supplement

A disk containing all the demonstration programs and answers to programming questions, is available free of charge, from DP Publications Ltd, to lecturers adopting the book as a course text.

BJH - Oxford June 1994

IMPORTANT NOTICE

To run the programs listed in this book you will need to have access to either version 3.0 or an earlier version of TopSpeed Modula-2. This can be purchased from Clarion Software(Europe) Ltd - see address below.

In addition you will need to install the modules that are listed in appendices III and IV. These modules are also available on the lecturers' supplement disk.

For further information about TopSpeed Modula-2 contact:

Clarion Software (Europe) Ltd.
Clare House,
Thompsons Close,
Harpenden,
Herts AL5 4ES

Tel: 0582 763200
Fax: 0582 768222

WARNING!

The *Information technology - Programming languages - Modula-2, 2nd Committee Draft Standard: CD 10514 December 1992 - document ISO/IEC JTC1/SC22/WG13 D181* is, at the time of going to print (June 1994), at the committee draft stage and, therefore, is in its first phase of development.

BSI Standards

Chapter 1
Programming Environment

The purpose of this chapter is to provide the reader with enough background information to be able to understand a computing environment in which to work as a programmer. An introduction is given to the hardware and software that make up a typical computer system which may be used for the development of computer programs written in Modula-2. By the end of the chapter the reader should have an understanding of the following topics.

- ☐ The stages involved in writing a computer program.

- ☐ The purpose of a computer program and its relationship to data and results.

- ☐ The hardware units that make up a computer system.

- ☐ The different levels of computer languages.

- ☐ The need to translate languages into a form that the computer can recognise.

- ☐ The necessary stages in the implementation of a computer program.

1.1 What is programming?

Before a computer can be programmed to solve a problem, it is necessary for the programmer to first understand how to solve the problem. This solution is known as an algorithm, and programming is the technique of designing an algorithm then coding the algorithm, using a suitable computer language, into a corresponding computer program. However, this is not the whole story. At the stages of design and after coding the program, it is necessary to test the solution to the problem and verify that it does indeed function correctly. A computer program is not usually static. Over a period of time it may be changed, and indeed evolve as the computer project to which it contributes also evolves. For this reason programming must also involve documenting the purpose of the program, the method of solution, the stages of testing that it has undergone, and other necessary facts. Programming, therefore, contains the activities of designing an algorithm, coding a program from the algorithm, and testing and documenting the program, as illustrated in figure 1.1.

Design and test an algorithm as a solution to a problem

Code the algorithm into a computer program using the appropriate language

Test the computer program to prove that it solves the problem

Document the computer program so that it can be maintained by others at a later time

figure 1.1 development of a computer program

The methods used in programming will vary between organisations. The production of the algorithm can take several forms, however, the use of diagrams such as flowcharts, structure charts and even textual descriptions of a solution are most common. An algorithm is converted into a computer program by either hand-coding the solution into statements from the programming language being used, or with the aid of a program generator. Program generators take the design in pseudo-diagrammatic/ textual form and convert it into a computer program. The advantage of this technique is that it saves time in coding a program, and the design and program always match.

Programs can be tested, by either the programmer tracing through the program, or by peer-group inspection. The latter technique involves a small group of staff in reviewing the accuracy of a program and whether it meets the original specification. Further testing, using suitable test data, is always carried out with the program being run on a computer.

The documentation of a program will usually conform to the in-house standards of an organisation.

1.2 Program, data and results

A computer program is a coded algorithm, represented by a series of instructions for the computer to obey and provides a method for processing data. Data is the name given to facts represented by characters and quantities. For example, in a business the names of employees and the number of hours worked by the employees represent data. Data is input into a computer, processed under the direction of a program into results, that are output in the form of, say, a report on the wages for hourly paid staff.

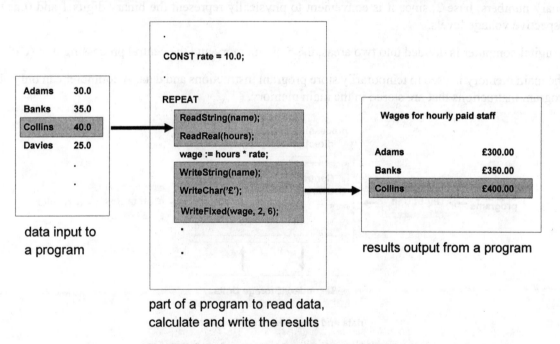

part of a program to read data,
calculate and write the results

figure 1.2 an example of a segment of program

In figure 1.2 data has been represented by a list of names and the number of hours worked by employees in a business. The segment of computer program contains instructions to read the name of an employee *ReadString(name)* and the number of hours worked by an employee *ReadReal(hours)*. The gross weekly wage of an employee is then calculated by the instruction *wage := hours * rate*, where all employees are paid at the same hourly rate of £10 per hour, declared by the statement *CONST rate = 10.0*. The result of this calculation can then be written to a report on the wages for hourly paid staff. The three instructions *WriteString(name)*, *WriteChar('£')* and *WriteFixed(wage,2,6)* are used to write the name and gross weekly wage for one employee.

3

In this example the name *Collins,* who worked a *40* hour week, has been read into the computer by the program. The gross weekly wage for employee *Collins* was then calculated to be *£400.00*, on the basis that all employees are paid at the hourly rate of £10 per hour. The name of the employee and the gross weekly wage are then written to the report. This sequence of statements is repeated until there is no more data available.

The program has been used to input data into the computer, process the data, then output the results from the computer in the form of a report.

1.3 A digital computer

A digital computer is an electronic machine capable of storing and obeying instructions at a very high speed. For example an instruction can be obeyed in one hundred millionth of one second. The term digital implies that all information is represented by numbers within the computer. The numbers are stored as binary numbers, base 2, since it is convenient to physically represent the binary digits 1 and 0 as two respective voltage levels.

A digital computer is divided into two areas, the main memory and the central processing unit (CPU).

The main memory is used to temporarily store program instructions and data. A computer can only obey program instructions that are stored in the main memory.

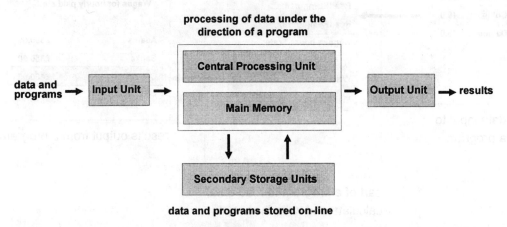

figure 1.3 a computer model

The CPU consists of two sub-units, the arithmetic and logic unit (ALU) and the control unit. The ALU performs the processes of arithmetic, logical operations and comparisons on data. Whereas the control unit fetches the instructions from main memory, interprets and obeys them, and coordinates the flow of information about the computer system.

Figure 1.3 illustrates a computer model containing the CPU, main memory and in addition three other units - input, secondary storage and output units, known as peripheral units.

An input unit allows data and computer programs to be input into the computer model.

Since the main memory is only used to temporarily store programs and data, it is necessary to have secondary storage units to provide a permanent storage facility. Programs and data are transferred to and from the secondary storage units to the main memory only when they are required. The information is said to be on-line to the computer. The rate of transfer of information is fast and dependent upon the type of secondary storage unit being used.

In order to transfer results from the main memory and secondary storage units to the outside world it is necessary to provide an output unit.

1.4 Input and output units

The most popular input unit used in a computer system is a keyboard. The layout of a popular keyboard is depicted in figure 1.4. Notice that a modern keyboard contains other banks of keys, in addition to the keys normally found on a typewriter that represent the letters of the alphabet. Both data and programs can be keyed into the computer by using such a keyboard.

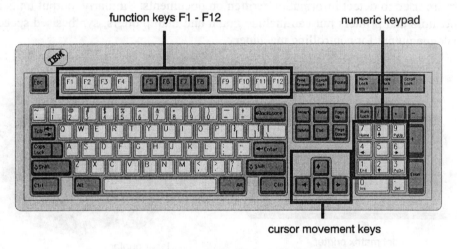

figure 1.4 the layout of a popular keyboard

A television screen or monitor can be used to simultaneously display the information that is being typed into a computer. Such a display is meant to provide a means of visually checking that the correct information is being entered. A monitor has a dual function, as well as displaying the information that is typed at a keyboard it is also used as an output unit in its own right. Information that has been processed by a computer can also be displayed on a screen. Figure 1.5 illustrates a typical monitor that is used in computer system.

The major disadvantage of using a monitor as an output unit stems from the inability of the unit to provide a hard copy of the output. Because information on a printed page is so convenient, it is necessary to include a printer as another output unit. Printers vary in their speed of output and include matrix printers that print characters composed from dots at a rate of up to 150 characters per second and laser printers that print complete pages in seconds. Figure 1.6 illustrates both types of printers.

figure 1.5 a monitor

It is worth mentioning in passing that there are other types of input and output units, however, these units are for specialised use and do not normally form part of a program development environment. Input units, for example bar code readers, are used to detect stock codes on supermarket merchandise. Magnetic ink character readers detect bank account numbers and branch codes on bank cheques. Optical character and mark readers are used to detect information written on documents. Similarly, output units are not only limited to monitors and printers but can include graph and map plotters, synthesised speech units and digital to analogue output for controlling machinery.

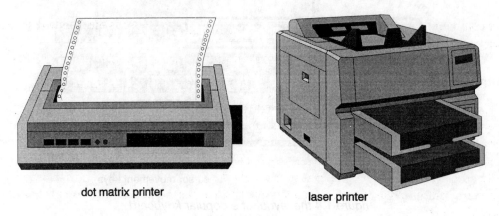

dot matrix printer   laser printer

figure 1.6 a selection of printers

1.5 Secondary storage units

These units can be broadly subdivided into:

(i) magnetic disk units with a storage capacity of up to many thousands of millions of characters; these are known colloquially as hard disks;

(ii) floppy disk units that have, depending upon their size and density, a storage capacity of up to several million characters, on one exchangeable magnetic disk;

(iii) optical and magneto/optical exchangeable disks with a storage capacity of up to hundreds of millions of characters on one exchangeable disk;

(iv) magnetic tape units with a storage capacity of up to a hundred million characters on one tape.

The magnetic and optical disk units transfer information to, and receive information from, the CPU at speeds of many millions of characters per second. When dealing with disk-based media access to the information is direct and fast. By comparison access speeds to information held on magnetic tape is slow, since the contents of the tape must be read sequentially before information can be retrieved.

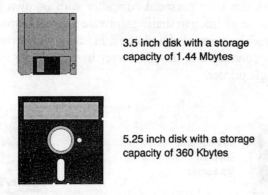

3.5 inch disk with a storage capacity of 1.44 Mbytes

5.25 inch disk with a storage capacity of 360 Kbytes

figure 1.7 popular floppy disks

The most common form of secondary storage medium the reader will use is the floppy disk. Figure 1.7 illustrates two popular sizes of floppy disk.

1.6 Computer configurations

The reader is likely to come across two different, but popular ways, in which computer equipment is configured. The first is a stand alone personal computer as shown in figure 1.8. This consists of an outer casing or box that contains the central processing unit, main memory, secondary storage devices such as a hard disk, and floppy disk drives, a power supply and various interface cards to permit linking the CPU to other devices. The personal computer has as standard a keyboard and monitor. In addition to these, a device known as a mouse is used to point at items displayed on the monitor, and the computer will probably be connected to a printer.

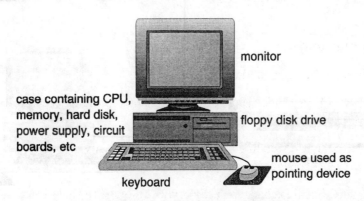

monitor

case containing CPU, memory, hard disk, power supply, circuit boards, etc

floppy disk drive

mouse used as pointing device

keyboard

figure 1.8 a stand-alone personal computer

A second configuration that is extremely popular is a network of computers. There are several ways in which the computers can be joined together on a network, but this is of little importance in this chapter. The main points to consider are that a network usually contains a larger more powerful computer known as a file server to which all the other computers are connected. The purpose of the file server is to store and distribute essential software and information that is of common use to all the users on the network. Each terminal on the network can be a personal computer with its own local processing power and capability to store information. In addition to sharing software a computer network can permit the sharing of other peripheral devices, such as printers and plotters. Figure 1.9 illustrates a small network in which three personal computers are connected to the file server in order to obtain access to commonly used computer software, and a single printer.

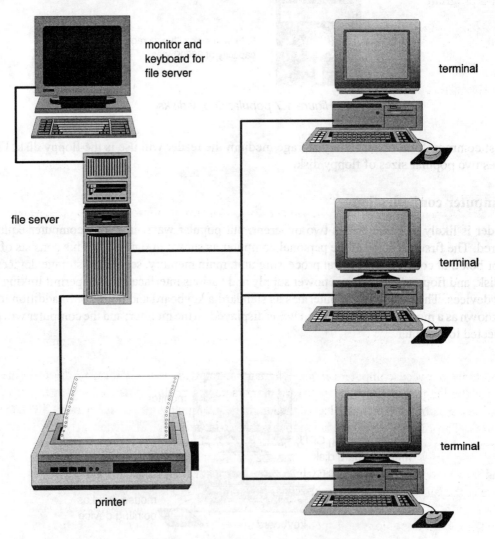

monitor and
keyboard for
file server

terminal

file server

terminal

terminal

printer

figure 1.9 a network of personal computers

1.7 Computer languages

A computer language is a set of instructions used for writing computer programs. There are essentially three levels of language, high, low and machine code.

Modula-2 is a high-level language, invented by Niklaus Wirth, a computer scientist at the Institute of Informatics in Zurich. Modula-2 is a direct descendant of two or Wirth's other languages, Pascal (1970) and Modula (1975). Modula-2 contains all aspects of Pascal and extends them for the construction of large-scale programs in a modular form. It is a general purpose language that is also suitable for systems programming and programming real-time systems. The first definition of Modula-2 was published in 1980 with subsequent revisions by 1983. The following segment of code illustrates several statements in a Modula-2 program.

```
ReadCard(GrossPay);
IF GrossPay < 1000 THEN
   Tax := 0;
ELSE
   Tax := TaxRate * GrossPay DIV 100;
END;
WriteCard(Tax,4);
```

As this example illustrates, high-level languages contain statements that are written with English words and symbols. Such languages are not designed specifically for any one brand of computer.

The architecture of a computer may be defined as the type of CPU, memory size, and internal features of the hardware. A program written in Modula-2 to run on one computer architecture, for example a DECstation, that also runs without modification on a different architecture, for example an IBM PC, is said to be portable between the two computers, if it produces exactly the same results.

Many computer languages are defined by a standard for the language. This is essentially a definition of the format or grammar of the language statements, the meaning or semantics of the statements and sometimes recommendations on how the language should be implemented on a computer.

The version of Modula-2 used in this book conforms to *TopSpeed Modula-2*, combined with a set of libraries that are based upon the *Draft Standard CD 10514* for Modula-2. High-level languages will only remain portable between computers if the language statements used conform to those defined in the standard for the language. However, software manufacturers tend to enhance languages with different extra facilities, creating in effect a dialect of the language. Computers also differ in their CPU and memory architectures. The more dialects of a language that exist and the difference in word sizes between computers, the less portable the language is likely to be.

Low level languages contain statements that are written using mnemonic codes (codes suggesting their meaning and, therefore, easier to remember) to represent operations and addresses that relate to the main memory and storage registers of a computer. Each low level language has instructions which correspond closely to the inbuilt operations of a specific computer. Since different brands of computer use different low level languages a program written for one brand of computer will not run on another brand. Despite the many low level languages in existence they all adhere to the same broad principles of language structure. An example of statements from a typical low level language is:

```
LDA 5000
ADD 6000
STA 5000
```

This program segment adds two numbers and stores the result in a memory location! This type of programming is obviously not as clear as writing **sum := sum + number;** which is the equivalent operation in Modula-2.

Machine level statements are even worse to mentally interpret. They are normally written using one of the number bases 2, 8 or 16. For example the following program segment coded in base 2 binary, would require the aid of a reference manual in order to decipher the meaning of each code.

```
11011101 1011011
01001100 1011100
11011100 1011011
```

1.8 Program implementation

There are four phases associated with the implementation of a program on a computer system. These phases are illustrated in figure 1.10, and are explained as follows.

Phase 1. In order to type a Modula-2 program at the keyboard and save the program on a disk it will be necessary to run a program called an editor. In addition to program entry, an editor allows a program to be retrieved from disk and amended as necessary. A Modula-2 program is stored in text mode so that the programmer can read the program as it was written. No translation of the Modula-2 program to a machine recognisable form has been necessary at this stage.

Phase 2. A computer stores and uses information in a binary format, therefore, the computer cannot understand programs written in either high or low level languages. Program code written in either a high or low level language must be translated into a binary machine code that the computer can recognise. Translation is possible by using a supplied program to translate high or low level language statements into machine code.

Translation to machine code from a high level language is by compiler, and from a low level language by assembler. The translator, compiler or assembler, is resident in the main memory of the computer and uses the high or low level program code as input data. The output from the translator is a program in machine readable code. In addition to translation, a compiler or assembler will report on any grammatical errors made by the programmer in the language statements of the program.

There are several dialects of Modula-2 available, with each dialect having its own compiler for a specific brand of computer. A program written in Modula-2 for an IBM PC computer would require translation using, say, a JPI TopSpeed compiler. However, the same program, in text form, could be transferred to a DECstation and be translated into machine-oriented language using the DEC Modula-2 compiler. Note the portability of the language only refers to the language in text mode not machine code.

Phase 3. Before a compiled Modula-2 program can be run or executed by the computer it must be converted into an executable form. One function of the link/loader is to take the machine oriented program and combine it with any necessary software (already in machine oriented form) to enable the program to be run. For example, input and output routines that are supplied by the system will need linking into the

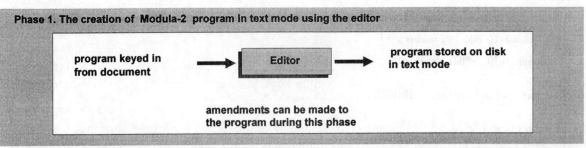

Phase 1. The creation of Modula-2 program in text mode using the editor

program keyed in
from document

Editor

program stored on disk
in text mode

amendments can be made to
the program during this phase

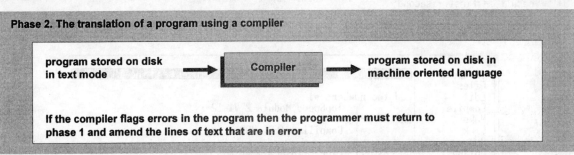

Phase 2. The translation of a program using a compiler

program stored on disk
in text mode

Compiler

program stored on disk in
machine oriented language

If the compiler flags errors in the program then the programmer must return to
phase 1 and amend the lines of text that are in error

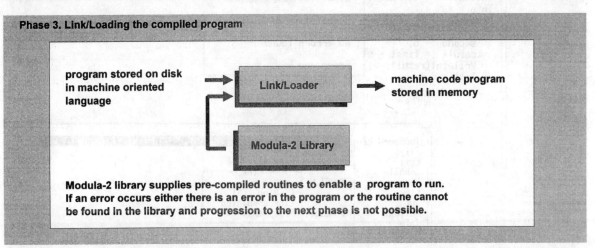

Phase 3. Link/Loading the compiled program

program stored on disk
in machine oriented
language

Link/Loader

machine code program
stored in memory

Modula-2 Library

Modula-2 library supplies pre-compiled routines to enable a program to run.
If an error occurs either there is an error in the program or the routine cannot
be found in the library and progression to the next phase is not possible.

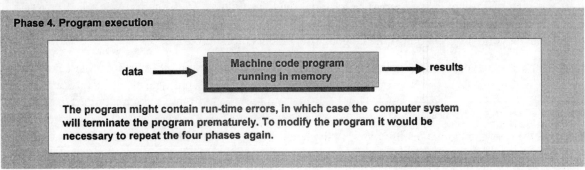

Phase 4. Program execution

data

Machine code program
running in memory

results

The program might contain run-time errors, in which case the computer system
will terminate the program prematurely. To modify the program it would be
necessary to repeat the four phases again.

figure 1.10 four phases of program implementation

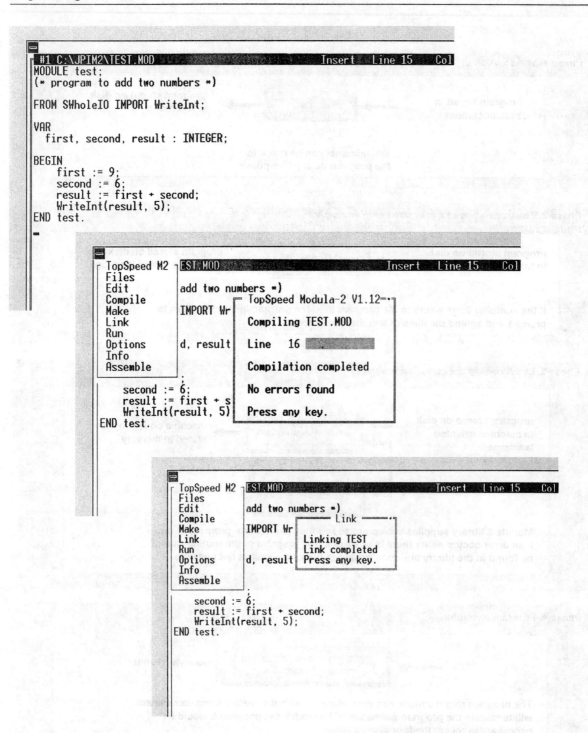

figure 1.11 TopSpeed
Environment

program to allow data to be input at a keyboard and results displayed on a monitor. The complete machine code program is then loaded into memory ready for execution. Figure 1.11 illustrates the phases of editing, compiling and linking a program in the TopSpeed Modula-2 environment.

Phase 4. After the command to run the program is invoked the screen is cleared and the result of the addition of the two numbers is displayed as depicted in figure 1.12.

There exists a higher layer of software known as an operating system, above the user's program, that controls the computer system. The role of an operating system covers many areas, however, one important aspect is that of supervising the execution of user written programs. Such supervision includes the premature termination of user programs in the event of attempting to execute illegal operations such as dividing a number by zero or reading from a data file that has not been opened.

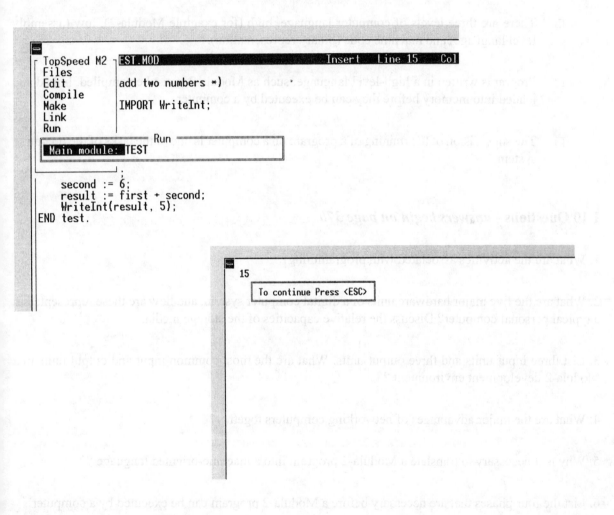

figure 1.12 Running a program

1.9 Summary

☐ Programming consists of designing an algorithm, coding the algorithm into a computer program, testing the computer program and finally supplying sufficient documentation with the program so that it can easily be understood and modified by others.

☐ A digital computer consists of input, output and secondary storage units that are peripheral to the central processing unit and main memory.

☐ Data is input to the computer and processed under the direction of a program to produce results at an output unit.

☐ There are three levels of computer language, high (for example Modula-2), low (assembly level language) and machine code (binary representation).

☐ Programs written in a high-level language, such as Modula-2, must be compiled, linked and loaded into memory before they can be executed by a computer.

☐ The supervision of the running of a program on a computer is one of the tasks of the operating system.

1.10 Questions - *answers begin on page 370*

1. What are the activities associated with programming?

2. What are the five major hardware units of a digital computer system, and how are these represented in a typical personal computer? Discuss the relative capacities of the storage media.

3. List three input units and three output units. What are the most common input and output units in a Modula-2 development environment ?

4. What are the major advantages of networking computers together?

5. Why is it necessary to translate a Modula-2 program into a machine-oriented language ?

6. List the four phases that are necessary before a Modula-2 program can be executed by a computer.

7. What is meant by program portability ? Why are low level languages not considered to be portable ?

Chapter 2
Data

This chapter contains information about data found in everyday life. It explores the different characteristics of data such as type, size and format, and introduces the reader to five data types integer, cardinal, real, character and string. The methods of declaring these types of data and documenting their meaning in a Modula-2 program is also examined. By the end of the chapter the reader should have an understanding of the following topics.

- ☐ How to recognise data and classify it by type.

- ☐ The format of data.

- ☐ How data is stored inside the memory of a computer.

- ☐ The identification of variables and constants.

- ☐ How to represent variables and constants in a program.

15

2.1 What is data?

The reader's first introduction to the meaning of data in this book was given in the first chapter, where data was defined as the name given to facts represented by characters and quantities. The word data has found its way into everyday language. The Concise Oxford Dictionary definition of data is "..1 known facts or things used as a basis for inference or reckoning. 2 quantities or characters operated on by a computer etc..". Put another way, data can be numbers and/ or groups of characters that represent facts. There are plenty of examples of data to be found. Consider the diagram of the road sign in figure 2.1, it represents a typical everyday example of data. The road sign contains two items of data, the name of the town Keswick, and a distance to Keswick of 15 miles. Hence a group of characters represent the name and a number represents the distance.

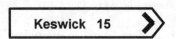

figure 2.1 a road sign

Figure 2.2 illustrates a thermometer to indicate the temperature outside. The scale on the thermometer is graduated in both degrees Fahrenheit and degree Centigrade. From the illustration it is clear that the temperature is cold outside, and can be either $+14^{\circ}$ Fahrenheit or -10° Centigrade. The temperature is represented by either a positive or a negative number.

Figure 2.3 illustrates a typical menu in a cafe. The names of the items of food or drink are represented by groups of characters and the price of each item by a number.

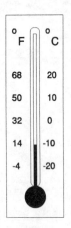

Greasy Spoon Cafe	
M E N U	
fruit juice	£ 0.30
soup	£ 0.50
cold meat salad	£ 2.50
sausages (2)	£ 1.00
bacon & egg	£ 1.00
cod	£ 1.50
plaice	£ 2.00
portion of chips	£ 0.75
tea	£ 0.25
coffee	£ 0.35
all prices exclude VAT	

figure 2.2   *figure 2.3*

Figure 2.4 illustrates part of a railway timetable. The names of the stations are represented by groups of characters, the departure or arrival of a train by a single character **d** or **a**, and the times of departure or arrival of a train by numbers that represent the time of day.

Figure 2.5 illustrates a bank cheque. The cheque number, bank clearing code and bank account number, written in magnetic characters at the bottom of the cheque, are all numbers. The payee name and the name of the account are represented by groups of characters. The amount in the box is represented as a number. The date can either be represented as a group of characters, or the values for day, month and year as numbers.

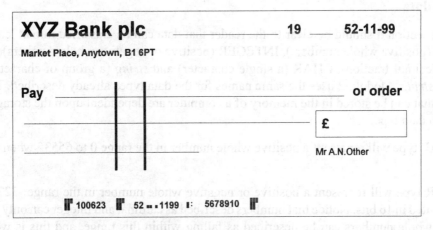

figure 2.4

figure 2.5 a bank cheque

From these few examples it should be evident that data can take the form of whole numbers, such as road distances, temperatures and times of arrival or departure; numbers with a decimal fraction, such as amounts of money; single characters such as departure **d** or arrival **a** codes; and finally groups of characters such as place names, items of food and bank account names.

2.2 Types of data

Examine the data that has been presented in the previous five examples. In figure 2.1 the name of the town Keswick is composed from a group of characters and is known as a *string* data type. The number of miles, 15, on the road sign is a whole number and must always be positive, therefore is known as a CARDINAL data type.

The thermometer shown in figure 2.2 contains two different temperature scales. Both temperature scales use positive and negative numbers. If you assume that the accuracy of the scale is to a whole number of degrees, then this scale too consists of whole numbers. However, because the numbers can be positive or negative the data type for the numbers is known as an INTEGER data type.

The menu shown in figure 2.3 contains a mixture of data, the names of items of food and drink are of the data type *string*; the prices contain a decimal fraction and are numbers of data type REAL.

The railway timetable shown in figure 2.4 contains the names of the towns and cities of data type *string*, a single character to denote departure or arrival of data type CHAR and whole numbers that represent times, in a 24-hour clock format, of data type CARDINAL.

The bank cheque shown in figure 2.5 contains the payee name and the name of the account of data type *string*. The amount shown in the box is REAL. However, despite the cheque number, bank clearing number and account number containing digits, they could each be represented as type *string*. This fact will become clearer after the next section on sizes of data. The date can either be three numbers representing day, month and year, each of data type CARDINAL, or the complete date of type *string*. Note - a string can contain digits as well as letters and other characters.

2.3 Sizes of data

From the last section it should be clear to the reader that data can be classified into at least five types - CARDINAL (positive whole numbers), INTEGER (positive or negative whole numbers), REAL (numbers with a decimal fraction), CHAR (a single character) and *string* (a group of characters). With the exception of *string*, Modula-2 uses the same names for the data types already described. The maximum sizes of data that can be stored in the memory of a computer are dependent upon the storage capacity set aside for each data type.

A CARDINAL type will represent a positive whole number in the range 0 to 65535 when represented in 16 bits.

An INTEGER type will represent a positive or negative whole number in the range -32768 to +32767 when represented in 16 bits. Notice that numbers described as cardinal and integer can only be of a limited size. Not all whole numbers can be described as falling within this range, and this is why the cheque number, bank clearing number, account number and date were described as being of data type *string*.

A REAL type will represent a positive or negative number containing a decimal fraction. The range of real numbers that can be stored is between 1.2×10^{-38} to 3.4×10^{38} with a precision of six digits. This implies that very large numbers cannot be represented completely accurately and the least significant digits in the number may be lost!

The type declaration CHAR is used to denote a single character taken from the ASCII character set. This set is given in figure 2.8 and appendix V. Notice that characters are not confined to letters of the alphabet, but can be digits and other symbols.

The type declaration *string* is **not** implicitly defined as part of the Modula-2 language. However, a *string* data type can be explicitly defined and used to describe a group of up to 255 characters. The use of a *string* data type will be explained in more detail in the next chapter.

2.4 Data representation

This section may be omitted on the first reading.

The main memory of a computer is made up from many millions of storage cells called bytes. Each byte has a unique address in the memory of the computer and is capable of storing eight bits (binary digits) worth of information.

Integers are stored within a fixed number of bytes. A common size for integer storage is two bytes, which gives the range of integers that can be stored as -32768 to +32767. Any integer that lies outside this range cannot be stored in the memory of the computer as an integer. A representation of the integer 1225 in two bytes is given in figure 2.6.

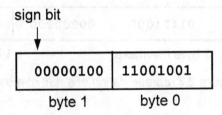

figure 2.6 addressable bytes in main memory

This is known as a pure binary representation of the number. Each bit represents a multiple of 2, with the rightmost bit of byte 0 having a value of 1, the next bit a value of 2, the next a value of 4, the next a value of 8 and so on. Summing only those bits that are set at 1 results in $2^0+2^3+2^6+2^7+2^{10}$ =1+8+64+128+1024=1225. Notice that the leftmost bit of byte 1 is reserved as the sign bit. A sign bit set at 0 represents a positive number, and set at 1 represents a negative number. Negative numbers are stored using a 2's complement representation. For example the number -1225 will be stored using the following bit pattern.

+1225	= 00000100 11001001
1's complement	= 11111011 00110110 interchange 1's and 0's
2's complement	= 11111011 00110111 add 1 to rightmost bit

The result of this bit manipulation is a two byte representation of -1225. Notice that the sign bit has been automatically set to 1. Larger integers, than those stated in the range above, can be stored, provided the number of bytes used to store the integers is increased. Many computers use long integer storage by increasing the number of bytes to four. This gives an effective storage range of -2,147,483,648 to +2,147,483,647.

A cardinal number is a non-negative integer. The mode of storage is normally a pure binary representation without the sign bit. Therefore, the range of cardinal numbers that can be stored in two bytes is 0 to 65535, and the range that can be stored in four bytes is 0 to 4,294,967,295.

Real numbers are stored within a fixed number of bytes using a floating point representation of the number. The number of bytes can vary between four, six and eight, however, four is common. Real numbers have two parts, a mantissa (the fractional part) and an exponent (the power to which the base of the number must be raised in order to give the correct value of the number when multiplied by the mantissa). For example 437.875 can be re-written as 0.437875×10^3, where 0.437875 is the mantissa, 3 the exponent.

The number +437.875 has a binary equivalent of 110110101.111 and when the binary point is floated to the left and exponent adjusted the number is represented as $0.110110101111 \times 2^9$. The organisation of this number in a floating point representation is shown in figure 2.7.

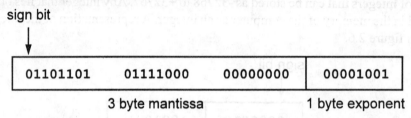

sign bit

01101101	01111000	00000000	00001001

3 byte mantissa   1 byte exponent

figure 2.7 representation of a real number

The mantissa (f) must always lie in the ranges $0.5 <= f < 1$ for a positive fraction and $-1 <= f < 0.5$ for a negative fraction. It is then said to be normalised. A negative mantissa can be represented using the 2's complement technique described in the previous section. There are various techniques for representing the exponent, however, a pure binary representation is shown here.

A four byte organisation of a real number will give a maximum value of 3.4×10^{38} and a minimum value of 1.2×10^{-38} with an accuracy of 6 decimal digits. The majority of decimal fractions do not convert exactly into binary fractions, therefore, the representation of a real number is not always accurate. Accuracy of storage can be improved by using a greater number of bytes to represent the mantissa.

By increasing the number of storage bytes for the mantissa, it is possible to increase the accuracy of representation of fractions. Similarly by increasing the storage capacity for the exponent the range of real numbers must also increase. A real number represented using eight bytes will give a maximum value of 1.8×10^{308} and a minimum value of 2.2×10^{-308}, with an accuracy of 15 decimal digits.

Modula-2 defines a type LONGREAL to permit the representation of larger real numbers to a greater accuracy.

When the result of a computation is too large to be represented the number has over-flowed storage. Conversely, when a result is too small to be represented the number has under flowed storage, and the computer will probably return the result as zero.

Characters are stored in the memory by using 7-bit binary codes. For example, the character 'A' is coded 65, 'B' is coded 66, 'C' is coded 67 etc. The list of ASCII (American Standard Code for Information Interchange) character codes is given in figure 2.8 and appendix V.

Code	Character	Code	Character	Code	Character
000	NUL	043	+	086	V
001	SOH	044	,	087	W
002	STX	045	-	088	X
003	ETX	046	.	089	Y
004	EOT	047	/	090	Z
005	ENQ	048	0	091	[
006	ACK	049	1	092	\
007	BEL	050	2	093	]
008	BS	051	3	094	^
009	HT	052	4	095	_
010	LF	053	5	096	'
011	VT	054	6	097	a
012	FF	055	7	098	b
013	CR	056	8	099	c
014	SO	057	9	100	d
015	SI	058	:	101	e
016	DLE	059	;	102	f
017	DC1	060	<	103	g
018	DC2	061	=	104	h
019	DC3	062	>	105	i
020	DC4	063	?	106	j
021	NAK	064	@	107	k
022	STN	065	A	108	l
023	ETB	066	B	109	m
024	AN	067	C	110	n
025	EM	068	D	111	o
026	SUB	069	E	112	p
027	ESC	070	F	113	q
028	FS	071	G	114	r
029	GS	072	H	115	s
030	RS	073	I	116	t
031	US	074	J	117	u
032	space	075	K	118	v
033	!	076	L	119	w
034	"	077	M	120	x
035	#	078	N	121	y
036	$	079	O	122	z
037	%	080	P	123	{
038	&	081	Q	124		
039	'	082	R	125	}
040	(	083	S	126	~
041	)	084	T	127	del
042	*	085	U		

figure 2.8 ASCII codes

2.5 Syntax notation

Tokens are the simplest textual elements of Modula-2, and can be classified into *keywords*, *delimiters*, *generic tokens* and *separators*. A formal notation is used to describe how sequences of tokens can be assembled to form programs. This notation consists of productions involving syntactical constructs and tokens. Each construct can have several productions associated with it, each expressing a possible expansion of the construct. For example a decimal number might be defined as:

decimal number ::= [sign] digit {digit}
sign ::= '+' | '-'
digit ::= **'0'|'1'|'2'|'3'|'4'|'5'|'6'|'7'|'8'|'9'**

where the definition symbol **::=** is used to separate the syntactical construct being defined from its expansion; the brackets **[ ]** are used to enclose parts of a production that are optional; the braces **{ }** are used to enclose parts of a production which may be repeated zero or more times; the bar **|** is used to separate alternative definitions within a production; and single quotes **' '** are used to enclose non-alphabetic tokens. Similarly a real number might be defined as:

real literal ::= [sign] digit {digit} '.' {digit} [scale factor]
scale factor ::= **'E'** [sign] digit {digit}

The following production can be used to define the syntax of a program:

program module ::= **MODULE** module identifier [priority]';'
  import lists, module block, module identifier '.'
module identifier ::= identifier
identifier ::= letter | underscore {alphanumeric | underscore}
priority ::= '[' constant expression ']'

All tokens appear with emboldened characters. Keywords, such as **MODULE**, appear in upper-case letters; delimiters, such as ';' and generic tokens, such as '0', '1', '2', etc, are enclosed in single quotes. Lists of productions, for example import lists, module block, module identifier, are separated by commas.

Separators consist of white spaces (blanks, tabs and line breaks) and comments. Separators have no meaning to the compiler other than to separate tokens.

A full description of the Modula-2 syntax is given in appendix II.

2.6 Variables.

The main memory of a computer is made up from many millions of storage cells, each with a unique numeric address, as illustrated in figure 2.9.

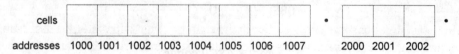

figure 2.9 addressable memory cells

22

Data can be thought of as occupying areas of the computer's memory in the same way as people occupy houses in a street. To distinguish different families in different houses we could use either the surname of the family or the number of the house. To distinguish data in different areas of memory we could give the data a name or use the numeric memory address where the data is stored.

In Modula-2 it is much easier to refer to data by name and let the computer do the work of finding out where in memory the data is stored. Figure 2.10 illustrates how data can be stored across the storage cells and accessed by the names given to the groups of cells and not the addresses of the cells.

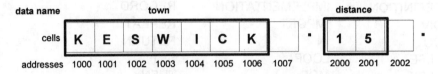

figure 2.10 data can be accessed by name

When a program that uses these data names is executed, the instructions may change the contents of some, if not all, of the groups of bytes. Because of this change or variation in the data the data names are known as variables. A programmer is required to compose many different types of names in a program, of which variables are just one type. The collective name given to all these names is identifiers. Modula-2 uses the following rules for the composition of identifiers.

An identifier may contain combinations of letters of the alphabet (both upper case A-Z and lower case a-z), an underscore character _ and decimal digits, provided the identifier begins with either a letter or an underscore character. Modula-2 distinguishes between the use of upper and lower case letters in an identifier. Identifiers can normally be of any length. The particular implementation of Modula-2 being used may only recognise up to a certain number of characters. An identifier must not be the same as those Modula-2 words found in figure 2.11.

The syntax of an identifier can be re-expressed as:

identifier ::= letter | underscore {letter | digit | underscore}

A programmer should always compose identifiers so they convey the meaning of the data. The identifiers name, street, town, postcode imply the meaning of the data that they represent, rather than the identifiers N, S, T and P. When an identifier is constructed from more than one word, each word should either begin with an upper case letter, or be separated by an underscore, so that the identifier can be clearly read and its meaning understood. Example of legal identifiers are *SubTotal*, *VAT*, *total*, *rate_of_pay*.

2.7 Variable declaration

When investigating the data that is to be used in a computer program it can be helpful to document this information on a data analysis form as shown in figure 2.12. The form has been completed from the study of the five everyday situations presented earlier in the chapter. A description of the data helps to provide a clearer meaning of the identifiers being used. The data type is established and approximate sizes of data recorded. Where sizes of data cannot be predicted the maximum size for the data type has been recorded.

keywords			
AND	EXIT	NOT	TYPE
ARRAY	EXPORT	OF	UNTIL
BEGIN	FOR	OR	VAR
BY	FORWARD	POINTER	WHILE
CASE	FROM	PROCEDURE	WITH
CONST	IF	QUALIFIED	
DEFINITION	IMPLEMENTATION	RECORD	
DIV	IMPORT	REPEAT	
DO	IN	RETURN	
ELSE	LOOP	SET	
ELSIF	MOD	THEN	
END	MODULE	TO	

pervasive identifiers			
ABS	EXCL	MAX	REAL
BITSET	FALSE	MIN	SIZE
BOOLEAN	FLOAT	NEW	TRUE
CARDINAL	HALT	NIL	TRUNC
CAP	HIGH	ODD	VAL
CHR	INC	ORD	
CHAR	INCL	PROC	
DEC	INTEGER	REAL	
DISPOSE	LONGREAL	SIZE	

figure 2.11 words that must not be used as identifiers

A Modula-2 program can be divided into two areas, data declarations and instructions. The data declarations must appear before the instructions since they describe the type of data used by the instructions.

If the values of the data in the storage cells can be changed by the instructions in a computer program, then the values of the data vary, and the data identifiers are known as variable names. The data declaration for such items must be headed by the word VAR. A data declaration contains the variable name followed by the data type.

The abbreviation VAR only appears once. The syntax for the variable declaration is given as:

variable declaration ::=   identifier list ':' type denoter
identifier list ::=   identifier { ',' identifier }

For example the data declaration for the road sign shown in figure 2.1 might be:

DATA ANALYSIS FORM

description	identifier	data type	size
name of town	town	string	<=255 chars
distance to town in miles	distance	CARDINAL	<=65535
temperature	temp	INTEGER	<=32767
item of food or drink	item	string	<=255 chars
price of item	price	REAL	<=2.50
name of town	town	string	<=255 chars
arrival or departure code	a_d_code	CHAR	1 char
time of day - 24 hour format	time	CARDINAL	<=2359
cheque number	ChequeNumber	string	6 chars
clearing code number	ClearingCode	string	6 chars
account number	AccountNumber	string	7 chars
name of acount	name	string	<=255 chars
name cheque made out to	payee	string	<=255 chars
amount cheque made out for	amount	REAL	<=1,000,000.00
date cheque written	date	string	<=19 chars

figure 2.12 the use of a data analysis form

```
VAR
   NameOfTown      : string;
   distance        : CARDINAL;
```

Similarly the data declarations for the thermometer and the menu shown in figure 2.2 and figure 2.3 respectively might be:

```
VAR
   temp            : INTEGER;
```

and

```
VAR
   Item            : string;
   price           : REAL;
```

Notice that the declaration of the name of the cafe, the title and the last line of the menu and the currency sign have not been included since these are not variable quantities. Only the item of food and the price will vary according to the data being used. The data declarations for the railway timetable shown in figure 2.4 might be:

```
VAR
   NameOfTown   : string;
   a_d_code     : CHAR;
   time         : CARDINAL;
```

The heading has been ignored since this is not a variable quantity. Clearly the name of the town, arrival/departure code and time do vary according to the data being used.

Finally, the data declarations for the bank cheque shown in figure 2.5, ignoring the name and address of the bank, and the amount in words, might be:

```
VAR
    ChequeNumber   : string;
    ClearingCode   : string;
    AccountNumber  : string;
    name           : string;
    payee          : string;
    amount         : REAL;
    date           : string;
```

2.8 Constants

In many programs there will be data values that do not change, but remain constant during the running of the program. Examples of items of data that remain constant could be Value Added Tax (VAT) currently at 17.5%, and mathematical PI 3.14159. Such constants can be declared in a Modula-2 program as :

```
CONST
    VAT    = 0.175;
    PI     = 3.14159;
```

The abbreviation CONST only appears once. A *simplified* syntax of the constant declaration can be expressed as:

constant declaration ::=	identifier '=' [sign] term
term:: =	constant literal
constant literal ::=	numeric literal | string literal
numeric literal ::=	whole number literal | real literal
string literal ::=	quoted string | quoted character | character number literal
quoted string ::=	''' {character} ''' | '"' {character} '"'

The data type associated with each constant is inherent in the value of the constant, notice that 0.175 and 3.14159 are both REAL. Should the rate of VAT change during the life of the program, the only amendment necessary to the program would be to the line VAT = 0.175; no further changes would be necessary to the constant VAT in the remainder of the program. Although the value of PI could be written as the literal 3.14159 in the instructions, the programmer may, as a matter of convenience, find it easier to use PI as a meaningful identifier in the program.

Strings can be represented as constants, for example:

```
CONST
    alphabet = 'abcdefghijklmnopqrstuvwxyz';
```

Single characters can be represented as constants in one of two formats. Either as a single character delimited by apostrophes, for example:

```
CONST
   comma = ',';
```

or by using the octal (base 8) value of the ASCII code post fixed by the letter C.

```
CONST
   comma = 54C;
```

A table of octal codes corresponding to the ASCII character set is given in appendix V.

2.9 Summary

☐   Data is composed from numbers and characters that represent facts.

☐   There are at least four implicit data types in Modula-2, CARDINAL, INTEGER, REAL, and CHAR.

☐   The data type *string* is not implicitly defined in the language and must be explicitly defined in a program.

☐   The size of data is limited by its type, and must fit between pre- defined ranges.

☐   Data must conform to set formats.

☐   A formal notation is used to denote the syntax or grammar of statements in a computer language.

☐   Data stored in the memory of a computer can be referenced through a data name invented by the programmer.

☐   Data names must conform to the rules for identifiers.

☐   A data analysis form should be used for documenting the description, name, type and size of all variables.

☐   All the variables used in a Modula-2 program must be declared, before they can be used by instructions contained in the program.

☐   Variable data declaration specifies the name of the data, followed by the type of the data.

☐   Data values that do not change during the running of a program may be declared as constants.

☐   Character constants can be declared using the octal value of the ASCII code, post fixed by the letter C.

2.10 Questions - *answers begin on page 370*

1. From the illustrations in figures 2.13, 2.14 and 2.15 of items found in everyday life, discuss what you consider to be data, and show how the data is classified by type as variables declared in a Modula-2 program. Assume that the data type string is available in the program.

used cars for sale	
Astra 1.4 L, 5 door, 91 (H), blue	£6750
BMW 316, 2 door, 87 (E), black	£6590
BMW 320i SE, 4 door, 88 (E), blue	£7990
Escort 1.6 Ghia Estate, 91 (J), silver	£9750
Fiesta 1.1 LX, 5 door, 91 (H), white	£6490
Granada 2.0 LXI, 90 (H), white	£6390
Jaguar 2.9 Auto, ABS, air con, 90 (G), grey	£12990
Nissan Sunny 1.6 GSX, 4 door, 89 (F), white	£5690
Sierra Sapphire 1.8 LX, 89 (F), white	£4990
Toyota Corolla, 89 (G), silver	£3990
VW Golf 1.6, 5 door, 87 (E), blue	£4790

figure 2.13

XYZ Bank plc

Mr A.N.Other

Market Place, Anytown, B1 6PT

Statement of Account

1993 sheet 90 Account No. 5678910	DEBIT	CREDIT	BALANCE Credit C Debit D
JAN18 BALANCE BROUGHT FORWARD			550.50 C
JAN21 cheque 100642	55.86		494.64 C
JAN26 cheque 100644	10.08		484.56 C
JAN27 SWEET HOME BUILDING SOCIETY	280.14		204.42 C
JAN28 cheque 100643	51.69		152.73 C
FEB 1 SALARY		650.00	802.73 C
FEB 4 cheque 100645	38.11		764.62 C
FEB 8 GAS COMPANY	32.00		732.62 C
FEB 9 ELECTRICITY COMPANY	22.00		710.62 C
FEB10 cheque 100647	10.08		700.54 C
FEB11 cheque 100648	41.96		658.58 C
FEB15 SUNDRIES		15.00	673.58 C
FEB18 BALANCE CARRIED FORWARD			673.58 C

figure 2.14

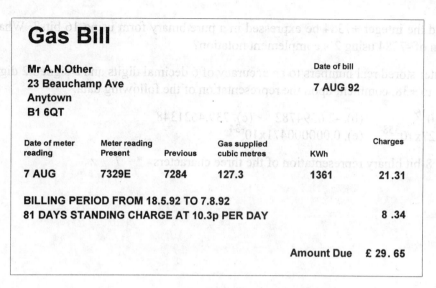

figure 2.15

2. Identify the illegal variable names in the following list of identifiers. State why you think the names are illegal.

(a). PriceOfBricks (b). net-pay (c). X1 (d). cost of paper
(e). INTEGER (f). ?X?Y (g). 1856AD (h) cardinal

3. Describe the types of the following items of data.

(a). 'OXFORD' (b). -0.789 (c). +156 (d). 'X'
(e). 65456 (f). 65456.0 (g). -329 (h). -32768
(i). +32767 (j). +32768 (k). 31851976.28

4. Using figure 2.8 or appendix V, what are the ASCII codes of the following characters?

(a). A (b). M (c). * (d). a (e). m
(f). NUL (g). 9

5. Write the following numbers using the E notation for real numbers, such that there is only one non-zero digit to the left of the decimal point.

(a). -874.458 (b). +0.00123456 (c). 123456789.0

6. State, giving reasons, why the following numbers cannot be stored as REAL numbers in Modula-2.

(a). 30.16E+38 (b). 1234567890.1234567 (c). -0.000456E-39

7. How would the integer +7384 be expressed in a pure binary form using 16 bits? What is the 16 bit representation of -7384 using 2's complement notation?

8. If a computer stored real numbers to an accuracy of 6 decimal digits and a signed 2 digit exponent in the range -38 to +38, comment upon the representation of the following data.

(a). 3.7948×10^{16}.   (b). -2.6394782   (c). 739.4621348
(d). $-17694.327 \times 10^{3584}$ (e). $0.000000471 \times 10^{-34}$

9. Derive the 8-bit binary representation of the three characters * 7 z.

Chapter 3

Instruction Sequence

This chapter contains work on the following topics - arithmetic applied to variables and constants; the use of library modules for the input of data at a keyboard and the output of results to a screen; and the development of a sequence of instructions into a computer program. By the end of the chapter the reader should have an understanding of the following topics.

☐   The construction of arithmetic expressions for the purposes of calculation.

☐   The order of evaluation of arithmetic expressions.

☐   The use of library routines for the input and output of data and information.

☐   The construction of a sequence of instructions that form the basis of simple programs for the input and processing of data and the output of results.

☐   The use of constants and variables in a program.

☐   An introduction to several Modula-2 standard functions.

31

3.1 Assignment

In section 2.6 of the previous chapter it was shown that data can be referenced by name in the memory of a computer. Figure 3.1 illustrates numbers being referenced by names A, B and C in three separate locations in memory.

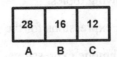

figure 3.1 numbers stored by name

The arithmetic operators + (addition) - (subtraction) * (multiplication) and / (division) can be used to make calculations on the stored numeric data. For example A := B + C would add the contents of B to the contents of C and store the result in A, destroying or overwriting the previous contents of A. Therefore, after the statement A := B + C had been executed by the computer the contents of A changed, and the result of the computation is shown in figure 3.2.

28	16	12
A	B	C

figure 3.2 result of the computation A:=B+C

The symbol := is known as an assignment operator and must not be confused with the symbol = which has a different meaning in the Modula-2 language.

Similar before and after situations can be applied to other computations as illustrated in figure 3.3.

In the last example of figure 3.3 the expression counter := counter + 1 may seem a little unusual, since the variable counter appears on both sides of the expression. The statement should be read as follows. On the right-hand side of the expression the current value of counter (3) is increased by 1, giving a result of (4). This result is then assigned to the variable on the left-hand side of the expression, that also happens to be the variable counter. The old value of counter (3) is overwritten or destroyed by the new value (4). The effect of this statement has been to increase the value of the variable counter by 1.

The destination of a result will always be on the left-hand side of an assignment. Therefore A:=9 implies that A is assigned the value 9. The statement 9:=A has no meaning since 9 is an illegal variable name. However, A:=B would imply that A is assigned the value of B, whereas, B:=A would imply that B is assigned the value of A. In order to exchange the values of the two variables A and B it is necessary to introduce a third, temporary variable T.

T:=A duplicates the value of A in T, A:=B overwrites the value of A with the value of B, B:=T overwrites the value of B with the value of T, hence the original contents of A and B have been exchanged.

Modula-2 defines a number of arithmetic operators which take integer/ cardinal operands and return integer/ cardinal results. These operators are + addition, - subtraction, * multiplication, DIV division resulting in truncation and MOD remainder after division. These operators are known as dyadic since

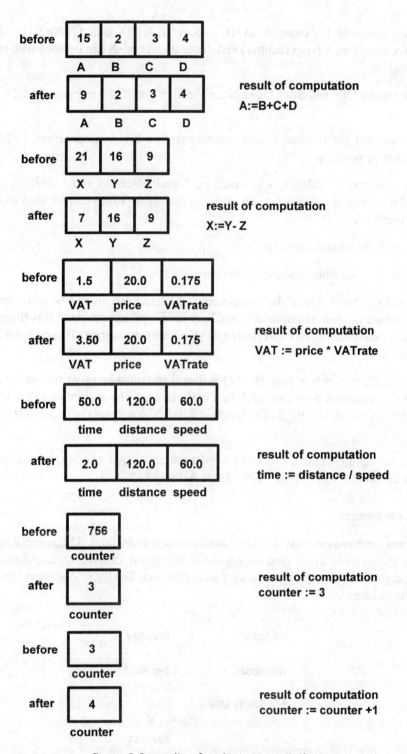

figure 3.3 results of various computations

they operate on two operands. For example, A+B, A-B, A*B, A DIV B and A MOD B. There also exists two monadic prefix operators + (sign identity) and - (negation) which can be used with single operands, for example +A and -B.

The dyadic infix operator DIV truncates the result of the division of two integers, 14 DIV 4 = 3 and (-14) DIV 4 = -3.

The dyadic infix operator MOD returns the remainder from a division operation, 14 MOD 4 =2. The second operand must be positive.

The dyadic infix operators + addition, - subtraction, * multiplication and / division can be used for arithmetic on real numbers. Similarly + (sign identity) and - (negation) can be used as monadic prefix operators on real numbers.

The format of an assignment statement is:

assignment statement ::= variable designator ':=' expression

The data type on the left-hand side of the assignment statement must always be consistent with the data type on the right-hand side. For example, if variable A is of type integer A:=3.0 is illegal since 3.0 is a real literal. The assignment should be expressed as A:=3, where the absence of the decimal fraction implies an integer constant.

Similarly, if the variable B is of type real, B:=A/3 is illegal and must be re-written as B:=FLOAT(A)/3.0 The function FLOAT converts the value of A to a real number. The assignment A:=B*3 is illegal and must be re-written as A:=TRUNC(B)*3. The function TRUNC truncates the value of B and uses only the integer result.

A Modula-2 function that gives the absolute value of a real or integer number, regardless of operational sign, is ABS. For example, ABS(-3)=3; ABS(+3)=3; ABS(-3.84)=3.84.

3.2 Operator precedence

If an expression was written as A + B * C - D / E how would it be evaluated? There is a need to introduce a set of rules for the evaluation of such expressions. All operators have an associated hierarchy that determines the order of precedence for evaluating an expression. The list of operators illustrated in figure 3.4 summarises this hierarchy.

operator	priority
monadic -	highest
* / MOD DIV	↓
+ -	lowest

figure 3.4

Expressions are evaluated by taking the operators with the highest priority before those of a lower priority. Where operators are of the same priority the expression is evaluated from left to right. Expressions in parenthesis will be evaluated before non-parenthesised expressions. Parenthesis, although not an operator, can be considered as having an order of precedence after monadic - (minus).

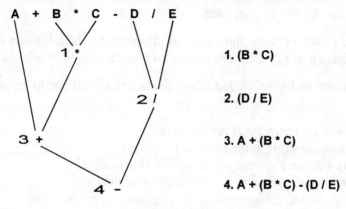

figure 3.5

The expression A + B * C - D / E can be evaluated by inspecting the operators and grouping operations according to the above rules. The numbers in figures 3.5 and 3.6 indicate the order of evaluation. The equivalent algebraic expression is given at each stage of the evaluation.

The expression (X * X + Y * Y) / (A + B) can be evaluated in the same way.

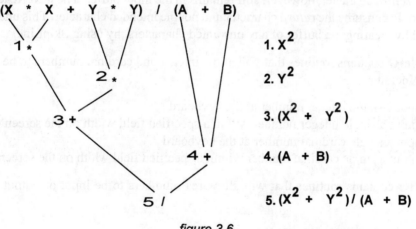

figure 3.6

The reader should adopt the habit of using parenthesis in order to make the meaning of an expression as clear as possible. For example, the algebraic expression: U.V / W.X is written in Modula-2 as U*V/W/X however, (U*V)/(W*X) is easier to understand. Similarly, $X^2 + Y^2 + \dfrac{4}{Z^2}*(X+Y)$

would be written in Modula-2 as: (X*X)+(Y*Y)+4*(X+Y)/(Z*Z).

3.3 Library modules

In common with such languages as C and Ada, Modula-2 contains no statements in the definition of the language for the input and output of data. These languages are supplied with libraries that contain routines for input and output as well as other functions. Whenever data is to be input or results output, the most appropriate routines from the libraries are used.

There are many libraries for the input and output of information. The following three library modules are based on those defined in the *Draft Standard* and will be considered in this chapter.

Module **STextIO** contains routines that will allow characters and strings to be input or output. These routines include:

ReadChar	input a single character at the keyboard
ReadString	input a single string at the keyboard
WriteChar	display a single character on the screen of a monitor
WriteString	display a single string on the screen of a monitor
WriteLn	move the screen cursor down to the beginning of the next line
SkipLine	ignore any remaining characters on the current line input from the keyboard

All data entered at the keyboard is held in a temporary storage area known as an input buffer. The behaviour of the ReadChar statement is to scan the input buffer, if it is empty it waits for data to be input, if it is not empty it consumes the data that it requires. Any subsequent ReadChar statement in a program would consume the data that remained in the buffer. Thus if three characters, BH*return* are typed in response to the statements ReadChar(initial1); ReadChar(initial2); you can assume that initial1=B and initial2=H, the *return* character, however, still remains in the input buffer. The next ReadChar statement in a program would consume the *return* character and not the intended character. This undesirable feature can be rectified by clearing the buffer of any unwanted characters, by using SkipLine.

Module **SWholeIO** contains routines that will allow integer and cardinal numbers to be input or output. These routines include:

ReadInt	input a single integer number at the keyboard
WriteInt	output a single integer number within a specified field width on the screen of a monitor
ReadCard	input a single cardinal number at the keyboard
WriteCard	output a single cardinal number within a specified field width on the screen of a monitor

Module **SRealIO** contains routines that will allow real numbers to be input or output. These routines include:

ReadReal	input a single real number at the keyboard
WriteFloat	output a single real number in floating-point form, with a specified number of significant figures and within a specified field width, on the screen of a monitor
WriteFixed	output a single real number in fixed-point form, rounded to a specified number of decimal places and within a specified field width, on the screen of a monitor

Whenever any of these routines are to be used they must be imported into the program from the appropriate library module and be declared at the beginning of the program. For example, if it was necessary to input and output numbers of type REAL the declaration: FROM SRealIO IMPORT ReadReal, WriteFixed; would be made.

3.4 Input and output routines

Consider a problem in which the gross weekly wage of an hourly paid employee was to be calculated. The information that would need to be collected about the employee would be the number of hours worked and the hourly rate of pay. From the library STextIO the routine WriteString will permit text to be displayed on the screen of a monitor. Therefore, it is possible to prompt a user to input data by coding into a program the statements:

WriteString('input number of hours worked ') and WriteString('input hourly rate of pay ').

From the library SRealIO the routine ReadReal will permit numbers of data type REAL to be input at a keyboard.

The statement ReadReal(HoursWorked) would enable a real value, 35.0 say, to be entered at a keyboard. The end of the line of data is indicated by depressing the *return* or *entry* key on a keyboard. After the execution of this statement the variable HoursWorked would be set at 35.0.

Similarly the statement ReadReal(RateOfPay) would enable a real value, 10.00 say, to be entered at a keyboard. After the execution of the statement the variable RateOfPay would be set at 10.00.

By combining both input and output statements into a series of statements it is possible to prompt when the input of data is required, as follows.

```
WriteString('input number of hours worked  ');
ReadReal(HoursWorked);
WriteString('input hourly rate of pay  ');
ReadReal(RateOfPay);
```

From the library SRealIO the routine WriteFixed will permit a real number to be displayed on a screen in a fixed-point format. The statement WriteFixed(GrossWage,2,7) would display, say 350.00, where the value of the variable GrossWage, 350.00, is output with a maximum field width of 7 characters and to a precision of 2 decimal places, hence the notation GrossWage,2,7. This assumes that the variable GrossWage is real, and has been assigned a value using the following statement.

```
GrossWage := HoursWorked * RateOfPay.
```

This value for the gross weekly wage can be displayed in an informative way, on a screen, by the following series of statements.

```
WriteString('gross weekly wage £');
WriteFixed(GrossWage,2,7);
WriteLn;
```

The statement WriteLn causes the cursor on the screen to be moved to the left-hand edge of the next line. When the code shown in this section is executed by the computer it would give the following display on a screen.

```
input number of hours worked 35.0
input hourly rate of pay 10.00
gross weekly wage £ 350.00
```

where 35.0*return* and 10.00*return* have been typed in response to the prompts.

3.5 Format of a program module

The following format should be adopted when constructing programs in Modula-2.

MODULE *name of module*;

FROM *name of library module* IMPORT *list of input/ output routines*;

CONST *list of constants*;

VAR *list of variables*;

BEGIN

   sequence of program statements;

END *name of module*.

This format can be adopted when constructing the program to calculate the gross wage of an hourly paid employee.

Since HoursWorked and GrossWage can be input as decimal fractions they will need to be declared as REAL data types and input using the routine ReadReal from the library module SRealIO. The result of the computation GrossWage:=HoursWorked*RateOfPay will also be of type REAL, hence GrossWage is also declared as type REAL and must be output using the routine WriteFixed from the library module SRealIO. Since screen prompts are used to signal the input of data and output of a result, the routines WriteString and WriteLn are both imported from the library module STextIO.

```
MODULE wages;
(* program to calculate a gross weekly wage based on hourly paid work *)

FROM STextIO IMPORT WriteString, WriteLn;
FROM SRealIO IMPORT ReadReal, WriteFixed;

VAR
  HoursWorked : REAL;
  RateOfPay   : REAL;
  GrossWage   : REAL;

BEGIN
    WriteString('input number of hours worked ');
    ReadReal(HoursWorked);
    WriteString('input hourly rate of pay ');
    ReadReal(RateOfPay);
```

```
    GrossWage:=HoursWorked * RateOfPay;
    WriteString('gross weekly wage £');
    WriteFixed(GrossWage,2,7);
    WriteLn;
END wages.
```

Notice that every statement has been separated from the next by a semi-colon(;). The syntax of a statement sequence can be expressed as: statement sequence ::= statement '; {statement ';'}. Notice also that comments can be inserted into programs by delimiting the beginning and ending of the comment with the characters (* and *) respectively.

3.6 Implementing a Modula-2 program

Assuming that the reader is using a JPI TopSpeed programming environment, the following stages are necessary to implement the Modula-2 program discussed in the previous section. Having invoked the editor, it is now possible to type the program at the keyboard.

In the transcription of this program typical errors that are made by beginners to programming have been deliberately introduced.

After the program has been typed it is saved to disk using the filename *wages.mod*. The program is then compiled. The result of the compilation is that six errors have been found as shown in figure 3.7. By returning to the editor the nature of these errors are revealed to the programmer. The error diagnostics are as follows.

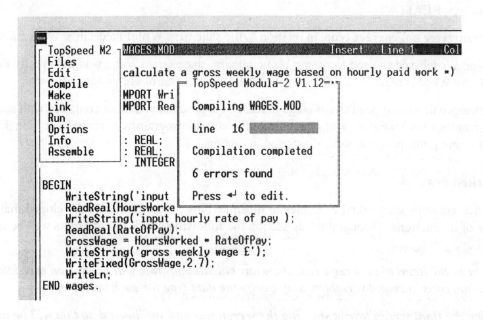

figure 3.7

Error: Syntax Error, expected: END . ; ^, in relation to the line ReadReal(HoursWorked).

This can be very misleading since the error occurred on the previous line. You may notice that the WriteString statement has not been separated from the ReadReal statement by a semicolon. Remember that the semicolon is used to separate statements in a program.

Error: (Lexical) String not terminated, in relation to the line WriteString('input hourly rate of pay).

All string literals are delimited by matching single apostrophes or matching inverted commas. The right-hand apostrophe is missing in this string.

Error: "HoursWorked" is undefined, in relation to the line ReadReal(HoursWorked).

By inspecting the declaration of the variables it is clear to see that HoursWorked has been typed as Hoursworked (notice the lower case w). Modula-2 is a case sensitive language, therefore, the variable name HoursWorked appears to the compiler not to have been declared.

Error: Syntax Error, expected: END . ; { (: := ^ in relation to the line:

GrossWage = HoursWorked * RateOfPay.

Clearly the equals sign in the assignment is wrong, it must contain the assignment operator.

Error: Illegal assignment (incompatible types), in relation to the statement

GrossWage := HoursWorked * RateOfPay. By inspecting the declaration of the variables in this statement it becomes obvious that GrossWage has been incorrectly declared as being an integer type. Since you cannot assign a real value to a variable defined as an integer type the variable GrossWage must be amended to the data type REAL.

Error: parameter not correct type, in relation to the statement WriteFixed(GrossWage,2,7).

The routine WriteFixed is used to output real numbers, since GrossWage was incorrectly declared as integer, GrossWage is regarded by the compiler to be a parameter of the wrong data type.

Having changed the data type of GrossWage to REAL the program is then re-compiled with success! The program can then be linked and run. A listing of the correct program was given in section 3.5, and the results of running this program were illustrated in section 3.4.

3.7 Worked examples

This section contains six worked examples to illustrate how programs can be developed that contain a sequence of instructions. Throughout this section the following check list of points will be used in the design of every program.

(i) Determine the items of data required; show any calculations that will be used on this data. Classify this data into constants and variables, and specify the data type for each variable.

(ii) Design the final screen layout showing the screen text and specimen data that will be used. From this it is possible to state the libraries and routines that are required for input/ output, and in addition show test data and expected results.

When inventing test data the type and nature of the data should be representative of the problem. Numerical data should be chosen for ease of calculation.

(iii) Document in English, NOT Modula-2 code, the sequence of operations that are necessary to solve the problem. This is in fact the algorithm or method of solving the problem, and is represented in a pseudo-code.

(iv) From the information documented in parts (i), (ii) and (iii) code the program using Modula-2.

(v) Compile and link the program. Only if these two stages are successful can you run the program using the same test data that was invented in part (ii).

In the first example a program is required that will allow a user to input a distance to travel, in miles, and the speed of travel, in m.p.h., from a town. The program is required to calculate the time it will take, in hours, to reach the town.

(i) Three items of data can be identified in this problem, distance, speed and time. If distance and speed are whole numbers then because of the calculation of time (distance/speed), the data type for the time must be a real number. Since the data types on both sides of an assignment expression must be of the same type it will be necessary to FLOAT both the variables for distance and speed. An alternative strategy would be to define both distance and speed as real numbers, however, for the sake of instruction this simplification will not be considered further.

distance : CARDINAL; speed : CARDINAL; time : REAL;

(ii) Screen layout

    input distance to town 15
    input speed of travel 60
    time taken to reach town is 0.25 hours

Since two cardinal values are to be input to the computer it will be necessary to import the routine ReadCard from the module SWholeIO. The calculated value for time is of type real, therefore, WriteFixed will need to be imported from the module SRealIO, if this value is to be displayed on a screen. Finally it will be necessary to display several prompts on the screen so that the user knows when to input a value for the distance and a value for the speed. Similarly it is far better to say what the figure for the time relates to, rather than just a figure on the screen. The routines WriteString and WriteLn will need to be imported from the module STextIO if textual screen output is to be used.

If the distance = 15 miles and the average speed of travel = 60 m.p.h., then using the expression time = distance / speed, the time of travel will be 15/60 or 0.25 hour. Ensure that the format of the WriteFixed routine caters for at least two decimal places, since any less will display the wrong result!

(iii) Sequence of instructions

    input distance
    input speed
    calculate time using the expression distance / speed
    display time

(iv) Program.

```
MODULE travel;
(* program to calculate and output the time in hours, to travel a
   distance input in miles, at an average speed input in m.p.h. *)

FROM STextIO IMPORT WriteString, WriteLn;
FROM SWholeIO IMPORT ReadCard;
FROM SRealIO IMPORT WriteFixed;

VAR
  distance : CARDINAL;
  speed    : CARDINAL;
  time     : REAL;

BEGIN
    WriteString('input distance to town ');
    ReadCard(distance);
    WriteString('input speed of travel ');
    ReadCard(speed);
    time := FLOAT(distance) / FLOAT(speed);
    WriteString('time taken to reach town is ');
    WriteFixed(time,2,4);
    WriteString(' hours');
    WriteLn;
END travel.
```

(v) Results from program travel being run

```
input distance to town 15
input speed of travel 60
time taken to reach town is 0.25 hours
```

The second example is only a refinement of the previous example. Here the user is first invited to enter the name of the town, so that it can be used in future textual output. This program brings in the use of a string variable. Remember it was stated in the previous chapter that the Modula-2 language did not implicitly contain the data type string, and it would be necessary to explicitly declare such a type.

The data type string can be explicitly imported from the module StringType. This module has been written by the author and needs to be included as part of the Modula-2 system if any of the programs using the string data type are to be compiled and run successfully. The definition of this module is included in appendix III and its implementation in appendix IV.

(i) The only additional item of data is the name of a town which is of type string. The other variables remain the same as in the previous example.

(ii) Screen layout

    input name of town Keswick
    input distance to Keswick 15
    input speed of travel 60
    time taken to reach Keswick is 0.25 hours

(iii) Sequence of instructions

    input name of town
    input distance
    input speed
    calculate time using the expression distance / speed
    display time

(iv) Program

```
MODULE journey;
(* program to calculate and output the time in hours, to travel a
   distance input in miles, at an average speed input in m.p.h. *)

FROM STextIO IMPORT ReadString, WriteString, WriteLn;
FROM StringType IMPORT string;
FROM SWholeIO IMPORT ReadCard;
FROM SRealIO IMPORT WriteFixed;


VAR
   town     : string;
   distance : CARDINAL;
   speed    : CARDINAL;
   time     : REAL;

BEGIN
    WriteString('input name of town ');
    ReadString(town);
    WriteString('input distance to ');
    WriteString(town);
    WriteString(' ');
    ReadCard(distance);
    WriteString('input speed of travel ');
    ReadCard(speed);
    time := FLOAT(distance) / FLOAT(speed);
    WriteString('time taken to reach ');
    WriteString(town);
    WriteString(' ');
    WriteString('is ');
    WriteFixed(time,2,4);
    WriteString(' hours');
    WriteLn;
END journey.
```

(v) Results from program journey being run

```
input name of town Keswick
input distance to Keswick 15
input speed of travel 60
time taken to reach Keswick is 0.25 hours
```

In the third example, if a person buys three newspapers, the Courier, Globe and Mercury; write a program to input the name and cost in pence of each newspaper, calculate the total cost and average cost in pence and display the result of these two computations.

(i) The names of the three newspapers, the individual costs of the three newspapers, the total cost and average price are all items of data. The names of the newspapers are string variables, and the prices, total cost and average price are cardinal variables.

NamePaper1, Namepaper2, Namepaper3 : string;
PricePaper1, PricePaper2, Pricepaper3 : CARDINAL; TotalCost, average ; CARDINAL;

The total cost is the sum of the costs of the three newspapers: TotalCost := PricePaper1 + PricePaper2 + PricePaper3, and the average price is: average := TotalCost DIV 3 - notice that DIV is used and not / since the average and TotalCost are both cardinal numbers

(ii) Screen layout

```
name of first newspaper Globe
price of Globe 40
name of second newspaper Mercury
price of mercury 50
name of third newspaper Courier
price of Courier 60
total cost of three newspapers is 150p
average cost of newspapers is   50p
```

The input and output of cardinal types is possible by using the routines ReadCard and WriteCard from the library module SWholeIO. The declaration of data type string must import the type from the module StringType. The input and output of strings is possible by using the routines ReadString, WriteString and WriteLn from the module STextIO.

In the previous example it was necessary to introduce a space after the name of the town, otherwise the information that followed would not be formatted correctly. Similarly a space is introduced after the name of each newspaper and before the price is input. In place of the statement WriteString(' ') it should be possible to define a space as a constant having a value of 40C, and use the statement WriteChar(space) to display a single space. If the respective prices of the three newspapers are 40p, 50p and 60p then the total cost is 150p and the average price is 150 DIV 3 = 50p.

(iii) Sequence of instructions

input name of the first paper
input the price of the first paper
input name of the second paper
input the price of the second paper
input the name of the third paper
calculate the total cost of all three papers
calculate the average cost of the three papers
display the total cost
display the average cost

(iv) program

```
MODULE newspapers;
(*
program to find the names and prices of three newspapers, calculate
and output the total cost and average price of the papers
*)

FROM StringType IMPORT string;
FROM STextIO IMPORT ReadString, WriteString, WriteChar, WriteLn;
FROM SWholeIO IMPORT ReadCard, WriteCard;

CONST
    space = 40C;

VAR
  NamePaper1, NamePaper2, NamePaper3   : string;
  PricePaper1, PricePaper2, PricePaper3 : CARDINAL;
  TotalCost, average                    : CARDINAL;

BEGIN
    WriteString('name of first newspaper ');
    ReadString(NamePaper1);
    WriteString('price of '); WriteString(NamePaper1); WriteChar(space);
    ReadCard(PricePaper1);
    WriteString('name of second newspaper ');
    ReadString(NamePaper2);
    WriteString('price of '); WriteString(NamePaper2); WriteChar(space);
    ReadCard(PricePaper2);
    WriteString('name of third newspaper ');
    ReadString(NamePaper3);
    WriteString('price of '); WriteString(NamePaper3); WriteChar(space);
    ReadCard(PricePaper3);

    TotalCost:=PricePaper1+PricePaper2+PricePaper3;
    average:=TotalCost DIV 3;
```

```
    WriteString('total cost of three newspapers is ');
    WriteCard(TotalCost, 4); WriteChar('p'); WriteLn;
    WriteString('average price of newspapers is ');
    WriteCard(average, 4); WriteChar('p'); WriteLn;
END newspapers.
```

(v) Results from program newspapers being run

```
name of first newspaper Globe
price of Globe 40
name of second newspaper Mercury
price of Mercury 50
name of third newspaper Courier
price of Courier 60
total cost of three newspapers is   150p
average price of newspapers is    50p
```

The menu provided by the Greasy Spoon Cafe was illustrated in the previous chapter (figure 2.3). If meals are categorised into three courses as starter, main course and beverage, then the next program will allow the name and price of items for each course to be input and the final bill to be output that includes the sub-total, value added tax at 17.5% and total for the meal. The motto of the Greasy Spoon cafe is "chips with everything", so you are billed for a portion of chips whether you eat them or not!

(i) The data will be the names of the three courses and the respective prices of these courses, the sub total, value added tax, and total.

The variables for the starter, main course and beverage are strings, and the corresponding prices for these courses are real. The sub total, value added tax and total are also real.

starter, main course, beverage : string;
PriceStarter, PriceMain, PriceBeverage ; REAL;
SubTotal, VAT, total : REAL;

Since chips are provided with every meal, the price of chips can be regarded as a constant, so too can the rate of value added tax and the character space (see previous example).

priceChips = 0.75; VATrate = 0.175 and space = 40C.

In calculating the final bill, the sub total, value added tax and final total are calculated as follows.

SubTotal:=PriceStarter+PriceMain+PriceChips+PriceBeverage;
VAT:=VATrate * SubTotal;
total:=SubTotal+VAT;

(ii) Screen layout

starter? soup
price of soup 0.50
main course? cold meat salad
price of cold meat salad 2.50
beverage? coffee
price of coffee 0.35

Greasy Spoon Cafe

soup
                    0.50
cold meat salad
                    2.50
portion of chips
                    0.75
coffee
                    0.35

SUBTOTAL   4.10
VAT   0.72
TOTAL   4.82

In order to input and output data of type string it will be necessary to import string from StringType; ReadString, WriteString and WriteLn from STextIO. The real numbers can be input and output by importing from SRealIO the routines ReadReal and WriteFixed respectively. If the cost of the three courses is £0.50, £2.50 and £0.35 respectively, the sub total (including chips at £0.75) will be £4.10, VAT at 17.5% on the sub total is £0.72, and the total bill will come to £4.82.

(iii) Sequence of instructions

input name of starter, input price of starter
input name of main course, input price of main course
input name of beverage, input price of beverage
calculate sub total
calculate value added tax
calculate total
display name of cafe
display name and cost of starter
display name and cost of main course
display name and cost of beverage
display sub total
display value added tax
display total

(iv) program

```
MODULE meal;
(*
program to input the name and cost of items of food in a cafe, and output
the bill for the meal
*)

FROM SRealIO IMPORT ReadReal, WriteFixed;
FROM StringType IMPORT string;
FROM STextIO IMPORT ReadString, WriteString, WriteChar, WriteLn;

CONST
    VATrate = 0.175;
    space = 40C;
    PriceChips = 0.75;

VAR
  starter, MainCourse, beverage            : string;
  PriceStarter, PriceMain, PriceBeverage   : REAL;
  SubTotal                                 : REAL;
  VAT                                      : REAL;
  total                                    : REAL;

BEGIN
    WriteString('starter? '); ReadString(starter);
    WriteString('price of '); WriteString(starter); WriteChar(space);
    ReadReal(PriceStarter);
    WriteString('main course? '); ReadString(MainCourse);
    WriteString('price of '); WriteString(MainCourse); WriteChar(space);
    ReadReal(PriceMain);
    WriteString('beverage? '); ReadString(beverage);
    WriteString('price of '); WriteString(beverage); WriteChar(space);
    ReadReal(PriceBeverage);

    SubTotal := PriceStarter + PriceMain + PriceChips + PriceBeverage;
    VAT := VATrate * SubTotal;
    total := SubTotal + VAT;

    WriteLn; WriteLn;
    WriteString('G r e a s y   S p o o n   C a f e');
    WriteLn; WriteLn;
    WriteString(starter); WriteLn;
    WriteFixed(PriceStarter, 2, 30); WriteLn;
    WriteString(MainCourse); WriteLn;
    WriteFixed(PriceMain, 2, 30); WriteLn;
    WriteString('portion of chips'); WriteLn;
    WriteFixed(PriceChips, 2, 30); WriteLn;
    WriteString(beverage); WriteLn;
```

```
      WriteFixed(PriceBeverage,2,30); WriteLn;
      WriteString('SUBTOTAL  '); WriteFixed(SubTotal,2,20);
      WriteLn;
      WriteString('VAT      '); WriteFixed(VAT,2,20);
      WriteLn;
      WriteString('TOTAL    '); WriteFixed(total,2,20);
END meal.
```

(v) Results from program meal being run

```
starter? soup
price of soup 0.50
main course? cold meat salad
price of cold meat salad 2.50
beverage? coffee
price of coffee 0.35


G r e a s y   S p o o n   C a f e

soup
                        0.50
cold meat salad
                        2.50
portion of chips
                        0.75
coffee
                        0.35

SUBTOTAL                4.10
VAT                     0.72
TOTAL                   4.82
```

In the fifth example, write a program to solve the following problem. A rectangular living room has a window area of 3 square metres and a door area of 1.5 square metres. Write a program to input the length, width and height of the room and calculate the area of available wall space. If a 1 litre tin of emulsion will cover 25 square metres, calculate and display the number of tins required to emulsion the walls of the room.

(i) In this problem the window and door areas, and area of coverage of a tin of emulsion can all be treated as constants. Since the problem requests that the dimensions of the room are to be input at the keyboard, the length, width and height should be treated as variables of type real. Before the number of tins of emulsion can be calculated it would be useful, but not necessary, to calculate the area of the walls to be emulsioned. This variable will again be of type real. If it assumed that only 1 litre tins of emulsion can be used then the number of tins will be of type cardinal.

Three constants can be identified in this problem: EmulsionCover = 25.0; WindowArea = 3.0; DoorArea=1.5.

The variables are length, width, height, WallArea : REAL; NumberOfTins : CARDINAL;

In calculating the number of tins to purchase it will be necessary to adjust the result of dividing the wall area by emulsIon coverage to give a whole number of tins, otherwise, the calculation will result in fractional parts of a tin of emulsion. If the smallest amount of paint used is 1mL from a tin, then a constant of 0.999 should be added to the theoretical number of tins before the result is truncated.

wall area := (2 * height * length) + (2 * height * width) - window area - door area
        := 2 * height * (length + width) - (window area + door area)
number of tins := (wall area / emulsion cover), rounded to the next whole tin
           := TRUNC ((wallarea / emulsion cover) + 0.999)

(ii) Screen design

    input room dimensions
    length? 7.0
    width? 5.0
    height? 2.5
    number of tins to purchase 3

The routine necessary for the input of Real variables is ReadReal from the library module SRealIO. The output of the number of tins of emulsion requires the routine WriteCard from SWholeIO, and the output of screen prompts requires the routines WriteString and WriteLn from the library module STextIO.

(iii) Sequence of instructions

    input length
    input width
    input height
    calculate wall area
    calculate number of tins
    display number of tins

(iv) Program

```
MODULE tins;
(*
program to calculate the amount of emulsion needed to paint a room
*)

FROM SRealIO IMPORT ReadReal;
FROM SWholeIO IMPORT WriteCard;
FROM STextIO IMPORT WriteString, WriteLn;

CONST
  EmulsionCover = 25.0;
  WindowArea    = 3.0;
```

```
    DoorArea        = 1.5;

VAR
    length, width, height : REAL;
    WallArea              : REAL;
    NumberOfTins          : CARDINAL;

BEGIN
    WriteString('input room dimensions'); WriteLn;
    WriteString('length? '); ReadReal(length);
    WriteString('width? '); ReadReal(width);
    WriteString('height? '); ReadReal(height);

    WallArea := 2.0 * height * (length+width) - (WindowArea+DoorArea);
    NumberOfTins := TRUNC((WallArea/EmulsionCover) + 0.999);
    WriteString('number of tins to purchase  = ');
    WriteCard(NumberOfTins,2); WriteLn;
END tins.
```

(v) Results from program tins being run

```
input room dimensions
length? 7.0
width? 5.0
height? 2.5
number of tins to purchase  = 3
```

The final example introduces two standard functions in Modula-2. If you want to find the ASCII code for a character then the function ORD will provide the solution. For example, ORD('A')=65, ORD('B')=66, etc. Similarly there exists an inverse function CHR, such that if you know the ASCII code for a character then it is possible to find the character by using the function CHR. For example, CHR(65)='A', CHR(66)='B', etc. The last program of this section demonstrates the use of the functions ORD and CHR. A character is input at the keyboard and its ASCII code is displayed, followed by an ASCII code being input at the keyboard and the corresponding character is displayed. Notice from figure 2.9, in the previous chapter, that all the characters from code 0 to code 32 are not easily recognisable as characters that can be displayed on the screen. For this reason the user of the program is advised to input an ASCII code in the range 33 to 126 only.

(i) There are only two variables in this program, one representing a character and the other representing an ASCII code - character : CHAR; code ; CARDINAL. The conversion of character to ASCII code uses the expression code := ORD (character), and from ASCII code to character uses the expression character := CHR (code).

(ii) Screen layout

    input a single character R
    ASCII code for R is 82
    input an ASCII code in the range 33 to 126 64
    character with ASCII code 64 is @

(iii) Sequence of instructions

    input a character
    convert the character to the appropriate ASCII code
    display the ASCII code
    input an ASCII code
    convert the ASCII code to a character
    display the character

(iv) Program

```
MODULE codes;
(*
program to input a single character and display its ASCII code
then input an ASCII code and display the corresponding character
*)

FROM STextIO IMPORT ReadChar, WriteChar, WriteString, WriteLn;
FROM SWholeIO IMPORT ReadCard, WriteCard;

VAR
   character : CHAR;
   code      : CARDINAL;

BEGIN
    WriteString('input a single character ');
    ReadChar(character);
    code := ORD(character);
    WriteString('ASCII code for '); WriteChar(character);
    WriteString(' is '); WriteCard(code, 3); WriteLn; WriteLn;

    WriteString('input an ASCII code in the range 33 to 126 ');
    ReadCard(code);
    character := CHR(code);
    WriteString('character with ASCII code '); WriteCard(code,3);
    WriteString(' is '); WriteChar(character); WriteLn;
END codes.
```

(v) Results from program codes being run

```
input a single character R
ASCII code for R is   82

input an ASCII code in the range 33 to 126 64
character with ASCII code 64 is @
```

3.8 Summary

☐ Arithmetic can be used on the contents of the memory locations, allowing computations to be made on numeric data.

☐ Numbers can be added, subtracted, multiplied and divided by using the operators +, -, * and / respectively.

☐ When two integer/ cardinal numbers are divided then use the function DIV, to calculate an integer/ cardinal quotient and the function MOD to calculate an integer/ cardinal remainder.

☐ All operators are given a priority. Expressions are evaluated by taking the operators with the highest priority before those of a lower priority. Where operators are of the same priority the expression is evaluated from left to right.

☐ Expressions in parenthesis will be evaluated before non-parenthesised expressions.

☐ The result of a computation is assigned to a variable using the := assignment operator.

☐ The resultant data type of a computation is dependent upon the data types being computed. Data types cannot be mixed in an expression.

☐ Use the function FLOAT to convert an integer/ cardinal value to real, and the function TRUNC to convert a real number to an integer value.

☐ All input and output is dependent upon the use of appropriate library routines.

☐ The names of the constants should be used in the program and not their literal values.

☐ Constants must be declared before variables.

☐ All variables must be declared in a VAR statements before they can be used in the program.

☐ A semi-colon is used to separate statements in a Modula-2 program.

3.9 Questions - *answers begin on page 372*

1. What are the values of the following variables after the execution of the respective assignments?

(a). B := A;   A   B   C   D
      C := A;   36   98   45   29
      D := A;

(b). D := A + B + C + D;   A   B   C   D
                           10   14   29   36

(c). A := B - 2;   A   B
                           17   50

(d). Y := X - Y;   X   Y
                           19   32

(e). Z := X * Y;   X   Y   Z
                           18   3   27

(f). B := B / A;   A   B
                          12.5 25.0

(g).   X := A DIV B;   A   B   X
                           16   3   25

(h).   Y := C MOD D;   C   D   Y
                           18   5   2

(i).   D := TRUNC(E)   D   E
                           34 -16.9

2. How are the following expressions written in Modula-2?

(a). $\dfrac{A+B}{C}$ (b). $\dfrac{W-X}{(Y+Z)}$ (c). $\dfrac{D-B}{2A}$ (d). $\dfrac{1}{2}(A^2+B^2)$

(e). (A - B).(C - D)   f. B.B - 4.A.C   g. A.X.X+B.X.X+C

3. Find the errors in the following Modula-2 expressions.

(a). AB   (b). X*-Y   (c). (64+B2)/-6   (d). (A-B)(A+B)

(e). -2 / A + -6   (f). $\dfrac{1}{2}*(X-Y)$

4. Re-write the following Modula-2 expressions as algebraic expressions.

(a). X + 2 / Y + 4   (b). A * B / (C + 2)   (c). U / V * W / X
(d). B * B - 4 * A * C   (e). A / B + C / D + E / F

5. (a) Write a program to display the message 'Hello World' on the screen.

(b) Write a program to input a short message of your choice and display the message on the screen.

6. Write a program to store the numbers 5 and 9 as integer variables A and B respectively. Compute the sum, difference, product, integer quotient and remainder of these variables taken in the order A+B, A-B, A*B, A DIV B, A MOD B, and display the results on a screen.

7. Write a program to input your name, height in inches and weight in stones; convert the height to centimetres and weight to kilogrammes and display the following results. Note: 1 inch = 2.54 cm and 1 stone = 6.364 Kg.

PERSONAL DETAILS
NAME: Bert Smith
HEIGHT (cm): 180
WEIGHT (Kg): 75

8. Write a program to input a temperature in degrees Fahrenheit and display the equivalent temperature in degrees Centigrade. The formula for conversion is: Centigrade = (Fahrenheit-32)*(5/9).

9. Write a program to input the length and width of a rectangular-shaped garden, calculate the area of the garden and the cost of turfing a lawn, if a 0.5m border is left around the perimeter of the garden. Assume the cost of turf is 0.75 per square metre. Display the result of these calculations.

10. Write a program to input an amount of money as a whole number, for example 157, and display an analysis of the minimum number of £20, £10, £5 notes and £1 coins that make up this amount. Hint: use the DIV and MOD functions.

11. Write a program to input the length, width and depths at the deepest and shallowest ends of a rectangular swimming pool. Calculate the volume of water required to fill the pool and display this volume.

12. Write a program to input a character in the range 0 to 9, convert the mode of storage to an integer, multiply the value by pi (3.14159) and output the result. Hint: use the ORD function to obtain the value of the ASCII code, for example ORD('0') = 48. Thus integer 0 = ORD('0')-48.

13. In each of the following questions you are expected to write MODULE, Input/Output and data declarations to fit the sequence of instructions given. When you have completed the declarations for each program, file, compile and run the programs on your computer.

a. The instruction sequence calculates the arithmetic mean of three integers and displays the result to an accuracy of two decimal places.

```
BEGIN
   WriteString('input three integers separated by spaces e.g.  2 5 7');
```

```
    WriteString('then press the RETURN key'); WriteLn;
    ReadInt(x);ReadInt(y);ReadInt(z);
    mean:=FLOAT(x+y+z)/3.0;
    WriteString('arithmetic mean of integers = ');
    WriteFixed(mean,2,10); WriteLn;
END C3Q13a.
```

b. The instruction sequence calculates the surface area and volume of a sphere.

```
BEGIN
    WriteString('input cardinal value for radius of sphere ');
    ReadCard(radius);
    SurfaceArea := 4.0 * pi * FLOAT(radius*radius);
    volume := SurfaceArea * FLOAT(radius)/3.0;
    WriteString('surface area of sphere = '); WriteFixed(SurfaceArea,2,10);
    WriteLn;
    WriteString('volume of sphere = '); WriteFixed(volume,2,10);
    WriteLn;
END C3Q13b.
```

c. The instruction sequence prepares a sales invoice.

```
BEGIN
    WriteString(' SALES INVOICE');WriteLn;WriteLn;
    WriteString('input cost of item 1 '); ReadReal(item1);
    WriteString('input cost of item 2 '); ReadReal(item2);
    WriteString('input cost of item 3 '); ReadReal(item3);
    SubTotal:=item1+item2+item3;
    Tax:=SubTotal*VAT;
    total:=SubTotal+Tax;
    WriteString(' Sub Total               ');
    WriteFixed(SubTotal,2,10);WriteLn;
    WriteString(' VAT @ 17.5%             ');
    WriteFixed(Tax,2,10);WriteLn;
    WriteString(' Total                   ');
    WriteFixed(total,2,10);WriteLn;
END C3Q13c.
```

14. The following formulae are used in calculating sizes of objects.

(a) Cylinder. Area=2.pi.r(h+r); volume=pi.r.r.h where r is the radius of the base and h is the height of the cylinder.

(b) Cone. Area of curved surface=pi.r.l where l is the slant height of the cone and r is the radius of the base; volume = 1/3.A.h where A is the base area and h the height.

Write a program to input the various measurements of the cylinder and cone, calculate and display the areas and volumes for each shape.

Chapter 4
Selection

In chapter 3 the reader was introduced to programs that were based upon the input of data, calculations made using the data and the output of results. Programs written in this manner are fine for solutions to problems that require no more than the computer to follow a sequence of instructions, but are of little use if decisions are to be made within a program. This chapter introduces the reader to coding decisions and branching on the result of a decision to alternative statements in a program. By the end of the chapter the reader should have an understanding of the following topics.

☐ The syntax and use of the statements IF..THEN and IF..THEN..ELSE.

☐ The construction and evaluation of a Boolean expression

☐ Embedding selection statements one within another.

☐ The declaration of a variable of type BOOLEAN.

☐ The use of AND and OR in the construction of Boolean expressions.

☐ The syntax and use of the CASE statement.

4.1 If .. then

Consider the following simple program which informs the user of what garment to wear depending on whether it is raining or not.

```
MODULE weather1;
(*
program to demonstrate the IF .. THEN statement
*)

FROM STextIO IMPORT ReadChar, WriteString, WriteLn;
FROM StringType IMPORT string;

CONST
    yes = 'Y';

VAR
    reply   : CHAR;
    garment : string;

BEGIN
    garment:='overcoat';
    WriteString('is it raining outside? answer Y[es] or N[o] ');
    ReadChar(reply); reply:=CAP(reply);

    IF reply = yes THEN
        garment := 'raincoat';
    END;

    WriteString('before you go out today take your ');
    WriteString(garment); WriteLn;
END weather1.
```

Results from program weather1 being run twice

```
is it raining outside? answer Y[es] or N[o] N
before you go out today take your overcoat

is it raining outside? answer Y[es] or N[o] Y
before you go out today take your raincoat
```

In tracing through the program the following operations take place.

The string variable garment is assigned the value *overcoat*. The user is then requested to input whether it is raining or not. If the answer to the question is *yes*, then the value of garment is changed to *raincoat*.

However, if the answer to the question is *no*, then the value of garment remains unaltered. Finally the user is advised the type of garment to take before venturing outdoors.

When assigning a value to a string variable the string must be enclosed between apostrophes, for example garment:='overcoat'. However, when typing a string value at a keyboard the string is NOT enclosed between apostrophes.

In the program it has been possible to ask a question, and depending upon the answer, select an alternative statement for the computer to execute. This is possible by using the if..then statement

```
IF reply = yes THEN
   garment := 'raincoat';
END;
```

The expression *reply = yes* is known as a Boolean expression, since it will either equate to TRUE (when the reply is equal to yes) or FALSE (when the reply is NOT equal to yes, therefore by implication may be equal to no). Only when the Boolean expression equates to TRUE will the statement immediately after the reserved word THEN be executed by the computer. If the Boolean expression equates to FALSE, the computer will ignore the statement after THEN and branch to the next executable statement after the reserved word END. The end of the IF .. THEN statement, as far as the computer is concerned, follows the ; (semicolon) at the end of the reserved word END.

The user is asked to input Y or N in response to the question *is it raining outside?* To safeguard the input being in upper case it has been necessary to introduce the statement *reply := CAP(reply)*, where the function CAP will convert the input character to upper case if it is not already a capital letter. This function only applies to letters of the alphabet.

In the Boolean expression *reply = yes*, pay particular attention to the data types being used. The data type for reply is CHAR, and the identifier *yes* is declared as a constant assigned the value 'Y'. This technique has been used to improve the readability of the program. An alternative method of coding the Boolean expression could have been *reply = 'Y'*, which is not as clear.

4.2 If .. then .. else

The following syntax notation indicates that there is more to the if..then statement than was indicated in the previous section.

if statement ::=   guarded statements [if else part] **END**
guarded statements ::=   **IF** Boolean expression **THEN** statement sequence
if else part ::=   **ELSE** statement sequence

Consider the following modification to the previous program to include the statement if..then..else.

The function of the program is exactly the same as before. If it was executed using the same data as the first program then there would be no change in the output.

```
MODULE weather2;
(*
program to demonstrate the IF .. THEN .. ELSE statement
*)

FROM STextIO IMPORT ReadChar, WriteString, WriteLn;
FROM StringType IMPORT string;

CONST
    yes = 'Y';

VAR
    reply   : CHAR;
    garment : string;

BEGIN
    WriteString('is it raining outside? answer Y[es] or N[o] ');
    ReadChar(reply); reply := CAP(reply);

    IF reply = yes THEN
        garment := 'raincoat';
    ELSE
        garment := 'overcoat';
    END;

    WriteString('before you go out today take your ');
    WriteString(garment); WriteLn;
END weather2.
```

There are two differences in the construction of the program. Firstly there has been no initial assignment to the string variable garment, and secondly an if..then ..else statement of the form

```
IF reply = yes THEN
   garment := 'raincoat';
ELSE
   garment := 'overcoat';
END;
```

has replaced the if .. then statement in the previous program. The manner in which this statement functions is very straightforward. If the result of the Boolean expression *reply = yes* is TRUE then the statement after THEN *garment := 'raincoat'* will be executed. However, if the result of the Boolean expression is FALSE, as a result of *no* being input, then the statement after ELSE *garment := 'overcoat'* will be executed by the computer. In both cases the computer will then branch to the next statement after the reserved word END.

4.3 Nested if 's

The statement that follows THEN and/or ELSE can also be an IF statement. In the previous examples if the weather had been warm then wearing either a raincoat or an overcoat could prove to be very uncomfortable. If a second item of data is included about the temperature then it is possible to more accurately specify what to wear whether it is raining or not.

If it is raining and the temperature is less than 15 degrees Centigrade then wear a raincoat, otherwise if it is warmer then take an umbrella. However, if it is not raining and the temperature is less than 15 degrees Centigrade then wear an overcoat, otherwise if it is warmer then wear a jacket. The program has been reconstructed to take these new facts into account. The outer if..then..else statement is used to determine which path to take depending upon whether it is raining. The inner if..then..else statements are used to determine which path to take depending upon the temperature.

Notice also the use of the relational operator in the expression *temperature < 15*. The relational operator < means less than. A list of relational operators that can be used in Boolean expressions is given in figure 4.1.

operator	meaning
>	greater than
<	less than
=	equal to
>=	greater than or equal to
<=	less than or equal to
<> or #	not equal to

figure 4.1 relational operators

```
MODULE weather3;
(*
program to demonstrate the IF .. THEN .. ELSE statements
*)

FROM STextIO IMPORT ReadChar, WriteString, WriteLn, SkipLine;
FROM StringType IMPORT string;
FROM SWholeIO IMPORT ReadInt;

CONST
    yes = 'Y';

VAR
    reply       : CHAR;
    garment     : string;
    temperature : INTEGER;
```

61

```
BEGIN
    WriteString('what is the temperature outside today? ');
    ReadInt(temperature); SkipLine;
    WriteString('is it raining outside? answer Y[es] or N[o] ');
    ReadChar(reply); reply := CAP(reply); SkipLine;

    IF reply = yes THEN
        IF temperature < 15 THEN
            garment := 'raincoat';
        ELSE
            garment := 'umbrella';
        END;
    ELSE
        IF temperature < 15 THEN
            garment := 'overcoat';
        ELSE
            garment := 'jacket';
        END;
    END;

    WriteString('before you go out today take your ');
    WriteString(garment); WriteLn;
END weather3.
```

Results from program weather3 being run four times

```
what is the temperature outside today? 10
is it raining outside? answer Y[es] or N[o] Y
before you go out today take your raincoat

what is the temperature outside today? 10
is it raining outside? answer Y[es] or N[o] N
before you go out today take your overcoat

what is the temperature outside today? 15
is it raining outside? answer Y[es] or N[o] Y
before you go out today take your umbrella

what is the temperature outside today? 15
is it raining outside? answer Y[es] or N[o] N
before you go out today take your jacket
```

In the program, after both the *temperature* and *reply* have been input, if the Boolean expression *reply = yes* is TRUE, then the statement after THEN will be obeyed. But this is another if statement! If the Boolean expression *temperature < 15* is TRUE then the statement after THEN *garment := 'raincoat'* will be executed, however, if the Boolean expression *temperature < 15* is FALSE then the statement after ELSE *garment := 'umbrella'* will be executed. In either case the computer will then branch to the next executable statement after the reserved word END in the outer if .. then .. else statement. If the Boolean expression *reply = yes* is FALSE, then the statement after ELSE, in the outer if..then..else, will be obeyed, and if the Boolean expression *temperature < 15* is TRUE then the statement after THEN *garment := 'overcoat'* will be executed, however, if the Boolean expression *temperature < 15* is FALSE then the statement after ELSE *garment := 'jacket'* will be executed.

When IF statements are embedded one within another, they are said to be nested. It is essential, as part of the syntax, that each IF..THEN or IF..THEN..ELSE statement is terminated with END, and that IF..END or IF..ELSE..END are aligned. The following code illustrates that the indentation of respective IF statements indicates the level of nesting.

```
IF condition_1 THEN
   statement_1;
ELSE
   IF condition_2 THEN
      statement_2;
   ELSE
      IF condition_3 THEN
         statement3;
      ELSE
         statement4;
      END;
   END;
END;
```

The final form of syntax for the IF statement is:

if statement ::=	guarded statements [if else part] **END**
guarded statements ::=	**IF** Boolean expression **THEN** statement sequence
	{**ELSIF** Boolean expression **THEN** statement sequence}
if else part ::=	**ELSE** statement sequence

Therefore, the ELSE IF statements in the previous example can be combined to form:

```
IF condition_1 THEN
   statement_1;
ELSIF condition_2 THEN
   statement_2;
ELSIF condition_3 THEN
   statement_3;
ELSE
   statement_4;
END;
```

4.4 Boolean data type

In the previous example how would the computer cater for data being input that did not match either *yes* or *no* in response to a reply? If the reply was neither Y or N then the Boolean expression *reply = yes* would be false and the computer would assign *overcoat* to the variable *garment* if the temperature was less than fifteen degrees, or would assign *jacket* to the variable *garment* if the temperature was warmer. This is clearly an undesirable feature of the program, and it is the responsibility of the programmer to trap any invalid data and report the exceptional circumstances to the user of the program.

The next program traps and reports on data being input that does not conform to the reply *yes* or *no*. The program introduces a new data type whose values are FALSE or TRUE only. This data type is known as a BOOLEAN type. A variable *error*, has been declared as being BOOLEAN, which means that the values FALSE or TRUE can be assigned to it. In the program the variable *error* is initialised to FALSE on the assumption that no invalid data will be input. However, as soon as invalid data is recognised, the value of *error* is changed to TRUE.

Since *error* is of type BOOLEAN and only has the values FALSE or TRUE assigned to it, the variable may be used in place of a Boolean expression. Notice in the last segment of the program code that if there has been an error, the message of what garment to take is suppressed and replaced by a data error message.

```
MODULE weather4;
(*
program to demonstrate the use of a Boolean variable
*)

FROM STextIO IMPORT ReadChar, WriteString, WriteLn, SkipLine;
FROM StringType IMPORT string;
FROM SWholeIO IMPORT ReadInt;

CONST
      yes = 'Y';
      no  = 'N';

VAR
      reply       : CHAR;
      garment     : string;
      temperature : INTEGER;
      error       : BOOLEAN;

BEGIN

      WriteString('what is the temperature outside today? ');
      ReadInt(temperature); SkipLine;
      WriteString('is it raining outside? answer Y[es] or N[o] ');
      ReadChar(reply); reply := CAP(reply); SkipLine;

      error := FALSE;
```

```
      IF reply = yes THEN
          IF temperature < 15 THEN
              garment := 'raincoat';
          ELSE
              garment := 'umbrella';
          END;
      ELSE
          IF reply = no THEN
              IF temperature < 15 THEN
                  garment := 'overcoat';
              ELSE
                  garment := 'jacket';
              END;
          ELSE
              error:=TRUE;
          END;
      END;

      IF error THEN
          WriteString('DATA ERROR - reply not input as either Y or N');
          WriteLn;
      ELSE
          WriteString('before you go out today take your ');
          WriteString(garment); WriteLn;
      END;
END weather4.
```

Results from the program weather4 being run twice

```
what is the temperature outside today? 25
is it raining outside? answer Y[es] or N[o] Y
before you go out today take your umbrella

what is the temperature outside today? 25
is it raining outside? answer Y[es] or N[o] ?
DATA ERROR - reply not input as either Y or N
```

4.5 Boolean expressions

From the discussion so far it should be clear to the reader that Boolean expressions can only equate to one of two values, either TRUE or FALSE. Examples of Boolean expressions given so far have been *temperature < 15*, *reply = yes*, *reply = no* and *error*.

The next example is a program that will input the name of a person and decide whether they are a suspect to a crime. It has been reported that the crime was committed by a person aged between 20 and 25 years, and between 66 to 70 inches tall. The program displays the name of the suspect if they fit this description.

```
MODULE suspect;
(*
program to display the name of a suspect to a crime who is aged between
20 and 25 years and between 66 inches and 70 inches tall
*)

FROM StringType IMPORT string;
FROM STextIO IMPORT ReadString, WriteString, WriteLn;
FROM SWholeIO IMPORT ReadCard;

VAR
   name   : string;
   age    : CARDINAL;
   height : CARDINAL;

BEGIN
    WriteString('input name of suspect '); ReadString(name);
    WriteString('age? '); ReadCard(age);
    WriteString('height? '); ReadCard(height);

    IF (age >= 20) AND (age <= 25) THEN
        IF (height >= 66) AND (height <= 70) THEN
            WriteString(name);
            WriteString(' is a suspect and should be held for interrogation');
            WriteLn;
        END;
    END;
END suspect.
```

Results from program suspect being run

```
input name of suspect Artful Dodger
age? 23
height? 69
Artful Dodger is a suspect and should be held for interrogation
```

The conditions used in this program are (age >=20), (age <=25), (height >= 66) and (height <=70). It has been possible to combine these conditions into (age >= 20) AND (age <= 25), and (height >= 66) AND (height <= 70) by using the Boolean operator AND. A truth table for AND is given in figure 4.2. This table can be interpreted as follows.

If the (age >= 20) is condition X and (age <= 25) is condition Y, then X AND Y can only be TRUE if both condition X is TRUE AND condition Y is TRUE. In other words both conditions (age >= 20) AND (age <= 25) must be TRUE for the expression to be TRUE. Therefore, if either condition X or condition Y or both, happen to be FALSE the complete expression given by X AND Y is FALSE.

Similarly both conditions in the Boolean expression (height >= 66) AND (height <=70) must be TRUE for the condition to be TRUE. If either one condition or both conditions are FALSE then the Boolean expression is FALSE.

condition X	condition Y	X AND Y
FALSE	FALSE	FALSE
FALSE	TRUE	FALSE
TRUE	FALSE	FALSE
TRUE	TRUE	TRUE

figure 4.2 truth table for logical AND

In the program, if the age is between 20 and 25 years, then the computer executes the next if statement, and if the height is between 66 and 70 inches then the name of the suspect is printed.

This program can be reconstructed, by omitting the second if..then statement, and combining the Boolean conditions for age and height as follows.

```
IF (age >= 20) AND (age  <= 25) AND (height >= 66) AND (height  <= 70) THEN
   WriteString(name);
   WriteString(' is a suspect and should be held for interrogation');
END;
```

condition X	condition Y	X OR Y
FALSE	FALSE	FALSE
FALSE	TRUE	TRUE
TRUE	FALSE	TRUE
TRUE	TRUE	TRUE

figure 4.3 truth table for logical OR

The same program can be reconstructed yet again using different Boolean conditions and the logical operator OR. By considering the age and height to lie outside the ranges it is possible to construct the following Boolean expressions:

$$(age < 20) \text{ OR } (age > 25)$$
$$(height < 66) \text{ OR } (height > 70)$$

From the truth table for logical OR, given in figure 4.3, if (age < 20) is condition X, and (age >25) is condition Y, then X OR Y is TRUE if X is TRUE, or Y is TRUE, or both are TRUE.

Similarly, if (height < 66) is condition X, and (height > 70) is condition Y, then X OR Y is TRUE if X is TRUE, or Y is TRUE, or both are TRUE.

The conditions for age and height can also be combined into (age < 20) OR (age > 25) OR (height < 66) OR (height > 70).

Thus if any one of the conditions is TRUE the entire Boolean expression is TRUE, and the suspect is released. However, if all the conditions are FALSE, then the entire Boolean expression must be FALSE, the suspect is between 20 and 25 years of age and between 66 and 70 inches tall, and is held for further interrogation, as depicted in the next program.

Boolean expressions and variables can have their values changed by using the NOT operator. If the Boolean variable *error* was TRUE, then NOT *error* would be FALSE. Similarly if *error* was FALSE then NOT *error* would be TRUE.

```
MODULE NewSuspect;
(*
program to display the name of a suspect to a crime who is aged between
20 and 25 years and between 66 inches and 70 inches tall
*)

FROM StringType IMPORT string;
FROM STextIO IMPORT ReadString, WriteString, WriteLn;
FROM SWholeIO IMPORT ReadCard;

VAR
    name    : string;
    age     : CARDINAL;
    height  : CARDINAL;

BEGIN
    WriteString('input name of suspect '); ReadString(name);
    WriteString('age? '); ReadCard(age);
    WriteString('height? '); ReadCard(height);

    WriteString(name);
    IF (age < 20) OR (age > 25) OR (height < 66) OR (height > 70) THEN
        WriteString(' is not a suspect and should be released');
    ELSE
        WriteString(' is a suspect and should be held for interrogation');
    END;
    WriteLn;
END NewSuspect.
```

Results from program NewSuspect being run twice

```
input name of suspect Bill Sykes
age? 44
height? 68
Bill Sykes is not a suspect and should be released

input name of suspect Artful Dodger
age? 23
height? 69
Artful Dodger is a suspect and should be held for interrogation
```

4.6 Case

An ordinal type has a value that belongs to an ordered set of items. For example integers are ordinal types since they belong to the set of values from -32768 to +32767. A character is an ordinal type since it belongs to the ASCII character set of values from the null character to the del character. Real numbers and strings are not ordinal types.

If selection is to be based upon an ordinal type then a CASE statement can be used in preference to if..then..else statements.

The syntax of the case statement follows.

case statement ::=	**CASE** case selector **OF** case list **END**
case selector ::=	ordinal expression
case list ::=	case alternative {'|' case alternative } [case else part]
case else part ::=	**ELSE** statement sequence
case alternative ::=	[case label list ':' statement sequence]
case label list ::=	case label {',' case label}
case label ::=	constant expression ['..' constant expression]

The expression must evaluate to an ordinal value. Each possible ordinal value is represented as a case label, which indicates the statement to be executed corresponding to the value of the expression. Those values that are not represented by case labels will result in the statement after ELSE being executed.

In the example that follows a user is invited to input a value for a motorway junction on the M2 in Kent. Depending upon the value of the junction from 1 to 7, the destination of the adjoining roads at that junction are displayed. If the value input is not in the range 1..7 the statement after the ELSE will warn the user of the data error. After the appropriate statement has been executed the computer branches to the END of the case statement.

69

```
MODULE motorway;
(*
program to demonstrate the use of the CASE statement
*)

FROM SWholeIO IMPORT ReadCard;
FROM STextIO IMPORT WriteString, WriteLn;

VAR
  junction : CARDINAL;

BEGIN
    WriteString('input junction number on the M2 motorway ');
    ReadCard(junction);

    CASE junction OF
    1: WriteString('A2 only')|
    2: WriteString('A228 Snodland Rochester')|
    3: WriteString('A229 Maidstone Chatham')|
    4: WriteString('A278 Gillingham')|
    5: WriteString('A249 Sittingbourne Sheerness')|
    6: WriteString('A251 Ashford Faversham')|
    7: WriteString('A2 Canterbury Dover/ A299 Margate Ramsgate');
    ELSE
        WriteString('DATA ERROR - incorrect junction number');
    END;
    WriteLn;
END motorway.
```

Results from program motorway being run three times

```
input junction number on the M2 motorway 5
A249 Sittingbourne Sheerness

input junction number on the M2 motorway 3
A229 Maidstone Chatham

input junction number on the M2 motorway 66
DATA ERROR - incorrect junction number
```

By comparing the case statement in the program with the syntax notation, the reader should note the following points.

An expression is any expression that will evaluate to an item of ordinal type. In this example the expression consists of a single variable of type integer, which evaluates to an integer in the range 1 .. 7.

A case label is any value that corresponds to the ordinal type in the expression. Case labels in this example represent the junction numbers 1, 2, 3, 4, 5, 6 and 7. Case labels must be unique.

The use of else is optional, and used for the purpose of trapping any values of the expression that are not represented as case labels.

The case statement terminates with the reserved word END.

4.7 Worked examples

This section contains two programs to further demonstrate the use of if..then..else and case statements.

The first program in this section validates a date in the twentieth century. It checks that the number of months in a year should not exceed 12, and that the number of days in each month has not been exceeded. The program also reports on Leap Years.

Notice the use of the Boolean variable *error* to trap a possible error in the value for months.

The method of determining a Leap Year has been to divide the year by 4, and testing for a zero remainder. For example, if the year is 1992, then 1992 MOD 4 is 498 after division with a remainder 0. Therefore the condition (1992 MOD 4 = 0) would be TRUE for a Leap Year. Clearly if the year was 1993, then 1993 MOD 4 is 498 after division with a remainder 1. Therefore the condition (1993 MOD 4 = 0) would be FALSE for a non Leap Year.

```
MODULE validate;
(*
program to validate a date in the format dd mm yy
*)

FROM STextIO IMPORT WriteString, WriteLn;
FROM SWholeIO IMPORT ReadCard, WriteCard;

VAR
   day, month, year : CARDINAL;
   NumberOfDays     : CARDINAL;
   error            : BOOLEAN;

BEGIN
    WriteString('input a date in the twentieth century'); WriteLn;
    WriteString('day '); ReadCard(day);
    WriteString('month '); ReadCard(month);
    WriteString('year '); ReadCard(year);

    error := FALSE;
```

71

```
       (* calculate the number of days in a month and check for Leap Year *)
       CASE month OF
       1,3,5,7,8,10,12 : NumberOfDays := 31 |
       4,6,9,11          : NumberOfDays := 30 |
       2                 : IF year MOD 4 = 0 THEN
                             NumberOfDays := 29;
                             WriteCard(year,4);
                             WriteString(' is a Leap Year');
                             WriteLn;
                           ELSE
                             NumberOfDays := 28;
                           END;
       ELSE
           error := TRUE;
       END;

       IF (day > NumberOfDays) OR error THEN
           WriteString('DATA ERROR - check day or month');
       ELSE
           WriteString('date checked and is valid');
       END;

       WriteLn;
END validate.
```

Results from program validate being run three times

```
input a date in the twentieth century
day 18
month 3
year 1987
date checked and is valid

input a date in the twentieth century
day 12
month 2
year 1992
1992 is a Leap Year
date checked and is valid

input a date in the twentieth century
day 30
month 2
year 1987
DATA ERROR - check day or month
```

In the final example of this chapter, a program is written to mimic a simple calculator. The user is invited to type the value of two real numbers, and to state whether the numbers are to be added (+), subtracted (-), multiplied (*) or divided (/).

A case statement is used to select the appropriate calculation corresponding to the arithmetic operator that was input. Since the result of a division by zero will give a meaningless answer, the program includes an if..then..else statement to trap a zero divisor.

```
MODULE calculator;
(*
program to add, subtract, multiply or divide two numbers
*)

FROM STextIO IMPORT ReadChar, SkipLine, WriteString, WriteLn;
FROM SRealIO IMPORT ReadReal, WriteFixed;

VAR
   first, second : REAL;
   result        : REAL;
   operator      : CHAR;
   error         : BOOLEAN;

BEGIN
    WriteString('input first number '); ReadReal(first);
    WriteString('input second number '); ReadReal(second);
    SkipLine;
    WriteString('input operator '); ReadChar(operator);

    error := FALSE;

    CASE operator OF
    '+' : result := first + second |
    '-' : result := first - second |
    '*' : result := first * second |
    '/' : IF second = 0.0 THEN
                error := TRUE;
          ELSE
                result := first / second;
          END;
    ELSE
        error:=TRUE;
    END;
```

```
    IF error THEN
        WriteString('DATA ERROR - illegal operator or attempt to divide by
                    zero');
    ELSE
        WriteString(' = '); WriteFixed(result,2,10);
    END;
END calculator.
```

Results from program calculator being run four times

```
input first number 250.0
input second number 75.0
input operator +
=         325.00

input first number 18.0
input second number 26.0
input operator *
=         468.00

input first number 35.0
input second number 0.0
input operator /
DATA ERROR - illegal operator or attempt to divide by zero

input first number 121.0
input second number 11.0
input operator x
DATA ERROR - illegal operator or attempt to divide by zero
```

4.8 Summary

☐ A Boolean expression or variable of Boolean type, equates to either TRUE or FALSE.

☐ Depending upon the result of the Boolean expression or variable it is possible for the computer to select different statements in an if statement.

☐ Boolean variables can be used in place of a Boolean expression in an if statement.

☐ Boolean expressions and Boolean variables can be combined into one Boolean expression by using the Boolean operators AND and OR.

☐ If statements may be nested, one within another.

☐ When selection is based upon an ordinal type, a case statement may be used.

☐ All case labels must be unique and of an ordinal type compatible with the selector type.

4.9 Questions - *answers begin on page 375*

1. If A=1, B=-2, C=3, D=4, E='S' and F='J' then state whether the following conditions are true or false.

(a). A=B

(b). A>B   (c). (A<C) AND (B<D)

(d). (A<C) AND (B>D)

(e). (A>B) OR (C<D)

(f). E>F

(g). ((A+C)>(B-D)) AND ((B+C)<(D-A))

2. How would you code the following conditions in Modula-2?

(a). X is equal to Y   (b). X is not equal to Y

(c). A is less than or equal to B

(d). Q is not greater than T   (e). X is greater than or equal to Y

(f). X is less than or equal to Y and A is not equal to B

(g). A is greater than 18 and H is greater than 68 and W is greater than 75

(h). G is less than 100 and greater than 50

(i). H is less than 50 or greater than 100.

3. Trace through the following segment of code for each new value of A,B and C, and state the output in each case.

(a). A=16, B=16, C=32   (b). A=16, B=-18, C=32

(c). A=-2, B=-4, C=16

```
IF A>0 THEN
   IF B<0 THEN
      WriteChar('x');
   ELSE
      IF C>20 THEN
         WriteChar('y');
      END;
   END;
ELSE
   WriteChar('z');
END;
```

4. Modify the suspect program given in the chapter to cater for both sexes, and eliminate all women from the list of suspects.

5. A worker is paid at the hourly rate of 8 per hour for the first 35 hours worked. Thereafter overtime is paid at 1.5 times the hourly rate for the next 25 hours worked and 2 times the hourly rate for further hours worked. Write a program to input the number of hours worked per week, calculate and output the overtime paid.

6. A salesperson earns commission on the value of sales. Figure 4.4 shows the scale of the commission. Write a program to input a figure for the value of sales, calculate and output the commission.

value of sales	% commission
£1 - £999	1
£1000 - £9999	5
£10000 - £99999	10

figure 4.4

7. A barometer dial is calibrated into the following climatic conditions STORM RAIN CHANGE FAIR and VERY DRY. Write a program that will input one of these readings abbreviated to the first letter, and output what to wear from the following rules.

STORM   wear overcoat and hat.
RAIN   wear raincoat and take umbrella.
CHANGE   behave as for FAIR if it rained yesterday and as for RAIN if it did not.
FAIR   wear jacket and take umbrella.
VERY DRY wear jacket.

8. A bicycle shop in Oxford hires bicycles by the day at different rates throughout the year, according to the season - see figure 4.5. The proprietor also gives a discount on the number of days a bicycle is hired. If the hire period is greater than 7 days, then a reduction of 25% is made. For every bicycle hired a returnable deposit of £50 must be paid. Write a program to input the season and the number of days hire, calculate and display the cost of the hire including the returnable deposit.

season	charge
Spring	£5.00
Summer	£7.50
Autumn	£3.75
Winter	£2.50

figure 4.5

Chapter 5
Repetition

In writing computer programs it is often necessary to repeat part of a program a number of times. One way of achieving this would be to write out that part of the program as many times as it was needed. This however, is a very impractical method, since it would produce a very lengthy computer program and the number of times part of the program is to be repeated, is not always known in advance. The purpose of this chapter is to introduce the reader to three methods for repetition that overcome the disadvantages just mentioned. These methods are based on the control structures known as WHILE, REPEAT and LOOP. By the end of the chapter the reader should have an understanding of the following topics.

☐   The syntax and use of WHILE, REPEAT and LOOP control statements.

☐   A knowledge of when it is appropriate to use each statement.

☐   The comparison of strings, using an imported library function, in a Boolean expression.

☐   The detection of characters input at a keyboard.

5.1 While..do

A while loop will allow a statement to be repeated zero or more times. The syntax of the while loop is:

while statement ::= **WHILE** Boolean expression **DO** statement sequence **END**

Consider the use of a while loop to display numbers on a screen while the numbers are not zero. A segment of the program follows.

```
ReadInt(number);
WHILE number # 0 DO
   WriteInt(number,3);
   ReadInt(number);
END;
```

If the first number to be read is zero then the Boolean expression *number # 0* will be FALSE. The computer will not enter the loop but branch to the next executable statement after the reserved word END at end of the while loop. Since the loop was not entered the contents of the loop is said to have been repeated zero times.

However, if the first number to be read was non-zero, the Boolean expression would be TRUE, and the computer would execute the statements contained within the loop. To this end the number would be written on the screen and the next number input at the keyboard. The computer then returns to the line containing the Boolean expression which is re-evaluated to test whether the new number is not zero. If the condition is TRUE the computer continues to execute the statements in the loop. If the condition is FALSE the computer will branch to the next executable statement after the reserved word END that effectively marks the end of the loop.

Restating the behaviour of the while loop, if the first number read is zero then the loop is not entered, the statements within the loop have been repeated zero times. If the second number to be read is zero the statements in the loop will have been repeated once. If the third number to be read is zero the statements in the loop will have been repeated twice, etc. Therefore, if the hundredth number to be read is zero the statements inside the loop will have been repeated ninety-nine times.

The outline program has been developed into the following Modula-2 program.

```
MODULE WhileDemo;
(*
program to demonstrate the WHILE loop
*)

FROM STextIO IMPORT WriteString, WriteLn;
FROM SWholeIO IMPORT ReadInt, WriteInt;

VAR
  value : INTEGER;

BEGIN
    WriteString('input an integer - terminate with 0 ');
    ReadInt(value);
```

```
    WHILE (value # 0) DO
            WriteInt(value,3); WriteLn;
            WriteString('input an integer - terminate with 0 ');
            ReadInt(value);
    END;
END WhileDemo.
```

The specimen outputs from the program shows (i) the statements within the loop being repeated twice, and (ii) the statements within the loop not being repeated at all.

(i) Results from program WhileDemo being run

```
input an integer - terminate with 0 36
 36
input an integer - terminate with 0 18
 18
input an integer - terminate with 0 0
```

(ii) Results from program WhileDemo being run

```
input an integer - terminate with 0 0
```

The program *suspect*, taken from section 4.5 in the previous chapter, has been re-constructed to include a while loop to allow the program to be repeated many times without the need to re-run the program.

Before the while loop is entered the user is requested to input the name of a suspect. If the word END is input, then this is a cue to exit from the while loop. The reader might expect to construct the Boolean expression *name <> 'END'* to control the while loop, for example, *WHILE name <> 'END' DO*. However, in Modula-2 you cannot compare strings in this manner. There exists a library module named *Strings* that contains a function *Equal* that will allow two strings to be compared, and returns the value TRUE if both strings are the same, otherwise it returns the value FALSE. To compare the *name* with the string 'END', it is necessary to construct the Boolean expression *Equal(name, 'END')*. If the contents of the string variable *name* is equal to the string 'END', then the result is TRUE. If this expression is to be used in a while loop it will be necessary to negate the condition, for example,

WHILE NOT Equal(name, 'END') DO

The while loop will then be exited only when the Boolean expression *Equal(name, 'END')* is NOT TRUE.

As long as the string END is not input in response to the prompt to input the name of a suspect, the computer will continue to process the details of all suspects to the crime.

```
MODULE SuspectDemo;
(*
program to display the name of a suspect to a crime who is aged between
20 and 25 years and between 66 inches and 70 inches tall
*)

FROM StringType IMPORT string;
FROM STextIO IMPORT ReadString, WriteString, WriteLn;
FROM SWholeIO IMPORT ReadCard;
FROM Strings IMPORT Equal;

VAR
  name   : string;
  age    : CARDINAL;
  height : CARDINAL;

BEGIN
    WriteString('input name of suspect - terminate with END ');
    ReadString(name);

    WHILE NOT Equal(name, 'END') DO
            WriteString('age? '); ReadCard(age);
            WriteString('height? '); ReadCard(height);

        IF (age >= 20) AND (age <= 25) THEN
            IF (height >= 66) AND (height <= 70) THEN
                WriteString(name);
                WriteString(' is a suspect and should be held
                            for interrogation');
                WriteLn;
            END;
        END;

        WriteString('input name of suspect - terminate with END ');
        ReadString(name);
    END;
END SuspectDemo.
```

Results from program SuspectDemo being run

```
input name of suspect - terminate with END Smith
age? 20
height? 68
Smith is a suspect and should be held for interrogation
input name of suspect - terminate with END Jones
age? 26
height? 68
```

```
input name of suspect - terminate with END Evans
age? 25
height? 69
Evans is a suspect and should be held for interrogation
input name of suspect - terminate with END END
```

5.2 Repeat..until

Unlike a while loop a repeat..until loop will permit the statements within the loop to be executed at least once by the computer. The syntax of the repeat..until loop is:

repeat statement ::= **REPEAT** statement sequence **UNTIL** Boolean expression

The program *motorway*, taken from section 4.6 in the previous chapter, has been re-constructed to include a repeat..until loop to allow the program to be repeated many times without the need to re-run the program. In this program the user is given the option to continue executing the statements in the loop until the reply to the question is *no*.

Notice that the computer enters the loop without any test for entry being made. Hence the contents of a repeat..until loop will always be executed at least once. There can be many executable statements between the REPEAT and UNTIL reserved words. If the reply to continue is *no* then the Boolean expression, *reply = no*, will be TRUE and the computer will branch to the next executable statement after the Boolean expression. However, if the reply is *yes* then the Boolean expression will be FALSE and the computer will repeat all the statements within the loop.

In this example the Boolean expression that controls the exit from the repeat..until loop compares the contents of a character variable with a character constant. The character constant *no* had been declared under the CONST section of the program.

```
MODULE roads;
(*
program to demonstrate the use of the REPEAT..UNTIL statement
*)

FROM SWholeIO IMPORT ReadCard;
FROM STextIO IMPORT SkipLine, ReadChar, WriteString, WriteLn;

CONST
    no = 'N';

VAR
  junction : CARDINAL;
  reply    : CHAR;

BEGIN
    REPEAT
        WriteString('input junction number on the M2 motorway ');
```

```
        ReadCard(junction);

        CASE junction OF
        1: WriteString('A2 only')|
        2: WriteString('A228 Snodland Rochester')|
        3: WriteString('A229 Maidstone Chatham')|
        4: WriteString('A278 Gillingham')|
        5: WriteString('A249 Sittingbourne Sheerness')|
        6: WriteString('A251 Ashford Faversham')|
        7: WriteString('A2 Canterbury Dover/ A299 Margate Ramsgate');
        ELSE
            WriteString('DATA ERROR - incorrect junction number');
        END;
        WriteLn; SkipLine;
        WriteString('continue? - answer Y[es] or N[o] ');
        ReadChar(reply); reply:=CAP(reply);
    UNTIL reply = no;
END roads.
```

Results from program roads being run

```
input junction number on the M2 motorway 5
A249 Sittingbourne Sheerness
continue? - answer Y[es] or N[o] Y
input junction number on the M2 motorway 7
A2 Canterbury Dover/ A299 Margate Ramsgate
continue? - answer Y[es] or N[o] Y
input junction number on the M2 motorway 8
DATA ERROR - incorrect junction number
continue? - answer Y[es] or N[o] Y
input junction number on the M2 motorway 1
A2 only
continue? - answer Y[es] or N[o] N
```

5.3 Loop

The third control structure for repetition is a generalised form of REPEAT..UNTIL and WHILE..DO. The syntax of the statement is:

loop statement ::= **LOOP** statement sequence **END**

which upon inspection, has no means of controlling an exit from the loop. For example:

```
LOOP
  WriteString('help there is no way out!');
  WriteLn;
END;
```

would cause the message *help there is no way out!* to be repeated until the program was abandoned by the user. When there is no exit point within the loop, the loop is said to be infinite.

In order to create a termination of the loop, it is necessary to include an EXIT statement within the loop. The EXIT statement may appear anywhere inside the LOOP statement and causes the computer to move to the next executable statement after the loop END. The examples in figure 5.1 show how the LOOP statement can be used in place of WHILE and REPEAT. The variable counter is used as a control variable to ensure that only five iterations of the loop are performed.

```
(i)   counter:=0;                    (* simulation of a WHILE loop *)
      WHILE counter#5 DO             counter:=0;
                                     LOOP
                                       IF counter=5 THEN EXIT END;
          counter:=counter+1;
      END;                             counter:=counter+1;
                                     END;

                                     (* simulation of a REPEAT loop *)
(ii)  counter:=0;                    counter:=0;
      REPEAT                         LOOP
          counter:=counter+1;          counter:=counter+1;

      UNTIL counter = 5;

                                       IF counter=5 THEN EXIT END;
                                     END;
```

figure 5.1 simulation of WHILE and REPEAT

If data is input to a program using WHILE, it is necessary to use two read statements, as illustrated in section 5.1. This is not the case when using a LOOP statement, since the test to exit from the loop can be placed anywhere inside the loop.

```
LOOP
   ReadReal(value);
   IF value = 0.0 THEN EXIT END;
   .
   .
   .
END;
```

5.4 Worked examples

The following program illustrates how a sentence is input at the keyboard and the number of words in the sentence counted. It is assumed that only one space is used between words and the sentence is terminated by a full-stop.

```
MODULE WordsCount;
(*
program to count the number of words in a sentence
*)

FROM STextIO IMPORT ReadChar, WriteString, WriteLn;
FROM SWholeIO IMPORT WriteCard;

CONST
    space=40C;
    FullStop=56C;

VAR
    character    : CHAR;
    NumberOfWords : CARDINAL;

BEGIN
    NumberOfWords := 0;
    WriteString('input a sentence on one line - terminate with a full stop ')
    WriteLn;
    ReadChar(character);
    WHILE character # FullStop DO
        IF character = space THEN
            NumberOfWords := NumberOfWords + 1;
        END;
        ReadChar(character);
    END;
    NumberOfWords := NumberOfWords + 1;
    WriteString('number of words in sentence is ');
    WriteCard(NumberOfWords, 3);
END WordsCount.
```

Result from program WordsCount being run

```
input a sentence on one line - terminate with a full stop
To be or not to be that is the question.
number of words in sentence is  10
```

In this last example the end of the sentence was detected by using the full- stop as a sentinel. However, it is possible to detect the end of a line of data by testing for the end of line character. This is given in the ASCII codes as FF with a decimal code of 12 or an octal code of 15C.

In the second example of this section a program is to be written that will edit a single line of text. Within the input text will be found an opening parenthesis (, followed some characters later by a closing parenthesis). The text is to be output, with the characters between and including the parentheses removed.

In this example you may assume that the character (always appears before the character), and both characters will always be present.

```
MODULE edit;
(*
program to input a line of text, edit a portion of the text and output
the edited text
*)

FROM STextIO IMPORT ReadChar, WriteChar, WriteString, WriteLn;

CONST
    EndOfLine = 15C;
VAR
    character : CHAR;

BEGIN
    WriteString('input one line of text');
    WriteLn;

    (* read and write characters up to ( *)
    ReadChar(character);
    WHILE character # '(' DO
            WriteChar(character);
            ReadChar(character);
    END;

    (* read characters up to ) *)
    WHILE character # ')' DO
            ReadChar(character);
    END;

    (* read and write characters as far as the end of the line *)
    ReadChar(character);
    WHILE character # EndOfLine DO
            WriteChar(character);
            ReadChar(character);
    END;
END edit.
```

Results from program edit being run

```
input one line of text
WriteString('all the text between parenthesis should be suppressed');
WriteString;
```

85

In the last worked example of this chapter, a program has been written to allow a sentence to be input at the keyboard. The sentence may be written over several lines, be punctuated by commas, semi-colons, colons, and spaces, and be terminated by a question mark, exclamation mark or full-stop. The purpose of the program is to count the number of words in the sentence and display this value. The user is given the opportunity to type more than one sentence.

Every time a character is input, it is checked for being either a terminator (question mark, exclamation mark or full-stop), or a word separator (comma, semi-colon, colon, space, carriage return CR or line feed LF). In response to both types of word-delimiter, the word count must be increased by one. However, it is necessary to detect the occurrence of multiple spaces or two separators together, in which case the word count must not be increased again.

```
MODULE WordCount;
(*
program to count the number of words in a sentence
*)

FROM STextIO IMPORT WriteString, WriteLn, ReadChar, SkipLine;
FROM SWholeIO IMPORT WriteCard;

CONST
    no='N';
    QuestionMark=77C;
    ExclamationMark=41C;
    FullStop=56C;
    comma=54C;
    SemiColon=73C;
    colon=72C;
    space=40C;
    LF=12C;
    CR=15C;

VAR
    character: CHAR;
    words     : CARDINAL;
    reply     : CHAR;

BEGIN
    REPEAT
        words:=0;
        WriteString('input a sentence, terminate with ? ! or .');
        WriteLn;
        ReadChar(character);
        LOOP
            CASE character OF
            (* test for terminator *)
            QuestionMark,
            ExclamationMark,
```

```
        FullStop                : words := words + 1; EXIT |

        (* test for separator *)
        comma,
        SemiColon,
        colon,
        space,
        LF                      :   LOOP
                                        ReadChar(character);
                                        (* test for start of next word *)
                                        IF (character # space) AND
                                        (character # CR) AND
                                        (character # LF) THEN
                                            words := words + 1; EXIT;
                                        END;
                                    END;

        ELSE
            ReadChar(character);
        END;
    END;
    WriteLn;  SkipLine;
    WriteString('number of words in sentence ');
    WriteCard(words,3); WriteLn; WriteLn;
    WriteString('more sentences - answer Y[es] or N[o] ');
    ReadChar(reply);
    reply:=CAP(reply);
    SkipLine;
  UNTIL reply = no;
END WordCount.
```

Results from program WordCount being run

```
input a sentence, terminate with ? ! or .
Mary had                        a little
lamb; it's fleece was white as snow
and everywhere that Mary went
the lamb was sure to go.

number of words in sentence  22

more sentences - answer Y[es] or N[o] Y
input a sentence, terminate with ? ! or .
This is a test of the program,
a full sentence can be input
over
as many lines as are required,
and, full account, will be taken of all
punctuation.
```

87

```
number of words in sentence 29

more sentences - answer Y[es] or N[o] N
```

5.5 Summary

☐   The statements within a while loop can be executed zero or more times.

☐   The statements within a repeat..until loop are executed at least once.

☐   Both loops use Boolean expressions to control the amount of repetition.

☐   In a while loop all statements within the loop will be executed while the Boolean expression is TRUE.

☐   In a repeat..until loop all the statements within the loop will be executed until the Boolean expression becomes TRUE.

☐   A loop statement will permit a conditional exit from anywhere inside the loop

5.6 Questions - *answers begin on page 377*

1. Write a program to display the message 'HELLO WORLD' ten times on the screen.

2. Write a program to input a message of your choice and the number of times you want to repeat it, then repeatedly display the message.

3. Return to your solution to question 8 in section 3.9 of chapter 3, and modify your program to output a table of values for temperatures in degrees Fahrenheit and the equivalent temperatures in degrees Centigrade. You should use a range of 32 degrees Fahrenheit through to 212 degrees Fahrenheit in steps of 10 degrees.

4. Write a program to output a table of conversion from miles to kilometres. The table should contain column headings for miles and kilometres. Miles should be output as cardinal values between 1 to 50, in steps of 1 mile, with a new headings being printed at the beginning of the table and after 20 and 40 miles respectively. Note 1 mile = 1.609344 Km

5. Write a program using REPEAT..UNTIL loops to output:

(a). The odd integers in the range 1 to 29.

(b). The squares of even integers in the range 2 to 20.

(c). The sum of the squares of the odd integers between 1 to 13 inclusive.

(d). the alphabet, both upper and lower case. Hint - use the CHR function and the ASCII code for the letter A through Z and a through z.

6. Write a program to find and print the arithmetic mean of a list of positive numbers. The number of numbers is not known in advance. Terminate the sequence of numbers with zero.

7. Write a program to calculate and output the overtime pay for ten employees and the total overtime paid. Overtime is paid at 12.00 per hour for every hour worked over 40 hours per week. Assume that employees do not work for fractional parts of an hour.

8. Write a program to input a phrase and display the ASCII code for each character of the phrase. Hint - use the ORD function.

9. Write a program to find and print the largest integer from ten integers input at the keyboard. Assume that numbers are input one per line.

10. Rewrite the program edit listed in section 5.4, so that it will output the contents of the parentheses only.

Chapter 6
Procedures

By now the reader has enough information to write small programs. At this stage it is important to explain how specific programming activities can be formed into building blocks known as procedures. The procedures can then be used as the basis for constructing larger programs. By the end of this chapter the reader should have a knowledge of the following topics.

☐ The construction of a procedure and its place within a program.

☐ How to call a procedure from within a program.

☐ How to pass data into a procedure and return data from a procedure.

☐ How to document and test a procedure.

☐ The importance of the use of a test harness.

6.1 What is a procedure?

A procedure can be regarded as a group of self-contained declarations and executable statements that can be used to perform a particular activity. It is very important to stress the words self-contained, since a procedure can be written and tested in isolation from the final program. A procedure can be thought of as a building block. Different building blocks are written for different activities within a program. A complete program is built from many different building blocks or procedures, each having been tested, before being used as part of the whole program.

6.2 Where are procedures written?

Procedures are embedded into a program. They are written after the global constant and variable declarations of the program and before the executable statements of the main program. The position that procedures occupy in a program is depicted in figure 6.1.

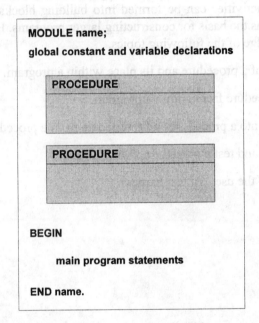

figure 6.1 procedures contained within a program

6.3 Procedure format

One of the rectangles that depicts a procedure, in figure 6.1, has been expanded to show the format of a procedure in figure 6.2.

The format of a procedure is basically the same as a program. A procedure must be given a name, which may be followed by a list of data declarations known as a formal parameter list. A procedure may contain a list of local constant and variable declarations.

The executable statements of a procedure are found between the reserved words BEGIN and END.

The syntax of a procedure may be expressed as follows:

procedure declaration ::=	procedure heading ';' procedure block
procedure heading ::=	**PROCEDURE** identifier [formal parameters]
procedure block ::=	declarations [**BEGIN** statement sequence] **END** identifier

---

PROCEDURE name (formal parameter list);

---

local constant and variable declarations
BEGIN

    executable statements of procedure

END name;

---

figure 6.2 format of a procedure

6.4 Calling a procedure

The following procedure has been written to display a message on a screen a specific number of times.

```
PROCEDURE display(message : string; number : CARDINAL);
(*
procedure to display a message a number of times on the screen
*)
VAR
    counter : CARDINAL;
BEGIN
    counter := 0;
    WHILE counter # number DO
        WriteString(message);
        WriteLn;
        counter := counter + 1;
    END;
END display;
```

The first line of the procedure contains the name of the procedure, in this example *display*, followed by a list of data declarations known as the formal parameter list. In this example the declarations are:

(message : string; number : CARDINAL);

The formal parameter list has a dual role. In addition to specifying data declarations it informs the user about what data can be passed into the procedure, and what data can be passed out of the procedure. Remember a procedure is a self-contained mini-program, it should function where possible, independently of data that has been declared outside of the procedure. However, there will be a need to communicate with the procedure by calling it by name and possibly passing data to it and/or receiving data from it.

To call the procedure *display* it is necessary to

(i) state the name of the procedure, and

(ii) state two items of data that correspond with the two items in the formal parameter list.

A procedure call, therefore, may have two parts, the name of the procedure, and a list of data known as the actual parameter list.

The following statements, printed in italics, all represent possible ways of calling the procedure *display*, where the variable *information* is of type string and the variable *NumberOfTimes* is of type CARDINAL.

```
BEGIN
    display('Happy Birthday', 5);
END.

BEGIN
    information:='Happy Birthday';
    display(information, 5);
END.

BEGIN
    NumberOfTimes := 5;
    display('Happy Birthday', NumberOfTimes);
END.

BEGIN
    information:='Happy Birthday';
    NumberOfTimes:=5;
    display(information, NumberOfTimes);
END.
```

The following points must be observed when calling a procedure.

The list of constants or variables after the procedure name is known as the actual parameter list.

The number of actual parameters MUST be the same as the number of corresponding formal parameters.

The order of the actual parameters and the formal parameters MUST be the same.

The data types of the corresponding actual and formal parameters MUST be the same.

Having executed a procedure the computer returns to the next executable statement after the procedure call.

6.5 Parameters

The syntax of the formal parameter list follows:

formal parameters ::=   '(' [formal parameter list] ')'
formal parameter list ::=   formal parameter {';' formal parameter}
formal parameter ::=   [**VAR**] identifier list ':' formal type

It is possible to represent four different formats of a formal parameter list.

(i) No formal parameter list - the declarations between the parentheses are by-passed.

(ii) A formal parameter list that contains data declarations NOT preceded by the word VAR.

(iii) A formal parameter list that contains declarations that are proceeded by the word VAR.

(iv) A mixture of declarations, those preceded by VAR and those not preceded by VAR.

In the example, the procedure display has a formal parameter list that fits the second category:
(message : string; number : CARDINAL);

The parameters *message* and *number* are known as **value** parameters. The data is passed to the parameters in this procedure by making a copy of the actual parameter data available to the procedure. Figure 6.3 illustrates this fact.

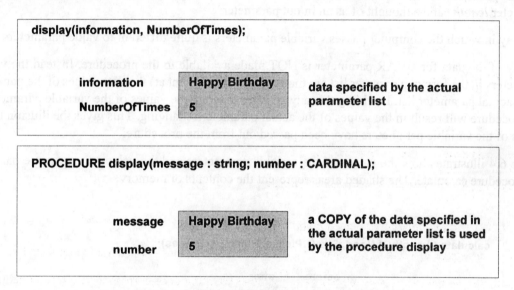

figure 6.3 data passed by value uses a copy of the data

Consider another example in which a procedure has been written to calculate the number of pieces of wood of set size that can be cut from a length of wood.

```
PROCEDURE calculate(VAR length : REAL; size : REAL; VAR pieces : CARDINAL);
(*
procedure to calculate the number of pieces of wood that can be cut to a
set size from a length of wood
*)
BEGIN
    pieces := 0;
    WHILE length >= size DO
        length := length - size;
        pieces := pieces + 1;
    END;
END calculate;
```

In the example, the procedure calculate has a formal parameter list that fits the fourth category:

(VAR length:REAL; size:REAL; VAR pieces:CARDINAL);

The parameters *length* and *pieces* are known as **variable** parameters, since they are preceded by the word VAR. The parameter size is a value parameter.

Variable (VAR) parameters are used if data is to be passed out from a procedure, or both into and out from a procedure. In this example *pieces* is a parameter that will pass the number of pieces cut from the length of wood, out from the procedure, since it is a result from a calculation. The parameter *length*, however, is a variable parameter that has passed into the procedure the length of wood, and will pass out from the procedure the amount of wood that has been wasted after the cutting has taken place. The variable parameter *length* can be thought of as an in/out parameter.

The way in which the computer passes variable parameters is quite different to value parameters.

A copy of the data for a VAR parameter is NOT made available to the procedure. Instead the variable parameters in the formal parameter list are made to reference (point at) the data values of the parameters in the actual parameter list. By doing this any changes made to the values of the variable parameters by the procedure will result in the values of the actual parameters changing. This gives the illusion that the values of the variable parameters have been passed out from the procedure.

Figure 6.4 illustrates how the values of the variable parameters and the value parameter are passed for the procedure calculate. The shaded areas represent the contents of memory.

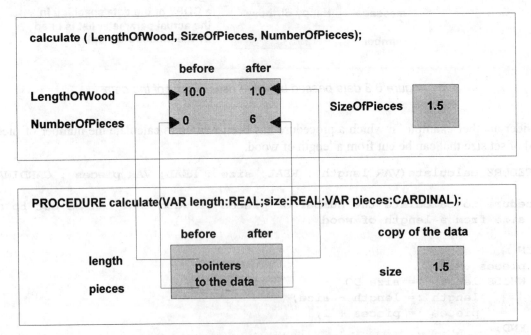

figure 6.4 VAR parameters point to the data

If on a first reading of this section the reader finds the subject difficult, then remember the following points when constructing a formal parameter list of a procedure.

A VAR parameter is used whenever an item of data is passed out from a procedure.

If a parameter is only to be passed into a procedure then it does NOT require to be preceded by the word VAR.

6.6 Local declarations

In figure 6.2, the statement after the formal parameter list, indicates that local constant and variable declarations are made before the executable statements of a procedure are written. These represent the constants and variables that are local ONLY to that procedure. The constants and variables declared here CANNOT be used outside of the procedure. Remember that a procedure should be viewed as a self-contained unit that contains its own constants and variables.

In the procedure *display* the only local variable was a *counter* of type CARDINAL, and the procedure *calculate* required no local constant or variable declarations.

6.7 Global declarations

Global declarations are not new to the reader. All the constant and variable declarations that have been made, in all the programs that have been written prior to this chapter, have been global. The word global implies that the constants and variables can be used anywhere in the program. If a procedure call is made from the main body of a program then any constant and/or variable names that are used in the actual parameter list MUST be declared as global constants and/or variables in the program.

The reader may question why it is necessary to use formal parameters if the actual parameters are global. Since global parameters can be used anywhere in a program, and that includes all the procedures, then why bother with parameter passing?

Programs should be developed from carefully designed, tested and documented procedures. Each procedure should behave like a well engineered component. The purpose or functionality of the procedure together with the data necessary to drive the procedure should be set out as a series of instructions on how to use the procedure.

In the development of a program that abandons the use of parameter passing, the developer would need to read through a procedure to distinguish between the local and global data in order to declare the global data. This in itself implies that such a procedure could not be treated as an off-the-shelf component that could be plugged into a program. In the production of a large complex program the sheer overhead of trying to manage global data would lead to poorly documented, error- prone programs.

6.8 Documentation

Before coding any procedures, regardless of how trivial, the reader should adopt the habit of completing a Procedure Documentation Form, shown in figure 6.5. This document is an aid to helping the programmer understand about the purpose or functionality of the procedure, determine what parameters are required and whether they are passed by value or as variables, and define the local constants and variables of the

Procedure Documentation Form

Procedure name:

Description of purpose of procedure and parameters:

number of parameters			VAR		
parameter name		type	in	out	in/ out

Local variables and/or constants			
description of variables and/or constants	identifier	type	max size

figure 6.5 layout of a procedure documentation form

procedure. Completing this document might seem a chore, and a far cry from cobbling together some code on the computer, but it is a necessary part of engineering a robust, reliable software component.

6.9 Worked examples

This section contains four examples on the use of procedures. Two of the procedures have already been used in this chapter, and two are new to the reader.

Each of the examples will contain the following documentation.

(i) A description of the problem to be solved.

(ii) A completed Procedure Documentation Form for the procedure to be coded.

(iii) A test program, known as a test harness, used to compile and test the procedure.

(iv) Specimen results from the test harness program being run.

98

The first example requires a procedure to display a message a specified number of times on a screen. The message and the number of times the message is to be repeated are both passed to the procedure as value parameters.

Procedure Documentation Form

Procedure name: display

Description of purpose of procedure and parameters:

To display a message a number of times on the screen.

number of parameters	2			VAR	
parameter name	type	in	out	in/ out	
message number	string cardinal	✓ ✓			

Local variables and/or constants

description of variables and/or constants	identifier	type	max size
a variable to count the number of times the message is displayed	counter	cardinal	65535

figure 6.6 documentation for procedure display

```
MODULE TestHar1;

FROM STextIO IMPORT ReadString, WriteString, WriteLn;
FROM StringType IMPORT string;
FROM SWholeIO IMPORT ReadCard;

VAR
     information   : string;
     NumberOfTimes : CARDINAL;
```

```
PROCEDURE display(message : string; number : CARDINAL);
(*
procedure to display a message a number of times on the screen
*)

VAR
     counter : CARDINAL;
BEGIN
     counter := 0;
     WHILE counter # number DO
           WriteString(message);
           WriteLn;
           counter := counter + 1;
     END;
END display;

BEGIN
     WriteString('input message '); ReadString(information);
     WriteString('repeat how many times? '); ReadCard(NumberOfTimes);
     display(information, NumberOfTimes);
END TestHar1.
```

Results from program TestHar1 being run

```
input message Happy Birthday
repeat how many times? 5
Happy Birthday
Happy Birthday
Happy Birthday
Happy Birthday
Happy Birthday
```

The second example involves developing a procedure that will calculate a modulus-11 check digit for a four-digit number. It is common practice to provide account numbers (e.g bank accounts, building society accounts, etc) with a check-digit. This digit provides a means for the computer to check that the account number has been correctly entered into the computer and that the digits have not been transposed.

A modulus-11 check-digit, for a four-digit number, is calculated in the following way.

Using the account number 9118 as an example: multiply each digit by its associated weight, here we have the weights 5,4,3,2 and calculate the sum of the partial products.

$(5x9) + (4x1) + (3x1) + (2x8) = 68$

The sum 68 is then divided by 11 and the remainder 2 is then subtracted from 11, the result 9 is the check digit. The account number, including the check-digit as the last digit, becomes 91189. If the value of the check-digit is computed to be 10 this is replaced by the character X and a check-digit of 11 will be replaced by 0.

Procedure Documentation Form

Procedure name: convert

Description of purpose of procedure and parameters:

To calculate a modulus-11 check digit of a four-digit   account number

number of parameters	2			VAR	
parameter name	type	in	out	in/ out	

parameter name	type	in	out	in/ out
number	cardinal	✓		
CheckDigit	cardinal		✓	

Local variables and/or constants

description of variables and/or constants	identifier	type	max size
individual digits of four-digit number	d1	cardinal	9
	d2	cardinal	9
	d3	cardinal	9
	d4	cardinal	9
sum of products	sum	cardinal	65535

figure 6.7 documentation for the procedure convert

```
MODULE TestHar2;

FROM STextIO IMPORT WriteString, WriteLn;
FROM SWholeIO IMPORT ReadCard, WriteCard;

VAR
     AccountNumber  : CARDINAL;
     CD             : CARDINAL;
```

```
PROCEDURE convert(number:CARDINAL; VAR CheckDigit : CARDINAL);
(*
procedure to calculate the check-digit of a four-figure number
*)

VAR
     d1, d2, d3, d4 : CARDINAL;
     sum            : CARDINAL;
BEGIN
     (* extract four digits from the number *)
     d1:=number DIV 1000;
     d2:=(number MOD 1000) DIV 100;
     d3:=(number MOD 100) DIV 10;
     d4:=number MOD 10;

     (* calculate the sum of the partial products *)
     sum := (5*d1) + (4*d2) + (3*d3) + (2*d4);
     CheckDigit := 11 - sum MOD 11;
END convert;

BEGIN
     WriteString('input a four-digit number '); ReadCard(AccountNumber);
     convert(AccountNumber, CD);
     WriteString('number with check digit '); WriteCard(AccountNumber, 4);

     IF    CD = 10 THEN
         WriteString('X');
     ELSIF CD = 11 THEN
         WriteString('0');
     ELSE
         WriteCard(CD,1);
     END;
END TestHar2.
```

Results from program TestHar2 being run three times

```
input a four-digit number 3456
number with check digit 34568

input a four-digit number 1001
number with check digit 10014

input a four-digit number 1234
number with check digit 12343
```

The third example involves writing a procedure to find the price of food at the Greasy Spoon Cafe, see figure 2.3, section 2.1 in chapter 2.

Procedure Documentation Form

Procedure name: **FindPrice**

Description of purpose of procedure and parameters:

To search for the price of items of food from a menu.

If the item is found then a Boolean variable success is set TRUE otherwise it is set FALSE

number of parameters	3			VAR	
parameter name	type	in	out	in/ out	
item	string	✓			
price	real		✓		
success	boolean		✓		

figure 6.8 documentation for procedure FindPrice

```
MODULE TestHar3;

FROM STextIO IMPORT ReadString, WriteString, WriteLn;
FROM SRealIO IMPORT ReadReal, WriteFixed;
FROM StringType IMPORT string;
FROM Strings IMPORT Equal;

VAR
    food  : string;
    cost  : REAL;
    found : BOOLEAN;

PROCEDURE FindPrice(item : string; VAR price : REAL;
                VAR success : BOOLEAN);
(*
procedure to find the price of an item on a menu at the Greasy Spoon Cafe
If the item of food is found then success remains TRUE and the price of the
item is assigned, otherwise success is set to FALSE and the price is set
to zero
*)
```

103

```
BEGIN
    success := TRUE;

    IF    Equal(item,'fruit juice')       THEN price:=0.30;
    ELSIF Equal(item,'soup')              THEN price:=0.50;
    ELSIF Equal(item,'cold meat salad')   THEN price:=2.50;
    ELSIF Equal(item,'sausages (2)')      THEN price:=1.00;
    ELSIF Equal(item,'bacon & egg')       THEN price:=1.00;
    ELSIF Equal(item,'cod')               THEN price:=1.50;
    ELSIF Equal(item,'plaice')            THEN price:=2.00;
    ELSIF Equal(item,'portion of chips')  THEN price:=0.75;
    ELSIF Equal(item,'tea')               THEN price:=0.25;
    ELSIF Equal(item,'coffee')            THEN price:=0.35;
    ELSE
            success:=FALSE;
            price:=0.0;
    END;
END FindPrice;

BEGIN
    WriteString('input name of food from menu '); ReadString(food);
    FindPrice(food, cost, found);
    IF found THEN
        WriteString('£'); WriteFixed(cost,2,4);
    ELSE
        WriteString(food); WriteString(' not on menu');
    END;
    WriteLn;
END TestHar3.
```

Results from program TestHar3 being run three times

```
input name of food from menu bacon & egg
£1.00

input name of food from menu lamb chops
lamb chops not on menu

input name of food from menu portion of chips
£0.75
```

In the fourth and final example of this section a procedure is written to calculate the number of pieces of wood that can be cut to a set size from a length of wood.

Procedure Documentation Form

Procedure name: calculate

Description of purpose of procedure and parameters:

To calculate the number of pieces that can be cut to a set size from a length of wood

number of parameters	3			VAR	
parameter name	type	in	out	in/out	
length	real			✓	
pieces	cardinal		✓		
size	real	✓			

figure 6.9 documentation for procedure calculate

```
MODULE TestHar4;

FROM STextIO IMPORT WriteString, WriteLn;
FROM SWholeIO IMPORT WriteCard;
FROM SRealIO IMPORT ReadReal, WriteFixed;

VAR
    LengthOfWood    : REAL;
    SizeOfPieces    : REAL;
    NumberOfPieces  : CARDINAL;

PROCEDURE calculate(VAR length : REAL; size : REAL; VAR pieces : CARDINAL);
(*
procedure to calculate the number of pieces of wood that can be cut to a
set size from a length of wood
*)

BEGIN
    pieces := 0;
    WHILE length >= size DO
            length := length - size;
            pieces := pieces + 1;
    END;
END calculate;
```

```
BEGIN
    WriteString('what is the length of the wood? ');
    ReadReal(LengthOfWood);
    WriteString('what size pieces do you want to cut? ');
    ReadReal(SizeOfPieces);
    calculate(LengthOfWood, SizeOfPieces, NumberOfPieces);
    WriteString('number of pieces '); WriteCard(NumberOfPieces,3); WriteLn;
    WriteString('size of off-cut '); WriteFixed(LengthOfWood,2,5);
END TestHar4.
```

Results from program TestHar4 being run

```
what is the length of the wood? 10.0
what size pieces do you want to cut? 1.5
number of pieces   6
size of off-cut  1.00
```

6.10 Summary

☐ A procedure should be written as a self-contained unit that represents a single programmed activity.

☐ A procedure may contain parameters and local constants and variables.

☐ When a procedure is called it is possible to pass data into the procedure.

☐ Upon return from a procedure it is possible to pass data out from the procedure.

☐ After the execution of a procedure the computer returns to the next executable statement after the procedure call.

☐ A parameter that is passed into a procedure only, is known as a value parameter, and is implemented by a copy of the actual parameter being made available to the procedure.

☐ A parameter that is passed out from, or into and out from a procedure is known as a variable parameter, and is implemented by the variables of the procedure making reference to the variables of the actual parameter list.

☐ A parameter that is passed out from, or into and out from a procedure is preceded by the reserved word VAR. Parameters that are only passed into a procedure may not be preceded by the word VAR.

☐ The number and type of actual parameters MUST match the number and type of formal parameters.

☐ The names of the actual and formal parameters can be the same or different.

- ☐ Constants and variables, including formal parameters, that are declared within a procedure remain local to that procedure.

- ☐ Constants and variables, including actual parameters, that are declared as global declarations at the beginning of a program can be used anywhere within the program, including all the procedures in the program.

- ☐ A procedure cannot be compiled on its own, and needs to be embedded within a test program.

- ☐ The test program, also known as a test harness, can be used to fully test the procedure.

- ☐ Procedures should be developed as off-the-shelf components that come complete with instructions for use.

6.11 Questions - *answers begin on page 380*

1. If the following variables are global:

```
VAR
   A,B,C : INTEGER;
   X,Y,Z : CHAR;
```

State the errors, if any, in the following procedure calls and procedure declarations.

	procedure call	procedure declaration
(a).	alpha	alpha(d,e,f);
(b).	beta(A,B,C)	beta;
(c).	delta(18'*')	delta(VAR C:INTEGER; Z:CHAR);
(d).	gamma(X,Y)	gamma(i,j,k:INTEGER);

2. Trace through the following procedure and determine the value of *result* after each of the following calls.

test('a', result); test('B', result); test('c', result);

```
PROCEDURE test(letter : CHAR; VAR capital : BOOLEAN);
BEGIN
   IF (ORD(letter) >=65) AND (ORD(letter) <=90) THEN
      capital:=TRUE
   ELSE
      capital:=FALSE;
END test;
```

3. Write and test a procedure to calculate the diameter, circumference and area of a circle. The input parameter is the radius, and the output parameters are the diameter, circumference and area; (diameter = 2 x radius; circumference = 2 x PI x radius; and area = PI x radius x radius where PI=3.14159).

4. Write and test a procedure to convert an octal digit (base 8) to a description of the digit, for example 0 zero, 1 one, 2 two ... 7 seven. The input parameter is an octal digit, and the output parameters are a variable of string type containing the description and a Boolean variable denoting success if the digit was correctly converted.

5. Write and test a procedure to analyse whether a character is a vowel or not. The input parameter is a letter of the alphabet, and the output parameter is a Boolean variable indicating success if a letter was a vowel.

6. Convert the program motorway in section 4.6, chapter 4, to a procedure containing the following formal parameter list - (JunctNo : CARDINAL; VAR destination : string; VAR error : BOOLEAN). The procedure will accept and validate a junction number and return the destination at that junction and whether the junction number was valid.

Chapter 7
Program development

This chapter explores the technique of dividing a programming solution into several parts, where each part is dedicated to a particular activity. The pencil and paper solution is tested and then coded into procedures that together form a Modula-2 program. The chapter also focuses the reader's attention on the need to develop documentation as a solution evolves. By the end of the chapter the reader should have a knowledge of the following topics.

☐ The place of program design in the context of developing a program.

☐ The use of pseudo-code as a means of expressing a program design in English.

☐ Testing a design for logical errors.

☐ Documenting procedures and coding procedures.

☐ Testing procedures as self-contained units.

☐ Bringing all the elements of the design and tested procedures together into a complete program.

7.1 Why design programs?

A beginner to programming may question why it is necessary to design programs at all. Indeed some programmers produce rough and ready solutions at a keyboard and continue to amend their programs until eventually the program appears to do what was expected. This approach often works for small programs, however, this is NOT a recommended approach to writing larger programs for the following reasons.

The final code is probably not easy to follow since it was no more than cobbled together.

The documentation of variable names and specific items of code are probably non-existent.

The program may not have been broken down into logical activities and written as separate procedures.

There was probably no test plan for testing the program or procedures and indeed the program might easily fail. Remember that such programs are produced by continuous amendments until the program appears to work. This changing or tinkering with code often leads to unforeseen side effects that may not manifest themselves for quite some time.

Lastly, what of the programmer who is asked to modify the program at a later date? Without sufficient documentation such a task is normally preceded by tracing through the program in order to gain an insight into how the program functions. Since program maintenance accounts for a substantial proportion of programming budgets, clearly any improvement in programmer productivity must be a saving.

7.2 Pseudo-code

The simplest way of learning about the fundamental techniques of program design is to work through a problem.

A program is to be written that will allow a teacher to input examination marks at a keyboard, categorise the marks into one of four grades and after all examination marks have been entered into the computer, display a breakdown of the number of marks in each category of grade. The grade distribution is shown in the following table.

mark range	grade
100-85	distinction
84-65	merit
64-40	pass
39-0	fail

The number of examination marks is not known in advance, therefore, it will be necessary to introduce a sentinel mark, say 999, to signify the end of the marks being input. This value of course, must not be processed.

As early as chapter 3, it was evident that a simple order for processing data followed the sequence:

input data
process data
output results

In this problem each grade category represents the number of marks that fall into a particular mark range. For example, five distinctions would imply that five examination marks were within the range 100% to 85%. Each grade category must be initialised to zero before it can be used to tally the number of marks in each grade category. The simple processing model inferred in chapter 3 must now be modified to cope with initialisation.

> *initialisation*
> *input mark*
> *analyse mark*
> *output results*

The input of data, is the input of a single mark, one per line, at a keyboard. Since each mark must be processed BEFORE the next mark can be input it will be necessary to introduce a loop into the processing model.

> *initialisation*
> *input mark*
> *while mark not equal to sentinel do*
>   *analyse mark*
>   *input mark*
> *end while*
> *output results*

After the first examination mark has been input it is compared with the sentinel value 999. If the mark is NOT 999 then it is processed. A new mark is input and its value compared with the sentinel. This sequence of input mark, compare with sentinel and process mark continues while the mark is not the sentinel value. When the sentinel is input the computer will output the values stored in the four grade categories.

This first level of program design, provides the reader with an overview of the program to be written, and will form the basis for the main or control program.

The next stage is to examine each operation in the sequence and attempt to write down what is required. At present this is a pencil-and-paper exercise, and no attempt should be made to code the computer program or go anywhere near the computer!

Since initialisation consists of setting the value of each category of grade to zero the operation initialisation can be refined into the following design.

Pseudo-code for the procedure initialisation.

> *set distinction to zero*
> *set merit to zero*
> *set pass to zero*
> *set fail to zero*

The next operation to consider is input data. The data takes the form of percentage marks with the exception of the sentinel value 999. Whenever data is input, every attempt should be made to ensure that the data passed on for processing is valid. In this example the design of the part of the operation to input data should ensure that only valid data in the range 0 - 100 is passed on for processing, with the exception of the sentinel value.

Pseudo-code for the procedure input mark.

> *repeat*
> > *read mark*
> *until mark in range or sentinel*

The next operation to process each item of data, involves each mark being examined to see which range of marks it belongs to. When the appropriate range has been found the value of the grade category will be increased by one. For example if a mark was to be found in the range 85 to 100 then the value of distinction would be increased by one.

Pseudo-code for the procedure analyse mark.

> *if mark in range 85 to 100 then*
> > *increase distinction by 1*
> *else*
> > *if mark in range 65 to 84 then*
> > > *increase merit by 1*
> > *else*
> > > *if mark in range 40 to 64 then*
> > > > *increase pass by 1*
> > > *else*
> > > > *increase fail by 1*
> > > *end if*
> > *end if*
> *end if*

Finally the operation to output results is refined. This involves writing the values of the four grade categories to a screen.

Pseudo-code for the procedure output results.

> *write headings 'grade' and 'frequency'*
> *write sub-heading 'distinction' and value of distinction*
> *write sub-heading 'merit' and value of merit*
> *write sub-heading 'pass' and value of pass*
> *write sub-heading 'fail' and value of fail*

Notice that in designing the program, the structures if..then..else, repeat..until and while..do are used in the same context as though they were Modula-2 control statements in a program. However, at this stage there is no need for the statements to obey the syntax rules of statements in a Modula-2 program. The format of this design is to write statements in English, as a pseudo-code, that express ideas on how to initialise values, input data, process data and output results. The introduction of the Modula-2 look-alike control statements is to document how the sequence of statements are to be obeyed.

7.3 Test data and desk check

Having designed a solution to a programming problem using pseudo-code it is now possible to verify that the program is correct. Indeed there is little point in continuing beyond the design stage to coding and implementing a program if the design is fundamentally flawed.

In order to verify that the design represents a correct solution to a problem it is necessary to trace through the pseudo-code using suitable test data. When choosing test data the following points should be kept in mind.

The type and nature of the data is representative of the problem. Numerical data, where applicable, should be chosen for ease of calculation.

Data should be chosen to test all parts of the design.

Data is meaningful and within well defined ranges. However, this assumes that the design being tested will always use valid data. This is not always the case since some designs will be specifically written to trap bad data. In such circumstances the data must be chosen to cover all eventualities.

To initially test the design of the program to categorise marks by grades, the following approach is taken, using the Design Desk Check Document shown in figure 7.1.

Write the chosen test data and expected results from this data on the Design Desk Check Document.

Trace through the overall design of the program by starting with the call to initialisation. The name initialisation and the associated data identifiers are written on the form together with any values that are assigned to the data identifiers. In this case all four data identifiers are set to zero.

The next call is to input mark. The name input mark is documented together with the data identifier mark. The statement read mark is interpreted by using the first item of test data and assigning this value to mark. The condition associated with the repeat..until loop is documented and tested, the outcome of the test [T]rue or [F]alse is documented on the form.

In tracing the design the next statement to be executed is the while..do loop in the main program. The name main program and the condition in the while loop are both documented on the form. The condition is evaluated and the outcome written on the form.

Since the condition statement associated with the while..do loop is true, the next call is to analyse mark. The first condition in the series of tests is documented, and evaluated. Since this condition is true, the data identifier distinction is increased by 1 to the value 1.

The next statement to trace is input mark within the while loop of the main program. The next item of data from the test data list is tabulated and the condition associated with the repeat..until loop is evaluated. This value is false, therefore, another mark is read from the test data list. The condition is again evaluated, this time it is true, and the trace continues with testing the condition in the while loop in the main program.

The trace through the pseudo-code and the tabulation of data identifiers/ conditions and associated values continues until the sentinel value is read from the test data list. The final call is to output results. The four data identifiers and their respective current values documented on the form. The desk check appears to give the same results as those expected results predicted earlier, and at this stage it appears that the

113

Design Desk Check Document	1 OF 1

Test data	Expected results
100 101 75 65 55 45 35 999	distinction 1 merit 2 pass 2 fail 1

main program/ procedure	data identifier/ condition	value
initialisation	distinction merit pass fail	0 0 0 0
input mark	mark 0<=mark<=100 or 999	100, 101, 75, 65, 55, 45, 35, 999 T, F, T, T, T, T, T, T
main program	mark <> 999	T, T, T, T, T, T, F
analyse mark	85 <= mark <= 100 distinction 65 <= mark <= 84 merit 40 <= mark <= 64 pass mark < 40 fail	T, F, F, F, F, F 1 T, T, F, F, F 1, 2 T, T, F 1, 2 T 1
output results	distinction merit pass fail	1 2 2 1

figure 7.1 results of trace through pseudo-code

basic logical design of the program might function correctly. The pseudo-code and testing phase is a necessary and fundamental part in engineering the construction of a program. This phase is vital in establishing the following points.

(i) attempting to find a method of solving the problem;

(ii) verifying that the logical design for processing the data is correct;

(iii) determining which procedures are to be used in the program;

(iv) determining the order in which the procedures are called;

(v) identifying variables that are required in the procedures and main program.

7.4 Documenting procedures

Before any detailed coding is contemplated it is wise to establish what each procedure will do, and what parameters are necessary in order to process data. By examining the data identifiers recorded for each procedure on the Design Desk Check Document it is possible to determine:

(i) which data identifiers represent parameters and which represent local variables, and

(ii) which of the parameters are VAR parameters.

In the procedure initialisation the four identifiers are VAR parameters since their values are initialised in the procedure, and are required in other parts of the program, see figure 7.2.

In the procedure to input a mark, the only identifier is a VAR parameter since its value is required in other parts of the program, see figure 7.3.

In the procedure to analyse a mark, the identifier *mark* is an (in) parameter since it supplies a value to the procedure. However, the remaining identifiers are all VAR parameters since their values are needed in other parts of the program, see figure 7.4. Finally the procedure to display the results only requires the values of the four grades, and for this reason can be treated as (in) parameters, see figure 7.5.

Procedure Documentation Form				
Procedure name: initialisation				
Description of purpose of procedure and parameters: To set the four grade counters distinction, merit, pass and fail to zero				
number of parameters 4			VAR	
parameter name	type	in	out	in/ out
distinction merit pass fail	cardinal cardinal cardinal cardinal		✓ ✓ ✓ ✓	

figure 7.2

Procedure Documentation Form

Procedure name: **InputMark**

Description of purpose of procedure and parameters:

To input a mark in the range 0 to 100 or a sentinel value 999.
The procedure will not accept marks that are outside the range, except for
the sentinel value.
If a mark is outside the range the procedure will request that the mark is
input again.

number of parameters	1			VAR	
parameter name		type	in	out	in/ out
mark		cardinal		✓	

figure 7.3

Procedure Documentation Form

Procedure name: **analysis**

Description of purpose of procedure and parameters:

To classify a mark as belonging to a particular grade.
The number of marks in that grade is then increased by 1.

number of parameters	5			VAR	
parameter name		type	in	out	in/ out
mark		cardinal	✓		
distinction		cardinal		✓	
merit		cardinal		✓	
pass		cardinal		✓	
fail		cardinal		✓	

figure 7.4

```
                    Procedure Documentation Form

  Procedure name:     results

  Description of purpose of procedure and parameters:

  To display the number of distictions, merits, passes and failures.
```

number of parameters	4			VAR	
parameter name	type	in	out	in/ out	
distinction	cardinal	✔			
merit	cardinal	✔			
pass	cardinal	✔			
fail	cardinal	✔			

figure 7.5

7.5 Coding procedures

Having completed these forms it is now possible to extract enough information to code the name, formal parameter list and comments about the purpose of each procedure.

Each procedure is then coded directly from the corresponding pseudo-code, and should be embedded within a test harness program so that it can be compiled and tested before being copied as a well-engineered, off-the- shelf software component into the final program.

The pseudo-code design has been listed prior to the coding of each procedure. The reader should inspect the one-to-one correspondence that exists between the statements in the pseudo-code and the statements in the procedure.

At this stage each procedure is compiled and tested within its own separate test harness.

Pseudo-code for the procedure initialise.

set distinction to zero
set merit to zero
set pass to zero
set fail to zero

```
MODULE TH1;

FROM SWholeIO IMPORT WriteCard;

VAR
    distinction, merit, pass, fail : CARDINAL;

PROCEDURE initialisation(VAR distinction, merit, pass, fail : CARDINAL);
(*
procedure to set each of the grade counters to zero
*)
BEGIN
    distinction:=0;
    merit:=0;
    pass:=0;
    fail:=0;
END initialisation;

BEGIN
    initialisation(distinction, merit, pass, fail);
    WriteCard(distinction,3);
    WriteCard(merit,3);
    WriteCard(pass,3);
    WriteCard(fail,3);
END TH1.
```

Results of running test harness

```
0   0   0   0
```

Pseudo-code for the procedure to input a mark.

> *repeat*
> > *read mark*
> *until mark in range or sentinel*

```
MODULE TH2;

FROM STextIO IMPORT WriteString, WriteLn;
FROM SWholeIO IMPORT ReadCard, WriteCard;

CONST
    sentinel = 999;
VAR
    distinction, merit, pass, fail, mark : CARDINAL;
```

```
PROCEDURE InputMark(VAR mark : CARDINAL);
(*
procedure to input a mark, and validate that it is either a percentage or
a sentinel value
*)
BEGIN
    REPEAT
        WriteString('input a percentage mark - type 999 to stop ');
        ReadCard(mark);
    UNTIL ((mark >= 0) AND (mark <= 100)) OR (mark = sentinel);
END InputMark;

BEGIN
    REPEAT
        InputMark(mark);
        WriteCard(mark,3);
        WriteLn;
    UNTIL mark = sentinel;
END TH2.
```

Results from running test harness

```
input a percentage mark - type 999 to stop 56
 56
input a percentage mark - type 999 to stop 101
input a percentage mark - type 999 to stop 999
999
```

Pseudo-code for the procedure analysis used to process the data.

> *if mark in range 85 to 100 then*
> > *increase distinction by 1*
> *else*
> > *if mark in range 65 to 84 then*
> > > *increase merit by 1*
> > *else*
> > > *if mark in range 40 to 64 then*
> > > > *increase pass by 1*
> > > *else*
> > > > *increase fail by 1*
> > > *end if*
> > *end if*
> *end if*

Notice in the procedure *analysis* that else if has been combined to form ELSIF, hence only one END is necessary in the Modula-2 code.

```
MODULE TH3;

FROM SWholeIO IMPORT WriteCard;

VAR
    D,M,P,F : CARDINAL;

PROCEDURE analysis(mark : CARDINAL;
                   VAR distinction, merit, pass, fail : CARDINAL);
(*
procedure to increase the appropriate grade counter according to the
value of the mark
*)
BEGIN
    IF    mark >= 85 THEN
        distinction := distinction + 1;
    ELSIF mark >= 65 THEN
        merit := merit + 1;
    ELSIF mark >= 40 THEN
        pass := pass + 1;
    ELSE
        fail := fail + 1;
    END;
END analysis;

BEGIN
    D:=0; M:=0; P:=0; F:=0;
    analysis(100,D,M,P,F);
    analysis(75,D,M,P,F);
    analysis(65,D,M,P,F);
    analysis(55,D,M,P,F);
    analysis(45,D,M,P,F);
    analysis(35,D,M,P,F);
    WriteCard(D,3);
    WriteCard(M,3);
    WriteCard(P,3);
    WriteCard(F,3);
END TH3.
```

Results from running TestHarness

```
  1   2   2   1
```

120

Pseudo-code for the procedure to display the results on a screen.

write headings 'grade' and 'frequency'
write sub-heading 'distinction' and value of distinction
write sub-heading 'merit' and value of merit
write sub-heading 'pass' and value of pass
write sub-heading 'fail' and value of fail

```
MODULE TH4;

FROM STextIO IMPORT WriteString, WriteLn;
FROM SWholeIO IMPORT WriteCard;

PROCEDURE results(distinction, merit, pass, fail : CARDINAL);
(*
procedure to display the number of marks that fall into each of the cate-
gories of grades
*)
BEGIN
    WriteLn;
    WriteString('grade            frequency'); WriteLn;
    WriteString('distinction  ');      WriteCard(distinction,2); WriteLn;
    WriteString('merit        ');      WriteCard(merit,2); WriteLn;
    WriteString('pass         ');      WriteCard(pass,2); WriteLn;
    WriteString('fail         ');      WriteCard(fail,2); WriteLn;
END results;

BEGIN
    results(1,2,2,1);
END TH4.
```

Results from running test harness

```
grade           frequency
distinction     1
merit           2
pass            2
fail            1
```

7.6 Coding the main program

At this stage in the development of the program it is possible to record on a data analysis form, see figure 7.6, a description of the actual parameters, their identifiers, types and sizes. The names of the actual parameters can be the same as the formal parameters. Regardless of whether the names are the same or not, each procedure will either have a copy of the actual parameter in the case of (in) parameters or reference to the actual parameter in the case of VAR parameters.

DATA ANALYSIS FORM				
description		identifier	data type	size
grade counters	distinction	distinction	CARDINAL	<=65535
	merit	merit	CARDINAL	<=65535
	pass	pass	CARDINAL	<=65535
	fail	fail	CARDINAL	<=65535
examination mark		mark	CARDINAL	<=65535

figure 7.6

The first level program design forms the basis of the main or control program. Now the names and the actual parameters of the procedures have been defined, the main or control program can be coded.

Pseudo-code design of the main or control program.

> *initialisation*
> *input mark*
> *while mark not equal to sentinel do*
> > *analyse mark*
> > *input mark*
> *end while*
> *output results*

```
(* main control program *)
BEGIN
    initialisation(distinction, merit, pass, fail);
    InputMark(mark);
    WHILE mark <> sentinel DO
        analysis(mark, distinction, merit, pass, fail);
        InputMark(mark);
    END;
    results(distinction, merit, pass, fail);
END grades.
```

7.7 A complete program

A listing of the complete program follows. By using an editor it was possible to copy the compiled and tested procedures from their test harnesses directly into the final program. At this stage no attempt should be made to rewrite the procedures, otherwise typographical errors are likely to occur.

```
MODULE grades;
(*
program to input a number of examination marks, and classify each mark
into one of four grades. At the end of the data the number of marks in
each category of grade is displayed
*)

FROM STextIO IMPORT WriteString, WriteLn;
FROM SWholeIO IMPORT ReadCard, WriteCard;

CONST
    sentinel = 999;
VAR
    distinction, merit, pass, fail, mark : CARDINAL;

PROCEDURE initialisation(VAR distinction, merit, pass, fail : CARDINAL);
(*
procedure to set each of the grade counters to zero
*)
BEGIN
    distinction:=0;
    merit:=0;
    pass:=0;
    fail:=0;
END initialisation;

PROCEDURE InputMark(VAR mark : CARDINAL);
(*
procedure to input a mark, and validate that it is either a percentage or
a sentinel value
*)
BEGIN
    REPEAT
        WriteString('input a percentage mark - type 999 to stop ');
        ReadCard(mark);
    UNTIL ((mark >= 0) AND (mark <= 100)) OR (mark = sentinel);
END InputMark;

PROCEDURE analysis(mark : CARDINAL;
                   VAR distinction, merit, pass, fail : CARDINAL);
(*
procedure to increase the appropriate grade counter according to the value
of the mark
*)
BEGIN
    IF    mark >= 85 THEN
        distinction := distinction + 1;
    ELSIF mark >= 65 THEN
        merit := merit + 1;
```

123

```
    ELSIF mark >= 40 THEN
        pass := pass + 1;
    ELSE
        fail := fail + 1;
    END;
END analysis;

PROCEDURE results(distinction, merit, pass, fail : CARDINAL);
(*
procedure to display the number of marks that fall into each of the catego-
ries of grades
*)
BEGIN
    WriteLn;
    WriteString('grade            frequency'); WriteLn;
    WriteString('distinction  '); WriteCard(distinction,2); WriteLn;
    WriteString('merit        '); WriteCard(merit,2); WriteLn;
    WriteString('pass         '); WriteCard(pass,2); WriteLn;
    WriteString('fail         '); WriteCard(fail,2); WriteLn;
END results;

(* main control program *)
BEGIN
    initialisation(distinction, merit, pass, fail);
    InputMark(mark);
    WHILE mark <> sentinel DO
        analysis(mark, distinction, merit, pass, fail);
        InputMark(mark);
    END;
    results(distinction, merit, pass, fail);
END grades.
```

Results from running program grades

```
input a percentage mark - type 999 to stop 100
input a percentage mark - type 999 to stop 101
input a percentage mark - type 999 to stop 75
input a percentage mark - type 999 to stop 65
input a percentage mark - type 999 to stop 55
input a percentage mark - type 999 to stop 45
input a percentage mark - type 999 to stop 35
input a percentage mark - type 999 to stop 999

grade            frequency
distinction      1
merit            2
pass             2
fail             1
```

7.8 Summary

☐ Write a rough outline of how to solve the problem. This will be very brief and the first attempt at solving the problem. No detailed coding is expected at this stage. From this outline it is possible to state the initial procedures that can be used in the program.

☐ For each procedure derive an outline of the code required, and refine this code further until you reach a point when the code will form a 1-1 correspondence with statements in Modula-2.

☐ Invent simple test data and predict the corresponding results. Use this test data to trace through design of the program and produce a table of values for the intended variables. At the end of this desk check compare the values of the intended variables with the anticipated results. The results of the desk check and the anticipated results should agree, if not there is probably a logical error in the design of the program.

☐ Document the purpose and nature of all identifiers in each procedure.

☐ Code each procedure and embed it into a test harness program so that it can be independently compiled and tested.

☐ Code the global declarations and the main control program to form a skeleton of the final program.

☐ Copy, using an editor, the procedures from the test harnesses into the final program. This way the number of transcription errors that can occur in the procedures is drastically reduced.

☐ Compile and if necessary edit and recompile the program in order to remove any errors, including syntax errors.

☐ Test the program using the same test data that was used for the desk check. Ensure that the results are consistent with those expected. Apply more stringent tests on the program using data that, where possible, will test the program to its limits.

7.9 Questions - *answers begin on page 381*

Design, test and implement programs as answers to the following questions.

1. A school teacher keeps the names and addresses of his pupils on record cards. Pupils travel to school from many different villages in the rural region. The teacher wants to design a computer program to count those pupils in his class who fall into the following categories.

distance to school	category
0 to less than 1 mile	A
1 to less than 5 miles	B
5 to less than 10 miles	C
10 miles or further	D

The teacher has for reference a map of the region, with three concentric circles drawn from the school as centre having radii representing 1 mile, 5 miles and 10 miles respectively. From a pupil's record card the teacher knows the village where a pupil lives, therefore, the distance from the school in a straight line can be obtained from the map.

For a class of pupils the data input to the computer will be the number of pupils in the class followed by the distance each pupil lives from the school. When data input is complete the computer will output the number of pupils in each of the four categories.

The basic design for this program might be as follows.

initialise each category and pupil counter to zero
input class size
while pupil counter is not equal to class size do
    input distance
    analyse distance and update category value
    increase pupil counter by 1
end while
output values of categories

2. The lengths of four sides of a quadrilateral and one internal angle are input to a computer. Design a computer program to categorise the shape of the quadrilateral as a square, rhombus, rectangle, parallelogram or irregular quadrilateral.

The rules for determining the shape of the quadrilateral are given in the following table.

name	all sides equal?	opposite sides equal?	right angle
square	true	true	true
rectangle	false	true	true
rhombus	true	true	false
parallelogram	false	true	false

The basic design for this program might be as follows.

repeat
    input angle and lengths of four sides
    analyse shape
    display name of shape
    request for more data
until no more data

3. A motor insurance company uses the criteria of age, type of car and accident record in the last five years as a basis for estimating the type of insurance policy to issue to its customers.

The following table shows how each of the criterion are applied in issuing a policy.

age < 25?	foreign car?	accident?	type of policy
false	false	false	10% comprehensive
false	false	true	10% comprehensive + £50 excess
false	true	false	15% comprehensive
false	true	true	15% comprehensive + £50 excess

true	false	false	15% comprehensive
true	false	true	7.5% third party only
true	true	false	20% comprehensive
true	true	true	decline to issue policy

From the table if false is represented by 0, and true by 1, with the first column age < 25? having a weight of 4, the second column foreign car? having a weight of 2, and the third column accident? having a weight of 1, then each combination of true and false can represent a number. For example, false true false would be $(0x4) + (1x2) + (0x1) = 2$, similarly true false true would be $(1x4) + (0x2) + (1x1) = 5$, etc. If the result of each calculation is known as a score, then the score can be used to look- up using a case statement, the type of policy to issue.

Design a computer program to input the age of the driver, whether the car is of foreign manufacture, whether the driver has had an accident in the last five years, and the estimated value of the car. Calculate the score based upon this information. Look-up the type of policy to issue, and display the premium based upon a percentage of the estimated value of the car.

The basic design of the program might be as follows.

repeat
    input data and calculate score
    look up policy and premium percentage
    display type of policy and cost of premium
    request for more data
until no more data

4. A picture framer has a supply of picture mouldings of various lengths. he wants to cut from them as many 0.5m lengths as possible and where a 0.5m length cannot be cut he will cut 0.2m lengths. Design a program to input the length of a strip of moulding, and calculate and output the number of 0.5m, and 0.2m lengths and the amount of wasted moulding. Repeat the program for different lengths of moulding being input, and keep a running total of the number of 0.5m and 0.2m pieces and the cumulative length of wasted moulding. At the end of the data output the total number of 0.5m, 0.2m pieces and cumulative length of wasted moulding.

One of the procedures to calculate the number of pieces of wood cut to a set size has already been developed in chapter 5, section 5.9. This can be incorporated into the following design.

initialise totals for 0.5m, 0.2m lengths and waste
input length of moulding
while length not zero do
    calculate number of 0.5m lengths and waste
    update total for 0.5m lengths
    calculate number of 0.2m lengths and waste
    update total for 0.2m length
    update total waste
    display results for length of moulding
    input new length of moulding

end while
display results for all mouldings

5. Consider the following rules for calculating income tax in a country.

Personal allowances are £1200 for a single person and £2300 for a married man. A child allowance is £100 per child. Taxable income is the amount remaining after deducting the personal allowance and the total child allowance from the gross income. Income tax is calculated from taxable income according to the following table.

taxable income on	% rate of tax
first £1000	0
next £1000	20
next £2000	30
above £4000	40

If gross salary, personal status (married or single) and the number of children are input to a computer, design a program to calculate and display both the taxable income and the income tax.

Assume for the purposes of this problem that only married couples are entitled to a child allowance, and that married women are classified as single. The design for this program might be as follows.

repeat
    input data
    calculate income tax
    display results
    request for more data
until no more data

Chapter 8
Types, functions and sets

This chapter introduces a miscellany of topics that did not fit naturally into the previous chapters, yet should be covered before proceeding with the remainder of the book. It introduces the reader to subrange and enumerated data types. Subrange types enable a programmer to define legal ranges for data, whereas, enumerated types allow a programmer to create new data types that are more meaningful to the nature of the application that the program is written for.

The chapter also covers a building block that is similar to a procedure, however, unlike a procedure is declared as a specified type, and must return a value, and is known as a function. The use of functions from the mathematics library is also examined through worked examples and also in the context of procedure types.

The concept of a mathematical set is introduced together with operations upon a set. Finally yet another data type is introduced to describe a bitset.

By the end of the chapter the reader should have an understanding of the following topics.

- ☐ The integrity of data and the use of subranges to trap error data.

- ☐ User defined data types through the use of enumerated constants.

- ☐ Standard functions, that are implicit in the language, for using with enumerated types.

- ☐ An introduction to some of the functions found in the mathematics library.

- ☐ Explicitly creating user defined functions.

- ☐ The use of procedure types as parameters.

- ☐ The concept of sets and their use in manipulating bits within computer words.

8.1 Integrity of data

In writing a computer program it is vital to cater for both good and error data. There is a clear distinction to be made first between valid and invalid data. Valid data is expected data, a program has been written to process it and the results are predictable. Invalid data is unexpected data, a program has not been written to process it and, therefore, the results are unpredictable.

Good data is regarded as being correct valid data, whereas error data is incorrect valid data. Go back to the program *newspapers*, developed in Chapter 3, and consider for a moment what would happen if the value 4o had been input in response to the prompt *input cost of Globe* and the character o had been typed by mistake in place of the digit 0 (zero). The cost of the Globe had been declared as a cardinal, therefore, the computer was programmed to accept such a data type and not a combination of the digit 4 and the character o. Since the operating system supervises the running of all programs it should terminate this program and display an error message. This was clearly unexpected data, the program had not been written to cope with it and without the intervention of the operating system the results would have been unpredictable.

However, what if the value of the cost of the Globe had been input as 400 instead of 40? The program would have run correctly, yet the results would have been unreasonable. This value can be regarded as being in error, rather than being invalid, since the program has been written to cater for it but the data is too large to be realistic. Modula-2 will allow a programmer to specify the legal ranges for three of the data types already encountered - integer, cardinal and char.

8.2 Subranges

A reasonable range for the price of newspapers might be 15p to 65p. If there exists a variable CostOfPaper to replace the variables Courier, Globe and Mercury then this new variable can be declared of type cardinal with a subrange 15..65.

VAR
    CostOfPaper : CARDINAL [15..65];

The syntax of a subrange is given by:

subrange type ::=   [range type] '[' constant expression '..' constant expression ']'
range type ::=   ordinal type identifier
ordinal type identifier ::=   type identifier

If the statement *ReadCard(CostOfPaper)* is used to input the cost of a newspaper, the statement will not compile correctly since the compiler regards the subrange type as not strictly a cardinal value. A variable *cost* of type cardinal, that has not had a subrange declared, is used in the statement *ReadCard(cost)* to input the cost of a paper. This value is then assigned to the variable *CostOfPaper*. If a value for the *CostOfPaper* lies outside the range 15 to 65 the operating system will terminate the program.

The program given in section 3.7 to calculate the total and average cost of newspapers is re-written incorporating a sub-range type. The program is run three times. On the first and second occasions error data is deliberately introduced at the keyboard to illustrate to the reader how the program copes with the out-of-range data. To enable sub-range checking in *TopSpeed Modula-2*, the compiler directive (*$R+*) should be inserted on the next line, after the module name.

```
MODULE news;
(*$R+*)
(*
program to find the names and prices of three newspapers, calculate
and output the total cost and average price of the papers
*)

FROM StringType IMPORT string;
FROM STextIO IMPORT ReadString, WriteString, WriteChar, WriteLn;
FROM SWholeIO IMPORT ReadCard, WriteCard;

CONST
    space = 40C;

VAR
  NamePaper1, NamePaper2, NamePaper3 : string;
  CostOfPaper                        : CARDINAL[15..65];
  cost, TotalCost, average           : CARDINAL;

BEGIN
    WriteString('name of first newspaper ');
    ReadString(NamePaper1);
    WriteString('price of '); WriteString(NamePaper1); WriteChar(space);
    ReadCard(cost); CostOfPaper := cost; TotalCost := CostOfPaper;
    WriteString('name of second newspaper ');
    ReadString(NamePaper2);
    WriteString('price of '); WriteString(NamePaper2); WriteChar(space);
    ReadCard(cost); CostOfPaper := cost;
    TotalCost := TotalCost + CostOfPaper;
    WriteString('name of third newspaper ');
    ReadString(NamePaper3);
    WriteString('price of '); WriteString(NamePaper3); WriteChar(space);
    ReadCard(cost); CostOfPaper := cost;
    TotalCost := TotalCost + CostOfPaper;

    average:=TotalCost DIV 3;

    WriteString('total cost of three newspapers is ');
    WriteCard(TotalCost, 4); WriteChar('p'); WriteLn;
    WriteString('average price of newspapers is ');
    WriteCard(average, 4); WriteChar('p'); WriteLn;
END news.
```

Results from program newspapers being run three times

```
name of first newspaper Globe
price of Globe 4o
Run time error: Variable out of range

name of first newspaper Globe
price of Globe 40
name of second newspaper Mercury
price of Mercury 70
Run time error: Variable out of range

name of first newspaper Globe
price of Globe 40
name of second newspaper Mercury
price of Mercury 50
name of third newspaper Courier
price of Courier 60
total cost of three newspapers   150p
average cost of newspapers is    50p
```

The data types discussed so far, integer, cardinal real and char are known as scalar types. This means that their values cannot be sub-divided into further types. All scalar types have the property of being ordered. Given two values it is possible to say whether one value ranks greater than, equal to, or less than the other value. This is obvious for integers, cardinals and reals since -8 is less than 0, 5 is less then 6, and -1.75 is greater than -4.5. Since characters are coded according to the ASCII table given in chapter 2 and appendix V, A is less than B since the code for A is 65 which is less than the code for B (66).

From the sub-range ['A'..'Z']; the ordinal value (position in ASCII table) of A is 65, B is 66 and Z is 90.

From the subrange [-10..+10]; the ordinal value of the integer -10 is -10, 0 is 0 and +10 is +10.

The reader may recall from chapter 3, that Modula-2 has a function ORD that returns the ordinal value of an object in a sub-range. For example, ORD('A') = 65, ORD('B') = 66, ORD(-10) = -10, ORD(+10) = +10, etc.

Reals do not have subranges. Obviously the number of different values between, say, 0.0 and 1.0 is almost infinite. Type real, although a scalar, is not an ordinal type.

The standard functions MAX and MIN, as these identifiers suggest, compute the greatest and least values of ordinal types. For example, in a 16 bit 2's complement representation of an integer type MIN(INTEGER) = -32768 and MAX(INTEGER) = 32767. Using a 16 bit pure binary representation of a cardinal type MIN(CARDINAL) = 0 and MAX(CARDINAL) = 65535. If the data type CHAR contains values given in the ASCII code then MIN(CHAR) = null and MAX(CHAR) = del.

In the following worked example a food commodity is graded A,B,C,D and E where grade A represents a superior variety and grade E represents a poor variety. The price of the food reflects the quality of the food. Grade A food attracts the highest price (MaxPrice = 100), grade B food is priced at (MaxPrice/2), grade C at (MaxPrice/3), grade D at (MaxPrice/4) and grade E at (MaxPrice/5). Write a program to input a grade for food and the quantity of units of food required. Food is only sold in units from 1 to 12 inclusive. Calculate the cost of the purchase.

In calculating the price of the food it is necessary to convert the food grade to a proportion of the MaxPrice. Since ORD('A') is 65, ORD('B') is 66 etc, the expression ORD(FoodGrade)-64 will produce values in the range 1..5 for grades A..E, respectively.

```
MODULE FoodPrices;
(*$R+*)
(* program to calculate the cost of food from a food code *)

FROM STextIO IMPORT WriteLn, WriteString, ReadChar;
FROM SWholeIO IMPORT ReadCard;
FROM SRealIO IMPORT WriteFixed;

CONST
    MaxPrice    = 100;
    MaxQuantity = 12;

VAR
    FoodGrade      : ['A'..'E'];
    quantity       : CARDINAL[1..MaxQuantity];
    grade          : CHAR;
    amount         : CARDINAL;
    price          : REAL;
    CostOfPurchase : REAL;

BEGIN
    WriteString('input grade of food ');
    ReadChar(grade); FoodGrade := CAP(grade);
    WriteString('input quantity required ');
    ReadCard(amount); quantity := amount;
    price := FLOAT(MaxPrice) / FLOAT((ORD(FoodGrade)-64));
    CostOfPurchase := FLOAT(quantity) * price;
    WriteString('cost of purchase £');
    WriteFixed(CostOfPurchase,2,8);
END FoodPrices.
```

Results from program Foodprices being run three times

```
input grade of food a
input quantity required 10
cost of purchase £ 1000.00
```

```
input grade of food x
Run time error: Variable out of range

input grade of food C
input quantity required 100
Run time error: Variable out of range
```

8.3 Enumerated types

A programmer is allowed to create new data types in a Modula-2 program. The type declaration comes after the constant declaration and before the variable declaration.

The purpose of creating enumerated types is to improve the documentation of a program. It is not necessary to invent arbitrary numeric codes to quantify non-numeric values. The associated scalar values can be used directly in a program. For example, in a program that specifies different newspapers the type newspaper could be declared.

TYPE
    newspaper = (Times,Telegraph,Today,Mail,Express,Sun,Observer);

and an associated variable PaperName could be declared as having type newspaper.

VAR
    PaperName : newspaper;

The syntax of enumerated types is declared as:

enumeration type ::= '(' identifier list ')'

Within a program it would be legal to assign a scalar to PaperName:

PaperName := Telegraph;

Notice also that it is not necessary to enclose the scalar with apostrophes since the value is not a string. However, the objects associated with these new types cannot be read or written using any of the input output routines that have been discussed in the previous chapter.

Subranges can also be declared for enumerated types, however, the objects of such ranges cannot be used for input or output. For example:

TYPE
    newspaper = (Times,Telegraph,Today,Mail,Express,Sun,Observer);
    tabloid = [Today..Sun];
VAR
    PopularPress : tabloid;

Within a program the variable *PopularPress* can be assigned any of the values Today, Mail, Express or Sun. A further example of an enumerated type would be:

TYPE
    month = (Mar,Apr,May,Jun,Jul,Aug,Sep,Oct,Nov,Dec,Jan,Feb);

with a declaration of the following subranges.

    Spring = [Mar..May];
    Summer = [Jun..Aug];
    Autumn = [Sep..Nov];
    Winter = [Dec..Feb];

VAR
    SummerHoliday : Summer;
    WinterHoliday : Winter;

Both variables are of the type month with the subranges specified. The variable WinterHoliday can only be assigned the values Dec, Jan or Feb. Notice that if month had been specified as:

    month = (Jan,Feb,Mar,Apr,May,Jun,Jul,Aug,Sep,Oct,Nov,Dec);

the declaration of the subrange Winter = Dec..Feb would be illegal, since the ordinal value of Dec is greater than the ordinal value for Feb.

Scalar values in one list of an enumerated type cannot be used to form part of another list for a different enumerated type. For example:

TYPE
    DaysOfWeek = (Sun,Mon,Tue,Wed,Thu,Fri,Sat);
    DaysNotWorking = (Sun,Wed,Sat);

would be illegal.

8.4 Further functions

The scalar list for type char, although not specifically defined in a program, is implicitly taken to be the list of ASCII codes (see figure 2.8). Members of this list will have predecessors and successors. An exception to this statement is the character *null* which has no predecessor and *del* which has no successor.

For a variable *NextChar* of type CHAR, that has a current value of 'B', INC (NextChar) assigns 'C' to NextChar, DEC(NextChar) assigns 'A' to NextChar and NextChar:= VAL(CHAR,68) assigns the value 'D' to NextChar. In this last expression VAL(CHAR,68) returns the value of data type CHAR, whose ordinal number is 68. This value is 'D'.

In general, VAL(T,N), where T is the type-identifier of an ordinal type and N is a cardinal value, returns the value of the type T, whose ordinal number is N, if one exists. If no such value exists then a run-time error occurs. For variable V of an enumerated type T:

    INC(V) is the same as V:=VAL(T,ORD(V)+1)
    INC(V,N) is the same as V:=VAL(T,ORD(V)+N)

DEC(V) is the same as V:=VAL(T,ORD(V)-1), and
DEC(V,N) is the same as V:=VAL(T,ORD(V)-N).

Whenever INC and DEC cause their respective values to go out of range a run-time error will occur.

Given the declaration

```
TYPE
    month=(Mar,Apr,May,Jun,Jul,Aug,Sep,Oct,Nov,Dec,Jan,Feb);
VAR
    WhichMonth : month;
```

In each of the following examples if WhichMonth:=May has been taken to be the current value then:

INC(WhichMonth) increases WhichMonth by 1 to Jun
INC(WhichMonth,3) increases WhichMonth by 3 to Aug
DEC(WhichMonth) decreases WhichMonth by 1 to Apr
DEC(WhichMonth,2) decreases WhichMonth by 2 to Mar

Note that DEC(WhichMonth,3) or INC(WhichMonth,10) will both result in an out-of-range error.

Note, since data types integer, cardinal and char are ordinal types the functions INC and DEC may also be used on variables associated with these types.

In the worked example that follows the names of newspapers have been used to define constants of the enumerated type newspapers. These constants also have a sub-range depicting the most popular tabloid papers. The program computes the number of papers that have been defined as type newspapers and the number of papers that have been defined as tabloid.

```
MODULE Press;
(* program to demonstrate the use of the predefined functions ORD, MAX
and MIN when applied to an enumerated type *)

FROM STextIO IMPORT WriteString, WriteLn;
FROM SWholeIO IMPORT WriteCard;

TYPE
    newspapers = (Times,Telegraph,Today,Mail,Express,Sun,Observer);
    tabloid=[Today..Sun];

BEGIN
    WriteString('number of different newspapers is ');
    WriteCard(ORD(MAX(newspapers))+1, 2);
    WriteLn;
    WriteString('number of different tabloids is ');
    WriteCard(ORD(MAX(tabloid))-ORD(MIN(tabloid))+1, 2);
    WriteLn;
END Press.
```

Results from program Press being run

```
number of different newspapers is 7
number of different tabloids is 4
```

In the next example a numerical code for a secret agent is input to the computer and deciphered into the initials of the agent. The numerical code is composed of three numbers, each in the range 0 to 25. Each number is increased by 65 (ASCII code for 'A') and taken as the ordinal value in the ASCII character set. The character associated with this ordinal value is then output.

```
MODULE CodeBreaker;
(* program to decipher a numeric code *)

FROM STextIO IMPORT WriteLn, WriteString, WriteChar;
FROM SWholeIO IMPORT ReadCard;

VAR
  code                              : CARDINAL;
  initial_1, initial_2, initial_3 : CHAR;

BEGIN
    WriteString('input three digit code of secret agent '); WriteLn;
    ReadCard(code);
    INC(code, 65); initial_1:=VAL(CHAR, code);
    ReadCard(code);
    INC(code, 65); initial_2:=VAL(CHAR, code);
    ReadCard(code);
    INC(code, 65); initial_3:=VAL(CHAR, code);
    WriteString('the initials of the agent are ');
    WriteChar(initial_1); WriteChar(initial_2); WriteChar(initial_3);
    WriteLn;
    WriteString('his identity is revealed!'); WriteLn;
END CodeBreaker.
```

Results from program CodeBreaker being run

```
input three digit code of secret agent
1
9
7
the initials of the agent are BJH
his identity is revealed!
```

8.5 Mathematics library

The input/output routines that have been used in writing programs, were all pre-written and stored in the libraries STextIO, SWholeIO, and SRealIO. Whenever a routine was required it had to be imported from the appropriate library. Mathematical functions are imported into a program in a similar way. The following functions are based on the *Draft Standard* library RealMath, and can be imported into a program using:

FROM RealMath IMPORT   sqrt, exp, ln,
                                  sin, cos, tan,
                                  arcsin, arccos, arctan,
                                  power;

sqrt(X)   returns the positive square root of the argument. e.g sqrt(10) = 3.162277...
exp(X)   returns the exponential of X. e.g exp(1) = 2.71828 note: e= 2.71828...
ln(X)   returns the natural logarithm of X where X $\geq$ 0. e.g ln(2.71828) = 1; ln(1) = 0
sin(X)   returns the sine of X where X is in radians. e.g sin(0.5236) = 0.5
note: 30 degrees = 0.5236 radians.
cos(X)   returns the cosine of X where X is in radians. e.g cos(1.0472) = 0.5
note: 60 degrees = 1.0472 radians.
tan(X)   returns the tangent of X where X is in radians. e.g tan(0.7854) = 1.0
note: 45 degrees = 0.7854 radians
arcsin(X)   returns the arc sine of X in radians - i.e. the angle whose sine is X;
e.g arcsin(0.5)= 0.5236 since the sine of 30 degrees (0.5236 radians) = 0.5.
arccos(X)   returns the arc cosine of X in radians - i.e. the angle whose cosine is X;
e.g arccos(0.5)= 1.0472 since the cosine of 60 degrees (1.0472 radians) = 0.5.
arctan(X)   returns the arc tangent of X in radians - i.e. the angle whose tangent is X.
e.g arctan(1) = 0.7854... since the tangent of 45 degrees (0.7854..radians) = 1.
power(X,Y) returns the value of X raised to the power of Y.

8.6 Function procedures

Clearly it is impossible to provide all the functions (mathematical and non-mathematical) that a programmer may require in an application program. Therefore, incorporated into the Modula-2 language is a feature that allows a programmer to define explicitly any function. The syntax of a function is almost the same as that of a procedure. However, it is necessary to declare the data type of the function. The data type of each function defined in RealMath, is REAL. The format of each function heading follows, showing the data type expected for the input parameter (contained within the parenthesis), and the data type of the function.

PROCEDURE sqrt(X:REAL):REAL;
PROCEDURE exp(X:REAL):REAL;
PROCEDURE ln(X:REAL):REAL;
PROCEDURE sin(X:REAL):REAL;
PROCEDURE cos(X:REAL):REAL;

```
PROCEDURE tan(X:REAL):REAL;
PROCEDURE arcsin(X:REAL):REAL;
PROCEDURE arccos(X:REAL):REAL;
PROCEDURE arctan(X:REAL):REAL;
PROCEDURE power(X:REAL;Y:REAL):REAL;
```

The format of a function is given as:

function declaration ::=	function heading ';' function block
function heading ::=	**PROCEDURE** identifier [formal parameters] ':' function result type
function block ::=	declarations [**BEGIN** statement sequence] **END** identifier
function result type ::=	type identifier
formal parameters ::=	'(' [formal parameter list] ')'
formal parameter list ::=	formal parameter {';' formal parameter}

and can be interpreted as follow.

```
PROCEDURE NameOfFunction(formal parameter list): type identifier;
    (* local declaration section *)
BEGIN
    (* function body *)
    RETURN (* value for the function name *)
END NameOfFunction;
```

Note that when there are no parameters to pass into or out of the function, then the parenthesis must indicate null formal and actual parameter lists, for example RND().

The name of the function is assigned a value within the function body using the RETURN statement. It is for this reason that the first line of the function declaration must also include a type declaration for the name of the function.

Although the library RealMath contains a function for a tangent, as an academic exercise it is possible to define a new function for the tangent that imports both sin and cos from RealMath. A difference between this function over *tan* in the library RealMath, is that the angle is in degrees and not radians.

```
PROCEDURE  tan(angle:INTEGER):REAL;
CONST
   PI = 3.14159;
VAR
   radians:REAL; (* angle in radians *)
BEGIN
   radians := (FLOAT(angle) * PI)/180.0;
   RETURN Sin(radians)/Cos(radians)
END tan;
```

The formal parameter list can consist of both input and output parameters. In this example the parameter angle represents an input parameter, therefore, the word VAR may be omitted in the formal parameter list.

The following program prints the tangent of angles between 0 degrees and 20 degrees in steps of 1 degree. The function is called in exactly the same manner as any other function i.e. function name followed by argument(s). In this example the function has been called by *tan(angle_in_degrees)*. This function call has been deliberately written into the WriteFixed statement to save introducing an extra variable and assignment statement.

```
MODULE TrigTable;
(* program to print a table of tangents *)

FROM RealMath IMPORT sin, cos;
FROM STextIO IMPORT WriteString, WriteLn;
FROM SWholeIO IMPORT WriteCard;
FROM SRealIO IMPORT WriteFixed;

VAR
   angle_in_degrees : CARDINAL;

PROCEDURE tan(angle : CARDINAL):REAL;
CONST
    pi=3.14159;
VAR
    angle_in_radians : REAL;
BEGIN
    angle_in_radians:=(FLOAT(angle)*pi)/180.0;
    RETURN sin(angle_in_radians)/cos(angle_in_radians);
END tan;

BEGIN
    WriteString('angle tangent(angle)'); WriteLn;
    angle_in_degrees:=0;
    REPEAT
        WriteCard(angle_in_degrees, 2);
        WriteFixed(tan(angle_in_degrees),4,10);
        WriteLn;
        INC(angle_in_degrees);
    UNTIL angle_in_degrees > 20;
END TrigTable.
```

Results from program TrigTable being run

```
angle     tangent(angle)
0         0.0000
1         0.0175
2         0.0349
3         0.0524
4         0.0699
5         0.0875
6         0.1051
```

7	0.1228
8	0.1405
9	0.1584
10	0.1763
11	0.1944
12	0.2126
13	0.2309
14	0.2493
15	0.2679
16	0.2867
17	0.3057
18	0.3249
19	0.3443
20	0.3640

8.7 Graphical output

Often it is required to output a graphical display. The next example illustrates how this is achieved for the sine function. Since the average size of the screen of a monitor is approximately 80 characters wide and the absolute maximum value for the function is 1, it is necessary to introduce factors that increase the width of the sine wave and centralise the position of the wave on the screen. If a sine wave is to be output vertically, the central axis should be positioned approximately 40 characters from the left hand edge of the screen. The width of the sine wave must also be increased by a factor of, say, 30 characters. Figure 8.1 illustrates the positioning of such a wave on the screen. In the following example a plot for the sine wave is given every 15 degrees over two cycles.

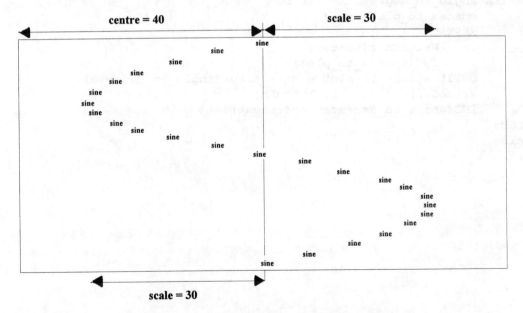

figure 8.1 position of a sine wave on the screen

```
MODULE sine;
(* program to output a sine wave *)

FROM RealMath IMPORT sin;
FROM STextIO IMPORT WriteChar, WriteString, WriteLn;

CONST
    scale     = 30;
    centre    = 40;
    increment = 15;
    pi        = 3.14159;
    space     = 40C;
VAR
    spaces_to_plot   : CARDINAL;
    angle_in_degrees : CARDINAL;

PROCEDURE sine_trace(angle:CARDINAL):CARDINAL;
(*
function to compute the distance from the central vertical axis of
the sine wave
*)
BEGIN
    RETURN TRUNC(FLOAT(centre) - FLOAT(scale)*sin(FLOAT(angle)*pi/180.0));
END sine_trace;

BEGIN
    angle_in_degrees := 0;
    WHILE angle_in_degrees <= 720 DO
            spaces_to_plot := 1;
            REPEAT
                WriteChar(space);
                INC(spaces_to_plot);
            UNTIL spaces_to_plot = sine_trace(angle_in_degrees);
            WriteString('sine'); WriteLn;
            INC(angle_in_degrees, increment);
    END;
END sine.
```

Results from program sine being run

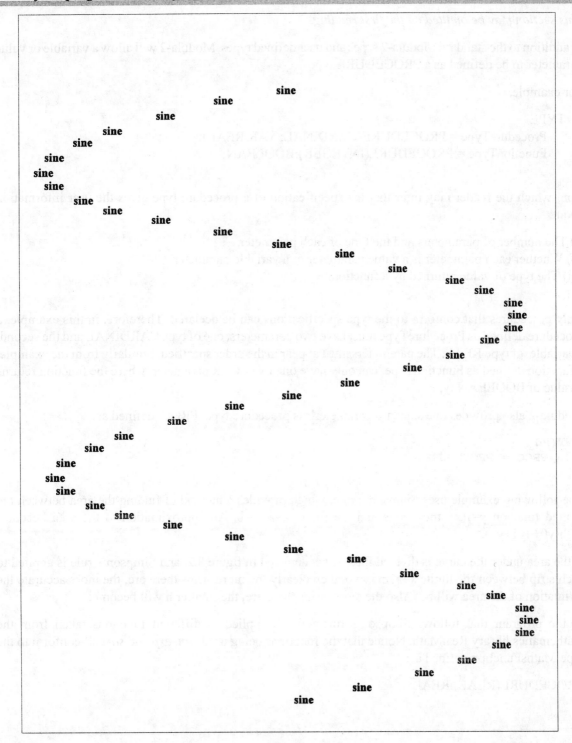

8.8 Procedure types

This section may be omitted on the first reading.

In addition to the standard Modula-2 types and user defined types, Modula-2 will allow a variable or value parameter to be defined as a PROCEDURE type.

For example,

```
TYPE
    ProcedureType = PROCEDURE(CARDINAL; VAR REAL);
    FunctionType = PROCEDURE(INTEGER):BOOLEAN;
```

from which the reader may infer that the specification of a procedure type gives the user information about:

(i) The number of parameters and the type of each parameter.
(ii) Whether each parameter is a value parameter or a variable parameter.
(iii) The type of value returned by a function.

Only procedures that conform to the type specifications can be declared. Therefore, in this example, a procedure defined as ProcedureType must have two parameters, one of type CARDINAL and the second, a variable, of type REAL. The parameters must appear in the order specified. Similarly from the example, a function defined as FunctionType, can only have one INTEGER parameter, where the function returns a value of BOOLEAN type.

Modula-2 also provides one standard parameterless procedure type, PROC, defined as:

```
TYPE
    PROC = PROCEDURE ;
```

The following example uses Simpson's rule, which provides a method of finding the area between the plotted function y=f(x), the x-axis and the limits x=a, x=b. An approximation to the area becomes 1/3h(y0+4y1+y2).

If the area under the curve is divided into strips, depicted in figure 8.2, and Simpson's rule is applied to each strip between the limits x=a and x=b, then clearly the more strips there are, the more accurate the estimation of the area will be. Also the more strips there are, the smaller h will become.

In the program that follows Simpson's rule will be applied to different functions taken from the mathematics library RealMath. Notice that the functions being used, *sin*, *exp* and *sqrt* all conform to the type MathsFunction defined as:

PROCEDURE(REAL):REAL;

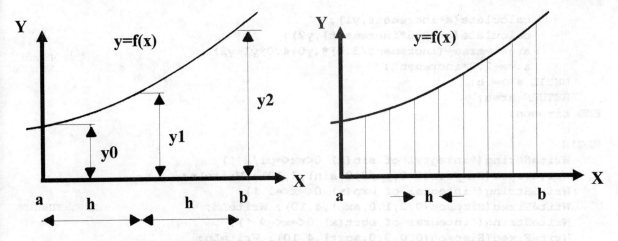

figure 8.2 Simpson's rule for the area under a curve

```
MODULE integration;
(*
program to calculate the integrals between defined limits of sin(x),
exp(x) and sqrt(x)
*)

FROM RealMath IMPORT sin, exp, sqrt;
FROM SRealIO IMPORT WriteFixed;
FROM STextIO IMPORT WriteString, WriteLn;

CONST
    pi        = 3.14159;
    increment = 0.001;

TYPE
    MathsFunction = PROCEDURE (REAL) :REAL;

PROCEDURE Simpson(a,b:REAL; function:MathsFunction):REAL;
VAR
  y0, y1, y2 : REAL;
  area       : REAL;

        PROCEDURE calculate(x:REAL; VAR y:REAL);
        BEGIN
            y:=function(x);
        END calculate;

BEGIN
    area:=0.0;
    REPEAT
        calculate(a,y0);
```

145

```
            calculate(a+increment,y1);
            calculate(a+(2.0*increment),y2);
            area:=area+(increment/3.0)*(y0+4.0*y1+y2);
            a:=a+2.0*increment;
        UNTIL a >= b;
        RETURN area;
    END Simpson;

BEGIN
    WriteString('integral of sin(x)  0<=x<=pi/2 ');
    WriteFixed(Simpson(0.0,pi/2.0,sin),4,10); WriteLn;
    WriteString('integral of exp(x)  0<=x<=1 ');
    WriteFixed(Simpson(0.0,1.0,exp),4,10); WriteLn;
    WriteString('integral of sqrt(x)  0<=x<=9 ');
    WriteFixed(Simpson(0.0,9.0,sqrt),4,10); WriteLn;
END integration.
```

Results from program integration being run

```
integral of sin(x)  0<=x<=pi/2      1.0012
integral of exp(x)  0<=x<=1       1.7183
integral of sqrt(x)  0<=x<=9      18.0042
```

8.9 Sets

A mathematical set is an unordered collection of elements without duplicates. The elements of a set come from a universe of possible values. Such a universe of names might be:

{Adams,Collins,Davies,Evans,Jones,Long,Morris,Peters,Smith,Thompson}

from which the sets

{Adams,Davies,Long} and {Adams,Collins,Evans,Thompson} could be formed.

Since sets are unordered, the sets {Adams,Davies,Long} and {Davies,Long,Adams} are the same. Duplicate elements do not change the value of a set, so the sets

{Adams,Davies,Long} and {Adams,Davies,Long,Davies,Adams} are the same.

A set may be empty, in which case it is denoted by {}.

The elements of the universal set given earlier in this section, can be defined as:

```
TYPE
    survey=(Adams,Collins,Davies,Evans,Jones,Long,Morris,Peters,Smith,Thompson);
    SetOfMembers = SET OF survey;
```

Notice that survey is the base type of SetOfMembers.

If in a survey of householders, sets of people were identified on the basis of high income and property owners, then the two sets might be coded as:

    HighIncome:=SetOfMembers{Collins,Long,Thompson}
    OwnProperty:=SetOfMembers{Adams,Collins,Davies,Morris,Thompson}

where the sets are defined as:

VAR
    HighIncome, OwnProperty : SetOfMembers;

Figure 8.3 indicates the operations that can be performed on sets. Notice that the operators + - * and / have also been used in the context of arithmetic. The use of the same operators, but in a different context, is known as operator overloading.

operator	meaning
union (+)	A+B is the set of elements belonging to A or B or both
difference (-)	A-B is the set of elements belonging to A but not to B
intersection (*)	A*B is the set of elements belonging to both A and B
symmetric difference (/)	A/B is the set of elements belonging to either A or B but not both

figure 8.3 operations on sets

With these operations it becomes possible to extract further information about the membership of the two sets.

The set that contains all the members of the high income set and all the members of the property owning set, or members from both sets is the *union* of the sets.

HighIncome+OwnProperty produces the set:

{Adams,Collins,Davies,Long,Morris,Thompson}

The set that contains members of high income that do not belong to the set of members that own properties is the *difference* between the sets.

HighIncome-OwnProperty produces the set {Long}

The set that contains members of high income and own property is the *intersection* of the sets.

HighIncome*OwnProperty produces the set {Collins,Thompson}

The set that contains either high income members or property owners, but not both, is the *symmetric difference* of the two sets.

HighIncome/OwnProperty produces the set {Adams,Long,Davies,Morris}

Consider the following declarations:

TYPE
    colours=(red,orange,yellow,green,blue,indigo,violet);
    rainbow = SET OF colours;
VAR
    set1, set2, set3, set4 : rainbow;
BEGIN
    set1:=rainbow{blue,indigo,violet};
    set2:=rainbow{red,orange,yellow};
    set3:=rainbow{yellow,blue,indigo,violet};
    set4:=rainbow{red,orange};
END;

Figure 8.4 lists the relational operations that can be performed on sets or members of sets

operator	meaning
=	equal
<> or #	not equal
<=	subset of
>=	superset of
IN	member of

figure 8.4 relational operators

Using these operations, the following expressions (i) to (v) inclusive, can be evaluated as either TRUE or FALSE

(i) set1=set2 is FALSE since two sets are only equal if they have the same elements;

(ii) set2#set4 is TRUE since both sets do not contain the same elements;

(iii) set1<=set3 is TRUE since every element of set1 is also an element of set3, set1 is a proper subset of set3 since set1#set3;

(iv) set2=set4 is TRUE since every element of set2 is also an element of set4, set2 is a proper superset of set 4 since set2#set4;

(v) blue IN set1 is TRUE since blue belongs to set1.

Modula-2 provides two procedures for including and excluding members of a set, these procedures are INCL and EXCL respectively.

(vi) INCL(set1,green) causes green to be included in set1 {blue,indigo,violet,green}

(vii) INCL(set4,red) causes no change to set4 {red,orange}

(viii) EXCL(set3,indigo) causes indigo to be removed from set3 {yellow,blue,violet}

(ix) EXCL(set2,violet) causes no change to set2 {red,orange,yellow}

8.10 Type bitset

The data type BITSET allows access to the individual bits of a computer word. This is the only standard set type in Modula-2 and is defined as

TYPE
   BITSET = SET OF [0..W-1]

where W is the wordlength of the computer. On an IBM PC compatible this value would be 16. The elements of a BITSET value normally correspond to the bits in one word of memory.

For example the BITSET value {0,6,9,15} represent a computer word containing the binary digit 1 in the positions 0,6,9 and 15. The remaining bit positions all contain the binary digit 0.

BITSET is a high-level type that is used for low-level programming. By performing operations on a BITSET value, a programmer can examine and change the individual bits of a word. Most Modula-2 systems store a BITSET value in a single computer word, where bit i of the word is 1 if i is a member of the set, and 0 if i is not a member of the set.

A programmer can perform various low-level operations on words by treating them as BITSET values. The following set operations on the contents of words illustrate how they represent low-level language operations on bits in words.

word1 + word2	logical OR on the bits of the two words;
word1 * word2	logical AND on the bits of the two words;
word1 / word2	logical exclusive OR on the bits of the two words;
{0..15} - word	one's complement of word;
i IN word	TRUE if bit i is set to 1 in word;
INCL(word,i)	set bit i to 1 in word;
EXCL(word,i)	clear bit i to 0 in word.

Modula-2 has a feature that will allow a value of one type to be treated as another, provided that the latter type has a name, and provided that values of the two types occupy the same amount of storage.

For example, if b is of type BITSET and i of type INTEGER, then the assignment b:=i; is strictly forbidden in Modula-2. However, BITSET can be used as a *type transfer function*, in which case the assignment b:=BITSET(i) is legal.

A call of a type transfer function has the same syntax as any function call. Because it is an expression and not a designator, it can appear only where Modula-2 allows an expression. A call of type transfer function cannot appear on the left side of an assignment statement.

A type transfer function does not transform its parameter. For example suppose that the value of i in the assignment b:=BITSET(i) was 25, then its representation in a 16-bit word would be: 0000000000011001, therefore, the value of i, interpreted as a BITSET, is {0,3,4}.

Note that type transfer functions can be used between any pairs of types, either standard or programmer defined, provided that the values of the two types occupy the same amount of storage.

The final program in this chapter illustrates how the BITSET type can be used to facilitate low-level operations on computer words.

```
MODULE bit;
(*
program to illustrate the use of bit sets
*)

FROM STextIO IMPORT WriteString, WriteLn, WriteChar;
FROM SWholeIO IMPORT ReadInt;

CONST
    Wordlength = 16;

VAR
  word_1, word_2 : INTEGER;
  reply          : CHAR;

PROCEDURE or(word1, word2 : INTEGER):BITSET;
(*
function to compute word1 + word2 giving bitwise OR
*)

BEGIN
    RETURN BITSET(word1) + BITSET(word2);
END or;

PROCEDURE and(word1, word2 : INTEGER):BITSET;
(*
function to compute word1 * word2 giving bitwise AND
*)

BEGIN
    RETURN BITSET(word1) * BITSET(word2);
END and;

PROCEDURE eor(word1, word2 : INTEGER):BITSET;
(*
function to compute word1 / word2 giving exclusive OR
*)

BEGIN
    RETURN BITSET(word1) / BITSET(word2);
END eor;
```

```
PROCEDURE complement(word : INTEGER):BITSET;
(*
function to compute ({0..Wordlength - 1} - word) giving the complement
*)
BEGIN
    RETURN {0..15} - BITSET(word);
END complement;

PROCEDURE display(word : BITSET);
(*
procedure to display the values of the bits of a word
*)

VAR
  BitPosition : CARDINAL;

BEGIN
    BitPosition := Wordlength;
    REPEAT
         DEC(BitPosition);
         IF BitPosition IN word THEN
             WriteChar('1');
         ELSE
             WriteChar('0');
         END;
    UNTIL BitPosition = 0;
    WriteLn;
END display;

BEGIN
    WriteString('input first integer  '); ReadInt(word_1);
    WriteString('input second integer '); ReadInt(word_2);
    WriteLn;
    WriteString('first integer  '); display(BITSET(word_1));
    WriteString('second integer '); display(BITSET(word_2));
    WriteString('OR             '); display(or(word_1,word_2));
    WriteString('AND            '); display(and(word_1,word_2));
    WriteString('EOR            '); display(eor(word_1,word_2));
    WriteString('complement     '); display(complement(word_1));
    WriteString('complement     '); display(complement(word_2));
END bit.
```

Results from program bit being run

```
input first integer   -32768
input second integer  +32767

first integer          1000000000000000
second integer         0111111111111111
OR                     1111111111111111
AND                    0000000000000000
EOR                    1111111111111111
complement             0111111111111111
complement             1000000000000000
```

8.11 Summary

- ☐ Data can be classified into subrange and enumerated types.

- ☐ Data of enumerated type can also have a subrange.

- ☐ Data of type INTEGER, CARDINAL, CHAR and enumerated types are known collectively as ORDINAL types.

- ☐ The predefined function ORD will return the ordinal position of an object of ordinal type.

- ☐ Modula-2 provides mathematical functions that can be accessed through the library RealMath.

- ☐ A programmer can explicitly define new functions that may include predefined functions that are either explicit, implicit or both.

- ☐ Since a function always has a value associated with its name, the function must be defined as being of a specific data type.

- ☐ A variable or value parameter can be defined as a PROCEDURE type.

- ☐ The language provides for the inclusion of mathematical sets and operations of union, difference, intersection and symmetric difference on sets.

- ☐ The contents of sets may be compared using relational operators.

- ☐ Data declared as type BITSET will permit access to the individual bits that represent the data.

8.12 Questions - *answers begin on page 386*

1. Declare a cardinal variable to have legal values in the range 1 to 31. Write a program to input a cardinal value, compute twice its value, and display the result. Investigate how your computer's operating system copes with computed numbers outside the declared range.

2. Declare subrange types for:

   (a). decimal digits;
   (b). a code number representing the week of a year.
   (c). the range of a compass used for navigation;
   (d). a three digit identity code that starts at 100;
   (e). the alphabet.

3. Declare enumerated types for:

   (a). the operators + - * / ;
   (b). four playing-card suits;
   (c). the thirteen cards of a suit;
   (d). the four points of a navigational compass.

4. Using figure 2.8 ASCII codes, evaluate the following expressions.

   (a). DEC(DEC(DEC('A'))); (b). INC(INC(INC('Z')));
   (c). ORD(DEC(INC(':')));   (d). INC(CHR(80)).

5. From the declaration

TYPE
    spectrum=(red,orange,yellow,green,blue,indigo,violet);
VAR
    colour:spectrum;

(a). What are the values of MAX(spectrum) and ORD(MAX(spectrum)) ?
(b). If the variable colour is assigned the value green, evaluate: DEC(colour,2) and ORD(INC(colour,3)).
(c). Is ORD(MIN(spectrum)) equal to 1? If not why not?
(d). What is VAL(spectrum,ORD(colour)+2) if colour is assigned the value green? Write a single Modula-2 standard function that will give the same result.
(e). Comment on the statement DEC(colour,3) if colour has been assigned the value orange.

6. If LOGb(X) = LOGa(X) / LOGa(b) then derive a function to calculate the logarithm of a number of any valid given base. Use this function in writing a computer program to find the logarithms of the numbers from 2 to 10 in steps of 0.5 to the bases 2 to 10 in steps of 2. Your output should be in the form of a table having the numbers down the page and the bases across the page.

7. Write a program to output a graph of the function Exp(-X)*Sin(2*PI*X) with x in the range 0 to 2.5 in increments of 0.1. What happens to the graph after a short period of time?

8. Write a program to test the accuracy of your computer by evaluating the following expressions.

(a). $(x^{0.5})^2 - x$ $0<=x<=1$ increment of 0.05
(b). $e.\log(x) - x$ $1<=x<=10$ increment of 1
(c). $\tan(\arctan(x)) - x$ $-100<=x<=100$ increment of 10.

9. Write a program containing procedure types to:

(a) compute the sum of the squares of the first twenty cardinal numbers;

(b) input two decimal digits at a keyboard and validate their values such that if the first digit is outside the range 0-9 inclusive issue a warning message to re-input the digit and sound the terminal bell; if the second digit is zero output a warning message and abandon the program, otherwise, validate as for the first digit.

Hint: You can abandon a program by executing the Modula-2 instruction HALT.

10. Devise procedures to:

(a). add two 16 bit positive binary integers;
(b). subtract two 16-bit positive binary integers.

Refer to chapter 2, section 2.4, for information on the storage of signed 16-bit integers. To subtract two binary numbers A - B, first find the two's complement of B and add the result to A.

11. Devise procedures to perform logical shifts on the contents of a 16-bit word. For example a logical shift right by five places on $0000001101110111 = 0000000000011011$. Notice that the five rightmost bits are lost, and zeros appear in the left of the word.

A logical shift left causes the most significant bits to be lost and zeros appear in the right of the word.

Chapter 9
Text Files

This chapter explores an alternative method for storing data using files. Two different methods are examined, together with a method of sorting data in files and writing reports. By the end of the chapter the reader should have an understanding of the following topics.

☐ The redirection of input and output from files held on a secondary storage medium, to replace keyboard input and screen output.

☐ The use of libraries that permit file processing.

☐ Sorting the contents of a file using operating system commands.

☐ Creating reports.

9.1 Redirection

The following program reads numbers input at a keyboard, displays on a screen the running total for the numbers input and calculates and displays the average of all the numbers input.

```
MODULE average;
(*
program to display the running total and average of numbers input
*)

FROM STextIO IMPORT WriteString, WriteLn;
FROM SWholeIO IMPORT ReadCard, WriteCard;

VAR
   number, sum, counter, mean : CARDINAL;

BEGIN
     counter := 0;
     sum := 0;
     ReadCard(number);
     WHILE number # 0 DO
          sum := sum + number;
          WriteString('sum of numbers so far ..');
          WriteCard(sum, 3);
          WriteLn;
          INC(counter);
          ReadCard(number);
     END;
     mean := sum DIV counter;
     WriteString('mean value of numbers ..');
     WriteCard(mean, 3);
END average.
```

When this program is executed it would be usual to input the data either on one line

```
8 4 2 9 2 0
```

or one number per line

```
8
4
2
9
2
0
```

The term stream is used to define any input source or output destination for data. The only streams that have been used in the previous chapters are from keyboard input and screen output. However, it is possible to define further streams that use other devices, such as a printer or a disk unit.

The use of a keyboard as a source, and a screen as a destination, can be changed by redirecting the standard input and output. In MSDOS it is possible to redirect standard input and standard output to other devices. For example, data can be input and output to a disk unit.

If the source of the data is to come from a disk-based file named **a:numbers.txt**, and the output is to be written to a file called **a:results.txt** then redirection is possible by modifying the command line statement used for running the program. The command line to redirect input and output for a program named **average** would be defined as:

C> **average <a:numbers.txt >a:results.txt**, where C> is an MSDOS prompt.

The contents of the file numbers.txt, resident on drive a, would contain the same data, in either format, that was input at the keyboard, and illustrated on the previous page. For example, **a:numbers.txt** contains

```
8 4 2 9 2 0
```

When the program is executed, using the command line shown above, the input is taken from the file **a:numbers.txt**, and the output does not appear on the screen, but is redirected to the file **results.txt** resident on drive a. After running the program if **results.txt** is listed it contains the following information.

```
8 4 2 9 2 0
sum of numbers so far .. 8
sum of numbers so far .. 12
sum of numbers so far .. 14
sum of numbers so far .. 23
sum of numbers so far .. 25
mean value of numbers .. 5
```

Both files, the first being created using an editor, and the second as output from a program, are both examples of text files.

A text data file is stored in the same character format as a source program file.

A text file is a stream of ASCII characters, divided into lines, each with an end of line marker, which is a carriage-return character, possibly followed by a line-feed character.

There are three ways in which a text file may be created. The first is by using the system editor in the same way as a program is created, via keyboard entry, with the text file stored on magnetic disk. The second is by redirecting the output from a program. The third is from within a program by using library procedures to direct output to, a text file held on magnetic disk, instead of the screen.

9.2 File processing activities

Since reading and writing data to and from files, is no more than input and output of data to a program, it should be of little surprise to the reader that all file processing activities are defined within a set of libraries and are not implicitly defined by statements in the Modula-2 language.

The good news is that the procedures found in the libraries STextIO, SWholeIO and SRealIO have a similar set of procedures for reading and writing to and from files, found in the libraries TextIO, WholeIO and RealIO. Notice from the listings that follow that every procedure includes an extra parameter cid (channel identifier) of type ChanId (Channel Identification).

Library Module TextIO

```
PROCEDURE ReadChar(cid:ChanId; VAR ch:CHAR);
(* If possible, removes a character from the input stream cid, and assigns
the corresponding value to ch. The read result is set to the value
allRight or endOfInput.
*)

PROCEDURE ReadString(cid:ChanId; VAR s:ARRAY OF CHAR);
(* Removes only those characters from the input stream cid before the next
line mark that can be accommodated in s as a string value, and copies them
to s. The read result is set to the value allRight or endOfInput.
*)

(* The following procedure reads past the next line mark *)

PROCEDURE SkipLine(cid:ChanId);
(* Removes successive items from the input stream cid up to and including
the next line mark or until the end of input is reached. The read result
is set to the value allRight or endOfInput.
*)

(* Output procedures *)

PROCEDURE WriteChar(cid:ChanId; ch:CHAR);
(* Writes the value of ch to the output stream cid. *)

PROCEDURE WriteLn(cid:ChanId);
(* Writes a line mark to the output stream cid. *)

PROCEDURE WriteString(cid:ChanId; s:ARRAY OF CHAR);
(* Writes the string value of s to the output stream cid. *)
```

Library Module WholeIO

```
PROCEDURE ReadInt(cid : ChanId; VAR int:INTEGER);
(* Skips leading spaces, and removes any remaining characters from cid
that form part of a signed whole number. The value of this number is as-
signed to int.
*)

PROCEDURE WriteInt(cid : ChanId; int:INTEGER; width:CARDINAL);
(* Writes the value of int to the default output channel in text form, in a
field of the given minimum width.
*)

PROCEDURE ReadCard(cid : ChanId; VAR card:CARDINAL);
(* Skips leading spaces, and removes any remaining characters from the de-
fault input channel that form part of an unsigned whole number. The value
of this number is assigned to card.
*)

PROCEDURE WriteCard(cid : ChanId; card:CARDINAL; width:CARDINAL);
(* Writes the value of card to the default output channel in text form, in
a field of the given minimum width.
*)
```

Library Module RealIO

```
PROCEDURE ReadReal(cid:ChanId; VAR real:REAL);
(* Skips leading spaces, and removes any remaining characters from cid
that forms part of the signed fixed or floating point number. The value of
this number is assigned to real.
*)

PROCEDURE WriteFloat(cid:ChanId;real:REAL;sigFigs:CARDINAL;width:CARDINAL);
(* Writes the value of real to cid in floating-point text form, with
sigFigs significant figures, in a field of the given minimum width.
*)

PROCEDURE WriteFixed(cid:ChanId;real:REAL;place:INTEGER;width:CARDINAL);
(* Writes the value of real to cid in fixed-point text form, rounded to
the given place relative to the decimal point, in a field of the given
minimum width.
*)
```

The input/output library allows for the reading and writing of data streams over one or more channels. Channels are connected to sources of input data, or to destinations of output data, known as devices or device instances.

When using STextIO, SWholeIO and SRealIO, the reader was using standard, or default channels, for input and output, hence there was no need to explicitly define the channel identifier. The standard input channel was connected to the keyboard device, and the standard output channel to the screen device.

Before any of the procedures belonging to TextIO, WholeIO and RealIO can be used it is necessary to request a channel, by calling an appropriate *open* procedure, in general supplying a name that identifies the source or destination to which the connection is to be made.

Opening a file

Before a file can be used it must be opened for either reading or writing by using the procedure *Open* from the library module StreamFile. This procedure is defined as follows:

```
PROCEDURE Open (VAR cid : ChanId; name : ARRAY OF CHAR;
                flags : FlagSet; VAR res : OpenResults);

(*
Attempts to obtain and open a channel connected to a sequential stream of
the given name.
If successful, assigns to cid the identity of the opened channel, and as-
signs the value opened to res.
If a channel cannot be opened as required, the value of res indicates the
reason, and cid identifies the invalid channel.
*)
```

If the call *Open(cid, name, flags, res)* is successful it will assign *cid* the identity of a channel that is connected to a sequential stream specified by *name*, and the enumerated constant *opened* shall be assigned to *res*. The value of flags can be *read*, *write* or *old*.

The inclusion of *read* in flags shall imply the inclusion of *old* and the source of the given *name* shall already exist if the call is to succeed.

If *write* is included, then a destination of the given *name* shall not already exist, unless the flag *old* is given or implied.

If a channel cannot be *opened* as required, the value of *res* shall indicate the reason, and *cid* shall identify the invalid channel.

Examples of the use of Open are *Open (data, 'a:numbers.txt', read, result);* which implies open a channel called *data*, connected to the device *a:numbers.txt*, for *reading*, and report the success of the open operation to the identifier *result*. Similarly *Open (report, 'a:stock.txt', write, result);* implies open a channel called *report*, connected to the device *a:stock.txt*, for *writing* and report the success of the open operation to the identifier *result*.

Figure 9.1 illustrates that after the file named *data* has been opened, a file position indicator is set to the first line in the file.

text file - data	ReadResult = endOfInput	ReadReal(data, price); ReadString(data, appliance);
file position → 395.95 television 550.00 music centre 149.95 freezer	FALSE	price = 395.95 appliance = television
file position → 395.95 television 550.00 music centre 149.95 freezer	FALSE	price = 550.00 appliance = music centre
395.95 television 550.00 music centre file position → 149.95 freezer	FALSE	price = 149.95 appliance = freezer
395.95 television 550.00 music centre 149.95 freezer file position →	TRUE	

figure 9.1 reading lines in a text file

Reading a text file

The lines of a text file can be read by using appropriate procedures from the library modules TextIO, WholeIO and RealIO. For example, the statement *ReadReal(data, price)* would read a real value for *price* and the statement *ReadString(data, appliance)* would read a string value for *appliance* from a line of the text file, that might contain the data depicted in figure 9.1. After each line of data has been read the file position indicator moves to the next line in the file, or points at the end of the file when there is no more data to read.

Detecting the end of a file

The repeated execution of *read* statements will cause all the data in the file to be read and an attempt would be made to read beyond the end of the file. This will result in a run-time error and the program will be terminated by the operating system. Therefore it is important that a method should exist for detecting the end of the file. There exists a function defined in the library IOResult, that returns the result for the last read operation on a specified channel. If the result equates to the enumerated constant *endOfInput*, then the end of file has been reached. Notice from figure 9.1 that the Boolean expression *ReadResult* = *endOfInput* is TRUE after the last line in the file has been read.

Writing to a file

Information is written to a file by using the appropriate write statements from the library modules TextIO, WholeIO and RealIO. For example, the statements *WriteFixed(results, price,2,7); WriteChar(results, space); WriteString(results, appliance); WriteLn(results);* would write the information for the *price* and the name of the *appliance* to one line of the file called results. Continued use of this statement would result in many lines containing prices and names of appliances to be written to the file.

Closing a file

When a file is no longer required it should be closed, resulting in the associated channel being closed. If the mode of use of the file is to change then it must first be closed before being opened in a different mode. For example a file that has been opened for writing, that is required to be read, must first be closed and then opened again for reading. The file position indicator then points to the first item in the file. The statement to close a file is give as follows.

```
PROCEDURE Close (VAR cid : ChanId);
```

Examples of the use of Close are: Close(data); Close(results);

9.3 Reading and writing

A text file contains the following lines of data that relate to the insured values of several domestic appliances. For example, a television is insured for £395.95, a music centre is insured for £550.00, etc.

```
395.95 television
550.00 music centre
995.95 desk-top computer
199.95 microwave oven
299.99 washing machine
149.95 freezer
```

The first program demonstrates how to open the file, and read and display the contents line by line. Notice if the file cannot be opened, this fact is reported and the program is abandoned. The keyword HALT can be used to terminate a program.

Notice that it has been necessary to import the type *ChanId* and enumerated type *OpenResults*, the constant *read* and the procedures *Open* and *Close* from the library *StreamFile*; the enumerated type *ReadResults* and the function *ReadResult* from the library *IOResult*. The type *ReadResults* is used to classify the result of a read operation, where *endOfInput* is just one of the enumerated constants that describes the end of file.

```
MODULE TextFile;
(* program to test the reading of a file *)

FROM StreamFile IMPORT ChanId, Open, Close, read, OpenResults;
FROM IOResult IMPORT ReadResult, ReadResults;
FROM StringType IMPORT string;
FROM RealIO IMPORT ReadReal;
FROM TextIO IMPORT ReadString;
FROM STextIO IMPORT WriteString, WriteLn;
FROM SRealIO IMPORT WriteFixed;

CONST
     space = 40C;
VAR
  price          : REAL;
  appliance      : string;
  data           : ChanId;
  results        : OpenResults;

BEGIN
    Open (data, 'a:\data.txt", read, results);
    IF results # opened THEN
        WriteString('file cannot be opened - ');
        WriteString('program abandoned');
        HALT;
    END;
    ReadReal(data, price);
    ReadString(data, appliance);
    WHILE ReadResult(data) # endOfInput DO
        WriteFixed(price, 2,7);
        WriteString(space);
        WriteString(appliance); WriteLn;
        ReadReal(data, price);
        ReadString(data, appliance);
    END;
    Close(data);
END TextFile.
```

Results displayed on a screen from program TextFile being run

```
395.95 television
550.00 music centre
995.95 desk-top computer
199.95 microwave oven
299.99 washing machine
149.95 freezer
```

When using files output does not necessarily need to be directed to a screen, it can in fact be directed to another text file. In the next example the contents of the file used in the previous program is modified such that the value of each appliance is increased by the rate of inflation, and the new value together with the name of the appliance is written to a text file.

```
MODULE CreateFile;
(* program to read the price and name of a domestic appliance from a text
file called old_data, increase the price of the appliance by the rate of
inflation and write the new price and appliance name to a new text file
called new_data *)

FROM StreamFile IMPORT ChanId, Open, Close, read, write, OpenResults;
FROM IOResult IMPORT ReadResult, ReadResults;
FROM StringType IMPORT string;
FROM RealIO IMPORT ReadReal, WriteFixed;
FROM TextIO IMPORT ReadString, WriteString, WriteLn;
IMPORT STextIO;

CONST
    space = 40C;
    inflation = 0.025; (* rate of inflation at 2.5% *)
VAR
  price        : REAL;
  appliance    : string;
  old_data     : ChanId;
  new_data     : ChanId;
  results      : OpenResults;

BEGIN
    Open (old_data, 'a:\data.txt", read, results);
    IF results # opened THEN
        STextIO.WriteString('a:\data.txt does not exist - ');
        STextIO.WriteString('program abandoned');
        HALT;
    END;
    Open(new_data, 'a:\new_data.txt", write, results);
    ReadReal(old_data, price);
    ReadString(old_data, appliance);
    WHILE ReadResult(old_data) # endOfInput DO
        price := price + (price * inflation);
        WriteFixed(new_data, price, 2,7);
        WriteString(new_data, space);
        WriteString(new_data, appliance); WriteLn(new_data);
        ReadReal(old_data, price);
        ReadString(old_data, appliance);
    END;
    Close(old_data);
    Close(new_data);
END CreateFile.
```

Results written to the file new_data.txt from program CreateFile being run

```
 405.85 television
 563.75 music centre
1020.85 desk-top computer
 204.95 microwave oven
 307.49 washing machine
 153.70 freezer
```

In this program two different methods of importing information have been used. According to appendix II, an import list can consist of either an *unqualified* import or a *simple* import. In the example given

FROM TextIO IMPORT ReadReal, WriteFixed; is regarded as an *unqualified* import, whereas

IMPORT STextIO; is a *simple* import.

All identifiers that are associated with a simple import, must be qualified with the name of the imported library. In this example STextIO.WriteString refers to writing a string to the default channel (the screen); whereas WriteString in an unqualified form refers to writing a string to a defined channel (new_data).

It would be wrong to use the unqualified form of import list for both libraries, since this would lead to a duplication of the name WriteString. The compiler could not resolve this duplicate entry, and would result in a compilation error.

9.4 Sort utility

The reader should be well aware of the need to present information in a usable form. Consider the organisation of a telephone directory, entries are ordered into strict alphabetical sequence by name. To find a telephone number, knowing the name of the person you want to call, is simply a matter of locating the appropriate section of the directory from the first few letters of the surname, and then searching several pages until a match is found for the surname. The address and telephone number of the person will be listed against the surname.

Another example of the organisation of information is that of a bus timetable. A timetable is organised into bus routes, often in ascending order of bus number, for example 131, 137, 137A, etc. For each bus route a chronological listing of bus departure times from a bus station, with arrival and departure times at places on route are given. Each route will normally have separate entries for buses travelling in opposite directions. If the time of a bus is to be found the bus number can easily be referenced since these are displayed in an ordered sequence. Departure times are listed chronologically, making reference to a specific part of the day simple. Bus arrival and departure times can then be selected from that part of the timetable.

In both these examples the information is required to be ordered or sorted on a part of the information. Telephone directories are sorted on names, bus timetables are sorted on bus routes and times of day. Such information is said to have been sorted on a key. Names of people, bus routes and times of the day all being examples of keys to information.

Computers are capable of storing very large amounts of information, and it is very important that the information is kept in an ordered format to provide fast access to information given an appropriate key and to allow for an orderly presentation of information when producing reports.

MSDOS provides a means of sorting the contents of text files into order. For example the file A:DATA.TXT created in the previous example, can be sorted into sequence by price, and stored in a different file named A:PRICE.TXT, by using the SORT command. For example:

C: **SORT <A:DATA.TXT A:PRICE.TXT** and the contents of A:PRICE.TXT would then appear as:

149.95 freezer
199.95 microwave oven
299.99 washing machine
395.95 television
550.00 music centre
995.95 desk-top computer

Since the price of an appliance starts in column 1, each line of the text file has been ordered by digits (the price). However, if it was required to sort the file into order by name of appliance then it is possible to state at which column sorting should take place. For example:

C: **SORT /+8 <A:DATA.TXT A:NAME.TXT** and the contents of A:NAME.TXT would then appear as:

995.95 desk-top computer
149.95 freezer
199.95 microwave oven
550.00 music centre
395.95 television
299.99 washing machine

The order of this file could also be reversed by modifying the command to:

C: **SORT /r/+8 <A:DATA.TXT A:NAME.TXT** and the contents of A:NAME.TXT would then appear as:

299.99 washing machine
395.95 television
550.00 music centre
199.95 microwave oven
149.95 freezer
995.95 desk-top computer

The reader is advised to refer to their MSDOS manual for further information about the SORT utility.

9.5 Report writing

Directing output to a screen is fine for a small amount of data, however, since the output scrolls off the screen, it is of little use if the file contains a considerable number of lines. Printed output on paper, of the contents of the file, is usually more acceptable. It is possible to direct the output that normally appears on a screen to a text file stored on magnetic disk. The contents of the text file can, at the users request, be printed on the paper.

For example if a text file had been created using the name A:REPORT.TXT then to obtain a print-out of the report in a PC-based environment, the following commands should be given from MSDOS, C: **PRINT A:REPORT.TXT.** Provided a printer is connected on-line, the contents of the report will be output to the printer. If you have any difficulties printing a text file then refer to your MSDOS manual for more information.

The following text file has been created using an editor, sorted into alphabetical sequence and stored under the name A:BOOKS.TXT. Each line in the file contains the quantity in stock, the price of the book and the title of a book.

```
1 8.95 Art in Athens
2 3.75 Birds of Prey
1 7.50 Eagles of Scotland
3 5.20 Gone with the Wind
2 3.75 Hate, Lust and Love
3 5.95 Maths for Adults
3 3.75 Modern Farming
3 5.20 Raiders of Planet X
1 8.95 Splitting the Atom
1 3.75 The Invisible Man
2 3.75 The Otter
4 5.95 The Tempest
2 5.95 The Trojan Wars
2 3.75 Under the Seas
2 7.50 Vampire Bats
```

A report is to be printed on the contents of this file. The design of a report is made considerably easier if the reader adopts the habit of planning the layout of the report on a report layout sheet, similar to the one shown in figure 9.2. If such a document cannot be obtained then paper pre-ruled into squares with numbered columns can be used. Such a document is an aid towards coding the Write and WriteLn statements in a program. Notice from the design of the document that when the stock level falls to one item the report indicates that the stock should be replenished. Notice also that totals are calculated for the number of books and value of all the books in stock and printed at the end of the report.

Report Layout Sheet　　　layout no. ☐

```
1 2 3 4 5 6 7 8 9 0 1 2 3 4 5 6 7 8 9 0 1 2 3 4 5 6 7 8 9 0 1 2 3 4 5 6 7 8 9 0 1 2 3 4 5 6 7 8 9 0

                        STOCK  REPORT  ON  BOOKS
quantity        price                       title
            1           8·95   *REORDER*  Art  in  Athens
            2           3·75              Birds  of  Prey




number of books in stock   3
value of books in stock £16 ·45
```

figure 9.2 layout of a report file

```
MODULE StockReport;
(*
program to read a file containing a stock list of books and print the con-
tents of the file, showing which books to re-order, and the total number
of books together with the total value of the stock
*)

FROM StreamFile IMPORT ChanId, Open, Close, read, write, OpenResults;
FROM IOResult IMPORT ReadResult, ReadResults;
FROM StringType IMPORT string;
FROM RealIO IMPORT ReadReal, WriteFixed;
FROM WholeIO IMPORT ReadCard, WriteCard;
FROM TextIO IMPORT ReadString, WriteString, WriteLn;
IMPORT STextIO;

CONST
    space = 40C;
    ReorderLevel = 1;

VAR
    quantity      : CARDINAL;
    price         : REAL;
    title         : string;
    TotalQuantity : CARDINAL;
    TotalPrice    : REAL;
    books         : ChanId;
```

```
    report          : ChanId;
    results         : OpenResults;

BEGIN
    Open (books, 'a:\books.txt", read, results);
    IF results # opened THEN
       STextIO.WriteString('a:\books.txt does not exist - ');
       STextIO.WriteString('program abandoned');
       HALT;
    END;
    Open(report, 'a:\report.txt", write, results);

    TotalQuantity := 0;
    TotalPrice := 0.0;
    WriteString(report, '               STOCK REPORT ON BOOKS');
    WriteLn(report); WriteLn(report);
    WriteString(report, 'quantity price           title');
    WriteLn(report); WriteLn(report);
    ReadCard(books, quantity);
    ReadReal(books, price);
    ReadString(books, title);

    WHILE ReadResult(books) # endOfInput DO
       WriteCard(report, quantity, 8);
       WriteFixed(report, price, 2, 6);
       IF quantity <= ReorderLevel THEN
          WriteString(report, ' *REORDER*  ');
       ELSE
          WriteString(report, '            ');
       END;
       WriteString(report, title);
       WriteLn(report);

       TotalQuantity:=TotalQuantity+quantity;
       TotalPrice:=TotalPrice+(price*FLOAT(quantity));

       ReadCard(books, quantity);
       ReadReal(books, price);
       ReadString(books, title);
    END;

    WriteLn(report);
    WriteString(report,'number of books in stock ');
    WriteCard(report, TotalQuantity, 3); WriteLn(report);
    WriteString(report, 'value of books in stock £');
    WriteFixed(report, TotalPrice, 2, 7); WriteLn(report);
    Close(books);
    Close(report);
END StockReport.
```

Results written to the file report.txt from program StockReport being run

```
            STOCK REPORT ON BOOKS

quantity price              title

       1   8.95 *REORDER*   Art in Athens
       2   3.75             Birds of Prey
       1   7.50 *REORDER*   Eagles of Scotland
       3   5.20             Gone with the Wind
       2   3.75             Hate, Lust and Love
       3   5.95             Maths for Adults
       3   3.75             Modern Farming
       3   5.20             Raiders of Planet X
       1   8.95 *REORDER*   Splitting the Atom
       1   3.75 *REORDER*   The Invisible Man
       2   3.75             The Otter
       4   5.95             The Tempest
       2   5.95             The Trojan Wars
       2   3.75             Under the Seas
       2   7.50             Vampire Bats

number of books in stock   32
value of books in stock £ 170.15
```

9.6 Worked example

A text file contains information about members of a swimming club. Each line of the file contains information on the age, competition results, sex and name for each member. For example the contents of the file members might contain the following data.

```
17 1 2 3 MJones
18 1 1 1 MHolmes
15 1 0 1 FEvans
14 1 1 0 FPeters
18 1 2 2 MNichols
15 1 1 2 FAdams
17 3 1 1 MBetts
16 1 0 1 MJenkins
15 2 0 1 FPatel
15 1 0 3 FMorgan
17 1 2 1 MPhillips
16 1 1 3 FSmith
```

The entry for competition results shows the placing (1) first, (2) second, (3) third and (0) not placed or absent from the competition for a member over the previous three swimming competitions.

This file of members is to be used to create two new files of swimmers. A file of male swimmers in the age range (16 < age <= 18) and a file of female swimmers in the age range (14 < age <= 16). the files will contain the names of the eligible members and the total number of points scored by each member over the previous three competitions.

A points system is used to signify how well a swimmer did in the last three competitions. Three points are awarded for first place, two points for second place and one point for third place. No points are awarded for not being placed or being absent from a competition. For example, a member with two first places and one second place would be awarded eight points.

The program that splits the members file into two files, based upon the criteria listed follows. Notice that a parameterless procedure has been created to read the contents each line in the text file. Without this procedure it would have meant duplicating six lines of code in the program.

```
MODULE swimmers;

(* program to produce two text files of swimmers from one text data file *)

FROM StreamFile IMPORT ChanId, Open, Close, read, write, OpenResults;
FROM IOResult IMPORT ReadResult, ReadResults;
FROM StringType IMPORT string;
FROM WholeIO IMPORT ReadCard, WriteCard;
FROM TextIO IMPORT ReadChar, WriteChar, ReadString, WriteString, WriteLn;
IMPORT STextIO;

CONST
    space  = 40C;
    male   = 'M';
    female = 'F';

VAR
  age                            : CARDINAL;
  result_1, result_2, result_3  : CARDINAL;
  sex                            : CHAR;
  name                           : string;
  members, males, females        : ChanId;
  points                         : CARDINAL;
  results                        : OpenResults;


PROCEDURE ReadFile(file : ChanId; VAR age : CARDINAL;
                   VAR result_1, result_2, result_3 : CARDINAL;
                   VAR sex : CHAR; VAR name : string);

(* procedure to read a single line of the original file *)
```

```
BEGIN
    ReadCard(file, age);
    ReadCard(file, result_1);
    ReadCard(file, result_2);
    ReadCard(file, result_3);
    ReadChar(file, sex);
    ReadString(file, name);
END ReadFile;

BEGIN
    Open (members, "a:\members.txt", read, results);
    IF results # opened THEN
        STextIO.WriteString('a:\members.txt does not exist - ');
        STextIO.WriteString('program abandoned');
        HALT;
    END;

    Open(males, "a:\males.txt", write, results);
    Open(females, "a:\females.txt", write, results);

    ReadFile(members, age, result_1, result_2, result_3, sex, name);

    WHILE ReadResult(members) # endOfInput DO

            points := 0;

            IF result_1 > 0 THEN points := points + 4 - result_1; END;
            IF result_2 > 0 THEN points := points + 4 - result_2; END;
            IF result_3 > 0 THEN points := points + 4 - result_3; END;

            IF (sex = male) AND (age > 16) AND (age <=18) THEN
                WriteCard(males, points, 2);
                WriteChar(males, space);
                WriteString(males, name);
                WriteLn(males);
            ELSIF (sex = female) AND (age > 14) AND (age <= 16) THEN
                WriteCard(females, points, 2);
                WriteChar(females, space);
                WriteString(females, name);
                WriteLn(females);
            END;

            ReadFile(members, age, result_1, result_2, result_3, sex, name);

    END;

    Close(members); Close(males); Close(females);

END swimmers.
```

172

Results showing the contents of the male and female swimmers files respectively

File males

```
6 Jones
9 Holmes
7 Nichols
7 Betts
8 Phillips
```

File females

```
6 Evans
8 Adams
5 Patel
4 Morgan
7 Smith
```

Having successfully split the members file into two separate files, it is required to read each file and produce a list of the three best male swimmers and the three best female swimmers, based upon the highest number of points scored over the previous three competitions.

The procedure SelectTeams reads the file specified by a formal parameter, and displays those three members who have scored the highest number of points. the file is first read for those with nine points, until the end of file is reached. It is then necessary to re-position the file position indicator to the start of the file, by closing the file and re-opening it. The file is then re-read for those members with eight points. This sequence of operations is repeated until three members have been listed.

```
MODULE selection;
(*
program to select a team of male swimmers and a team of female
swimmers who have had the most success in past swimming competitions
*)

FROM StreamFile IMPORT ChanId, Open, Close, read, OpenResults;
FROM IOResult IMPORT ReadResult, ReadResults;
FROM StringType IMPORT string;
FROM WholeIO IMPORT ReadCard;
FROM TextIO IMPORT ReadString;
FROM SWholeIO IMPORT WriteCard;
FROM STextIO IMPORT WriteString, WriteChar, WriteLn;

VAR
   name     : string;
   males    : ChanId;
   females  : ChanId;
```

173

```
PROCEDURE SelectTeams(file : ChanId; filename : ARRAY OF CHAR);
CONST
    space = 40C;
VAR
  count      : CARDINAL;
  MaxPoints  : CARDINAL;
  points     : CARDINAL;
  results    : OpenResults;

BEGIN
    count := 0;
    MaxPoints := 9;
    REPEAT
        Open (file, filename, read, results);
        IF results # opened THEN
           WriteString(filename);
           WriteString(' does not exist - ');
           WriteString('program abandoned');
           HALT;
        END;

        ReadCard(file, points);
        ReadString(file, name);

        WHILE (ReadResult(file) # endOfInput) AND (count # 3) DO

            IF points = MaxPoints THEN
               WriteCard(points,2);
               WriteChar(space);
               WriteString(name); WriteLn;
               INC(count);
            END;

            ReadCard(file, points);
            ReadString(file, name);
        END;

        DEC(MaxPoints);
        Close(file);
    UNTIL (count = 3) OR (MaxPoints = 0);
END SelectTeams;

BEGIN
    WriteString('Members of Male Swimming Team'); WriteLn; WriteLn;
    SelectTeams(males, `a:males.txt');
    WriteLn; WriteLn;
    WriteString('Members of Female Swimming Team'); WriteLn; WriteLn;
    SelectTeams(females, `a:females.txt');
END selection.
```

174

Results from program selection being run

```
Members of Male Swimming Team

 9 Holmes
 8 Phillips
 7 Nichols

Members of Female Swimming Team

 8 Adams
 7 Smith
 6 Evans
```

9.7 Summary

☐ A text file is a stream of ASCII characters, divided into lines, each with an end of line marker.

☐ A text file can be created (i) using an editor, (ii) as redirected output from a program, or (iii) as specific output from a program.

☐ Text files are normally stored on disk.

☐ A text file must be opened in the appropriate mode before it can be used.

☐ Whenever a file is opened, the file position is set to the first line to be read, or at the beginning of the file to be written.

☐ A text file is read by using the appropriate *Read* procedures from the libraries *TextIO*, *WholeIO* and *RealIO*.

☐ Whenever a line in a text file is read, the file position indicator is automatically advanced to the next line, until it points to the end of the file.

☐ The *ReadResult* function will return the value *endOfInput* when the file position indicator points beyond the last line of the file.

☐ Text is written to a file one item after another in the order in which the appropriate *Write* procedures from the libraries *TextIO*, *WholeIO* and *RealIO* occur in a program.

☐ Whenever a file is no longer required, or its mode of access is to change, then it should be closed.

☐ Before programming the output for a report, the layout of the report should first be designed on squared paper. The layout of the information can then be transferred directly into the appropriate *Write* procedures from the libraries TextIO, WholeIO and RealIO.

☐ Whenever possible data should be stored sorted.

9.8 Questions - *answers begin on page 390*

1. Create a text file *food.txt* containing the input data required for the "Greasy Spoon Cafe" program described in chapter 3, section 3.7. Using redirection, re-run this program so that data is read from the text file that you have created and the output is directed to a second text file of your choice. List the contents of both files.

2. Use an editor to create a text file *c9q2.txt* containing words and their meanings, with a word and its meaning written on one line. The size of a word should be less than fifteen characters and the size of the meaning less than 50 characters.

After the file has been created, write a program to read and display the contents of the file.

3. Use an editor to create a second file *c9q3.txt* with an identical format to that described in the previous question.

Write a program to open both files for reading, and a third file *c9q3file.txt* for writing. Copy the contents of the first file to the third file, then continue to copy the contents of the second file to the third file. Close all files.

Use the MSDOS SORT utility, or equivalent, to order the third file into alphabetical sequence using the word as the key.

If necessary, modify the program from the previous question so that it will read and display the contents of the sorted third file.

4. Create a text file *subscr.txt* containing the details of telephone subscribers. Lines are of fixed length and contain the following details.

previous meter reading and current meter reading
surname and initials of subscriber and telephone number

Invent a minimum of ten test data lines containing the data described. Assume that the previous meter reading is always less than the current meter reading. Using an editor, input and store the lines into a text file. Using a sorting utility, such as SORT in MSDOS, order the file on surname and initials as primary key.

Using the ordered text file write a program to output the following report file *telerept.txt*. Assume that charges for telephone calls are £0.04 per unit.

```
                TELEPHONE SUBSCRIBERS


NAME            NUMBER          UNITS   CHARGE
                                USED    £
Allen P         Abingdon 41937  2719    109.76
Brown J         Oxford 2245643  645     25.80
Carter F        Banbury 212     1768    70.72
  .               .               .       .
```

5. Create a file *beer.txt* that contains the details of items of stock in a brewery. Lines are of fixed length and contain the following details.

stock quantity
unit price
stock number and description

Assume that the lines are not in stock number order when they are input into the computer. Limit the number of test data lines to ten in this question. Using an editor, input and store the test data in a text file. Using an external sorting package, such as SORT in MSDOS, order the contents of the file on the stock number as primary key.

Using the ordered text file write a program to output the following report *stock.txt*.

```
                        STOCK REPORT
STOCK    DESCRIPTION      UNIT    LEVEL    VALUE
NUMBER                    COST
91189    Best Bitter      25.50   100      2550.00
92258    Master Brew Mild 20.00   200      4000.00
9238X    Stock Ale        15.00   100      1500.00
  .         .               .       .        .  .

                         TOTAL    £8050.00
```

6. A text file *viewers.txt* contains the following three fields per line.

    category of programme
    estimated size of viewing audience (millions)
    name of a television programme

where the category of programme is coded using a single character as follows:

    D - drama
    L - light entertainment
    N - natural history
    S - sport

A typical record from the file might contain the following data:

D12.5 Inspector Morse

and indicates that the television programme Inspector Morse was watched by 12.5 million viewers, and falls in the category of drama.

(a). Using an editor create the text file with programmes of your own choice.

(b). Sort the contents of this file on the **category** code as the key. This will group all the drama programmes together, all the light entertainment programmes together, etc.

(c). Write a program to input a category code and generate a report on the names of all the programs in that category, together with the audience viewing figures and finally the total number of viewers who watched programmes in that category.

7. Create a text file *bank.txt* that contains the following information about a persons transactions for a bank account.

    credit or debit C or D
    amount of a transaction
    date of transaction and a description of the transaction

A typical transaction record might appear in the file as follows:

D 32.00 MAR18 Electricity Company

The file is sorted on the date of the transaction, therefore it is important to limit the choice of your dates to only one month. The file should not contain more than, say ten transactions.

Write a program to read the file and print a bank statement *statement.txt* similar, but not necessarily identical to, the one shown in figure 2.14 in the second chapter. Assume for the purpose of this exercise that the name of the account, year, sheet number and account number are literals coded in the program and not variables. Ensure that strings are left-justified and right-filled with ... if necessary.

Chapter 10

Arrays and Records

Up to now little importance has been attached to the organisation of data in the memory of a computer. All variables have been associated with only discrete items of unstructured data. This chapter introduces the array, which is the commonest of the data structures and is available in most high-level languages, and uses methods for storing data that can lead to simple and more effective solutions. The chapter introduces two structures the array and the record. By the end of the chapter the reader should have an understanding of the following topics.

☐   The use of a FOR loop.

☐   Declaration and use of one-dimensional arrays.

☐   String processing.

☐   Passing arrays as parameters in a procedure.

☐   The format and organisation of records.

☐   An array of records.

☐   Variant records.

☐   Declaration and use of two-dimensional arrays.

☐   Declaration of multi-dimensional arrays.

10.1 For..do

For..do is another statement for controlling the number of times a sequence of statements is executed. In other words it ranks along-side the *while..do*, *repeat..until* and *loop* statements. The *for..do* statement was deliberately not introduced in chapter 5 since its use is more relevant to controlling the access to an array data structure.

In the following segments of code a *while..do* loop has been used to count from 1 to 10 and a *repeat..until* loop has been used to count from 10 to 0.

```
counter:=1;
WHILE counter <= 10 DO
BEGIN
   WriteInt(counter,3);
   INC(counter);
END;

counter:=10;
REPEAT
   WriteInt(counter,3);
   DEC(counter);
UNTIL counter = 0;
```

From these examples the reader should observe that in using either a *while..do* loop or *repeat..until* loop for counting it is necessary to include the following stages in the code.

(i) Initialise a control variable identifier (counter).

(ii) Increase or decrease the value of the control variable identifier (counter) each time the sequence of statements within the loop has been executed.

(iii) Test the value of the control variable identifier (counter) to determine whether to exit from the loop.

When using a *for..do* loop these stages are automatically taken care of by the *for..do* statement. To illustrate the point, the first *for..loop* is used to count from 1 to 10, and the second *for..do* loop to count from 10 to 0.

```
FOR counter:=1 TO 10 DO
   WriteInt(counter,3);
END;

FOR counter:=10 TO 0 BY -1 DO
   WriteInt(counter,3);
END;
```

The format of the *for..do* statement can be expressed as

for statement ::=   **FOR** control variable identifier ':=' initial value **TO** final value [**BY** step size] **DO**
statement sequence **END**

The *for..do* statement functions in the following way.

(i) The control variable identifier is automatically initialised to the value of the initial value.

(ii) The value of the control variable identifier is then tested against the value of the final value. If the initial value exceeds the final value the computer will exit from the loop and branch to the next executable statement after the body of the loop. If the initial value is less than or equal to the value of the final value then the computer will execute the statements within the body of the loop.

(iii) After the last statement in the loop has been executed the control variable identifier is automatically increased by the value of the step value. If the value of the step value is +1, then the BY clause may be omitted.

(iv) The computer branches back to stage (ii)

If the value of the initial value is greater than the value of the final value then the format of the *for..do* statement must include a BY clause with a negative step value. There are two differences in the manner in which this format functions.

(i) The computer will exit from the loop when the initial value is less than the final value.

(ii) The control variable identifier is decremented by the absolute value of the step value.

The lower and final values in the FOR statement can be scalar literals, variables, expressions and objects of enumerated type. Note that real numbers are not allowed as limits or incremental values. When the initial value is greater than the final value, the initial value should be decreased, otherwise the statements within the loop will not be executed. Always ensure that the initial value, final value and step value evaluate to values of the same type. The loop value should never be explicitly re-assigned a value from the statements within the loop. Figure 10.1 illustrates that FOR loops may be nested one within the other in the manner shown, but must never go out of scope.

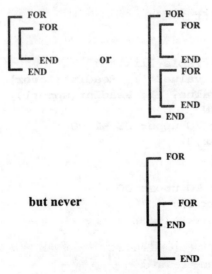

figure 10.1 Nested FOR loops

The following example program shows how *for..do* loops can be used to count from 1 to 10, 10 to 0, between limits that the user inputs at run-time, and between ordinal values other than integers or cardinals.

```
MODULE ForDemo;
(*
program to demonstrate the function of a FOR loop
*)

FROM STextIO IMPORT WriteString, WriteChar, WriteLn;
FROM SWholeIO IMPORT WriteInt, ReadInt;

TYPE
    compass = (North, South, East, West);

VAR
    index, lower, upper  : INTEGER;
    letter               : CHAR;
    points               : compass;

BEGIN
    (* counting up in steps of +1 *)
    FOR index:=1 TO 10 DO
        WriteInt(index,3);
    END;
    WriteLn;

    (* counting down in steps of -1 *)
    FOR index:=10 TO 0 BY -1 DO
        WriteInt(index,3);
    END;
    WriteString(' lift off');
    WriteLn;

    (* counting using variable limits *)
    WriteString('initial value? '); ReadInt(lower);
    WriteString('final value? '); ReadInt(upper);
    IF lower > upper THEN
        FOR index:= lower TO upper BY -1 DO
            WriteInt(index,3);
        END;
    ELSE
        FOR index:= lower TO upper DO
            WriteInt(index,3);
        END;
    END;
    WriteLn;

    (* using an ordinal type, other than a whole number, as an index *)
    FOR letter := 'A' TO 'Z' DO
```

182

```
        WriteChar(letter);
    END;
    WriteLn;

    (* using an enumerated type as an index *)
    FOR points := North TO West DO
        WriteInt(ORD(points),3);
    END;
    WriteLn;
END ForDemo.
```

Results from program ForDemo being run

```
 1  2  3  4  5  6  7  8  9 10
10  9  8  7  6  5  4  3  2  1  0 lift off
initial value? -5
final value? +3
-5 -4 -3 -2 -1  0  1  2  3
ABCDEFGHIJKLMNOPQRSTUVWXYZ
   0  1  2  3
```

10.2 One-dimensional array

Consider for a moment how you would store, say, five integer values. The obvious answer would be to create five variable names:

VAR
    number_1, number_2, number_3, number_4, number_5 : INTEGER;

and assign a value to each consecutive variable.

number_1 := 54;
number_2 := 26;
number_3 := 99;
number-4 := -25;
number_5 := 13;

If the same approach was adopted to store, say, fifty integer values then the amount of coding would become tedious to perform. Clearly there must be a better way of storing data of the same type, so that the amount of coding can be reduced to a minimum.

Well there is, and the answer is to use an *array*. Arrays come in various dimensions, however, within the scope of this text one and two dimensional arrays will be considered.

A picture of a one-dimensional array, containing five storage cells is illustrated in figure 10.2.

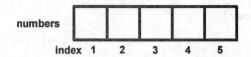

figure 10.2 a representation of a one-dimensional array

It is important to remember the following points.

(i) The contents of the array MUST be of the same data type. In other words an array can contain all integers, or all reals or all characters, or all strings, but not a mixture of each type.

(ii) Each item in the array is stored in a separate cell. If an array contained five integers, then each integer would occupy a single cell.

(iii) Each cell has a unique location value assigned to it showing its position within the array. This location value is known as either a subscript or an index.

(iv) The array is given only ONE name, irrespective of the number of items it contains.

(v) Before an array can be used it MUST be declared like any other variable.

The array depicted in figure 10.2 might be declared as follows.

VAR
    numbers : ARRAY[1..5] OF INTEGER;

This states that the name of the variable is *numbers* . It is an array containing five cells, having subscripts numbered 1 through to 5 respectively. The contents of the array is of type integer.

(vi) Access to an item of data within a cell is by using the name of the array followed by the position, subscript or index number, contained within square brackets.

To store the number 54 at cell position 1 in the array is possible by using the statement *numbers[1]:=54*; similarly to store number 26 at cell position 2 use *numbers[2]:=26*, etc.

10.3 Input and output of data

Figure 10.3 illustrates that the array called *numbers* contains five integers. These numbers can be stored in the array by direct assignment. For example the following five assignment statements would cause the numbers to be stored in the array as shown.

numbers[1]:=54;
numbers[2]:=26;
numbers[3]:=99;
numbers[4]:=-25;
numbers[5]:=13;

The contents of the array can be displayed on a screen by using WriteInt statements. For example:

WriteInt(numbers[1],3); WriteLn;
WriteInt(numbers[2],3); WriteLn;
WriteInt(numbers[3],3); WriteLn;
WriteInt(numbers[4],3); WriteLn;
WriteInt(numbers[5],3); WriteLn;

would display the contents of the array on five lines of a screen.

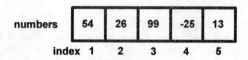

figure 10.3 a one-dimensional array containing integers

These statements have been incorporated into the following program so that the array *numbers* can be created and its contents displayed.

```
MODULE array_1;
(*
program to assign numbers directly to the cells of an array,
and display the contents of the cells
*)

FROM SWholeIO IMPORT WriteInt;
FROM STextIO IMPORT WriteString, WriteLn;

VAR
   numbers : ARRAY[1..5] OF INTEGER;

BEGIN
    (* direct assignment of numbers to cells of the array *)
    numbers[1]:=54;
    numbers[2]:=26;
    numbers[3]:=99;
    numbers[4]:=-25;
    numbers[5]:=13;

    (* the contents of the array can be displayed on a screen *)
    WriteString('contents of array'); WriteLn; WriteLn;
    WriteString('cell 1 '); WriteInt(numbers[1],3); WriteLn;
    WriteString('cell 2 '); WriteInt(numbers[2],3); WriteLn;
    WriteString('cell 3 '); WriteInt(numbers[3],3); WriteLn;
    WriteString('cell 4 '); WriteInt(numbers[4],3); WriteLn;
    WriteString('cell 5 '); WriteInt(numbers[5],3); WriteLn;
END array_1.
```

Results from program array_1 being run

```
contents of array

cell 1   54
cell 2   26
cell 3   99
cell 4  -25
cell 5   13
```

The original idea of introducing an array to store the integers, was to reduce the amount of coding required to assign the numbers to the store and output the numbers from the store. The previous example hardly inspires confidence that the original idea can be implemented! All it proves is that the same name, *numbers* , using different subscripts, 1 through 5, can be used in place of five different names. The program was introduced only to show the reader that it is possible to access explicitly any cell in the array.

To reduce the amount of coding it is necessary to replace the explicit use of the subscript or index by a control variable identifier. Instead of explicitly coding numbers[1], numbers[2], numbers[3], numbers[4] and numbers[5] it is far easier to use numbers[index], and embed this statement in a *for..do* loop changing the value of index from 1 TO 5. For example numbers can be input from a keyboard and stored in the array using:

```
FOR index:=1 TO 5 DO
    ReadInt(numbers[index]);
END;
```

and the contents of each cell of the array can be displayed on a screen using

```
FOR index:=1 TO 5 DO
    WriteInt(numbers[index],3); WriteLn;
END;
```

This idea of using the control variable identifier, in this case *index*, to control access to the contents of the array is demonstrated in the next program.

```
MODULE array_2;
(*
program to input numbers into a one-dimensional array and display the
contents of the array
*)

FROM SWholeIO IMPORT ReadInt, WriteInt;
FROM STextIO IMPORT WriteString, WriteChar, WriteLn;

CONST
    space = 40C;
```

```
VAR
  numbers : ARRAY[1..5] OF INTEGER;
  index   : CARDINAL;

BEGIN
    (* input numbers into the array *)
    WriteString('input five integers, one per line'); WriteLn; WriteLn;
    FOR index := 1 TO 5 DO
        WriteString('cell '); WriteInt(index,1); WriteChar(space);
        ReadInt(numbers[index]);
    END;
    WriteLn;

    (* output numbers from the array *)
    WriteString('contents of array'); WriteLn; WriteLn;
    FOR index:= 1 TO 5 DO
        WriteString('cell '); WriteInt(index,1); WriteChar(space);
        WriteInt(numbers[index],3); WriteLn;
    END;
    WriteLn;
END array_2.
```

Results from program array_2 being run

```
input five integers, one per line

cell 1 54
cell 2 26
cell 3 99
cell 4 -25
cell 5 13

contents of array

cell 1   54
cell 2   26
cell 3   99
cell 4  -25
cell 5   13
```

The use of a *for..do* control variable identifier is not confined to the input and output of data from an array but can be used to compare data between cells. In this next program five numbers are stored in an array, the contents of the array is then inspected to find the largest number.

The *for..do* control variable identifier index is used to gain access to consecutive items of data and compare each item with the largest number found so far.

```
largest:=numbers[1];
FOR index:=2 TO 5 DO
    IF numbers[index] > largest THEN
        largest := numbers[index];
    END;
END;
```

The variable *largest* is assigned the first value in the array. The control variable identifier is then set to access the remaining cells in the array. If a number in one of these cells is greater than the current value of the variable *largest* then *largest* is assigned this value.

```
MODULE array_3;
(*
program to input numbers into a one-dimensional array and find
and display the largest number in the array
*)

FROM STextIO IMPORT WriteString, WriteChar, WriteLn;
FROM SWholeIO IMPORT ReadInt, WriteInt;

CONST
    space = 40C;

VAR
  numbers : ARRAY[1..5] OF INTEGER;
  index   : INTEGER;
  largest : INTEGER;

BEGIN
    (* input numbers into array *)
    WriteString('input five integers, one per line'); WriteLn; WriteLn;
    FOR index := 1 TO 5 DO
        WriteString('cell '); WriteInt(index,1); WriteChar(space);
        ReadInt(numbers[index]);
    END;

    (* find largest number in the array *)
    largest := numbers[1];
    FOR index:= 2 TO 5 DO
        IF numbers[index] > largest THEN
            largest := numbers[index];
        END;
    END;

    WriteString('largest number in array is ');
    WriteInt(largest,3);
    WriteLn;
END array_3.
```

Results from program array_3 being run

```
input five integers, one per line

cell 1 54
cell 2 26
cell 3 99
cell 4 -25
cell 5 13
largest number in array is   99
```

10.4 Array of characters

A variable of *string* data type is represented as an array of characters, and is declared in the library *StringType* as:

TYPE
    string= ARRAY[0..MaxRdLength - 1] OF CHAR;

Notice that the lower bound for the subscript starts at 0 for a string and not 1. The end of a string is automatically marked by the inclusion of a *null* character. The value of *MaxRdLength* is implementation dependent, and for *TopSpeed Modula-2* is specified as 256.

Figure 10.4 illustrates an array that contains ten characters. In the program that follows, despite the data being defined as a variable of type *string*, it is possible to access each cell of this array to display the contents of the array.

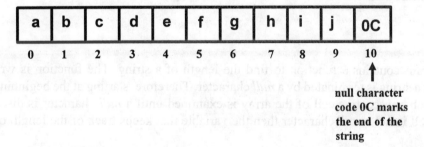

null character
code 0C marks
the end of the
string

figure 10.4 a string stored as an array of characters

```
MODULE StringDemo;
(*
program to demonstrate that a string data type is an array of characters
*)

FROM STextIO IMPORT ReadString, WriteString, WriteChar, WriteLn;
FROM StringType IMPORT string;


VAR
   characters : string;
   index      : INTEGER;

BEGIN
      (* input a string *)
      WriteString('input ten characters'); WriteLn;
      ReadString(characters);

      (* output the contents of the string one character at a time *)
      FOR index := 0 TO 9 DO
          WriteChar(characters[index]);
      END;
      WriteLn;
END StringDemo.
```

Results from program StringDemo being run

```
input ten characters
abcdefghij
abcdefghij
```

The next program contains a function to find the length of a string. The function is written with the knowledge that a string is terminated by a *null* character. Therefore, starting at the beginning of the string (index = 0), each consecutive cell of the array is examined until a *null* character is discovered. If the contents of a cell is not a *null* character then the variable that keeps track of the length of the string is increased by 1.

Notice in this program that the type declaration for the string in the formal parameter list makes no reference to the size of the one-dimensional array used to store the string. This declaration is known as an *open array parameter* and allows strings of different sizes to be used.

190

```
MODULE length_of_string;
(*
program to find the length of a string
*)

FROM STextIO IMPORT ReadString, WriteString, WriteLn;
FROM SWholeIO IMPORT WriteCard;
FROM StringType IMPORT string;

CONST
    null = 0C;

VAR
  data  : string;
  size  : CARDINAL;

PROCEDURE Length(data : ARRAY OF CHAR) : CARDINAL;
VAR
  size : CARDINAL;

BEGIN
    size:=0;
    WHILE data[size] # null DO
          INC(size);
    END;
    RETURN size;
END Length;

BEGIN
    WriteString('input text'); WriteLn;
    ReadString(data);

    WriteString('length of text is '); WriteCard(Length(data), 3);
    WriteLn;
END length_of_string.
```

Results from program LengthOfString being run

```
input text
How many characters in this string?
length of text is  35
```

The data type for the index of an open array parameter is always cardinal, whose lowest value is 0. The highest value depends upon the length of the array, or in this case string. There exists in the language, although not used in this example, a standard function HIGH, that returns the highest index of the **actual** array parameters. Since the lowest index is 0, HIGH(open array parameter) + 1, returns the size of the **actual** parameter array.

In the next example a string is passed to a procedure *Capitalize* that inspects the contents of the array containing the string for lower case characters only. When a lower case character is found it is converted into an upper case characters. All other characters in the array remain unchanged.

The procedure *Capitalize* makes no assumptions on what the function CAP does when it is used on non-lower case letters of the alphabet. Hence CAP is only applied to letters in the range a..z.

```
MODULE caps;
(* program to change every alphabetic character in a string to upper case *)

FROM STextIO IMPORT ReadString, WriteString, WriteLn;
FROM StringType IMPORT string;

CONST
    null = 0C;

VAR
  text       : string;

PROCEDURE Capitalize(VAR data : ARRAY OF CHAR);
(* procedure to convert lower case letters of the alphabet to upper case
all remaining characters remain unaltered *)

VAR
  size       : CARDINAL;
  character  : CHAR;

BEGIN

    size:=0;
    character := data[size];
    WHILE character # null DO
            IF  (character >= 'a') AND (character <= 'z') THEN
                character:=CAP(character);
            END;
            data[size] := character;
            INC(size);
            character := data[size];
    END;
END Capitalize;

BEGIN
    WriteString('input text'); WriteLn;
    ReadString(text);
    Capitalize(text);
    WriteString('capitalized text'); WriteLn;
    WriteString(text);
END caps.
```

Results from program caps being run

```
input text
This is a test of the procedure Capitalize .. and it works!
capitalized text
THIS IS A TEST OF THE PROCEDURE CAPITALIZE .. AND IT WORKS!
```

The purpose of the next program is to test a word for being a palindrome, that is a word spelt the same backwards as forwards. The method used to test the word is to inspect the characters at either end of the word, if these are the same then the next two characters at either end of the word are compared. The comparisons continue until there is no match between characters, or there are no further comparisons possible. The movement of the indices is shown in figure 10.5.

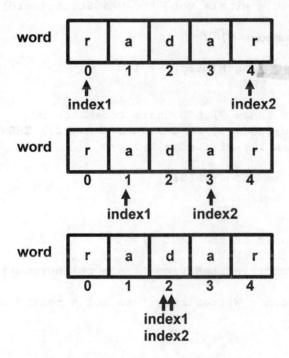

figure 10.5 testing for a palindrome

```
MODULE palindrome;
(*
program to input a word and test whether it is a palindrome
*)

FROM STextIO IMPORT WriteString, ReadString, WriteLn;
FROM StringType IMPORT string;
FROM Strings IMPORT Length;

VAR
    word                : string;
    index_1, index_2    : INTEGER;
    CharactersMatch     : BOOLEAN;

BEGIN
    (* input word *)
    WriteString('input a single word '); ReadString(word);

    (* test for palindrome *)
    index_1 := 0;
    index_2 := INTEGER(Length(word)) - 1;
    CharactersMatch := TRUE;

    WHILE (index_1 <= index_2) AND CharactersMatch DO
            IF CAP(word[index_1]) = CAP(word[index_2]) THEN
                INC(index_1); DEC(index_2);
            ELSE
                CharactersMatch:=FALSE;
            END;
    END;

    (* output the result of the test *)
    IF CharactersMatch THEN
        WriteString(word); WriteString(' is a palindrome');
    ELSE
        WriteString(word); WriteString(' is NOT a palindrome');
    END;
    WriteLn;
END palindrome.
```

Results from program palindrome being run twice

```
input a single word radar
radar is a palindrome
input a single word mouse
mouse is not a palindrome
```

In the final example of this section an array is used to store the names of the coloured balls in a game of snooker. The names are stored in cell positions such that the subscript or index to the cell represents the value of the coloured ball. For example red is stored in cell 1, yellow in cell 2, green in cell 3, .. black in cell 7. Figure 10.6 illustrates this data stored in the array *colours*.

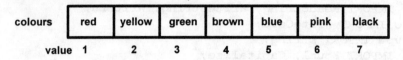

colours	red	yellow	green	brown	blue	pink	black
value	1	2	3	4	5	6	7

figure 10.6 array of colours of snooker balls

The purpose of the program is to keep the score for any break in snooker. The user is invited to type the colour of the ball potted, its corresponding value is displayed, followed by the total for the break. For each ball potted the total for the break is increased by the value of the ball until the user inputs the word NONE to signify the end of the break.

The procedure *search* is used to compare the colour of the ball potted with each colour stored in the array. If a match between the colours is found then the value for that ball can be determined, otherwise no value is assumed for the colour potted.

Had a *for..do* loop been used, in the *search* procedure, to access each cell of the array the coding might have been as follows.

```
FOR value:=1 TO 7 DO
    IF pot = colours[value] THEN
        score:=value;
        found:=TRUE;
    END;
END;
```

If the value for *pot* had been 'black', then this coding is perfectly satisfactory since the colour match is not found until value is 7, at the extreme end of the array. But what if the colour had been 'red'? The score would be set to 1 and *found* to true, then it would be necessary to exit from the loop, otherwise the computer would go round the loop a further six times, testing if there was a colour match.

An alternative to the coding can be achieved in several ways, in this example the *for..do* loop is replaced with a *while..do* loop, and includes a test in the *while..do* loop as to whether the colour has been found. In addition to this test it is necessary to include a test for the index or subscript to the array going out of bounds (value <=7). Combining the two conditions creates the statement:

WHILE (value <= 7) AND NOT found DO

Initially if found is set to FALSE and value is set to 1, the contents of the loop will continue to be executed until either the subscript value exceeds 7, or a colour match is found, and the Boolean variable found is set to TRUE.

```
MODULE BigBreak;
(*
program to calculate the amount scored in a break in snooker
*)

FROM STextIO IMPORT ReadString, WriteString, WriteLn;
FROM SWholeIO IMPORT WriteCard;
FROM StringType IMPORT string;
FROM Strings IMPORT Equal, Capitalize;

TYPE
    ArrayOfColour = ARRAY[1..7] OF string;

VAR
    colours       : ArrayOfColour;
    pot           : string;
    break, score  : CARDINAL;
    found         : BOOLEAN;

PROCEDURE initialise(VAR colours : ArrayOfColour);
(*
procedure to store each colour in consecutive cells of the array such
that the array subscript represents the value of the ball
*)

BEGIN
    colours[1] := 'RED';
    colours[2] := 'YELLOW';
    colours[3] := 'GREEN';
    colours[4] := 'BROWN';
    colours[5] := 'BLUE';
    colours[6] := 'PINK';
    colours[7] := 'BLACK';
END initialise;

PROCEDURE PotBall(VAR pot : string);
(*
procedure to input the colour of the potted ball
*)

BEGIN
    WriteString('input potted colour - type NONE to end break ');
    ReadString(pot);
    Capitalize(pot);
END PotBall;
```

```
PROCEDURE results(score : CARDINAL; break : CARDINAL);
(*
procedure to display the value of the ball potted and the current
value of the break
*)

BEGIN
    WriteString(pot); WriteString(' potted - score '); WriteCard(score,1);
    WriteLn;
    WriteString('break score '); WriteCard(break, 3);
    WriteLn;
END results;

PROCEDURE search (pot : string; VAR score : CARDINAL;
                  VAR colours : ArrayOfColour; VAR found : BOOLEAN);
(*
procedure to search an array for the name of a colour, when found the posi-
tion of the colour is the score for that ball
*)

VAR
  value : CARDINAL;

BEGIN
    found := FALSE;
    value := 1;
    WHILE (value <= 7) AND NOT found DO
        IF Equal(pot, colours[value]) THEN
            score := value;
            found := TRUE;
        ELSE
            INC(value);
        END;
    END;
END search;

BEGIN
    initialise(colours);
    break := 0;
    PotBall(pot);
    WHILE NOT Equal(pot, 'NONE') DO
        search(pot, score, colours, found);
        IF found THEN
            break:=break+score;
            results(score,break);
        END;
        PotBall(pot);
    END;
END BigBreak.
```

197

Results from program BigBreak being run

```
input potted colour - type NONE to end break red
RED potted - score 1
break score 1
input potted colour - type NONE to end break black
BLACK potted - score 7
break score 8
input potted colour - type NONE to end break red
RED potted - score 1
break score 9
input potted colour - type NONE to end break orange
input potted colour - type NONE to end break blue
BLUE potted - score 5
break score 14
input potted colour - type NONE to end break NONE
```

10.5 Records

It was stated earlier in the chapter that the contents of all the cells in an array MUST be of the same data type. In other words an array can contain all integers, or all cardinals or all reals, or all characters, or all strings, but not a mixture of each type.

This statement is perfectly true, however, it does not preclude a mixture of data types from being stored in the cell of an array provided that the types come under the umbrella of a record type.

A record is a collection of values, possibly of different types, whose components are accessed by name.

Figure 10.7 illustrates how a birthday date can be divided into the components *day*, *month* and *year*. Birthday is depicted as a record type, that contains the fields *day*, *month* and *year*, each of type cardinal.

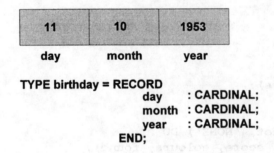

```
TYPE birthday = RECORD
                day   : CARDINAL;
                month : CARDINAL;
                year  : CARDINAL;
             END;
```

figure 10.7 record to represent a date

The type of record that is used to represent a date of birth is defined as having a type called *birthday*:

```
TYPE
     birthday =   RECORD
                     day        : CARDINAL;
                     month      : CARDINAL;
                     year       : CARDINAL;
                  END;
```

A variable that is used to store the date of birth is then defined as:

```
VAR
   date : birthday;
```

This implies that the variable *date* contains three fields, *day*, *month* and *year*. To access each field it is necessary to qualify the variable *date* with the name of the field. For example

```
date.day:=11;
date.month:=10;
date.year:=1953;
```

would assign the *day* as 11, *month* as 10 and *year* as 1953, thereby representing a date of 11 10 1953. In the program on the next page, the values for *day*, *month* and *year* are input via a keyboard, hence the statement:

ReadCard(date.day); ReadCard(date.month); ReadCard(date.year);

Since the variable *date* is a record, its fields CANNOT be output by simply writing WriteCard(date). It is necessary to specify every field that is to be output. For example

WriteCard(date.day,2); WriteCard(date.month,2); WriteCard(date.year,4);

or as stated in the program that follows as:

```
WriteString('day ');    WriteCard(date.day,2);     WriteLn;
WriteString('month '); WriteCard(date.month,2);   WriteLn;
WriteString('year ');   WriteCard(date.year,4);    WriteLn;
```

```
MODULE record_1;
(*
program to create a record and display the contents
*)

FROM SWholeIO IMPORT ReadCard, WriteCard;
FROM STextIO IMPORT WriteString, WriteLn;

TYPE
   birthday = RECORD
                     day    : CARDINAL;
                     month  : CARDINAL;
                     year   : CARDINAL;
              END;
```

```
VAR
    date : birthday;

BEGIN
    WriteString('input a date of birth as DD MM 19YY ');
    ReadCard(date.day); ReadCard(date.month); ReadCard(date.year);

    WriteString('day ');   WriteCard(date.day, 2);   WriteLn;
    WriteString('month '); WriteCard(date.month, 2); WriteLn;
    WriteString('year ');  WriteCard(date.year, 4);  WriteLn;
END record_1.
```

Results from program record_1 being run

```
input a date of birth as DD MM 19YY 11 10 1953
day 11
month 10
year 1953
```

The previous program can be extended to store more than one record. The variable name *date* needs to be changed and redefined as an array that will store records of type birthday:

dates : ARRAY [1..5] OF birthday;

Each record that is input at the keyboard can then be stored into consecutive locations of this five cell array, as depicted in figure 10.8. When all five records have been stored the contents of the array is then displayed on a screen.

index	day	month	year
1	11	10	1953
2	18	03	1948
3	14	06	1920
4	17	03	1960
5	25	09	1981

figure 10.8 array used to store records

```
MODULE record_2;
(*
program to create records, store them in an array and display
the contents of the array
*)

FROM SWholeIO IMPORT ReadCard, WriteCard;
FROM STextIO IMPORT WriteString, WriteLn;

TYPE
    birthday = RECORD
                        day   : CARDINAL;
                        month : CARDINAL;
                        year  : CARDINAL;
               END;

VAR
    dates : ARRAY[1..5] OF birthday;
    index : CARDINAL;

BEGIN
    (* input dates into the array *)
    WriteString('input five dates of birth as DD MM 19YY, one per line');
    WriteLn;
    FOR index := 1 TO 5 DO
        ReadCard(dates[index].day);
        ReadCard(dates[index].month);
        ReadCard(dates[index].year);
    END;
    WriteLn;

    (* display the contents of the array *)
    FOR index := 1 TO 5 DO
        WriteCard(dates[index].day, 2);
        WriteCard(dates[index].month, 3);
        WriteCard(dates[index].year, 5);
        WriteLn;
    END;
END record_2.
```

Results from program record_2 being run

```
input five dates of birth as DD MM 19YY, one per line
11 10 1953
18 03 1948
14 06 1920
17 03 1960
25 09 1981
```

```
11  10  1953
18   3  1948
14   6  1920
17   3  1960
25   9  1981
```

It is possible for a field of a record to also be of type record. For instance in figure 10.9 the record data type *Names_Dates* has two fields *name* and *DOB*. However, *DOB* has a data type *birthday*, where *birthday* has previously been defined as a record type. As figure 10.9 illustrates, a single field *DOB* of a record, can itself be a record containing the fields *day*, *month* and *year*.

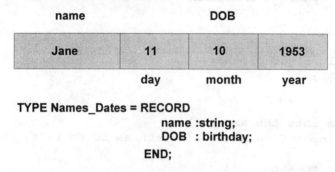

```
TYPE Names_Dates = RECORD
                   name :string;
                   DOB  : birthday;
                   END;
```

figure 10.9 a record used to represent name and date

The next program is merely an extension of the previous program. Instead of storing records containing dates of birth in an array it stores the names of people and their corresponding dates of birth in an array. Figure 10.10 illustrates the storage of the new records in the array.

index		name	day	DOB month	year
1		Jane	11	10	1953
2		Fred	18	03	1948
3		Henry	14	06	1920
4		Patrick	17	03	1960
5		Susan	25	09	1981

figure 10.10 array of records

```
MODULE record_3;
(*
program to create records, store them in an array and display
the contents of the array
*)

FROM SWholeIO IMPORT ReadCard, WriteCard;
FROM STextIO IMPORT ReadString, WriteString, WriteLn;
FROM StringType IMPORT string;

TYPE
   birthday = RECORD
                    day   : CARDINAL;
                    month : CARDINAL;
                    year  : CARDINAL;
              END;


   names_dates = RECORD
                      name : string;
                      DOB  : birthday;
                 END;

VAR
   list  : ARRAY[1..5] OF names_dates;
   index : CARDINAL;

BEGIN
    (* input names and dates of birth for five people into the array *)
    FOR index := 1 TO 5 DO
        WriteString('NAME '); ReadString(list[index].name);
        WriteString('DATE OF BIRTH ');
        ReadCard(list[index].DOB.day);
        ReadCard(list[index].DOB.month);
        ReadCard(list[index].DOB.year);
    END;
    WriteLn;
    (* display the contents of the array *)
    FOR index := 1 TO 5 DO
        WriteString(list[index].name);
        WriteCard(list[index].DOB.day, 4);
        WriteCard(list[index].DOB.month, 3);
        WriteCard(list[index].DOB.year, 5);
        WriteLn;
    END;
END record_3.
```

Results from program record_3 being run

```
NAME  Jane
DATE OF BIRTH 11 10 1953
NAME  Fred
DATE OF BIRTH 18 03 1948
NAME  Henry
DATE OF BIRTH 14 06 1920
NAME  Patrick
DATE OF BIRTH 17 03 1960
NAME  Susan
DATE OF BIRTH 25 09 1981

Jane   11 10 1953
Fred   18 03 1948
Henry  14  6 1920
Patrick  17  3  1960
Susan  25  9 1981
```

The amount of coding required to access a field within a record can be quite cumbersome. Consider the duplication of code necessary in displaying the fields for *day*, *month* and *year* in this program. A shorthand way of reducing the redundant code is to use a WITH statement. The code:

```
FOR index:=1 TO 5 DO
    WriteString(list[index].name);
    WriteCard(list[index].DOB.day,3):
    WriteCard(list[index].DOB.month,3);
    WriteCard(list[index].DOB.year,5);
END;
```

can be reduced to:

```
FOR index:=1 TO 5 DO
    WITH list[index] DO
        WriteString(name);
        WriteCard(DOB.day,3):
        WriteCard(DOB.month,3);
        WriteCard(DOB.year,5);
    END;
END;
```

or even:

```
FOR index:=1 TO 5 DO
   WITH list[index] DO
      WriteCard(name);
      WITH DOB DO
         WriteCard(day,3):
         WriteCard(month,3);
         WriteCard(year,5);
      END;
   END;
END;
```

The final program in this section is an extension of the program to create an array of names and dates of birth. Having input the data and stored it in an array, the user is invited to type the name of a person, the array is searched for that name, and if a match is found the date of birth for that person is displayed.

```
MODULE record_4;
(*
program to create records, store them in an array and search the array for
the name and display the date of birth
*)

FROM SWholeIO IMPORT ReadCard, WriteCard;
FROM STextIO IMPORT ReadString, WriteString, WriteLn;
FROM StringType IMPORT string;
FROM Strings IMPORT Capitalize, Equal;

TYPE
   birthday = RECORD
                    day    : CARDINAL;
                    month  : CARDINAL;
                    year   : CARDINAL;
              END;

   names_dates = RECORD
                    name : string;
                    DOB  : birthday;
                 END;

   many_names_dates = ARRAY[1..5] OF names_dates;

VAR
   list                : many_names_dates;
   person              : string;
   found               : BOOLEAN;
   position_in_array   : CARDINAL;
   NoMoreData          : BOOLEAN;
```

```
PROCEDURE InputData(VAR list : many_names_dates);
(*
procedure to create an array of names and corresponding birthdays
*)
VAR
  index : CARDINAL;

BEGIN
    WriteString('input names and dates of birth for five people'); WriteLn;
    FOR index := 1 TO 5 DO
        WriteString('NAME '); ReadString(list[index].name);
        WriteString('DATE OF BIRTH ');
        ReadCard(list[index].DOB.day);
        ReadCard(list[index].DOB.month);
        ReadCard(list[index].DOB.year);
    END;
    WriteLn;
END InputData;

PROCEDURE InputName(VAR person : string);
(*
procedure to input the name of a person whose birthday is to be looked up
*)
BEGIN
    WriteString('input name of person ');
    ReadString(person);
END InputName;

PROCEDURE search(list : many_names_dates; person : string;
                 VAR found : BOOLEAN; VAR position_in_array : CARDINAL);
(*
search for a matching name of a person and if found return the position
in the array of the match
*)
BEGIN
    position_in_array := 1;
    found := FALSE;
    WHILE (position_in_array <= 5) AND NOT found DO
        IF Equal(person, list[position_in_array].name) THEN
            found := TRUE;
        ELSE
            INC(position_in_array);
        END;
    END;
END search;
```

```
PROCEDURE continue(VAR NoMoreData : BOOLEAN);
(*
procedure to ask user whether to continue
*)

VAR
   reply : string;

BEGIN
    WriteString('do you want to continue? - answer yes or no ');
    ReadString(reply);
    Capitalize(reply);
    IF Equal(reply, 'NO') THEN
       NoMoreData := TRUE;
    ELSE
       NoMoreData := FALSE;
    END;
END continue;


BEGIN
    InputData(list);
    REPEAT
        InputName(person);
        search(list, person, found, position_in_array);
        IF found THEN
                WriteString('date of birth');
                WriteCard(list[position_in_array].DOB.day, 4);
                WriteCard(list[position_in_array].DOB.month, 3);
                WriteCard(list[position_in_array].DOB.year, 5);
                WriteLn;
        ELSE
                WriteString(person); WriteString(' not in list');
                WriteLn;
        END;
        continue(NoMoreData);
    UNTIL NoMoreData;
END record_4.
```

Results from program record_4 being run

```
input names and dates of birth for five people
NAME Jane
DATE OF BIRTH 11 10 1953
NAME Fred
DATE OF BIRTH 18 03 1948
```

```
NAME Henry
DATE OF BIRTH 14 06 1920
NAME Patrick
DATE OF BIRTH 17 03 1960
NAME Susan
DATE OF BIRTH 25 09 1981

input name of person Henry
date of birth 14  6 1920
do you want to continue? - answer yes or no yes
input name of person George
George not in list
do you want to continue? - answer yes or no yes
input name of person Patrick
date of birth 17  3 1960
do you want to continue? - answer yes or no
input name of person Jane
date of birth 11 10 1953
do you want to continue? - answer yes or no no
```

10.6 Two-dimensional arrays

An array is not confined to one dimension (one subscript or index), but can be extended to two-dimensions and beyond in order to provide a necessary flexible data structure for the solution to a problem. A two-dimensional array is a repetition of a one-dimensional array. The structure can be thought of as a matrix or grid structure. As a simple example of such a structure, a crossword may be composed of 15 rows and 15 columns, as depicted in figure 10.11.

The crossword puzzle can be defined as an array in Modula-2 by making the following declaration.

```
CONST
    MaxRow = 15;
    MaxColumn = 15;
TYPE
    (* the type line is a one-dimensional array *)
    line = ARRAY[1..MaxColumn] OF CHAR;
VAR
    (* an array of one-dimensional arrays *)
    puzzle : ARRAY[1..MaxRow] OF line;
```

However, a much preferred declaration would be:

```
VAR
    puzzle: ARRAY[1..MaxRow],[1..MaxColumn] OF CHAR;
```

columns

	1	2	3	4	5	6	7	8	9	10	11	12	13	14	15
1	J	U	I	C	E										
2	A				L	A	U	N	C	H					
3	M	O	D	E	M			A							
4								U							
5								G							
6								H							
7								T							
8								Y							
9															
10															
11															
12															
13															
14															
15															

rows

figure 10.11 crossword of 15 rows and 15 columns

This clearly indicates that the two-dimensional array is composed from 15 rows and each row is composed of 15 columns of the type char. The contents of the array is accessed through two indices, one for the row and one for the column, in that order, for example, puzzle[row, column]. Using the illustration given in figure 10.11 it should be clear to the reader that: puzzle[3,1] contains the character M,

puzzle[2,8] contains the character N,
puzzle[1,5] contains the character E and so on.

To build a new word THAT downwards from row 1 of column 10, the following assignment statements would be necessary.

puzzle[1,10]:='T';
puzzle[3,10]:='A';
puzzle[4,10]:='T';

If a program was required to allow the user to input words and display them on the board then the following routines would be necessary. The declaration of variables should then be extended to cater for the two indices.
VAR
    puzzle: ARRAY[1..MaxRow],[1..MaxColumn] OF CHAR;
    row, column: CARDINAL;

The reader must never assume that because an array has not been used that it will empty. Therefore, the first segment of code should initialise each square of the crossword to a blank space. This can be simply achieved by using two FOR loops, one to control the *row* index and the other to control the *column* index.

```
(* clear the crossword puzzle *)
FOR row:=1 TO MaxRow DO
    FOR column:=1 TO MaxColumn DO
        puzzle[row, column]:=space;
    END;
END;
```

This assumes that the constant space has already been declared i.e. CONST space = 40C;

If the start (Srow,Scol) and finish (Frow,Fcol) row and column co-ordinates, of a word to be input to the crossword, are known, and the word has already been input from a keyboard and stored as a string in a one- dimensional array called *word*, then the letters of the word can be transferred to the array *puzzle* using the following segment of code. In this code *row_index* and *col_index* are local control variable identifiers used as indices to the array *puzzle*, with the purpose of denoting the position of characters of the word on the same column or same line respectively.

```
(* transfer, letter by letter, the word to the crossword *)
index:=0;
IF Srow=Frow THEN (* horizontal word i.e. same row *)
    FOR col_index:=Scol TO Fcol DO
        puzzle[Srow,col_index]:=word[index];
        INC(index);
    END;
ELSE (* vertical word i.e. same column *)
    FOR row_index:=Srow TO Frow DO
        puzzle[row_index,Scol]:=word[index];
        INC(index);
    END;
END;
```

Having stored characters in the array puzzle it is useful if the contents of the crossword can be displayed on the screen so that new words can be invented and input to the computer. The output of the array is again controlled by two control variable identifiers *row* and *column*.

```
(* display the contents of the crossword *)
FOR row:=1 TO MaxRow DO
    FOR column:=1 TO MaxColumn DO
        write(puzzle[row, column]);
    END;
    WriteLn;
END;
```

These segments of code have been included in the following program that will allow the user to build words of a crossword puzzle. Note that the identifier *Xword* is used in the procedures and not the identifier *puzzle*. The identifier *puzzle* is, however, used as an actual parameter in the main program.

```modula2
MODULE crossword;
(*
program to construct and display a crossword
*)

FROM STextIO IMPORT ReadString, WriteString, WriteChar, WriteLn;
FROM SWholeIO IMPORT ReadCard, WriteCard;
FROM StringType IMPORT string;
FROM Strings IMPORT Equal, Capitalize;

CONST
    space   = 40C;
    MaxRow = 15;
    MaxCol = 15;

TYPE
    grid = ARRAY[1..MaxRow], [1..MaxCol] OF CHAR;

VAR
    puzzle : grid;
    reply  : string;

PROCEDURE display(Xword : grid);
(*
procedure to display the crossword
*)

VAR
  row, col : CARDINAL;

BEGIN
    WriteLn; WriteString('     1  2  3  4  5  6  7  8  9 10 11 12 13 14 15');
    WriteLn;
    FOR row:=1 TO MaxRow DO
        WriteCard(row, 2);
        FOR col := 1 TO MaxCol DO
            WriteChar(space); WriteChar(space); WriteChar(Xword[row, col]);
        END;
        WriteLn;
    END;
END display;

PROCEDURE clear(VAR Xword : grid);
(*
procedure to clear the letters from the crossword puzzle
*)
VAR
  row, col : CARDINAL;
```

```
BEGIN
    FOR row := 1 TO MaxRow DO
        FOR col := 1 TO MaxCol DO
            Xword[row, col] := space;
        END;
    END;
END clear;

PROCEDURE InputData(VAR Xword : grid);
(*
procedure to input the starting [Srow, Scol] and finishing [Frow, Fcol]
co-ordinates of a word and the word
*)

VAR
    index, col_index, row_index : CARDINAL; (* indices *)
    Srow, Scol, Frow, Fcol      : CARDINAL; (* co-ordinates *)
    word                        : string;

BEGIN
    WriteString('start? ');  ReadCard(Srow); ReadCard(Scol);
    WriteString('finish? '); ReadCard(Frow); ReadCard(Fcol);
    WriteString('word? ');   ReadString(word);

    index := 0;
    IF Srow = Frow THEN                       (* word in same row *)
        FOR col_index:= Scol TO Fcol DO    (* transfer word to crossword *)
            Xword[Srow,col_index] := word[index];
            INC(index);
        END;
    ELSE                                      (* word in same column *)
        FOR row_index:= Srow TO Frow DO    (* transfer word to crossword *)
            Xword[row_index,Scol] := word[index];
            INC(index);
        END;
    END;
END InputData;

BEGIN
    clear(puzzle);
    REPEAT
        InputData(puzzle);
        display(puzzle);
        WriteLn; WriteString('continue? ');
        ReadString(reply);
        Capitalize(reply);
    UNTIL Equal(reply, 'NO');
END crossword.
```

212

Partial results from program crossword being run

```
continue? YES
start? 2 8
finish? 8 8
word? NAUGHTY

   1  2  3  4  5  6  7  8  9 10 11 12 13 14 15
 1 J  U  I  C  E
 2 A           L  A  U  N  C  H
 3 M  O  D  E  M        A
 4                      U
 5                      G
 6                      H
 7                      T
 8                      Y
 9
10
11
12
13
14
15

continue? YES
start? 8 8
finish? 8 12
word? YACHT

   1  2  3  4  5  6  7  8  9 10 11 12 13 14 15
 1 J  U  I  C  E
 2 A           L  A  U  N  C  H
 3 M  O  D  E  M        A
 4                      U
 5                      G
 6                      H
 7                      T
 8                      Y  A  C  H  T
 9
10
11
12
13
14
15

continue? NO
```

10.7 Multi-dimensional arrays

As was hinted at the beginning of this section, it is possible to have an array of more than two-dimensions. A three-dimensional array is a repetition of a two-dimensional array, a four-dimensional array is a repetition of a three-dimensional array and so on.

The declaration of a three-dimensional array ThreeD could be coded as:

```
TYPE
    TwoD=ARRAY[1..10],[1..5] OF INTEGER;
VAR
    ThreeD: ARRAY[1..4] OF TwoD;
```

implying maximum dimensions of ThreeD[4,10,5]. Similarly, a four-dimensional array FourD could be coded as:

```
TYPE
    ThreeD=ARRAY[1..4],[1..10],[1..5] OF INTEGER;
VAR
    FourD: ARRAY[1..3] OF ThreeD;
```

implying maximum dimensions of FourD[3,4,10,5].

However, although these declarations fit nicely into the definition just given of multi-dimensional arrays the reader might prefer to declare the two arrays in the following alternative format.

```
VAR
    ThreeD: ARRAY[1..4],[1..10],[1..5] OF INTEGER;
```
and

```
VAR
    FourD: ARRAY[1..3],[1..4],[1..10],[1..5] OF INTEGER;
```

The method of access to the arrays will be through their respective indices. For example the following statements are all legal.

```
ThreeD[2,9,4]:=26;
ReadInt(ThreeD[1,8,3]);
WriteInt(ThreeD[plane, row, column],6);
FourD[a,b,c,d]:=48;
ReadInt(FourD[3,2,8,3]);
WriteInt(FourD[w,x,y,z],6);
```

10.8 Variant records

In the definition of a record type it has been assumed that all records in a file will conform to the type definition. However, it is possible that some records can have two parts - a fixed part and a variant part. Consider for a moment a record containing personal details of employees. If a person is married the details of their spouse is also included.

```
TYPE
    personnel = RECORD
                    (* fixed part *)
                    name        : string;
                    address     : string;
                    telephone   : string;
                    DateOfBirth : date;
                    department  : CHAR;
                    grade       : CHAR;

                    (* variant part *)
                    CASE married : BOOLEAN OF
                        TRUE :  SpouseName       : string;
                                DateOfMarriage   : date;
                                NumberOfChildren : CARDINAL|
                        FALSE : (* empty field *)
                    END;
                END;
```

From this example it can be seen that a *case* statement is used to represent the variant part of the record. The CASE selector, in this example married, is regarded as another field of the record structure, whose type is defined as BOOLEAN. The selector, however, can be of any previously defined ordinal type. The type BOOLEAN has been used here but any user defined type is possible. The labels of the CASE statement, here TRUE or FALSE, indicate the alternative variant record field components.

In this example if an employee is married, three additional fields are appended to the record; they are SpouseName, DateOfMarriage and NumberOfChildren. However, if an employee is not married these fields do not exist. More than one field in a record may be variant.

For example in the final program of this chapter a record contains descriptions of various forms of transport. The record description being given by:

```
data = RECORD
            name        : string;                    (* name of transport *)
            CASE tag    : CHAR OF
                'A'     : FixedWings : BOOLEAN |     (* Aircraft *)
                'B'     : use : string;              (* Boat *)
                        : TypeOfVessel : string |
                'V'     : description : string;      (* Vehicle *)
            END;
```

215

```
          CASE wheels   : BOOLEAN OF
              TRUE      : number     : CARDINAL |   (* number of wheels *)
              FALSE     : movement   : string;      (* description of how it moves *)
          END;
          CASE engine OF : BOOLEAN OF
              TRUE      : (* null *)|
              FALSE     : comment : string;          (* method of propulsion *)
          END;
      END;
```

Contents of data file a:transp.txt, where each field appears on a new line

```
helicopter
a
f
f
takes off vertically
t
tandem
v
bicycle
t
2
f
two people pedalling
firefly
b
sailing
dinghy
f
floats
f
wind in the sails
balloon
a
f
f
floats in air
f
a gas burner
rickshaw
v
light cart
t
2
f
a person pulling the cart
```

The purpose of this program is to read the transport file containing variant records, interpret the fields and output a suitable description of each form of transport.

```
MODULE transpt;
(*
program to demonstrate variant records
*)

FROM StreamFile IMPORT ChanId, Open, Close, read, OpenResults;
FROM IOResult IMPORT ReadResult, ReadResults;
FROM STextIO IMPORT WriteString, WriteChar, WriteLn;
FROM SWholeIO IMPORT WriteCard;
FROM StringType IMPORT string;
FROM TextIO IMPORT ReadString, ReadChar;
FROM WholeIO IMPORT ReadCard;

CONST
   space = 40C;

TYPE
   data = RECORD
             name       : string;

             CASE tag : CHAR OF
             'A'    : FixedWings   : BOOLEAN |
             'B'    : use          : string;
                      TypeOfVessel : string |
             'V'    : description  : string;
             END;

             CASE wheels : BOOLEAN OF
             TRUE   : number   : CARDINAL|
             FALSE  : movement : string;
             END;

             CASE engine : BOOLEAN OF
             TRUE   : (* null *) |
             FALSE  : comment : string;
             END;
          END;

VAR
        transport : data;
        data_file : ChanId;
        results   : OpenResults;
        LF        : CHAR;
```

```
PROCEDURE ReadBoolean(VAR value:BOOLEAN);
(* procedure to convert the characters t or f to TRUE or FALSE respec-
tively *)

VAR
   character : CHAR;
        truth     : string;
BEGIN
  ReadString(data_file, truth);
  character:=CAP(truth[0]);
  CASE character OF
    'T' : value:= TRUE |
    'F' : value:= FALSE;
  END;
END ReadBoolean;

PROCEDURE ReadRecord(VAR transport : data);
(* procedure to read the lines of a text file and store the information
into the fields of a variant record *)

VAR
   tags : string;
BEGIN
  WITH transport DO
    ReadString(data_file, name);
    ReadString(data_file, tags);
    tag:=CAP(tags[0]);
    CASE tag OF
      'A' : ReadBoolean(FixedWings)|
      'B' : ReadString(data_file, use);
            ReadString(data_file, TypeOfVessel)|
      'V' : ReadString(data_file, description);
    END;

    ReadBoolean(wheels);
    IF wheels THEN
      ReadCard(data_file, number);
      ReadChar(data_file, LF);
    ELSE
      ReadString(data_file, movement);
    END;

    ReadBoolean(engine);
    IF NOT engine THEN
      ReadString(data_file, comment);
    END;
  END;
END ReadRecord;
```

```
PROCEDURE WriteRecord(transport : data);
(* procedure to display the fields of a variant record *)

BEGIN
   WITH transport DO
      WriteString('A '); WriteString(name);
      CASE tag OF
         'A' :  WriteString(' is an aircraft ');
                IF NOT FixedWings THEN
                   WriteString('without fixed wings');
                END |
         'B' :  WriteString(' is a ');
                WriteString(use); WriteChar(space);
                WriteString(TypeOfVessel)|
         'V' : WriteString(' is a '); WriteString(description);
      END;

      IF wheels THEN
         WriteString(' it has'); WriteCard(number,2);
         WriteString(' wheels ');
      ELSE
         WriteString(' it '); WriteString(movement);
      END;
      WriteLn;

      IF NOT engine THEN
         WriteString('has no engine and is powered by ');
         WriteString(comment);
      END;
      WriteLn;
   END;
END WriteRecord;

BEGIN
   Open(data_file, 'a:transp.txt', read, results);
   IF results # opened THEN
      WriteString('file cannot be opened program abandoned');
      HALT;
   END;

   ReadRecord(transport);
   WHILE ReadResult(data_file) # endOfInput DO
      WriteRecord(transport);
      WriteLn;
      ReadRecord(transport);
   END;
   Close(data_file);
END transpt.
```

219

Results from program transpt being run

```
A helicopter is an aircraft without fixed wings it takes off vertically


A tandem is a bicycle it has 2 wheels
has no engine and is powered by two people pedalling

A firefly is a sailing dinghy it floats
has no engine and is powered by wind in the sails

A balloon is an aircraft without fixed wings it floats in air
has no engine and is powered by a gas burner

A rickshaw is a light cart it has 2 wheels
has no engine and is powered by a person pulling the cart
```

10.9 Summary

- [ ] A *for..do* loop provides a straightforward way of using a loop control variable as a counter.

- [ ] A *for..do* loop automatically initialises the loop control variable to the initial value, tests the variable to see if it has reached the final value, and increases the value of the control variable by the next ordinal value. When the value of the loop control variable exceeds the value of the final value the computer exits from the loop to the next executable statement after the end of the body of the loop.

- [ ] The value of the loop control variable is either increased by the step value if the initial value is less than the final value, or decreased by the step value if the initial value is greater than the final value. If the step value is omitted the default is taken to be one.

- [ ] A one-dimensional array is a data structure that can be used to store data of the same type.

- [ ] An array is subdivided into cells, with each cell having a unique subscript or index value.

- [ ] The maximum number of cells that an array contains is declared in a program and remains constant. For this reason an array is known as a static data structure.

- [ ] Access to any item of data in the array is through the name of the array, followed by the position of the data in the array, that is the subscript or index value of the cell that contains the data.

- [ ] A loop control variable in a for..do statement is a useful way of representing the subscript or index of an array. By varying the value of the loop control variable it is possible to access any cell within the array.

- [ ] Never use a *for..do* loop when searching for an item of data in an array, since the loop will not terminate when the item is found, unless the item happens to be the last item in the array.

☐ A variable of string data type is represented as an array of characters. The initial subscript is taken to be zero. The string is terminated by a null character.

☐ The contents of a variable of string data type can be accessed as individual characters stored from cell 0 in a one-dimensional array.

☐ An open array parameter is used when passing arrays of different sizes. However, the maximum size of the array to be passed must always be declared in the program.

☐ The function HIGH returns the value of the largest subscript of an actual array parameter.

☐ A record is a data type.

☐ A collection of data, of possibly different types, can be stored in a variable having a predefined record structure.

☐ The individual parts of a record are known as data fields. To access a specific field the variable name associated with the record must be qualified with the name of the field.

☐ A record may contain both a fixed number of fields and a number of fields that vary according to the data being stored. Such records are known as variant records.

☐ To simplify the qualification of a variable name with a field name a WITH statement may be used.

☐ By creating an array of records it is possible to store data of different types in an array.

☐ Multi-dimensional arrays are possible in Modula-2. A two-dimensional array is taken to be a repetition of one-dimensional arrays; a three-dimensional array is taken to be a repetition of two-dimensional arrays, and so on.

10.10 Questions - *answers begin on page 393*

1. Write a program using for..do loops to:

(a). Display the numbers 50 to 75 with an incremental value of 1.
(b). Display the numbers 20 to 5 with an incremental value of -1.
(c). Display the odd integers in the range 1 to 29 inclusive.
(d). Display the squares of the even integers in the range 2 to 20 inclusive.
(e). Display the sum of the squares of the odd integers in the range 1 to 13 inclusive.
(f). Display the alphabet in reverse order.

2. Write a program to store the alphabet as characters in an array. The program should display:

(a). The entire alphabet.
(b). The first six characters of the alphabet.
(c). The last ten characters of the alphabet.
(d). The tenth character of the alphabet.

3. Write a program to input eight integers in numerical order into a one-dimensional array X; copy the numbers from array X to another one-dimensional array Y such that array Y contains the numbers in descending order. Output the contents of array Y.

4. Write a program to input and store in an array, ten records that contain the names of telephone exchanges and their corresponding STD codes. For example Oxford 0865 might be one record in the array. Include a procedure to search for the name of the exchange when given the STD code. Display the result of the search.

5. Write a procedure to store only the score-draws of football matches in a one-dimensional array. The maximum number of matches played is fifty-eight, and the results are recorded as the Boolean value TRUE for a score-draw, otherwise the Boolean value FALSE.

If one line on the football pools is stored in another one-dimensional array as twelve predicted score-draws by integers in the range 1 to 58, corresponding to the matches being played, check the contents of this array for the number of score draws that actually happened, and display this result.

6. Write a program to store the names of foods and their prices, as displayed in the Greasy Spoon Cafe (section 2.1), as records in an array. Extend the program to:

(a). Input the name of an item of food and display the price.
(b). Input an amount of money and display all the individual items of food that cost the same or less than the amount of money.
(c). Generate a fully itemised bill, similar to that shown in section 3.7.

7. From the saying "thirty days hath September, April, June and November, and all the rest have thirty-one, except for February that has twenty-eight days clear and twenty-nine in a Leap Year", write a program to:

(a). store the names and number of days in each month as records in an array;
(b). display a calendar for any year remaining in the twentieth century (1993 .. 1999), printing the year and the names of the months; the value for the date is to be printed under the name of the day.

8. Write a program to store two twenty digit integers as characters of a string and perform the operations of addition and subtraction on the two integers. Output the answer as a string of digits.

9. Code and test the following procedures and functions.

DELETE(S,I,N) - procedure changes the value of string S by deleting N characters starting at the Ith character of S.

INSERT(S1,S2,I) - procedure changes the value of the string S2 by inserting the string S1 at the Ith position of S2.

COPY(S,I,N) - function that returns the substring of S which is the N characters starting at the Ith position.

CONCAT(S1,S2) - function that returns the result of the concatenation (joining together) of the strings S1 and S2.

LENGTH(S) - function that returns the length of string S.

POS(S1,S2) - function that scans through the string S2 to find the first occurrence of the substring S1 within S2. The value returned is the index within S2 of the first character of the matched substring.

10. A selection of towns in three counties in the South of England have populations as shown in figure 10.12.

county	town	population
Cornwall	Penzance	19210
	Truro	18557
	Newquay	15209
Dorset	Poole	124974
	Dorchester	14225
	Shaftesbury	4951
Hampshire	Southampton	214802
	Basingstoke	73492
	Winchester	35664

figure 10.12 populations of towns

Write a procedures to initialise the following arrays.

(a) A one-dimensional array containing the names of the counties.
(b) A two-dimensional array containing the names of the towns, where each row represents a different county, in the order given in the first table.
(c) A second two-dimensional array containing the population of each town, where each row represents a different county and each column a different town, in the order given in the first two-dimensional array.

Using the arrays from (a), (b) and (c) write procedures to input the name of a county and the name of a town, and perform a serial search on the one-dimensional array to match the county and obtain a row subscript, then perform a serial search on the first two-dimensional array, to match the town, and obtain a column subscript. Using the row and column subscripts, access the second two-dimensional array and display the value for the population of the chosen town.

Write further procedures to input the name of a county and output the total population for the towns listed in the county. Re-express this figure as a percentage of the population of all the towns defined in the array.

11. Write a program to play noughts and crosses against the computer. Use a two-dimensional array to represent the game board. Let the computer be player *nought* and the position of play by the computer is taken to be the **next free space** on the board, in the current row, then the next row and so on, from the co-ordinates generated by the following expression:

row = (4 - Xrow) MOD 4; column = (4 - Xcol) MOD 4; where Xrow and Xcol represent the co-ordinates of the position of the previous cross (X) placed on the board, and are always in the range 1..3.

The game player is *cross*, and always starts the game.

After every move display the board on the screen and at the end of a game final result.

Note. The reader may prefer to re-program this game after reading chapter 14, when the concept of a random number generator is understood. The position of play by the computer is then taken to be any free space on the board, generated as a random number within a specific range. An answer is not given for this modification.

12. A variant record for an animal file contains the following fields.

```
AnimalType = RECORD
            name : string;              (* name of animal *)
            CASE tag : CHAR OF
                'F' : habitat : string |     (* Fish *)
                'B' : fly : BOOLEAN |        (* Bird *)
                'I' : wings : CARDINAL|      (* Insect *)
                'R : description : string;   (* Reptile *)
            END;
            CASE Amble : BOOLEAN OF
                TRUE    : legs : CARDINAL;
                        : AmbleMode : string |
                FALSE : (* cannot walk *)
            END;
            CASE LivesInWater : BOOLEAN OF
                TRUE    : SwimmingMode : string|
                FALSE   : FearsWater : BOOLEAN;
            END;
        END;
```

Invent a test data file for different animals, conforming to the record description given above. Write a program to process records of this type and output a report showing the description of each animal.

Chapter 11
Sorting and Searching

The purpose of this chapter is to provide the reader with an insight into methods used to organise information. Such methods must provide for a means of sorting information using a defined key or keys, and a means of searching through the information efficiently using a particular key, such that the access time to information is fast. By the end of the chapter the reader should have an understanding of the following topics.

☐ The development of the algorithms for a selection sort and an insertion sort.

☐ A method of merging two text files together to form a third file where the information is sorted on a particular key.

☐ A method of searching for information in an array that contains data that has been sorted.

11.1 Selection sort

Sorting methods used in computing can be classified into two areas - internal sorting and external sorting. Internal sorting involves the storage in main memory of all the data to be sorted. However, when the amount of data is too large to be stored and sorted in the main memory, it is stored on an external secondary storage medium, such as tape or disk, and successive parts of the data are sorted in the main memory. Such a technique is known as external sorting. The type of sorting method that is used will depend upon at least one of the following factors.

The amount of information to be sorted. Clearly it would be very time consuming to use a relatively inefficient sorting method on a large quantity of data.

The computer configuration being used - the size of the main memory and the number of tape/ disc units.

The nature of the application and the urgency of the results.

In the chapter on text files the MSDOS utility SORT was explained as a method for ordering information held in a file. In this chapter two internal methods for sorting numbers held in an array will be explained. The first is known as the *selection* sort.

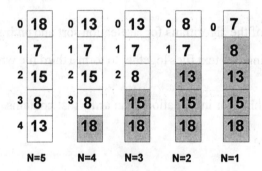

figure 11.1 an illustration of a selection sort

Figure 11.1 illustrates the movement of integers in a one- dimensional array, when a selection sort is used to place the integers into ascending order (lowest value to highest value). The contents of the cells from 0 to 4 are inspected for the largest number (18), and when found swapped with the number in cell 4. The contents of the cells from 0 to 3 are inspected for the largest number (15), and when found swapped with the number in cell 3. The contents of the cells from 0 to 2 are inspected for the largest number (13), and when found swapped with the number in cell 2. The contents of the cells from 0 to 1 are inspected for the largest number (8), and when found swapped with the number in cell 1. When there is only the contents of cell 0 to inspect the numbers are assumed to have been sorted into ascending order.

To generalise, if N represents the number of integers to be sorted, stored in the cells of an array from 0 to N-1, the largest number in 0 to N-1 cells is found, and swapped with the number in cell N-1. The process is repeated, with N being decreased by 1 each time until N=0.

This method of sorting numbers can be developed into a procedure in two parts. The first part is to define a function that will find the position of the largest element in any sized array.

```
PositionOfLargest(limit : CARDINAL) : CARDINAL;
(* function to return the position of the largest integer in the array bounds 0..limit *)
VAR
    largest              : INTEGER;
    cell                 : CARDINAL;
    index_of_largest     : CARDINAL;
BEGIN
    largest := numbers[0];
    index_of_largest := 0;
    FOR cell:=1 TO limit DO
        IF numbers[cell] > largest THEN
            largest := numbers[cell];
            index_of_largest := cell;
        END;
    END;
    RETURN index_of_largest;
END PositionOfLargest;
```

The second part of the development of a procedure to sort the numbers uses this function embedded within a procedure that passes through the array many times until all the numbers are sorted.

```
PROCEDURE selection_sort(VAR numbers : ARRAY OF INTEGER; size : CARDINAL);
VAR
    index, position :CARDINAL;
    temp            : INTEGER;

    PROCEDURE PositionOfLargest(limit : CARDINAL) : CARDINAL;

BEGIN
    FOR index:= size-1 TO 1 BY -1 DO
        (* find the position of the largest number in the array bounds 0..index *)
        position := PositionOfLargest(index);
        (* swap numbers *)
        temp := numbers[index];
        numbers[index] := numbers[position];
        numbers[position] := temp;
    END;
END selection_sort;
```

The following program reads a text file containing integers. The number of integers is not known in advance, but must not exceed MaxNumbers (=100). The program then displays the numbers that it has stored in an array, sorts the numbers into ascending order using the selection sort, and finally displays the contents of the sorted array.

```
MODULE sort;
(* program to demonstrate a selection sort *)

FROM STextIO IMPORT WriteString, WriteLn;
FROM SWholeIO IMPORT WriteInt;
FROM WholeIO IMPORT ReadInt;
FROM StreamFile IMPORT ChanId, Open, Close, read, OpenResults;
FROM IOResult IMPORT ReadResult, ReadResults;


CONST
    MaxNumbers=100;
TYPE
    table = ARRAY[0..MaxNumbers-1] OF INTEGER;
VAR
    numbers : table;
    size    : CARDINAL;

PROCEDURE selection_sort(VAR numbers : ARRAY OF INTEGER; size : CARDINAL);
(* procedure to sort an array of integer numbers into ascending order *)

VAR
  index, position : CARDINAL;
  temp            : INTEGER;


        PROCEDURE PositionOfLargest(limit : CARDINAL) : CARDINAL;
        (*  function to return the position of the largest number in the
            array bounds 0..limit *)

        VAR
          largest          : INTEGER;
          cell             : CARDINAL;
          index_of_largest : CARDINAL;

        BEGIN
            largest := numbers[0];
            index_of_largest := 0;
            FOR cell := 1 TO limit DO
                IF numbers[cell] > largest THEN
                    largest := numbers[cell];
                    index_of_largest := cell;
                END;
            END;
            RETURN index_of_largest;
        END PositionOfLargest;

BEGIN
    FOR index := size-1 TO 1 BY -1 DO
        position:=PositionOfLargest(index);
        temp:=numbers[index];
```

```
        numbers[index]:=numbers[position];
        numbers[position]:=temp;
    END;
END selection_sort;

PROCEDURE DataInput(VAR numbers: ARRAY OF INTEGER; VAR size : CARDINAL);
(* procedure to input numbers from a data file and store them in an array *)
VAR
   file    : ChanId;
   results : OpenResults;

BEGIN
    Open (file, 'a:\file.txt", read, results);
    IF results # opened THEN
       WriteString('a:file.txt does not exist - ');
       WriteString('program abandoned');
       HALT;
    END;
    size := 0;
    ReadInt(file, numbers[size]);
    WHILE ReadResult(file) # endOfInput DO
          INC(size);
          ReadInt(file, numbers[size]);
    END;
    Close (file);
END DataInput;

PROCEDURE DataOut(numbers:ARRAY OF INTEGER; size:CARDINAL);
(* procedure to display an array of any size *)
VAR
   index : CARDINAL;

BEGIN
    FOR index := 0 TO size-1 DO
        IF index MOD 10 = 0 THEN
            WriteLn;
        END;
        WriteInt(numbers[index], 6);
    END;
    WriteLn;
END DataOut;

BEGIN
    DataInput(numbers, size);
    DataOut(numbers, size);
    selection_sort(numbers, size);
    DataOut(numbers, size);
END sort.
```

229

Results from program sort_1 being run

```
 56   89   -4   67   13  389    5  234   36  -88
 21  -30  101    3   10   16  678  -99  111    2

-99  -88  -30   -4    2    3    5   10   13   16
 21   36   56   67   89  101  111  234  389  678
```

11.2 Insertion sort

The second sorting method known as the insertion sort follows. Figures 11.2 and 11.3 illustrate how integer numbers stored in a one-dimensional array are ordered within the array, using this method.

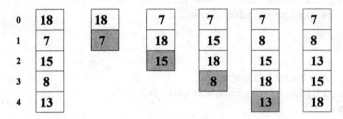

figure 11.2 an illustration of an insertion sort

The second number (7) in the array, is compared with the first (18) and ordered into ascending sequence (7,18). The next number (15) in the array, is then inserted into the correct position (7,15,18) in relation to the previously ordered numbers. The next number (8) in the array, is inserted into the correct position (7,8,15,18) in relation to the previously ordered numbers. Finally, the last number (13) in the array, is inserted into the correct position (7,8,13,15,18) in relation to the previously ordered numbers. Since this was the last number in the array, the numbers are now stored in ascending order.

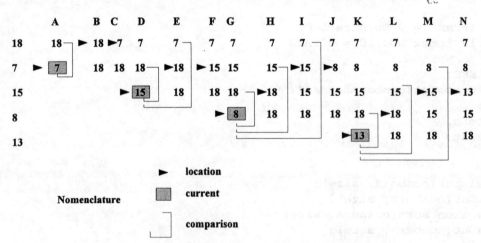

figure 11.3 movement of numbers in an insertion sort

The algorithm used to order the numbers can be represented by the following Modula-2 code, in which the array A is used to store the five numbers.

```
FOR index:=1 TO size-1 DO
    current:=A[index];
    location:=index;
    WHILE (location > 0) AND (A[location-1] > current) DO
        A[location]:=A[location-1];
        location:=location-1;
    END;
    A[location]:=current;
END;
```

Figure 11.4 illustrates a desk check of the insertion sort algorithm. The reader is recommended to trace through the insertion sort algorithm in order to gain a better understanding of the technique.

Desk Check of algorithm for Insertion Sort in conjunction with figure 11.3

column in fig 11.3	index	current	location	A[location-1]	A[location]	A[location-1] > current
A	1	7	1	18	7	TRUE
B			0		18	
C			0		7	
D	2	15	2	18	15	TRUE
E			1	7	18	FALSE
F			1		15	
G	3	8	3	18	8	TRUE
H			2	15	18	TRUE
I			1	7	15	FALSE
J			1		8	
K	4	13	4	18	13	TRUE
L			3	15	18	TRUE
M			2	8	15	FALSE
N			2		13	

figure 11.4 desk check of the insertion sort algorithm

The following insertion sort procedure can replace the selection sort procedure given in the program *sort* without any loss of functionality to the program.

```
PROCEDURE insertion_sort(VAR numbers : ARRAY OF INTEGER; size : CARDINAL);
(*
procedure to sort an array of integer numbers into ascending order
*)

VAR
  current            : INTEGER;
  location, index : CARDINAL;
```

```
BEGIN
    FOR index:=1 TO size-1 DO
        current := numbers[index];
        location := index;
        WHILE (location > 0) AND (numbers[location-1] > current) DO
            numbers[location]:=numbers[location-1];
            DEC(location);
        END;
        numbers[location]:=current;
    END;
END insertion_sort;
```

11.3 Merging

If two text files contain lines of information that are already sorted on a key, then it is possible to create a third file using the contents of the original two files such that the information held on the third file is also sorted on the same key.

The technique of merging two text files involves the interleaving of lines of text to form a new text file. The algorithm for merging the two files relies upon the fact that both files are already sorted on a key.

The keys of the two files to be merged are compared, if the keys are in ascending order, the line of text with the lower key value is written to the new file. The file that supplied the record is then read again and processing continues until the end of both files is encountered.

In the following algorithm to merge two files, it is necessary to compare the key of *file_a* with the key of *file_b*. However, when the end of either file is reached it is necessary to set the key field, of the file that has ended, to a higher value than all the other keys in the two files. The purpose of this practice is to force the remainder of the lines of text in the remaining file to be copied to *file_c*. The first character in the key field is substituted with CHR(127), thus setting the key to *high_key*.

The action of reading a line of text must be followed by testing for the end of the file, and if this condition is true, then setting the key field to a *high_key*.

open file_a and file_b for reading (the two files to be merged)
open file_c for writing (the file that eventually contains the lines of text from file_a and file_b)
read file_a, at end of file set key of file_a to high_key
read file_b, at end of file set key of file_b to high_key
WHILE not end of both files DO
   IF key file_a < key file_b THEN
     write file_a line to file_c
     read file_a, at end of file set key of file_a to high_key
   ELSE
     write file_b line to file_c
     read file_b, at end of file set key of file_b to high_key
   END
END
close all files

```
MODULE merge;
(* program to merge the contents of two ordered files into a third
ordered file *)

FROM StreamFile IMPORT ChanId, Open, Close, read, write, OpenResults;
FROM IOResult IMPORT ReadResult, ReadResults;
FROM StringType IMPORT string;
FROM Strings IMPORT Compare, less;
FROM TextIO IMPORT ReadString, WriteString, WriteLn;
CONST
    high_key = 127C;
VAR
    file_a, file_b, file_c : ChanId;
    results                : OpenResults;
    key_a, key_b           : string;
    eof_a, eof_b           : ReadResults;

BEGIN
    Open (file_a, 'a:file_a.txt", read, results);
    IF results # opened THEN HALT; END;
    Open (file_b, 'a:file_b.txt", read, results);
    IF results # opened THEN HALT; END;
    Open (file_c, 'a:file_c.txt", write, results);
    IF results # opened THEN HALT; END;

    ReadString(file_a, key_a);
    eof_a := ReadResult(file_a);
    ReadString(file_b, key_b);
    eof_b := ReadResult(file_b);
    WHILE  (eof_a # endOfInput) OR (eof_b # endOfInput) DO
           IF Compare(key_a, key_b) = less THEN
               WriteString(file_c, key_a);
               WriteLn(file_c);
               ReadString(file_a, key_a);
               eof_a := ReadResult(file_a);
               IF eof_a = endOfInput THEN key_a := high_key; END;
           ELSE
               WriteString(file_c, key_b);
               WriteLn(file_c);
               ReadString(file_b, key_b);
               eof_b := ReadResult(file_b);
               IF eof_b = endOfInput THEN key_b := high_key; END;
           END;
    END;
    Close (file_a); Close(file_b); Close(file_c);
END merge.
```

Results from program merge being run. All three files have been listed.

file_a

```
Adams, Rachel        414 Long Street London EC1 7GH
Davies, John         1 Short Street Oxford OX5 3ER
Farthing, Penelope   76 Grange View Poole BH15 6GH
```

file_b

```
Evans, Florence      17 High Court Witney OX8 4DF
Fielding, Michael    80 Baker Street Bournemouth BH7 6GH
Rankin, Robert       23 Sea View Southampton SO2 9QT
```

file_c

```
Adams, Rachel        414 Long Street London EC1 7GH
Davies, John         1 Short Street Oxford OX5 3ER
Evans, Florence      17 High Court Witney OX8 4DF
Farthing, Penelope   76 Grange View Poole BH15 6GH
Fielding, Michael    80 Baker Street Bournemouth BH7 6GH
Rankin, Robert       23 Sea View Southampton SO2 9QT
```

11.4 Searching

The concept of searching for information is not new to the reader. In the chapter 10 there were several examples of searching the contents of an array for information. However, in those examples it was necessary to search through the entire contents of the array to discover that the item was not in the array. Searching an array for data that does not exist in the array is clearly a waste of time. If the information held in the array was sorted into search key order then it would not always be necessary to search through an entire array before discovering that the information was not present.

Consider for a moment the following information held in the array depicted in figure 11.5. Alphabetically Adams is before Davies, Davies is before Evans, Evans is before Farthing, etc.

0	Adams,	Rachel	414 Long Street	London	EC1 7GH
1	Davies,	John	1 Short Drive	Oxford	OX5 3ER
2	Evans,	Florence	17 High Court	Witney	OX8 4DF
3	Farthing,	Penelope	76 Grange View	Poole	BH15 6GH
4	Fielding,	Michael	80 Baker Street	Bournemouth	BH7 6GH
5	Rankin,	Robert	23 Sea View	Southampton	SO2 9QT

figure 11.5 array of lines of text

If a search was to be made on the contents of the array for the key Ellis then the following comparisons, illustrated in figure 11.6, would be necessary before it was discovered that Ellis was not in the array. Ellis is alphabetically greater than both Adams and Davies so may be found further on in the array. Ellis is alphabetically less than Evans therefore, an entry for Ellis cannot exist in the array since the names are ordered into alphabetical sequence. By sorting the contents of the array into alphabetical order on the name of each person only three key comparisons were necessary before discovering that Ellis did not exist in the array. If the array had not been sorted by name then every name in the array would have been compared before it was discovered that the name did not exist in the array.

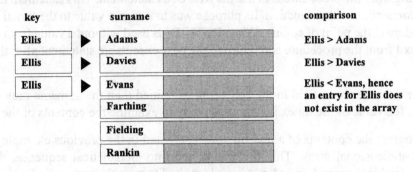

figure 11.6 sequential search on an array of text

Assuming that the lines of text are stored into consecutive array locations from 0 through to 5, the following algorithm is used in searching for a surname in the array.

```
set found to FALSE
set index to 0
WHILE (index < size) AND NOT found DO
    isolate the surname from the line table[index] in the array
    IF key = surname THEN
        set position to the current value of index
        set found to TRUE
    ELSE
        IF key < surname THEN
            RETURN
        ELSE
            increase index by 1
        END
    END
END
```

A Boolean variable *found* is initialised to FALSE, and the *index* used to access each cell of the array is initialised to 0, the first cell position of the array.

While the value of the *index* is within the limits of the array [0..5] and a key match is not found the search for the key continues. If the key is equal to the surname in the cell being examined, the information is found and the Boolean variable *found* is set to TRUE. The position in the array of the located line of text, that is the value of the index, is also assigned to a variable called *position*.

If the key is less than the name field in the cell being examined then the surname cannot exist in the array, and it is pointless to continue searching through the array. Since the Boolean flag *found* still remains at false no harm can result in exiting from the procedure as long as it is understood that the value of the variable *position* has not been determined and should not be used.

The method of exiting from the procedure is to use the RETURN statement. This statement has only been used up to now in connection with a function. Its purpose was to assign a value to the function name and exit from the procedure at the point of coding. When RETURN is used without a value from a procedure, the computer will exit from the procedure and return to the next executable statement after the procedure call.

If the key is greater than the name field in the cell being examined then the surname may exist further down the array, and the value of the index is increased ready to examine the contents of the next cell.

In the following program the contents of a text file *file_c*, created in the previous example is read, line by line, into a one-dimensional array. This file was sorted into alphabetical sequence, therefore the surnames are all ordered into ascending order. A user is invited to type the surname of a person, and the contents of the array is searched for the name of the same person. If a key match was possible the corresponding line of text is displayed, otherwise the user is notified that the person's name does not exist in the array.

```
MODULE search;
(* program to demonstrate a sequential search for information that is
ordered on a particular key *)

FROM StreamFile IMPORT ChanId, Open, Close, read, OpenResults;
FROM IOResult IMPORT ReadResult, ReadResults;
FROM StringType IMPORT string;
FROM Strings IMPORT Equal, Compare, less, Capitalize;
FROM TextIO IMPORT ReadString;
IMPORT STextIO;

CONST
    MaxLines = 99;
    NO = 'NO';
VAR
    datafile  : ChanId;
    line      : string;
    surname   : string;
    table     : ARRAY[0..MaxLines] OF string;
    position  : CARDINAL;
    found     : BOOLEAN;
    size      : CARDINAL;
    reply     : string;
```

```
PROCEDURE IsolateKey(VAR surname : string; line : string);
(*
procedure to isolate the surname as a key from a line in the text file
*)
CONST
    null  = 0C;
    comma = 54C;
VAR
    index : CARDINAL;

BEGIN
    index := 0;
    WHILE line[index] # comma DO
        surname[index]:=line[index];
        INC(index);
    END;
    surname[index]:=null;
END IsolateKey;

PROCEDURE ReadFile(datafile : ChanId; filename : string;
                   VAR table : ARRAY OF string; VAR size : CARDINAL);
(* procedure to open a text file and transfer the contents to an array *)

VAR
    results : OpenResults;
BEGIN
    Open (datafile, filename, read, results);
    IF results # opened THEN
        STextIO.WriteString(filename); STextIO.WriteString(' cannot be opened ')
        STextIO.WriteString('program abandoned'); STextIO.WriteLn;
        HALT;
    END;

    size:=0;
    ReadString(datafile, line);
    WHILE ReadResult(datafile) # endOfInput DO
        table[size] :=  line;
        INC(size);
        ReadString(datafile, line);
    END;

    Close(datafile);
END ReadFile;
```

```
PROCEDURE sequential_search(VAR table : ARRAY OF string; size : CARDINAL;
              key : string; VAR position : CARDINAL; VAR found : BOOLEAN);
(*
procedure to search an ordered array for a key
*)
VAR
   index :  CARDINAL;
   surname : string;

BEGIN
    found := FALSE;
    index := 0;
    WHILE (index < size) AND NOT found DO
          IsolateKey(surname, table[index]);
          IF Equal(key, surname) THEN
              position := index;
              found := TRUE;
          ELSE
              IF Compare(key, surname) = less THEN
                  RETURN;
              ELSE
                  INC(index);
              END;
          END;
    END;
END sequential_search;

BEGIN
    ReadFile(datafile, 'a:file_c.txt', table, size);
    REPEAT
        STextIO.WriteString('input a surname '); STextIO.ReadString(surname);
        sequential_search(table, size, surname, position, found);
        IF found THEN
            STextIO.WriteString(table[position]);
        ELSE
            STextIO.WriteString(surname); STextIO.WriteString(' not listed');
        END;
        STextIO.WriteLn; STextIO.WriteLn;
        STextIO.WriteString('continue search - yes or no? ');
        STextIO.ReadString(reply);
        Capitalize(reply);
    UNTIL Equal(reply, NO);
END search.
```

Results from program search being run

```
input a surname Farthing
Farthing, Penelope  76 Grange View Poole BH15 6GH

continue search - yes or no? yes
input a surname Ellis
Ellis not listed

continue search - yes or no? yes
input a surname Evans
Evans, Florence  17 high Court Witney OX8 4DF

continue search - yes or no? no
```

In this example the procedure *sequential_search* called the procedure *IsolateKey*. For the computer to resolve the identifier *IsolateKey* it was important to place this procedure before the procedure *sequential_search*. If the procedure *IsolateKey* was placed after the procedure *sequential_search* then the call to *IsolateKey* would result in a **forward** reference of the identifier and would result in an error. The topic of forward references is covered in more detail in the the next chapter in section 12.3.

11.5 Summary

☐ When data is stored in a structure in the memory of a computer any sorting algorithm used to order the data is referred to as an internal sorting algorithm.

☐ Data that is stored in external files that cannot physically be transferred as a whole to a structure in memory must be sorted in manageable groups of data. Such algorithms are referred to as external sorting algorithms.

☐ Examples of internal sorting algorithms are the selection sort and the insertion sort.

☐ In the selection sort the largest item of data is located and transferred to the end of the structure holding the data. The area over which the structure is examined is reduced by one storage unit, and the largest item of data is located and transferred to the end of the structure. These operations continue until the size of the structure is reduced to one storage unit. The contents of the original structure has then been ordered.

☐ In the insertion sort the contents of the first and second storage units are examined and ordered. This operation is extended to the first, second and third storage units and the data is ordered. The process continues extending the number of storage units to be examined by one. At every examination the contents of the storage units is ordered. After all the storage units have been examined the data will have been ordered.

☐ The ordered contents of two files can be merged together to form a third file that contains ordered data. The contents of each file is interleaved in key order and written to a third file.

☐ Searching for data held in key order in either an array or a file is made more efficient when the data is ordered. If the value of the key is greater than the item being inspected then the key may be found further on in the array or file. However, if the value of the key is less than the item being inspected then the key cannot exist in the array or file and the search must be abandoned.

11.6 Questions - *answers begin on page 404*

1. A list of ten different cardinal numbers in the range 1 to 100 are input at the keyboard and stored in a one-dimensional array. The numbers are not input in any order, however, the value of the number is used as an index to its position in the array. Without using a sorting algorithm, write a program to input this data and display the data on a screen, sorted into ascending order.

2. The median of a set of numbers is that number which has the same number of values above and below it. For example, in the set [1,3,9,18,7,5,4] the median is 5 since three numbers are larger [7,9,18] and three numbers are smaller [1,3,4] than 5. Write a program to compute the median of a set of non-zero cardinal numbers input to the computer.

(a) for an odd number of values;
(b) for an even number of values.

Note: clearly for an odd number of values the median will be the central value of the ordered set of numbers. An even number of values will not have one central value, but two central values. The median is taken to be the average of the two central values.

There exists a standard BOOLEAN function ODD, that can be used to test whether a cardinal number is odd or even. For example ODD(3) would return the value TRUE, and ODD(2) would return the value FALSE.

3. Write a program to store twenty cardinal numbers in a one-dimensional array, such that the numbers are not in any predefined order.

Compare adjacent numbers in the array, and swap the numbers such that the first number of the pair is always smaller than the second number of the pair. Repeat the process for all the adjacent numbers in the array.

Repeat the process described in the previous paragraph until all the numbers are sorted into ascending order, that is no swapping of pairs of numbers was necessary.

4. Modify the program merge listed in section 11.3 such that three ordered text files are merged into a fourth ordered text file.

5. Modify the program search listed in section 11.4 such that the array is not used, and only the text file file_c is searched for a surname.

Chapter 12
Recursion

Procedures and functions have been used by calling them in either the main program or from within another procedure. By now this method of access to such units of code should be familiar to the reader. The calling of one procedure from within another procedure is quite acceptable. But what if the procedure being called is the same procedure that is doing the calling? The procedure is in effect calling itself. The reason for allowing a procedure to call itself is, in many instances, to simplify the programming of a solution. By the end of the chapter the reader should have an understanding of the following topics.

- [ ] A definition of recursion and its implications.
- [ ] The use of recursive procedures.
- [ ] Sorting and searching using a recursive algorithms.

12.1 Definition

It would be tempting to offer a simple definition of recursion as a procedure or function that called itself. However, this would be incomplete, since there is no mention of how the called procedure gets closer to the solution or how to stop the procedure repeatedly calling itself.

Recursion can be regarded as a technique for performing routine R, by performing a similar routine R_i. The routine R_i is exactly the same in nature as the original routine R, however, it represents a solution to a smaller problem than R.

Thus routine R recursively calls routine R_1; routine R_1 recursively calls routine R_2; routine R_{n-1} recursively calls routine R_n. Where R_n is a solution to a smaller problem than R_{n-1}; R_2 is a solution to a smaller problem than R_1; R_1 is a solution to a smaller problem than R. Eventually the recursive calls must lead to a solution R_n, which cannot allow for further recursive calls, since a terminating criterion has been reached.

With these facts in mind, the reader should always address the following three questions before constructing a recursive solution.

How can you define the solution in terms of a smaller solution of the same type?

How is the size of the solution being diminished at each recursive call?

What instance or level of the solution, can serve as the degenerate case, and does the manner in which the solution size is diminished ensure that this degenerate case will always be reached?

12.2 Worked Examples

In this section three worked examples will be fully explained with the aid of diagrams. The reader is advised to spend some time on this section in order to understand the technique of recursion.

The following program contains a procedure to output the value of variable i , in the range from 1 to 5 inclusive. Rather than constructing a FOR i:=1 TO 5 DO loop, the value of i is updated and output in a procedure, the procedure is then called again recursively to repeat updating i and to output the value of i . The procedure is recursively called until i becomes equal to 5.


```
MODULE demo_1;
(*
program to demonstrate recursive calls and returns
*)

FROM STextIO IMPORT WriteString, WriteLn;
FROM SWholeIO IMPORT WriteCard;

VAR
   level : CARDINAL;
```

```
PROCEDURE output(level : CARDINAL);
BEGIN
    INC(level);
    WriteString('recursive call to level ');
    WriteCard(level,2); WriteLn;
    IF level < 5 THEN
        output(level); (* recursive call made here *)
    ELSE
        RETURN;
    END;
    WriteString('returning through level ');
    WriteCard(level,2); WriteLn;
END output;

BEGIN
    level := 0;
    output(level);
END demo_1.
```

Results from program demo_1 being run

```
recursive call to level 1
recursive call to level 2
recursive call to level 3
recursive call to level 4
recursive call to level 5
returning through level 4
returning through level 3
returning through level 2
returning through level 1
```

In the context of this solution, consider the three questions about constructing recursive algorithms, given in the last section.

A smaller solution has been defined since only one value of i is output by the procedure, and not all five values. Since i is being increased by 1, after each recursive call, the size of the solution is being diminished since i will eventually become equal to 5. The degenerate case is when i is equal to 5. No further recursion is then possible, and all values in the range 1..5 have been output.

In figure 12.1 on the next page, a recursive call produces another instance or level of the procedure, depicted by the code being superimposed upon the calling code.

The remaining code after *output(i)*, has been blacked-out in the recursive calls to levels 1,2,3 and 4, since this is not yet executed.

Level 5 serves as the degenerate case in which i=5. No further recursion is possible and the code:

243

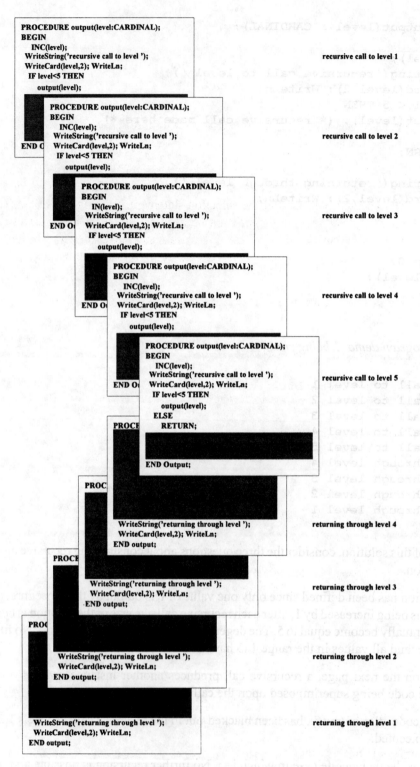

figure 12.1 recursive calls to procedure output

```
IF level < 5 THEN
    output(level);
ELSE
    RETURN;
END;
```

will cause RETURN to be executed. The computer must return through each level or instance of the code, before the program can finish.

Since the computer is returning to the procedure that invoked the call, the next statement after the call, *output(level)*, will be executed. However, *output(level)*, was in one branch of a selection, therefore, the next statement to be executed will be after the selection statement. For this reason all the code that had been executed is now blacked-out, since it will not be used as the computer returns back through the levels, or instances, of the procedure. Notice also, that within each level the value of i has remained the same as it was when the level was originally invoked. Hence, in returning through the levels, i is output as 4,3,2 and 1 respectively.

The second program in this section illustrates how a procedure can be called recursively to output the contents of a string backwards.

```
MODULE demo_2;
(*
program to print a string backwards
*)

FROM STextIO IMPORT WriteChar;
FROM StringType IMPORT string;

CONST
    alphabet = 'abcdefghijklmnopqrstuvwxyz';

PROCEDURE WriteBackward(alpha:string; index:INTEGER);
BEGIN
    IF index >=0 THEN
        WriteChar(alpha[index]);
        WriteBackward(alpha, index-1);
    END;
END WriteBackward;

BEGIN
    WriteBackward(alphabet, 25);
END demo_2.
```

Results from program demo_2 being run

```
zyxwvutsrqponmlkjihgfedcba
```

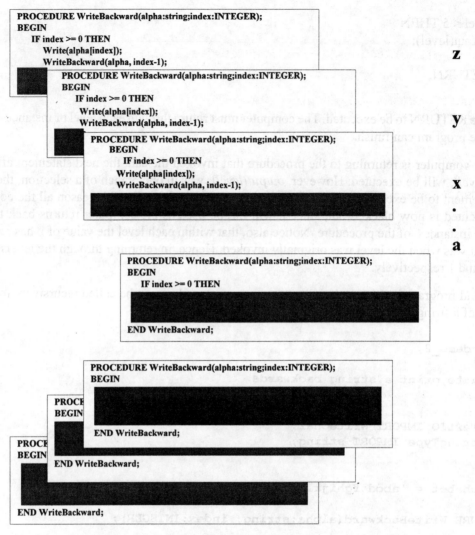

figure 12.2 recursive calls to procedure WriteBackward

There are two observations to make from the program and figure 12.2. The identifier *index* is set at the last cell of the array and the contents, z, output; *index* is then reduced by 1 and a recursive call to WriteBackward outputs y, *index* is then reduced by 1 and WriteBackward is recursively called again. The output of characters continues until the index is less than zero. Since the recursive call WriteBackward(alpha, index-1) is the last executable statement of the procedure WriteBackward, although the computer must return through each instance of procedure WriteBackward, no further output is possible.

The last program in this section illustrates how a function can be called recursively to calculate the factorial value of a number.

```
MODULE demo_3;
(*
program to calculate the factorial value of a number
*)

FROM STextIO IMPORT WriteString, WriteLn;
FROM SRealIO IMPORT ReadReal, WriteFixed;

VAR
   n : REAL;

PROCEDURE factorial(n:REAL) : REAL;
BEGIN
     IF n=0.0 THEN
         RETURN 1.0;
     ELSE
         RETURN n * factorial(n-1.0);
     END;
END factorial;

BEGIN
     LOOP
        WriteString('input a real number - 0.0 to exit ');
        ReadReal(n);
        IF n<=0.0 THEN EXIT; END;
        WriteString('n!'); WriteFixed(factorial(n),0,10); WriteLn;
     END;
END demo_3.
```

Results from program demo_3 being run

```
input a real number - 0.0 to exit 3.0
n!         6
input a real number - 0.0 to exit 4.0
n!        24
input a real number - 0.0 to exit 5.0
n!       120
input a real number - 0.0 to exit 6.0
n!       720
input a real number - 0.0 to exit 0.0
```

In this example the value of the factorial of a number cannot be calculated until the procedure has recursively reached factorial(0). Upon returning to the next instance of factorial(1), the value 1*factorial(0) can then be calculated. Returning to the instance of factorial(2), the value 2*factorial(1) can then be calculated. Finally returning to the instance of factorial(3), the value 3*factorial(2) can be calculated. This information is illustrated in figure 12.3.

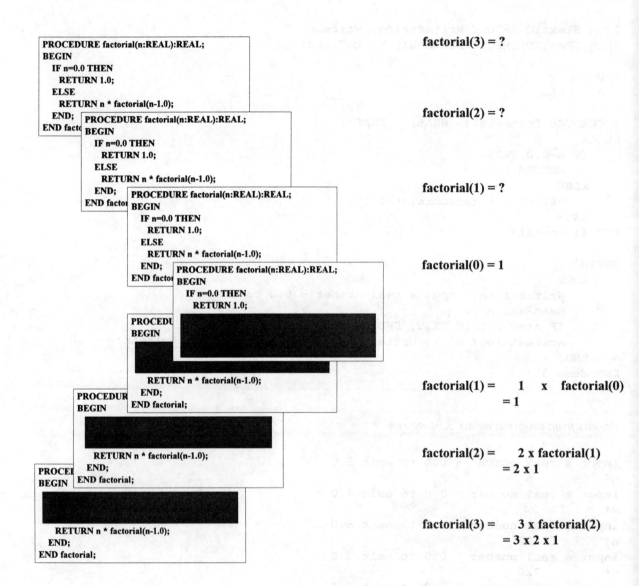

figure 12.3 recursive call to the function factorial

12.3 Indirect recursion

Forward referencing of procedures/ functions was briefly mentioned in the previous chapter. The examples of direct recursion given in this chapter do not cause any problems regarding forward referencing. However, if indirect recursion is contemplated, then it is necessary to declare one of the recursive procedures as a FORWARD reference. For example

```
PROCEDURE alpha(x:CARDINAL); FORWARD;

PROCEDURE beta(y:CARDINAL);
  .
BEGIN
  .
  .
  alpha(a);
  .
END beta;

PROCEDURE alpha(x:CARDINAL);
  .
BEGIN
  .
  .
  beta(b);
  .
END alpha;
```

To resolve the problem of the forward reference of *alpha(a)* in procedure *beta*, it has been necessary to declare the full heading of the procedure alpha followed by the keyword FORWARD. In addition to this declaration it is also necessary to specify fully the procedure *alpha* after the procedure *beta*.

12.4 Binary Search

This method requires that the keys are sorted, in this example into ascending order, prior to the search. In this example the key is a field in a record and the records are stored in a one- dimensional array. The list is divided into two parts and the relative position of the key with regard to one of the two lists is found. This sub-list is again divided into two lists and the relative position of the key with regard to one of the two new lists is found. The method continues until either a key match is found or the size of the sub-list is reduced to two keys and neither key matches. Figure 12.4 illustrates the sub-dividing of a list until a key match is found. When a sub-list contains an even number of keys the mid-point is taken to be the next lowest key from the centre. The key to be matched in this illustration is Quayle. Notice that only three comparisons are necessary compared with ten comparisons if a serial or sequential search had been performed.

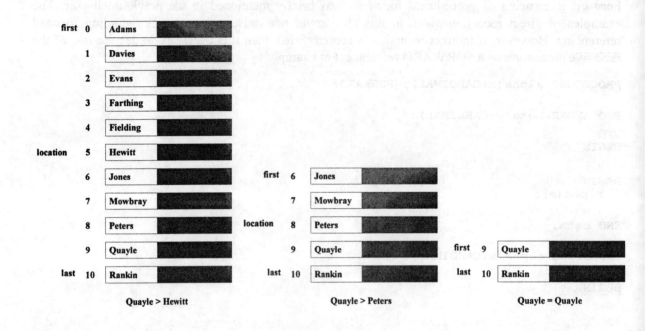

figure 12.4 binary search for a surname in an array

```
MODULE demo_4;
(*
program to demonstrate a binary search for information held in an array
*)

FROM StreamFile IMPORT ChanId, Open, Close, read, OpenResults;
FROM IOResult IMPORT ReadResult, ReadResults;
FROM StringType IMPORT string;
FROM Strings IMPORT Equal, Compare, equal, greater, Capitalize;
FROM TextIO IMPORT ReadString;
IMPORT STextIO;

CONST
    MaxLines = 99;
    NO = 'NO';
VAR
    datafile  : ChanId;
    line      : string;
    surname   : string;
    table     : ARRAY[0..MaxLines] OF string;
```

```
    position    : CARDINAL;
    found       : BOOLEAN;
    size        : CARDINAL;
    reply       : string;

PROCEDURE IsolateKey(VAR surname : string; line : string);
(* procedure to isolate the surname as a key from a line in the file *)
CONST
    null  = 0C;
    comma = 54C;
VAR
    index : CARDINAL;

BEGIN
    index := 0;
    WHILE line[index] # comma DO
        surname[index]:=line[index];
        INC(index);
    END;
    surname[index]:=null;
END IsolateKey;


PROCEDURE ReadFile(datafile : ChanId; filename : string;
                   VAR table : ARRAY OF string; VAR size : CARDINAL);
(* procedure to open a text file and transfer the contents to an array *)

VAR
    results : OpenResults;

BEGIN
    Open (datafile, filename, read, results);
    IF results # opened THEN
        STextIO.WriteString(filename);
        STextIO.WriteString(' cannot be opened ');
        STextIO.WriteString('program abandoned'); STextIO.WriteLn;
        HALT;
    END;

    size:=0;
    ReadString(datafile, line);
    WHILE ReadResult(datafile) # endOfInput DO
        table[size] :=  line;
        INC(size);
        ReadString(datafile, line);
    END;

    Close(datafile);
END ReadFile;
```

251

```
PROCEDURE binary_search(VAR table : ARRAY OF string; key : string;
                        first, last : CARDINAL;
                        VAR location : CARDINAL):BOOLEAN;
VAR
    surname : string;

BEGIN
    IF first > last THEN
        RETURN FALSE;
    ELSE
        location := (first+last) DIV 2;
        IsolateKey(surname, table[location]);
        IF Compare(surname, key) = equal THEN
            RETURN TRUE;
        ELSIF Compare(surname, key) = greater THEN
            RETURN binary_search(table, key, first, location-1, location);
        ELSE
            RETURN binary_search(table, key, location+1, last, location);
        END;
    END;
END binary_search;

BEGIN
    ReadFile(datafile, 'a:file_c.txt', table, size);
    REPEAT
        STextIO.WriteString('input a surname '); STextIO.ReadString(surname);
        IF binary_search(table, surname, 0, size-1, position) THEN
            STextIO.WriteString(table[position]);
        ELSE
            STextIO.WriteString(surname); STextIO.WriteString(' not listed');
        END;
        STextIO.WriteLn; STextIO.WriteLn;
        STextIO.WriteString('continue search - yes or no? ');
        STextIO.ReadString(reply);
        Capitalize(reply);
    UNTIL Equal(reply, NO);
END demo_4.
```

The results are similar to those found in section 11.4 in the previous chapter, only the method of searching for a key is different.

Figure 12.5 illustrates the recursive calls to the function BinarySearch.

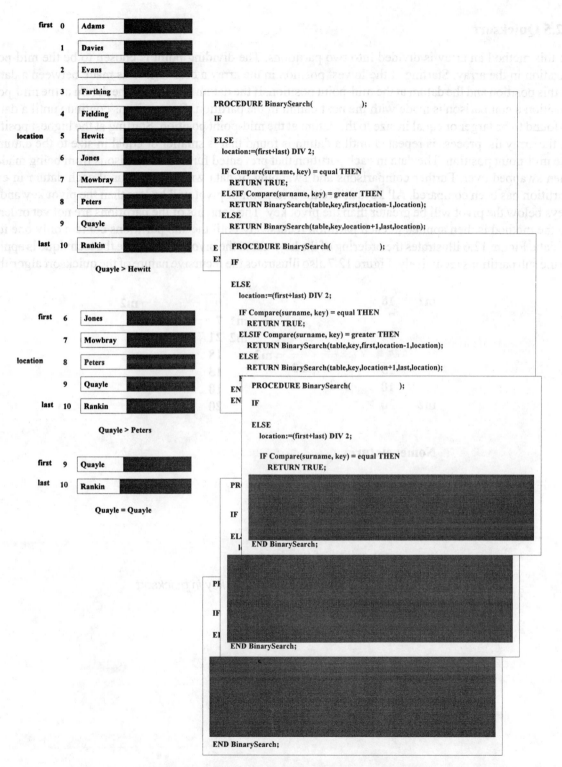

figure 12.5 recursive calls to function BinarySearch

12.5 Quicksort

In this method an array is divided into two partitions. The dividing point is chosen to be the mid-point position in the array. Starting at the lowest position in the array a comparison is made between a datum at this position and the datum at the mid-point position. If the datum is less than the datum at the mid-point position a comparison is made with the next datum in the partition. Comparisons continue until a datum is found to be larger or equal in size to the datum at the mid-point position. Starting at the highest position in the array the process is repeated until a datum is found that is smaller or equal in size to the datum at the mid-point position. The data in each partition that prevented further comparisons from being made is then swapped over. Further comparisons and swapping of data will continue until each datum in each partition has been compared. All keys above the mid-point or pivot will be less than the pivot key and all keys below the pivot will be greater than the pivot key. The contents of the partitions are not yet ordered, so the method is then applied to each partition recursively until the sub partitions contain only one item of data. Figure 12.6 illustrates the ordering of the keys about the pivot point before the technique is applied to the sub partitions recursively. Figure 12.7 also illustrates the recursive nature of the quicksort algorithm.

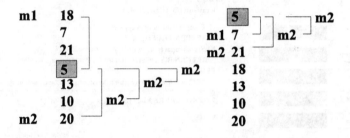

Nomenclature:

m1 - marker1
m2 - marker2

[ ] **mid point or pivot key**

[ ] **comparison of two keys**

figure 12.6 ordering about a pivot key in quicksort

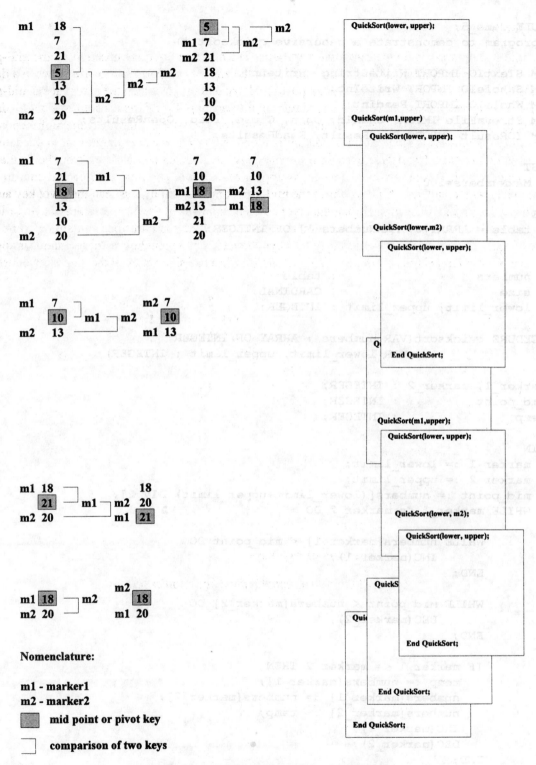

Nomenclature:

m1 - marker1

m2 - marker2

▨ mid point or pivot key

⌐ comparison of two keys

figure 12.7 recursive nature of quicksort

```
MODULE demo_5;
(* program to demonstrate a recursive quicksort *)

FROM STextIO IMPORT WriteString, WriteLn;
FROM SWholeIO IMPORT WriteInt;
FROM WholeIO IMPORT ReadInt;
FROM StreamFile IMPORT ChanId, Open, Close, read, OpenResults;
FROM IOResult IMPORT ReadResult, ReadResults;

CONST
    MaxNumbers=100;

TYPE
    table = ARRAY[0..MaxNumbers-1] OF INTEGER;

VAR
    numbers                     : table;
    size                        : CARDINAL;
    lower_limit, upper_limit : INTEGER;

PROCEDURE quicksort(VAR numbers : ARRAY OF INTEGER;
                    VAR lower_limit, upper_limit : INTEGER);
VAR
  marker_1, marker_2 : INTEGER;
  mid_point          : INTEGER;
  temp               : INTEGER;

BEGIN
    marker_1 := lower_limit;
    marker_2 := upper_limit;
    mid_point := numbers[(lower_limit+upper_limit) DIV 2];
    WHILE marker_1 <= marker_2 DO

        WHILE numbers[marker_1] < mid_point DO
            INC(marker_1);
        END;

        WHILE mid_point < numbers[marker_2] DO
            DEC(marker_2);
        END;

        IF marker_1 <= marker_2 THEN
            temp := numbers[marker_1];
            numbers[marker_1] := numbers[marker_2];
            numbers[marker_2] := temp;
            INC(marker_1);
            DEC(marker_2);
        END;
    END;
```

```
        IF lower_limit < marker_2 THEN
            quicksort(numbers, lower_limit, marker_2);
        END;

        IF marker_1 < upper_limit THEN
            quicksort(numbers, marker_1, upper_limit);
        END;
END quicksort;

PROCEDURE DataInput(VAR numbers: ARRAY OF INTEGER; VAR size : CARDINAL);
(* procedure to input numbers from a data file and store them in an array *)

VAR
  file    : ChanId;
  results : OpenResults;

BEGIN
    Open (file, 'a:\file.txt', read, results);
    IF results # opened THEN
        WriteString('a:file.txt does not exist - ');
        WriteString('program abandoned');
        HALT;
    END;

    size := 0;
    ReadInt(file, numbers[size]);
    WHILE ReadResult(file) # endOfInput DO
        INC(size);
        ReadInt(file, numbers[size]);
    END;
    Close (file);
END DataInput;


PROCEDURE DataOut(numbers:ARRAY OF INTEGER; size:CARDINAL);
(* procedure to display an array of any size *)
VAR
  index : CARDINAL;

BEGIN
    FOR index := 0 TO size-1 DO
        IF index MOD 10 = 0 THEN
            WriteLn;
        END;
        WriteInt(numbers[index], 6);
    END;
    WriteLn;
END DataOut;
```

```
BEGIN
    DataInput(numbers, size);
    DataOut(numbers, size);
    lower_limit := 0;
    upper_limit := size-1;
    quicksort(numbers, lower_limit, upper_limit);
    DataOut(numbers, size);
END demo_5.
```

The results are the same as those in section 11.1, only the method of sorting the numbers has changed.

12.6 Summary

- A recursive routine will repeatedly call itself until a criterion for terminating is satisfied.

- The computer must return through each instance of the routine that has been invoked.

- Each instance of a routine represents a smaller solution to a problem, where all the instances represent the complete solution to the problem.

- With indirect recursion a forward reference of a procedure/ function is necessary.

- The binary search algorithm relies upon the fact that the contents of the array must be ordered. The technique repeatedly divides an array into smaller arrays that are likely to contain the key, until either a key match is possible or the array cannot be subdivided further.

- In the quicksort algorithm an array is divided into two partitions by a pivot key. Keys in each partition are compared for an ordered sequence with the pivot key. When an ordered sequence in each partition is no longer possible the offending keys are swapped. Further comparisons and swapping of keys continues until each key in each partition has been compared. All the keys above and below the pivot key will then be ordered, however, the partitions themselves are not yet ordered. The algorithm is then applied to each partition recursively until the sub partitions contain only one item of data.

12.7 Questions - *answers begin on page 407*

Write recursive procedures in answers to the following questions.

1. Write a program to sum a one-dimensional array containing cardinal numbers.

2. Write a program to raise a number to a power, for example $X^n = X * X^{n-1}$ if $n > 0$.

3. Write a program to generate the first fifteen numbers in a Fibonacci series.

4. Write a program to find the largest element in an array.

5. Implement the selection sort, from the previous chapter, as a recursive procedure.

Chapter 13

Pointers and Linked Lists

Within this chapter a new data type will be introduced, the pointer. Since pointers are the basis of data structures such as linked lists, stacks, queues, trees and graphs, these structures will be explained to the reader in this and future chapters. By the end of the chapter the reader should have an understanding of the following topics.

- ☐ The concept of a pointer.

- ☐ Dynamic storage allocation and de-allocation.

- ☐ Constructing a linked list.

- ☐ Accessing information in a linked list.

- ☐ Updating the contents of a linked list.

- ☐ Restricted forms of linked lists that represent queues.

13.1 Introduction

The only internal static data structure that has been explained so far, is the array. The term **internal refers** to the entire structure being stored in the main memory of the computer. The array is described as being static since its size must be declared before it can be used in a program. For example in the following declaration:

```
CONST
    StringLength = 80;
TYPE
    buffer = ARRAY [0..StringLength-1] OF CHAR;
```

the size of the array will always be a maximum 80 characters, irrespective of whether it is completely or partially filled.

A file structure does have the advantage that the number of records it contains does not have to be declared in advance. Files will vary in their sizes according to the amount of data available and the processing requirements of the program. Files are not stored in the main memory of the computer, therefore, to access file-based information tends to be slower than to access information stored in an array. The data structures to be introduced in this and subsequent chapters, have the following advantages over arrays and files.

The maximum size of the structures does not need to be declared in advance.

The structures can grow or shrink in size, depending upon how large or small the volume of data being processed.

The structures are stored in the main memory of the computer, therefore, access to the data tends to be faster than using files.

13.2 Pointers

The fundamental scalar data types used within this book have been cardinal, integer, real and char. Declarations such as:

```
VAR
    W : CARDINAL;
    X : INTEGER;
    Y : REAL;
    Z : CHAR;
```

imply that W, X, Y and Z are identifiers of memory addresses that store data of the type cardinal, integer, real and char, respectively, as depicted in figure 13.1.

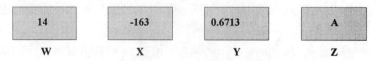

figure 13.1 identifiers that represent different types

A pointer is an identifier that does not store a scalar data value, but stores an address of where to find the data in memory. This address literally points to where the data is stored. The following declarations:

```
VAR
    W : POINTER TO CARDINAL;
    X : POINTER TO INTEGER;
    Y : POINTER TO REAL;
    Z : POINTER TO CHAR;
```

correspond to the diagrammatic representation given in figure 13.2.

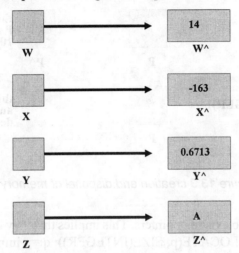

figure 13.2 pointers for storage of different types

The declaration of a pointer is given as POINTER TO identifier, whereas the contents of the memory location that is being pointed at is given as *identifier^*. Therefore, W^, X^, Y^ and Z^ are the values 14, -163, 0.6713 and 'A' respectively. In the following example P has been declared as a pointer to an address containing an integer. The pointer can be declared as:

```
TYPE    pointer = POINTER TO INTEGER;
VAR     P : pointer;
```

or as:

```
VAR     P : POINTER TO INTEGER;
```

Pointers are allocated memory from the system heap (a storage area for dynamically allocated variables) by the procedure ALLOCATE, and de-allocated memory, so that it is returned to the system heap, by the procedure DEALLOCATE.

Figure 13.3 illustrates typical operations for the allocation, use and deallocation of a pointer to memory.

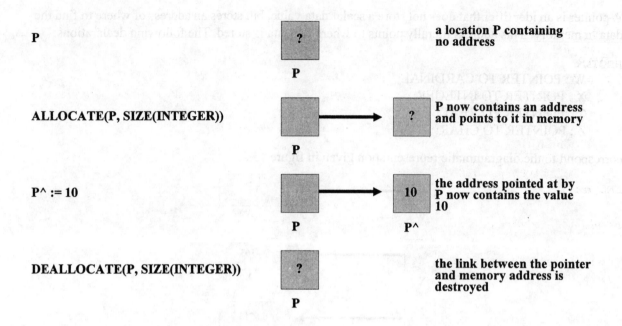

P   ?   a location P containing no address

P

ALLOCATE(P, SIZE(INTEGER))   ?   P now contains an address and points to it in memory

P

P^ := 10   10   the address pointed at by P now contains the value 10

P   P^

DEALLOCATE(P, SIZE(INTEGER))   ?   the link between the pointer and memory address is destroyed

P

figure 13.3 creation and disposal of memory

Other pointers can be assigned to existing pointers. This implies that they both point at the same address. For example the statements ALLOCATE(p, SIZE(INTEGER)); q:=p implies that both p and q point at the same address. Niklaus Wirth suggested that within implementations of Modula-2, a library module named **Storage** should be supplied that contained the two procedures ALLOCATE and DEALLOCATE. Thus given a variable P of type POINTER TO INTEGER, then the variable is created by ALLOCATE(P, SIZE(INTEGER)) and disposed of by DEALLOCATE(P, SIZE(INTEGER)). SIZE is a standard function that gives the number of bytes or words required to store the defined data type. In the *Draft Standard* implicit procedures NEW and DISPOSE have been recommended as alternative procedures to ALLO-CATE and DEALLOCATE, and in this example would be used as NEW(P) and DISPOSE(P) respectively, with no reference to the size of the data being stored. However, both NEW and DISPOSE use ALLOCATE and DEALLOCATE respectively, so it is still necessary to explicitly import ALLOCATE and DEALLOCATE into a module with calls to NEW and DISPOSE.

The first program demonstrates the facts that have been presented in this section.

```
MODULE ex_1;
(*
program to reference an integer via a pointer
*)

FROM Storage IMPORT ALLOCATE, DEALLOCATE;
FROM STextIO IMPORT WriteString, WriteLn;
FROM SWholeIO IMPORT ReadInt, WriteInt;
TYPE
   pointer = POINTER TO INTEGER;
```

```
VAR
   p, q : pointer;

BEGIN
    ALLOCATE(p, SIZE(INTEGER));
    WriteString('input a single integer '); ReadInt(p^);
    q := p;
    WriteString('value of integer being pointed at is ');
    WriteInt(q^, 5);
    WriteLn;
    DEALLOCATE(p, SIZE(INTEGER));
END ex_1.
```

Results from program ex_1 being run

```
input a single integer 12345
value of integer being pointed at is 12345
```

13.3 Linked lists

In the previous section it was implied, from the examples, that pointers could point to memory locations containing either of the four scalar types - cardinal, integer, real or char. It is common practice for pointers to point to records. For example, a pointer P could point to a record, called *node*, containing two fields, *word* and *link*. The declaration for this structure would be:

```
TYPE
    pointer = POINTER TO node;
    node =   RECORD;
                word : ARRAY [1..3] OF CHAR;
                link : pointer;
             END;
VAR
    head : pointer;
```

Diagramatically this structure can be represented as shown in figure 13.4.

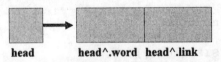

head   head^.word head^.link

figure 13.4 a pointer can point at a record

According to the declaration of the record the contents of head^.link is a pointer. If this pointer points at a second node then the two nodes have been linked together and formed a linked list as illustrated in figure 13.5.

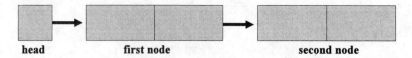

head   **first node**   **second node**

figure 13.5 records linked together as nodes

A linked list containing three nodes could be built as depicted in figure 13.6. The beginning of the linked list is indicated by the pointer *head* and the end of the list by the NIL (/) pointer. A NIL pointer implies there are no further nodes to be pointed at. The contents of nodes are output by making reference to the identifiers *head^.word*, *pointer1^.word* and *pointer2^.word* respectively.

The next program in this chapter is a summary of the segments of code that have been illustrated in this section. The program builds the three-node linked list that is illustrated in figure 13.6, and displays the contents of the nodes on the screen of a monitor.

```
MODULE ex_2;
(*
program to build and display a linked list containing three nodes
*)

FROM Storage IMPORT ALLOCATE, DEALLOCATE;
FROM STextIO IMPORT WriteString, WriteLn;
FROM StringType IMPORT string;

TYPE
   pointer = POINTER TO node;

   node = RECORD
               word : string;
               link : pointer;
           END;

VAR
   head, pointer_1, pointer_2 : pointer;

BEGIN
    ALLOCATE(head, SIZE(node));
    head^.word := 'THE';
    ALLOCATE(pointer_1, SIZE(node));
    head^.link := pointer_1;
    pointer_1^.word := 'CAT';
    ALLOCATE(pointer_2, SIZE(node));
    pointer_1^.link := pointer_2;
    pointer_2^.word := 'SAT';
    pointer_2^.link := NIL;
```

```
    WriteString(head^.word); WriteLn;
    WriteString(pointer_1^.word); WriteLn;
    WriteString(pointer_2^.word); WriteLn;

    DEALLOCATE(pointer_2, SIZE(node));
    DEALLOCATE(pointer_1, SIZE(node));
    DEALLOCATE(head, SIZE(node));
END ex_2.
```

Results from program ex_2 being run

```
THE
CAT
SAT
```

A disadvantage of the code used to build the last linked list was that it was limited to only three nodes, since it used two temporary pointers *pointer1* and *pointer2*.

.. continued

```
ALLOCATE(head, SIZE(node));
head^.word := 'THE';
```

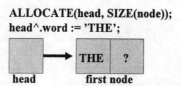

```
ALLOCATE(pointer1, SIZE(node));
head^.link := pointer1;
```

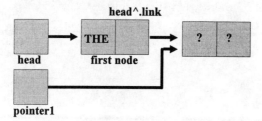

A new pointer has been created (pointer1), however, since head^.link is also of type pointer, it is necessary to make head^.link point at the new node pointed at by pointer1.

```
pointer1^.word := 'CAT';
```

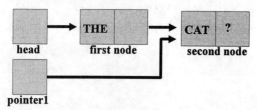

```
ALLOCATE(pointer2, SIZE(node));
pointer1^.link := pointer2;
```

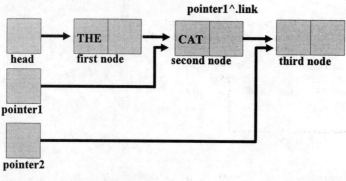

```
pointer2^.word := 'SAT';
pointer2^.link := NIL;
```

figure 13.6 a linked list containing three nodes

The second program in this section illustrates how to create and display a linked list of any size containing words. The process of building nodes is illustrated in figure 13.7. This figure should be read in conjunction with the procedures *CreateList* and *CreateNode* listed in the program that follows. Initially the pointer *head* is assigned the value NIL, and *head* and *text* are passed to the procedure *CreateNode*. CreateNode allocates storage for a node, inserts the text into the node and sets the pointer in the node to NIL. Since *next* is a VAR parameter the value of *head* effectively points to the first node. Another pointer *last* in procedure *CreateList* is then assigned the value of *head*. To build a new node at the end of the list, the value of *last^.link* is passed to procedure *CreateNode* along with the text to be inserted into the new node. Since *next* is a VAR parameter the value of *last^.link* effectively points to the second node in the list. The value of *last^.link* is then assigned to *last* in the procedure *CreateList* and the process of building the next node continues.

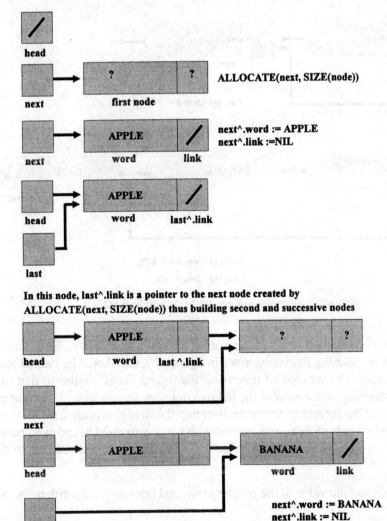

figure 13.7 building a linked list of any size

267

Figure 13.8 illustrates how to traverse this linked list, in order to display its contents. The technique requires writing the contents of *current^.word*, then replacing the contents of the pointer *current* by *current^.link* which is a pointer to the next node. When the value of *current^.link* is NIL, the end of the list will have been reached. This figure should be studied in conjunction with the procedure *ListOut*.

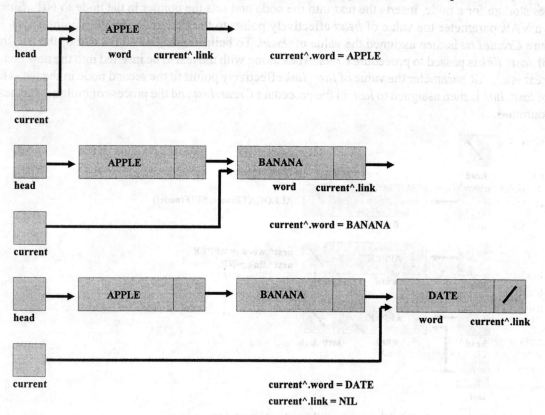

figure 13.8 output the contents of a linked list

Finally when the linked list is no longer required the storage allocated to the linked list should be returned to the heap. The method of performing this is illustrated in figure 13.9, and should be studied in conjunction with the procedure *CleanUp*. The method of traversing the linked list is similar to that to output the contents of a linked list. Starting at the *head* of the list two pointers are introduced, *current* points at the first node, and *temp* points at the second node. By deallocating the storage requirement for the node being pointed at by *current*, this leaves both *head* and *current* with nothing to point at and as a consequence are known as dangling pointers. Dangling pointers can lead to some error prone situations, so care must be maintained!

The pointer *current* is assigned the value of the pointer *temp*, and later in the algorithm, the pointer *head* is assigned a NIL value.

The pointer *current* is in effect pointing at the first node in the list, and the pointer *temp* must be arranged to point at the second node in the list. The node being pointed at by *current* is deallocated, and the algorithm continues as before. Eventually, *temp* will be assigned the value NIL when there is only one node

268

remaining in the linked list. After this node has been de-allocated, current is assigned to *temp*, and therefore is set to NIL.

Since there is no more de-allocation of storage to perform on the linked list, and the linked list is in effect empty, *head* is set at the value NIL.

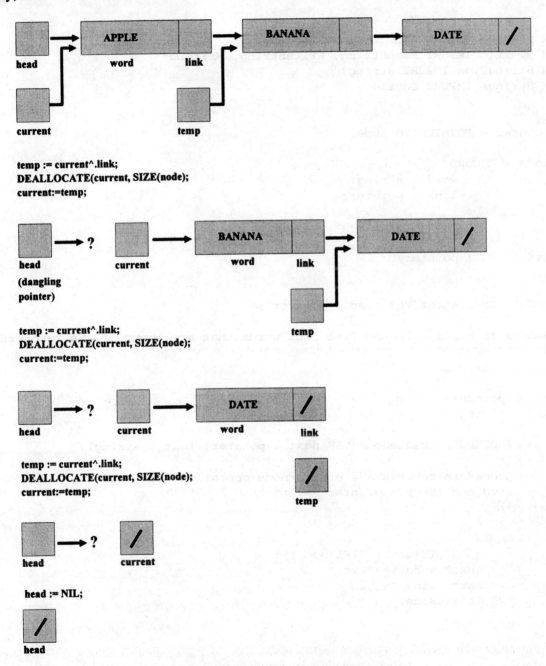

figure 13.9 de-allocation of storage space

```
MODULE ex_3;
(*
program to build a linked list of any size containing words, display
the contents of the linked list after it has been completed and finally
re-assign the storage space used to build the linked list back to the heap
*)

FROM Storage IMPORT ALLOCATE, DEALLOCATE;
FROM STextIO IMPORT ReadString, WriteString, WriteLn;
FROM StringType IMPORT string;
FROM Strings IMPORT Equal;

TYPE
   pointer = POINTER TO node;

   node = RECORD
                 word : string;
                 link : pointer;
             END;

VAR
   head        : pointer;


PROCEDURE CreateList(VAR head : pointer);
(*
procedure to build a linked list from words that are input at the keyboard
*)

VAR
   last : pointer;
   text : string;

        PROCEDURE CreateNode(VAR next : pointer; text : string);
        (*
        procedure to create a single node containing the input
        word and the NIL pointer
        *)

        BEGIN
            ALLOCATE(next, SIZE(node));
            next^.word := text;
            next^.link := NIL;
        END CreateNode;
```

```
BEGIN
    head := NIL;
    WriteString('input word - enter ! to exit ');
    ReadString(text);
    WHILE NOT Equal(text, '!') DO
            IF head = NIL THEN
                    CreateNode(head, text);
                    last := head;
            ELSE
                    CreateNode(last^.link, text);
                    last:=last^.link;
            END;
            WriteString('input word - enter ! to exit ');
            ReadString(text);
    END;
END CreateList;


PROCEDURE ListOut(head : pointer);
(*
procedure to display the contents of the linked list
*)

VAR
   current : pointer;


BEGIN
    current := head;
    IF head = NIL THEN
        WriteString('list empty'); WriteLn;
    ELSE
        WHILE current # NIL DO
            WriteString(current^.word); WriteLn;
            current:=current^.link;
        END;
    END;
END ListOut;


PROCEDURE CleanUp(VAR head : pointer);
(*
procedure to re-allocate the storage space used by the linked list
back to the heap
*)

VAR
   current : pointer;
   temp    : pointer;


BEGIN
    current := head;
```

271

```
        WHILE current # NIL DO
                temp := current^.link;
                DEALLOCATE(current, SIZE(node));
                current := temp;
        END;
        head := NIL;
    END CleanUp;

BEGIN
    CreateList(head);
    ListOut(head);
    CleanUp(head);
END ex_3.
```

Results from program ex_3 being run

```
input word - enter ! to exit APPLE
input word - enter ! to exit BANANA
input word - enter ! to exit DATE
input word - enter ! to exit FIG
input word - enter ! to exit LEMON
input word - enter ! to exit ORANGE
input word - enter ! to exit PLUM
input word - enter ! to exit !
APPLE
BANANA
DATE
FIG
LEMON
ORANGE
PLUM
```

13.4 Linked-List maintenance

In order to maintain a linked list it will be necessary to insert new nodes into the list and delete redundant nodes from the list. The method of insertion and deletion of nodes is straightforward. Consider a linked list in which the records are ordered on the word key field. In traversing such a linked list of words, the words would appear in an alphabetical sequence. In the following example a new node is to be created containing the word GRAPE. The linked list will be traversed until the position for insertion into the list is located. In figure 13.10 the position is between the nodes containing the words FIG and MELON. To insert a new node it is necessary to introduce a new pointer temp, that will be used to point at the new node. The sequence of statements that are required to insert the node are as follows.

ALLOCATE(temp, SIZE(node)); - create a new node
temp^.text:=line; - store the text to be inserted in the new node

temp^.link:=current; -   the new node points to the next node in the list
last^.link:=temp; -   the last node points to the inserted node

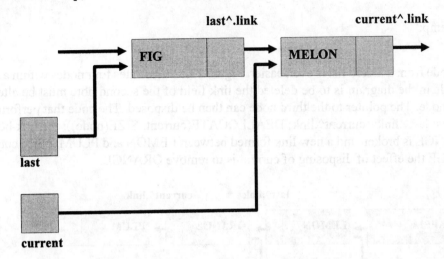

If temporary pointers, last and current, are used to denote the
positions of the preceding and following nodes then the insertion
of a new node can be drawn as:

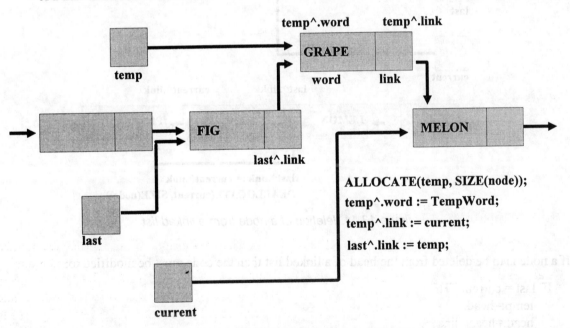

```
ALLOCATE(temp, SIZE(node));
temp^.word := TempWord;
temp^.link := current;
last^.link := temp;
```

figure 13.10 insertion of a node into a linked list

If the last node is the same as the current node then the new node must be inserted at the head of the list,
therefore, the statement last^.link:=temp should be changed to:

273

```
IF last = current THEN
    head := temp;
ELSE
    last^.link:=temp;
END;
```

The deletion of a node from a linked list is even easier. Figure 13.11 illustrates four nodes within a linked list. If the third node in the diagram is to be deleted the link field of the second note must be altered to point at the fourth node. The pointer to the third node can then be disposed. The code that performs this deletion of a node is: last^.link:=current^.link; DEALLOCATE(current, SIZE(node)); the link between LEMON and ORANGE is broken and a new link formed between LEMON and PLUM. Since current is pointing to ORANGE the effect of disposing of current is to remove ORANGE.

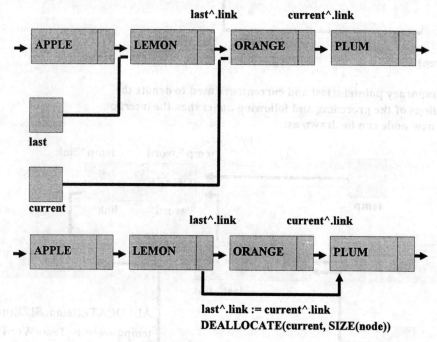

figure 13.11 deletion of a node from a linked list

If a node is to be deleted from the head of a linked list then the code must be modified to:

```
IF last = current THEN
    temp:=head;
    head:=head^.link;
    DEALLOCATE(temp, SIZE(node));
ELSE
    last^.link:=current^.link;
    DEALLOCATE(current, SIZE(node));
END;
```

In both these examples it is necessary to search the linked list for the position of the node to be inserted or the position of the node to be deleted. When the list is being searched for the insertion of a new word it is possible that the word may already exist in the list. Similarly, when the list is being searched prior to the deletion of a word, it is possible that the word may not exist in the list. Both exceptions must be catered for in the algorithm. The procedure that follows performs a linear search on the contents of an ordered linked list. The reader is advised to study and desk-check this code, since it will appear again in a slightly modified form in the final program.

```
PROCEDURE search(VAR head, last, current : pointer; key : string; VAR found : BOOLEAN);
(* search for the position of a key in the linked list *)

BEGIN
    found:=FALSE;
    current:=head; (* point at head of list with variables current and head *)
    last:=current;
    WHILE (current # NIL) AND NOT found DO
        IF Equal(key, current^.word) THEN
            found := TRUE;
            RETURN;
        ELSIF Compare(key, word) = less THEN
            RETURN;
        ELSE
            last:=current; (* move to next node in list and continue search *)
            current:=current^.link;
        END;
    END;
END search;
```

In the final program nodes of a linked list contain part of a dictionary of words and their meanings. For example a typical entry in the linked list might contain: *adobe an unburnt sun-dried brick.* The linked list is created by reading a text file containing lines of text similar to the example given here. The user is invited to either *insert* a new entry, *delete* an existing entry, *examine* the linked list, *copy* the linked list to a file or *quit* from the program. These options are displayed from the function *menu.* The format of a record stored in a node of the linked list is:

```
text : string;
link : pointer;
```

In the text field a dictionary word appears first, followed by at least one space followed by the meaning of the word, for example *adobe an unburnt sun-dried brick.* To obtain the word from the line of text it is necessary to use a procedure *IsolateKey* that separates the word from its meaning.

```
MODULE ex_4;
(* program to allow the user to inspect, insert and delete information
found in a dictionary - for the purpose of testing the program the
dictionary is limited to only ten items, however more can be accommodated
by increasing the number of entries in the original data file *)

FROM Storage IMPORT ALLOCATE, DEALLOCATE;
FROM StreamFile IMPORT ChanId, Open, Close, read, write, OpenResults;
FROM IOResult IMPORT ReadResult, ReadResults;
FROM TextIO IMPORT ReadString, WriteString, WriteLn;
FROM StringType IMPORT string;
FROM Strings IMPORT Compare, Equal, less;
IMPORT STextIO;

TYPE
    pointer = POINTER TO node;

    node = RECORD
                text        : string;
                link        : pointer;
            END;

VAR
    head, last, current : pointer;
    key, line           : string;
    found               : BOOLEAN;


PROCEDURE CreateList(VAR head : pointer);
(* procedure to build a linked list by reading successive records from
a text file, that has already been created *)

VAR
    datafile : ChanId;
    filename : string;
    last     : pointer;
    results  : OpenResults;


        PROCEDURE CreateNode(VAR next : pointer; line : string);
        (*
         procedure to build a single node in the linked list
        *)

        BEGIN
            ALLOCATE(next, SIZE(node));
            next^.text := line;
            next^.link := NIL;
        END CreateNode;
```

```
BEGIN
    STextIO.WriteString('input name of file ');
    STextIO.ReadString(filename);
    Open (datafile, filename, read, results);
    IF results # opened THEN
        STextIO.WriteString(filename);
        STextIO.WriteString(' cannot be opened program abandoned');
        STextIO.WriteLn;
        HALT;
    END;

    head := NIL;
    ReadString(datafile, line);
    WHILE ReadResult(datafile) # endOfInput DO
        IF head = NIL THEN
            CreateNode(head, line);
            last := head;
        ELSE
            CreateNode(last^.link, line);
            last:=last^.link;
        END;
        ReadString(datafile, line);
    END;
END CreateList;

PROCEDURE ListOut(head : pointer);
(* procedure to display the contents of the linked list *)

VAR
    current : pointer;

BEGIN
    current := head;
    IF head = NIL THEN
        STextIO.WriteString('list empty'); STextIO.WriteLn;
    ELSE
        WHILE current # NIL DO
            STextIO.WriteString(current^.text); STextIO.WriteLn;
            current:=current^.link;
        END;
    END;
END ListOut;

PROCEDURE CleanUp(VAR head : pointer);
(*
procedure to re-allocate the storage space used by the linked list
back to the heap
*)
```

```
VAR
  current : pointer;
  temp    : pointer;

BEGIN
    current := head;
    WHILE current # NIL DO
         temp := current^.link;
         DEALLOCATE(current, SIZE(node));
         current := temp;
    END;
    head := NIL;
END CleanUp;

PROCEDURE IsolateKey(VAR word : string; line : string);
(*
procedure to isolate the word as a key from line of text
*)

CONST
     null = 0C;
     space = 40C;

VAR
  index : CARDINAL;

BEGIN
    index := 0;
    WHILE (line[index] # space) AND (line[index] # null) DO
         word[index] := line[index];
         INC(index);
    END;
    word[index]:=null;
END IsolateKey;

PROCEDURE search(VAR head, last, current : pointer; key : string;
                 VAR found : BOOLEAN);
(*
search for the position of a key in the linked list
*)

VAR
  word : string;

BEGIN
    found := FALSE;
    current := head;
    last := current;
    WHILE (current # NIL) AND NOT found DO
```

```
          IsolateKey(word, current^.text);
          IF Equal(key, word) THEN
              found := TRUE;
              RETURN;
          ELSIF Compare(key, word) = less THEN
              RETURN;
          ELSE
              last := current;
              current := current^.link;
          END;
      END;
END search;

PROCEDURE insert(VAR head, last, current : pointer; line : string);
(* insert a new node into the linked list *)

VAR
   temp : pointer;

BEGIN
    ALLOCATE(temp, SIZE(node));
    temp^.text := line;
    temp^.link := current;
    IF last = current THEN
        head := temp;
    ELSE
        last^.link := temp;
    END;
END insert;

PROCEDURE delete(VAR head, last, current : pointer);
(*
procedure to delete an existing node from a linked list
*)

VAR
   temp : pointer;

BEGIN
    IF last = current THEN
        temp:=head;
        head:=head^.link;
        DEALLOCATE(temp, SIZE(node));
    ELSE
        last^.link := current^.link;
        DEALLOCATE(current, SIZE(node));
    END;
END delete;
```

279

```
PROCEDURE copy(head:pointer);
(*
procedure to copy the contents of the linked list to a named file
*)

VAR
  datafile : ChanId;
  filename : string;
  results  : OpenResults;

BEGIN
    STextIO.WriteString('input name of file ');
    STextIO.ReadString(filename);
    Open (datafile, filename, write, results);
    IF results # opened THEN
       STextIO.WriteString(filename);
       STextIO.WriteString(' cannot open file - program terminated');
       HALT;
    END;

    current := head;
    WHILE current # NIL DO
          WriteString(datafile, current^.text);
          WriteLn(datafile);
          current:=current^.link;
    END;
    Close (datafile);
END copy;

PROCEDURE menu():CHAR;
(* function to return the value of the menu item *)

VAR
  reply : CHAR;

BEGIN
    STextIO.WriteLn;
    STextIO.WriteString('Do you want to:'); STextIO.WriteLn;
    STextIO.WriteString('[I]nsert a new entry'); STextIO.WriteLn;
    STextIO.WriteString('[D]elete an existing entry'); STextIO.WriteLn;
    STextIO.WriteString('[E]xamine the list'); STextIO.WriteLn;
    STextIO.WriteString('[C]opy list to file'); STextIO.WriteLn;
    STextIO.WriteString('[Q]uit'); STextIO.WriteLn;
    STextIO.WriteString('input I, D, E, C or Q ');
    STextIO.ReadChar(reply); reply:=CAP(reply); STextIO.SkipLine;
    STextIO.WriteLn;
    RETURN reply;
END menu;
```

```
BEGIN
    CreateList(head);
    LOOP
        CASE menu() OF
        'I' : STextIO.WriteString('input line'); STextIO.WriteLn;
              STextIO.ReadString(line); IsolateKey(key, line);
              search(head, last, current, key, found);
              IF NOT found THEN
                  insert(head, last, current, line);
              ELSE
                  STextIO.WriteString('key exists in list');
                  STextIO.WriteLn;
              END|
        'D' : STextIO.WriteString('input key ');
              STextIO.ReadString(key);
              search(head, last, current, key, found);
              IF found THEN
                  delete(head, last, current);
              ELSE
                  STextIO.WriteString('key not in list');
                  STextIO.WriteLn;
              END|
        'E' : ListOut(head) |
        'C' : copy(head) |
        'Q' : CleanUp(head);
              HALT;
        ELSE
              STextIO.WriteString('error- wrong code'); STextIO.WriteLn;
        END;
    END;
END ex_4.
```

Contents of file used to create the linked list

```
adobe an unburnt sun-dried brick
adorn add beauty or lustre to; be an ornament to
commis a junior waiter or chef
dan any of the twelve degrees of advanced proficiency in judo
guru Hindu spiritual teacher or head of a religious sect
isotonic having the same osmotic pressure
logic the science of reasoning, proof, thinking or inference
nova a star showing a sudden large increase of brightness then subsiding
propel drive or push forward
serein a fine rain falling in tropical climates from a cloudless sky
```

Results from program ex_4 being run

```
input name of file a:ex_4data.txt
Do you want to:
[I]nsert a new entry
[D]elete an existing entry
[E]xamine the list
[C]opy list to file
[Q]uit
input I, D, E, C or Q I

input line
plural more than one in number


Do you want to:
[I]nsert a new entry
[D]elete an existing entry
[E]xamine the list
[C]opy list to file
[Q]uit
input I, D, E, C or Q E

adobe an unburnt sun-dried brick
adorn add beauty or lustre to; be an ornament to
commis a junior waiter or chef
dan any of the twelve degrees of advanced proficiency in judo
guru Hindu spiritual teacher or head of a religious sect
isotonic having the same osmotic pressure
logic the science of reasoning, proof, thinking or inference
nova a star showing a sudden large increase of brightness then subsiding
plural more than one in number
propel drive or push forward
serein a fine rain falling in tropical climates from a cloudless sky

Do you want to:
[I]nsert a new entry
[D]elete an existing entry
[E]xamine the list
[C]opy list to file
[Q]uit
input I, D, E, C or Q D

input key adobe

Do you want to:
[I]nsert a new entry
[D]elete an existing entry
[E]xamine the list
```

```
[C]opy list to file
[Q]uit
input I, D, E, C or Q E

adorn add beauty or lustre to; be an ornament to
commis a junior waiter or chef
dan any of the twelve degrees of advanced proficiency in judo
guru Hindu spiritual teacher or head of a religious sect
isotonic having the same osmotic pressure
logic the science of reasoning, proof, thinking or inference
nova a star showing a sudden large increase of brightness then subsiding
plural more than one in number
propel drive or push forward
serein a fine rain falling in tropical climates from a cloudless sky

Do you want to:
[I]nsert a new entry
[D]elete an existing entry
[E]xamine the list
[C]opy list to file
[Q]uit
input I, D, E, C or Q C

input name of file a:amended.txt

Do you want to:
[I]nsert a new entry
[D]elete an existing entry
[E]xamine the list
[C]opy list to file
[Q]uit
input I, D, E, C or Q Q
```

13.5 Queues

Queues are a familiar aspect of everyday life. People queue in orderly lines to wait for buses, or to wait to be served in a post office or bank. There are many examples in computing of the use of queues. In a real-time system queues of processes wait to use a processor or queues of jobs wait to use a resource such as a printer. The general concept of a queue is a line of objects that has a front and a rear. The first object in the queue is said to be at the front of the queue, whereas the last object in the queue is said to be at the rear of the queue. In a First In First Out (FIFO) queue, an object can only join the queue at the rear and leave the queue at the front.

Queues can be built out of linked lists. The rear of a queue is depicted in figure 13.12. Notice that a pointer *rear* is used to indicate the last node in the queue.

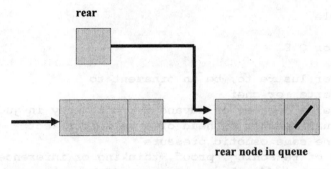

figure 13.12 rear of FIFO queue

To allow another node to join a FIFO queue requires a new node *temp*, to be introduced. This node will contain the details of the latest member to join the queue. The code required to insert a new node at the rear of the queue follows. This code should be read in conjunction with the illustration in figure 13.13.

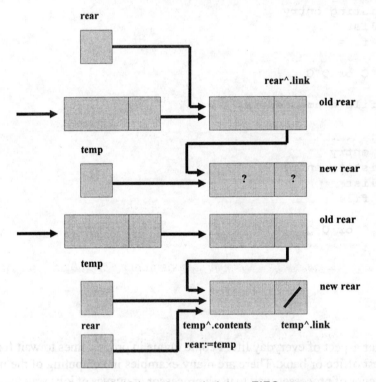

figure 13.13 insert a node into a FIFO queue

ALLOCATE(temp, SIZE(node));
rear^.link := temp;

will allocate a new node, *temp*, and point the old rear node in the queue to this new node;

temp^.contents:=data;
temp^.link:=NIL;

will store the new data in the new node and set the pointer of this node to NIL since it is the new rear node;

rear:=temp

will force the rear pointer to point at the last node in the queue i.e. the node that has just been inserted into the rear of the queue.

Members of a FIFO queue can only leave from the front. The coding required to remove a member from the front of a queue follows, and should be read in conjunction with figure 13.14.

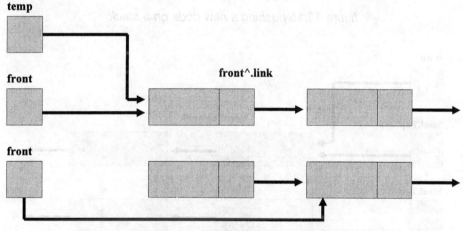

figure 13.14 removing a node from a FIFO queue

temp := front;

will assign a temporary pointer to also point at the front of the queue

front := front^.link;

will change the front of the queue to point at the second node in the queue and has the effect of by-passing the first item in the queue;

DEALLOCATE(temp, SIZE(node));

since temp was pointing at the original first node in the queue this node is no longer required and can be disposed.

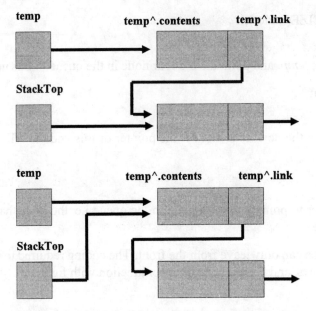

figure 13.15 pushing a new node on a stack

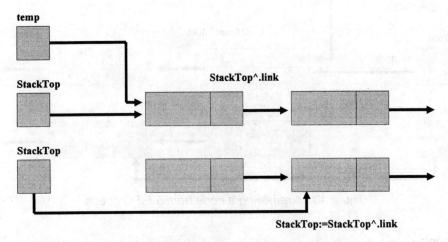

figure 13.16 popping a node from a stack

13.6 Stacks

A stack is a form of queue in which members of the queue can join and leave at one end only. The queue is known as a LIFO queue - Last In First Out. The entry/ exit point of the stack is known as the stack top and the position of this stack top is controlled by a stack pointer. An item that joins the queue is said to be pushed on to the stack. An item that leaves the queue is said to be popped from the stack. The methods for pushing and popping items from a stack are illustrated in figures 13.15 and 13.16 respectively, and should be used in conjunction with the code that follows.

To push a new node on the stack requires the following code.

```
ALLOCATE(temp, SIZE(node));
temp^.contents:=item;
temp^.link:=StackTop;
```

will assign a new node *temp*, store the new item in this node and force the new node to point to the original top of the stack;

```
StackTop:=temp;
```

will force the pointer StackTop to point at the same node as the pointer *temp*, this will now point to the new node inserted into the top of the stack.

To pop an item from the top of a stack, is exactly the same process as removing an item from the front of a FIFO queue.

```
temp:=StackTop;
```

use temporary pointer to point at the top of the stack;

```
item:=StackTop^.contents;
StackTop:=StackTop^.link;
```

will store data from top node in stack and force StackTop pointer to point at next node in stack;

```
DEALLOCATE(temp, SIZE(node));
```

will remove node pointed at by temp - this will be the original first node in the stack.

13.7 Summary

- ☐ A pointer represents an address in the memory of a computer. This address contains the data that is being pointed at.

- ☐ Storage space to accommodate the data must be allocated from the heap, and when the storage space is no longer required should be de-allocated back to the heap.

- ☐ A linked list is represented as a series of records, where the first record is pointed at by a head pointer, and each record in turn points to the next record in the series, until the last record which contains a NIL pointer.

- ☐ If the keys representing data in a linked list are ordered then the insertion and deletion of records in the list is made easier.

- ☐ A linked list can be used to represent queues.

- ☐ A first in first out (FIFO) queue will have records inserted into the end of a linked list and records deleted from the head of a linked list.

- ☐ A last in first out (LIFO) queue will have records inserted (pushed) into the head of the queue and records deleted (popped) also from the head of the queue.

13.8 Questions - *answers begin on page 409*

1. Write a program to create a linked list of non-zero integers stored in key disorder. Build a second linked list that contains the integers from the first linked list sorted into key order. As each integer is used from the first linked list, delete it from the first linked list. When all the integers are sorted display the contents of the second linked list.

2. Write a program to input characters at a keyboard and store them on a stack. After the last character has been stored, pop all the characters from the stack, thereby reversing the order in which the characters were input.

3. Replace the procedures in MODULE ex_4, such that:

    (a) *ListOut* is a recursive procedure to output the contents of the linked list, and
    (b) *search* is a recursive procedure to search for a key in the ordered linked list.

4. A circular linked list is defined when the last node of the list points to the first node of the list. Illustrate what you understand by this statement and write procedures to:

    (a) Store and display integers held in the circular list, and
    (b) reverse the links in the circular list and re-display the integers.

5. The *Early Bird* organisation specialises in a computer-aided telephone call wake-up service. Customers telephone the company and state at what time of the day or night they want an alarm call. The data taken from each customer is:

    time of alarm call;
    telephone number;
    name of customer;
    special messages.

Write a program to store the data for each customer in the node of a linked list. Organise the list into chronological order based on a 24-hour clock. Assume that calls are only stored for a 24-hour period from noon of one day to noon the next day. The program should be menu driven and allow for the insertion, deletion and amendment of data. The next telephone alarm call to be made should be displayed on the screen, as a reminder to the operator.

Chapter 14
Modules

In chapter seven the reader was introduced to a pseudo-code refinement method for designing a computer program. The philosophy behind this method is to separate what is to be achieved by a program, from the details of how it is to be achieved. It was straightforward to write a first attempt at solving a problem in terms of what procedures would be required without becoming bogged down with the details of how the procedures should be written. This technique of separating the procedures required, from the detailed coding of the procedures, is known as procedural abstraction.

Modula-2 provides for the full realisation of procedural abstraction, through the use of modules. This chapter covers the construction and compilation of library modules, the portability of code, local modules and the advantages of using modules. By the end of the chapter the reader should have an understanding of the following topics.

☐ Program modules, library modules and local modules.

☐ The format of definition and implementation modules.

☐ Building libraries of re-usable code.

☐ The use of libraries to facilitate the portability of programs.

☐ Modular programming techniques.

14.1 Module description

There exists three distinct types of modules in the language. The first, the *program* module, is the most familiar to the reader. It is this type of module that has been used, so far, in the text.

The second, the *library* module, has been referenced in program modules, by using such statements as FROM *STextIO* IMPORT ReadString, WriteString, WriteLn; however, the reader has not yet come across the construction of library modules.

The third, the *local* module, can be regarded as a module nested within another module. Both program and library modules may contain local modules.

Modules act as walls that surround such entities as constants, types, variables, procedures and functions, that relate to a specific activity or group of activities. Such modules as STextIO and SWholeIO each contain entities that may be grouped by virtue of the nature of the activity to which they relate. STextIO contains procedures for the input and output of characters and strings, and SWholeIO contains procedures for the input and output of whole numbers.

Identifiers declared inside a module are not visible outside the module, unless the module exports them. In order for another module to gain access to any of the exported identifiers the module must import the identifier.

A module that imports an entity exported by a library module is said to be a client of the library module.

A library module can be separated into a public section, which is accessible to everyone, and a private section, which contains the working code and is hidden from the users.

A program module may import any number of library modules (FROM STextIO IMPORT ...; FROM SWholeIO IMPORT ...; FROM Strings IMPORT ...; etc), however, these modules may, in turn, import from other library modules.

A complete Modula-2 program consists of a set of interconnected modules.

14.2 Library modules

Every library module contains two sections, a definition section that is public and written in a DEFINITION MODULE and an implementation section that is private and written in an IMPLEMENTATION MODULE.

The definition module specifies the identifiers that the module exports, whereas the implementation section contains the code of the procedures and functions that supply these identifiers. In terms of procedural abstraction, the definition module describes what the module does and the implementation module describes how it does it.

Figure 14.1 illustrates an import graph of a program, where A represents the program module. Module A imports library modules B and C. In turn, library module B imports library module D, and library module C imports library modules D and E.

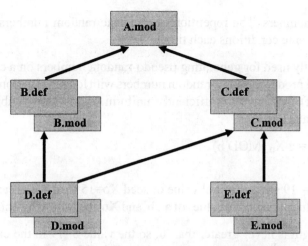

figure 14.1 import graph for a program

14.3 Random numbers

At this point in the chapter it is necessary to digress away from modules, and provide the reader with some background information about random numbers. The reason for this, is so that in the following section both definition and implementation modules can be created that export a random number generator function.

Computers are frequently used to simulate or model real-world events, such as the frequency of traffic on road systems, queues of shoppers in a supermarket, etc. The heart of any simulation is a source of random numbers to reproduce the random effects of the real world. For a series of values to be random they must exhibit at least two qualities.

The numbers must be unbiased. There can be no digit or number which is found more or less frequently than others.

The values must be non-predictive. A zero cannot foretell the appearance of another zero, or some other particular value. This also applies to the size of the values, the production of a small or large value should not give any clue about the size of subsequent values.

Rolling a die will generate random numbers with the values 1,2,3,4,5 and 6. If after numerous rolling all six numbers did not appear to occur with equal frequency then the numbers would not be random. Similarly if there was some pattern in their order which allowed predictions of future values then they would not be classed as being random. This illustrates the concept of randomness. The values must appear an equal number of times (unbiased), and sequences should not be repeated frequently (non-predictive).

Both of these attributes are intended to be observed over, say, a few million values.

In computer simulations it is often necessary to use the same set of random numbers over many trials. This repetition of the same random numbers implies that they are not truly random and they are, therefore, termed pseudo-random numbers. The repetition of the same random numbers allows the model to be tested under exactly the same conditions each time.

A method that is frequently used for generating pseudo-random numbers on a computer is a congruence method. This method will produce pseudo-random numbers with long cycles (long stream of values before the stream repeats itself) that have a sufficiently uniform distribution (unbiased). The formula for achieving such a set of values is:

$$X_{n+1} = a\,X_n\ (\text{MOD}\ b)$$

For example, if a = 2 , b = 19 and the initial value or seed Xo=15 then the stream of values illustrated in figure 14.2 would result. In choosing the values of **a** , **b** and **Xo** the following points should be considered.

The maximum cycle length is never greater than **b**, so the value b=19 in the example was too small. A suitable choice for **b** is b = 10^W where **w** is the number of significant figures used.

The constant **a** should be chosen such that a=8p+3 where **p** is a positive integer. This will improve the cycle length. The value of **a** should be close to $2^{W/2}$ in order to prevent successive values being too closely related. The initial seed X_0 is relatively prime to **b** (only common factor is 1).

n	Xn	Xn+1
0	15	11
1	11	3
2	3	6
3	6	12
4	12	5
5	5	10
6	10	1
7	1	2
8	2	4
9	4	8
10	8	16
11	16	13
12	13	7
13	7	14
14	14	9
15	9	18
16	18	17
17	17	15
18	15	11
19	11	3
20	..	..
21	..	..

figure 14.2 random numbers using a congruence method

These rules can be incorporated into the following function that when invoked will produce a random number RND in the range 0.1<=RND<1, where the initial value of seed is 19. It has been necessary to define **b** as a long integer to increase the cycle length. The reader is recommended to desk check the module and generate one random number.

```
PROCEDURE RND():LONGREAL;
CONST
    a=LONGINT(19);
    b=LONGINT(100000000);
VAR
  y                 : LONGINT;
  random_number : LONGREAL;
BEGIN
    y:=(a*seed) MOD b;
    seed := y;
    random_number := LONGREAL(ABS(y));
    REPEAT
        random_number := random_number / 10.0;
    UNTIL random_number < 1.0;
    RETURN random_number;
END RND;
```

14.4 Definition module

The purpose behind the use of a definition module is to convey to the public user of the module the name of the library, constants, types, variables, procedures and/or functions contained in the library, the names of the parameters used in the procedures and/or functions and their respective data types, and the purpose of each visible component of the library.

The syntax of a definition module is:

definition module ::= **DEFINITION MODULE** module identifier ';'
import lists, definitions **END** module identifier '.'

definitions ::=   {definition}
definition ::=   **CONST** {constant declaration ';'} |
                         TYPE {type definition ';'}|
                         VAR {variable declaration ';'} |
                         procedure heading ';'
procedure heading ::= proper procedure heading | function procedure heading

In the previous section a function was introduced to compute a pseudo-random number RND in the range 0.1<=RND<1. This procedure is an ideal candidate for a library module, since a random number generator is a useful feature in any programming language and by incorporating it into a library the function is available for all to use without the need for re-coding the procedure. The declaration for the module is given by:

```
DEFINITION MODULE Random;

PROCEDURE RND():LONGREAL;
(* function to compute a pseudo-random number in the range
0.1 <= RND < 1, using a congruence method *)

END Random.
```

The definition module is normally filed with a **.def** extension appended to the filename. This definition module informs the public user that within a library called Random, there exists a parameter-less function of type LONGREAL, that returns a pseudo-random number in the range 0.1<=RND<1.

All entities that are visible in a definition module can be exported to other modules without having to be explicitly listed in an EXPORT list. This is not the case for local modules, as will be explained later in the text.

When a programmer wants to use the RND function, the client program would be coded to include FROM Random IMPORT RND; and from within the module block accessed using RND() or alternatively IMPORT Random; and from within the module block accessed using Random.RND().

14.5 Implementation module

If the definition module describes what a module is to achieve, then an implementation module describes how the module does it. The syntax is:

implementation module ::=   **IMPLEMENTATION MODULE** module identifier '[' priority ']' ';'
                              import lists, module block, module identifier '.'
module block ::=   declarations [module body] **END**
module body ::=   **BEGIN** block body
block body ::=   statement sequence

The implementation module for the function RND would be coded as:

```
IMPLEMENTATION MODULE Random;
VAR
   seed : LONGINT;

PROCEDURE RND():LONGREAL;
CONST
    a=LONGINT(19);
    b=LONGINT(100000000);
VAR
   y                : LONGINT;
   random_number : LONGREAL;
BEGIN
   y:=(a*seed) MOD b;
   seed := y;
   random_number := LONGREAL(ABS(y));
```

294

```
    REPEAT
         random_number := random_number / 10.0;
    UNTIL random_number < 1.0;
    RETURN random_number;
END RND;

(* body of implementation module *)
BEGIN
    seed := 19;
END Random.
```

The implementation module is normally filed with a **.mod** extension appended to the filename.

Although the function RND will be called many times during the execution of a program, the body of the implementation module is only executed once, hence the value of the variable seed is only initialised once. An implementation module does not always contain a body.

The function RND can be used in an expression to compute a random number in the range 1 to 6 for the simulation of rolling a die a set number of times. Since 0.1<=RND<1 the expression (TRUNC(1000.0*RND()) MOD 6) +1 will generate random numbers in the range 1 to 6 with reasonable uniformity. The following program imports from Random the function RND and uses it to generate random integers in the range 1 to 6, as a simulation of rolling a die.

```
MODULE dice;
(*
program to count the number of times 1,2,3,4,5 and 6 appears when
a die is rolled a fixed number of times
*)

FROM STextIO IMPORT WriteString, WriteLn;
FROM SWholeIO IMPORT ReadCard, WriteCard;
FROM Random IMPORT RND;

VAR
   number_of_throws : CARDINAL; (* maximum number of throws of the die *)
   spots            : CARDINAL; (* number of spots on upwards face *)
   throw_counter    : CARDINAL; (* counts the number of throws *)
   frequency        : ARRAY[1..6] OF CARDINAL;

BEGIN
    WriteString('input number of throws of die (0 to exit) ');
    ReadCard(number_of_throws);
    WHILE number_of_throws > 0 DO

            (* initialise frequencies *)
            FOR spots := 1 TO 6 DO
                 frequency[spots] := 0;
            END;
```

```
                    (* simulate rolling die *)
                    FOR throw_counter := 1 TO number_of_throws DO
                        spots := TRUNC(1000.0 * RND()) MOD 6 + 1;

                        (* increase frequency by 1 *)
                        INC(frequency[spots]);
                    END;

                    (* display frequencies *)
                    WriteString('spots frequency');
                    WriteLn;

                    FOR spots := 1 TO 6 DO
                        WriteCard(spots,2);
                        WriteCard(frequency[spots],10);
                        WriteLn;
                    END;
                    WriteLn;

                    WriteString('input number of throws of die (0 to exit) ');
                    ReadCard(number_of_throws);
                END;
            END dice.
```

Results from program dice being run

```
input number of throws of die (0 to exit)  60000
spots frequency
 1       10026
 2       10035
 3       10103
 4        9845
 5       10001
 6        9990

input number of throws of die (0 to exit)  0
```

14.6 Module initialisation

From the last section it should now be clear that an implementation module can be composed of both procedures and/or functions, and where necessary have a body. Because a program may contain any number of library modules, each of which may have a body, it is necessary to know the order of module initialisation.

The bodies of all imported modules must be executed before the body of a client module can be executed. For example, in figure 14.3 the body of M3.mod must be executed before the body of M2.mod. Similarly the body of M2.mod must be executed before the body of M1.mod. The order of initialisation of the bodies of the three modules is M3, M2 and M1. This ensures the correct initialisation of each library module before a client performs any operations on it. The program module, is always executed last, after the bodies of all imported modules have been executed.

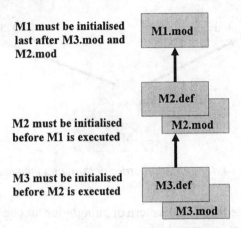

figure 14.3 initialisation order of modules with bodies

When a client module imports from several modules, they are initialised in the order in which they are imported. From figure 14.4 if M1 contains the code:

        FROM M2 IMPORT ....;
        FROM M3 IMPORT ....;

then the order of initialisation is M4,M2,M3,M1.

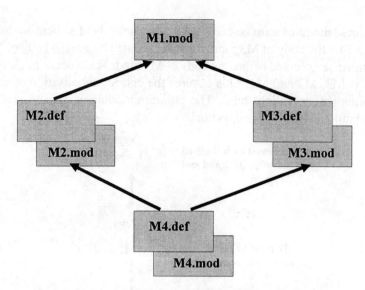

figure 14.4 importation order determines initialisation

The order of initialisation is undefined if the pattern of importation amongst two or more implementation modules forms a circle, as shown in figure 14.5.

In such a case the linker will probably choose the order in which the modules are initialised. Such arbitrary initialisation may cause the program to malfunction. The reader is advised to avoid creating this type of implementation module loop.

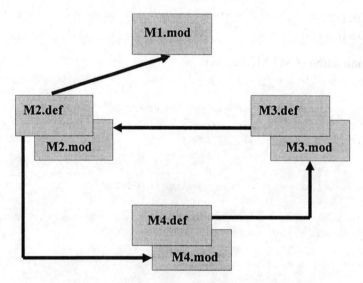

figure 14.5 circular pattern of imported modules

14.7 Portability

Since many of the features expected in a high-level language, such as the input and output of data, are not part of Modula-2, but rely on library routines, it is possible that a program written for one machine will not be portable to another owing to the different implementations of the input and output libraries.

To highlight this problem, consider for a moment part of the definition module for SWholeIO defined in the *Draft Standard*.

```
DEFINITION MODULE SWholeIO;

(*
Input and output of whole numbers in decimal text form over default channels.
*)

       _

       _

PROCEDURE ReadInt(VAR int:INTEGER);
(*
Skips leading spaces, and removes any remaining characters from the default
input channel that form part of a signed whole number. The value of this
number is assigned to int.
*)

PROCEDURE WriteInt(int:INTEGER; width:CARDINAL);
(*
Writes the value of int to the default output channel in text form, in a
field of the given minimum width.
*)

PROCEDURE ReadCard(VAR card:CARDINAL);
(*
Skips leading spaces, and removes any remaining characters from the default
input channel that form part of an unsigned whole number. The value of this
number is assigned to card.
*)

PROCEDURE WriteCard(card:CARDINAL; width:CARDINAL);
(*
Writes the value of card to the default output channel in text form, in a
field of the given minimum width.
*)

       _

       _

END SWholeIO.
```

Whereas, the corresponding procedures and functions provided by the *TopSpeed* Modula-2 library IO are:

```
DEFINITION MODULE IO;
(* functions for keyboard input and procedures for screen output *)

    _
    _

(* integer I/O *)
PROCEDURE RdInt():INTEGER;
PROCEDURE WrInt(V:INTEGER;length:INTEGER);

(* cardinal number I/O *)
PROCEDURE RdCard():CARDINAL;
PROCEDURE WrCard(V:CARDINAL;length:INTEGER);

    _
    _

END IO.
```

The reader should be aware of the following incompatibilities between the procedures that perform the same tasks in the two libraries.

The names of the libraries are different, SWhole and IO.

The Names of the corresponding procedures/ functions are different, WriteCard and WrCard, etc.

The procedures for reading integers and cardinals in *Draft Standard*, are implemented as functions in *TopSpeed* Modula-2. For example, the procedure ReadCard(VAR card:CARDINAL) in the *Draft Standard* is implemented as the function RdCard():CARDINAL in *TopSpeed* Modula-2.

A statement such as:

FROM SWholeIO IMPORT ReadInt, WriteInt;

written in the *Draft Standard*, has no chance of compiling correctly when using *TopSpeed* Modula-2, unless a new set of library routines, acting as an interface between the two dialects, are written to be used on a PC compatible computer.

By defining appropriate DEFINITION and IMPLEMENTATION modules for libraries on the *TopSpeed* Modula-2 system, portability with programs written for the *Draft Standard* becomes possible.

In the following example both a definition module and an implementation module have been defined for the library module SWholeIO running on a PC compatible machine that uses *TopSpeed* Modula-2. By supplying these two modules it is possible to implement a *Draft Standard* definition in an environment that was written before the *Draft Standard* was defined.

```
DEFINITION MODULE SWholeIO;

PROCEDURE ReadInt(VAR int:INTEGER);
PROCEDURE WriteInt(int:INTEGER; width:CARDINAL);
PROCEDURE ReadCard(VAR card:CARDINAL);
PROCEDURE WriteCard(card:CARDINAL; width:CARDINAL);

END SWholeIO.
```

Each procedure uses the respective procedure/ function found in the *TopSpeed* Modula-2 library to perform the necessary input / output.

```
IMPLEMENTATION MODULE SWholeIO;

IMPORT IO;

PROCEDURE ReadInt(VAR int:INTEGER);
BEGIN
   int:=IO.RdInt();
END ReadInt;

PROCEDURE WriteInt(int:INTEGER; width:CARDINAL);
BEGIN
   IO.WrInt(int, width);
END WriteInt;

PROCEDURE ReadCard(VAR card:CARDINAL);
BEGIN
   card:=IO.RdCard();
END ReadCard;

PROCEDURE WriteCard(card:CARDINAL; width:CARDINAL);
BEGIN
   IO.WrCard(card, width);
END WriteCard;

BEGIN
   IO.Prompt:=FALSE;
   IO.RdLnOnWr:=FALSE;
END SWholeIO.
```

14.8 Compilation

Modula-2 permits the separate compilation of program, definition and implementation modules. When compiling library modules the compiler checks that each entity imported from a library module is used in a manner that is consistent with the definition module for that library module.

The definition module must always be compiled before the implementation module. The result of the compilation of a definition module is a symbol table, which contains all constants, variables, type and procedure/ function declarations of the definition module. The symbol table is stored in the system and is available to all other modules.

When an implementation module is compiled, the compiler checks, using the symbol table, that it is consistent with the definition part of the module.

A change to a definition module requires a re-compilation of all modules which use the associated module, otherwise the compatibility of the definition module would not be assured.

A simple date/time stamp method is used in the *TopSpeed* Modula-2 system to ensure the viability of system modules.

For example if program module M1 imports from library module M2, then when the program file M1.mod is compiled the date and time of the last compilation of the definition module M2.def will be copied into the object code of the program M1. When the implementation module M2.mod is later compiled, the compiler copies the date and time of the last modification of the definition module M2.def to the object code of M2. When M1 and M2 are linked, the linker compares the dates and times. If the dates and times do not match then linking does not take place. Inconsistencies arise when M2.def is changed, and either M1.mod and M2.mod are not re-compiled.

14.9 Local modules

Modules that are declared within program modules, implementation modules, procedures and functions are known as local modules.

The format of a local module is exactly the same as a program module, except that:

A local module may contain an export list, which should appear immediately after the import lists.

A semi-colon, not a full-stop, follows the declaration of a local module.

Local modules, unlike program, definition and implementation modules, cannot be separately compiled.

Local modules are used to control the visibility of names within a program.

Local modules may have a body. The body of a local module is always executed immediately before the body of the enclosing module or procedure.

A local module acts like a wall around the entities inside it. Entities visible outside the module are not visible inside it, unless explicitly imported by the module. Similarly, entities visible inside the module are not visible outside unless exported by the module.

The body of a local module declared in a program or implementation module will be executed only once. Variables in the local module are static.

The body of a local module declared in a procedure will be executed every time the procedure is called. Values of variables in the local module and procedure are both lost when the procedure is exited.

The following example programs illustrate features of using local modules. In the first example, a variable declared within the local module is not accessible outside the scope of the module. Similarly a variable declared outside the local module is not accessible inside the local module.

```
MODULE demo1;
VAR
  a:CHAR;

  MODULE local;
  VAR
    b:CHAR;
      (* only b is visible *)
  END local;

(* only a is visible *)
END demo1.
```

The second example illustrates that a variable declared outside of a local module can be accessible to the local module, if it is imported into the local module.

```
MODULE demo2;
VAR
  a:CHAR;

  MODULE local;
  IMPORT a;
  VAR
    b:CHAR;
      (* both a and b are visible *)
  END local;

(* only a is visible *)
END demo2.
```

The third example shows how a variable declared within a local module can be exported to the surrounding module and becomes accessible outside the local module.

```
MODULE demo3;
VAR
  a:CHAR;

  MODULE local;
  EXPORT b;
  VAR
    b:CHAR;
      (* only b is visible *)
  END local;

(* both a and b are visible *)
END demo3.
```

In the fourth example routines that have been imported into the outer module are not accessible to the local module unless they are imported by the local module. Note also that an identifier can be exported from the local module in a qualified form. The identifier can only be used outside the local module if preceded by the name of the local module, in this example local.character.

```
MODULE demo4;
FROM STextIO IMPORT ReadChar, WriteChar, SkipLine, WriteString, WriteLn;

        MODULE local;
        IMPORT WriteString, ReadChar, SkipLine;
        EXPORT QUALIFIED character;

        VAR
          character : CHAR;
        BEGIN
            WriteString('from local module input character ');
            ReadChar(character);
            SkipLine;
        END local;

BEGIN
    WriteString('value of exported local variable ');
    WriteChar(local.character);
    WriteLn;
END demo4.
```

Results from program demo4 being run

```
from local module input character @
value of exported local variable @
```

A Fibonacci series is an infinite series of numbers such that the next term in the series is always the sum of the previous two terms, for example:

0, 1, 1, 2, 3, 5, 8, 13, 21, 34, 55 ...

A computer program can be written which uses a local module that contains a function to compute the next value in the series. The local module contains a body that is used to initialise the first two terms of the series. Zero is not strictly the first term of the series. Note that each time a number in the Fibonacci series is required a function call is made to the function number contained within the module Number-Generator. The body of NumberGenerator is only executed once, at the time of module initialisation.

```
MODULE demo5;
(* program to display the first ten terms in a Fibonacci series *)

FROM SWholeIO IMPORT WriteCard;

VAR
    loop_counter : CARDINAL;

        MODULE NumberGenerator;
        (* module to export the next Fibonacci number in sequence *)
        EXPORT number;
        VAR
            first, second : CARDINAL;

            PROCEDURE number() : CARDINAL;
            (* function to compute and return the next Fibonacci number *)
            BEGIN
                IF first < second THEN
                    first := first + second;
                    RETURN second;
                ELSE
                    second := second + first;
                    RETURN first;
                END;
            END number;

        BEGIN
            (*
            the body of the local module is used to hide the variables
            from the module demo5, and initialises the first and second
            values in the sequence
            *)

            first := 0;
            second := 1;
        END NumberGenerator;

BEGIN
    FOR loop_counter := 1 TO 10 DO
        WriteCard(number(), 4);
    END;
END demo5.
```

Results from program demo5 being run

```
   1    1    2    3    5    8   13   21   34   55
```

14.10 Modular programming

Writing a program as a collection of modules, rather than a single unit, offers the following advantages.

A large program can be designed as a collection of smaller modules. This has the advantage that each module can be designed, coded and tested independently of the remaining modules. A clear interface between the modules can be established through the definition of each module.

Members of a programming team can be assigned individual modules to develop, hence the allocation of work in project management can be improved.

Program modification is easier, since a programmer can change the details of an implementation module, without affecting the rest of the program, provided the definition module remains the same.

Program portability can be improved by the introduction of library modules that provide an interface between the libraries of two different Modula-2 systems.

Separate compilation of modules is possible, hence changes to modules do not result in the entire program having to be re- compiled.

Programmers can develop libraries of re-usable code. This not only saves time in the development of a system, but contributes towards the reliability of the system, since the modules have already undergone testing for other programs.

14.11 Summary

☐ Three different types of modules exist - program, library and local.

☐ A library module is composed of two parts - a definition module and an implementation module.

☐ A definition module defines the constants, types, variables, procedures and functions that can be exported.

☐ An implementation module contains the necessary types, procedures and functions to provide the functionality described by the corresponding definition module.

☐ An implementation module may import from other modules.

☐ An implementation module may have a body, in which case whatever is contained in the body is only executed once.

☐ The order of initialisation of implementation bodies is pre-defined, such that the module at the lowest point of the import graph is always initialised first. For two modules at the same level on the import graph the order of initialisation is governed by the order they appear in the import list of the client module that uses them.

☐ Circular import graphs should be avoided.

☐ Library modules can help facilitate the portability of programs.

☐ Local modules may be defined within program and implementation modules, procedures and functions.

14.12 Questions - *answers begin on page 414*

1. TopSpeed Modula-2 contains a library called SYSTEM where the resisters of the 8086 processor are defined, such that CL, CH and DL, DH pairs refer to the low and high bytes of the 16-bit registers C and D respectively. TopSpeed Modula-2 also contains a library called *Lib*, from which the procedure *Dos* can be exported to a client module. Dos permits access to DOS services through the DOS function handler. A call to *Dos* will return the time of day, such that registers CH, CL, DH and DL contain hours (0..23), minutes (0..59), seconds (0..59) and hundredths of a second (0..99) respectively, when the *Dos* call is used as indicated in the following procedure segment.

```
VAR
    r  :  SYSTEM.Registers;
BEGIN
    r.AH := 2CH; (* 2CH is the number of the DOS service requested *)
    Dos(r);
END;
```

Thus r.CH, r.CL, r.DH and r.DL will return hours, minutes, seconds and hundredths of a second respectively, which should be coerced to CARDINAL prior to printing or using in arithmetic.

Using this information write an implementation module that corresponds with the following definition module.

```
DEFINITION MODULE horologic;

PROCEDURE time_of_day(VAR hours, minutes, seconds:CARDINAL);
(* procedure to return the time of day in hours, minutes and seconds *)
PROCEDURE am(): BOOLEAN;
(* function to return TRUE if it is AM, otherwise FALSE depending upon the time of day *)
PROCEDURE clock_24;
(* procedure to display the time of day in 24-hour format as hh:mm *)
PROCEDURE clock_12;
(* procedure to display the time of day in a 12-hour format as hh:mm followed by either AM or PM *)
PROCEDURE elapsed_time() : LONGCARD;
(* function to return the number of seconds elapsed since midnight - the type LONGCARD is a type
defined in TopSpeed Modula-2 and not the Draft Standard *)

END horologic.
```

2. Write a program to test every procedure and function found in the library module horologic.

3. Write a procedure RANDOMIZE to be incorporated into the library Random in section 14.5. The RANDOMIZE procedure should be called before using RND whenever a different set of random numbers

are required. RANDOMIZE changes the starting position of the first number to be generated. This starting position could be input as a parameter taken as the elapsed time in seconds since midnight. For example if the current time was 10:50:20, using a 24-hour clock, then RANDOMIZE(39020), would start at the 39,020 th random number in the series.

4. Write a program to import RANDOMIZE and RND and generate different groups of random numbers.

5. Write the implementation module for CharClass given the following definition module for the *Draft Standard* library module CharClass.

DEFINITION MODULE CharClass;
(* Classification of values of the pervasive type CHAR *)

PROCEDURE IsNumeric (ch : CHAR) : BOOLEAN;
(* Tests if ch is classified as a numeric character *)
PROCEDURE IsLetter (ch : CHAR) : BOOLEAN;
(* Tests if ch is classified as a letter *)
PROCEDURE IsUpper(ch : CHAR) : BOOLEAN;
(* Tests if ch is classified as an upper case letter *)
PROCEDURE IsLower (ch : CHAR) : BOOLEAN;
(* Tests if ch is classified as a lower case letter *)
PROCEDURE IsControl (ch : CHAR) : BOOLEAN;
(* Tests if ch represents a control function *)
PROCEDURE IsWhiteSpace (ch : CHAR) : BOOLEAN;
(* Tests if ch represents either a space character or a format effector *)

END CharClass.

6. Write a program that tests every function found in the library module CharClass.

7. Write definition and implementation modules for calculating the following properties of a triangle.

   (a) Given length of one side and two angles, return the lengths of the two remaining sides and third angle.
   (b) Given the lengths of two sides and one angle, return the length of the remaining side and angles.
   (c) Given the lengths of the three sides, return the sizes of the three angles.
   (d) Given the lengths of the three sides return the area and the perimeter.
   (e) Given the lengths of the three sides, return the radii of the circumcircle and inscribed circles.

8. Import the necessary routines developed in the previous question into a program that requests the user to enter different available data on a triangle. Calculate and print comprehensive information about the triangle.

Chapter 15
Data abstraction

Data abstraction is the technique of combining a data type with a set of operations on data of the same type. By the end of this chapter the reader should have an understanding of the following topics.

☐ The meaning and implementation of an abstract data type.

☐ A stack implemented as an abstract data type.

☐ The introduction of a binary tree as an abstract data type.

15.1 Abstract data type

The concept of an abstract data type is not new. Consider for a moment the data type integer. Data of type integer can have the operations of *addition* (+), *subtraction* (-), *multiplication* (*) *division* (DIV) and *remainder* (MOD), as well as other standard functions, applied to the data. The method of implementing the integer type is hidden from the user. Many variables of the type integer can be declared. The implementation details for the various integer operators and functions are also hidden from the user.

The integer example demonstrates the necessary properties in the data abstraction model. The abstraction has created a data type *integer*. The type contains a minimal set of properties + - * *DIV MOD*. User access to the type is through a restricted interface, with the implementation details being hidden from the user of the type.

Modula-2 provides a facility for the programmer to define abstract data types and operations on such types. The detail of how the abstract data type is implemented is normally hidden from the user. The operations on the abstract data are conveyed to the user, only through the DEFINITION MODULE. The exact detail of how these operations are carried out is also hidden from the user, since such coding is only found in the IMPLEMENTATION MODULE.

The abstract data type is implemented in Modula-2 by the use of a pointer. Only the name of the data type appears in the DEFINITION MODULE, hence it is said to be *opaque*. Within the IMPLEMENTATION MODULE the abstract data type points to a declaration of how the data type is implemented. For example, imagine that the abstract data structure of a stack is given within a DEFINITION MODULE, that allows the user to specify and use the abstract data type stack, and the operators on the stack of initialise, empty, push and pop, as follows.

```
DEFINITION MODULE StackIO;

TYPE stack;

PROCEDURE initialise(VAR s:stack);
(* set the stack pointer to points at an empty stack *)
PROCEDURE empty(s:stack):BOOLEAN;
(* function returns TRUE if the stack is empty, otherwise returns FALSE *)
PROCEDURE push(VAR s:stack; character:CHAR);
(* insert a character on to the top of the stack *)
PROCEDURE pop(VAR s:stack; VAR character:CHAR);
(* remove a character from the top of the stack *)

END StackIO.
```

The reader's attention is drawn to the TYPE stack, since no definition of this type has been given to the user, hence the term *opaque*. The type stack, is defined in the IMPLEMENTATION MODULE as a pointer to a record structure. In general an abstract data type will be defined in the IMPLEMENTATION MODULE as a pointer to one of the regular Modula-2 data types. Having defined an abstract data type it is possible to generate many instances of that type. For example the declaration **VAR queue : stack** defines a variable *queue* of data type *stack*, and can have the operations initialise, empty, push and pop performed on it.

```
IMPLEMENTATION MODULE StackIO;

FROM Storage IMPORT ALLOCATE, DEALLOCATE;

TYPE stack = POINTER TO node;

     node = RECORD
                   data : CHAR;
                   link : stack;
             END;


PROCEDURE initialise(VAR s:stack);
BEGIN
    s:=NIL;
END initialise;

PROCEDURE empty(s:stack):BOOLEAN;
BEGIN
    IF s = NIL THEN
        RETURN TRUE;
    ELSE
        RETURN FALSE;
    END;
END empty;

PROCEDURE push(VAR s:stack; character:CHAR);
VAR
   temp_pointer : stack;
BEGIN
    ALLOCATE(temp_pointer, SIZE(node));
    temp_pointer^.data:=character;
    temp_pointer^.link:=s;
    s:=temp_pointer;
END push;

PROCEDURE pop(VAR s:stack; VAR character:CHAR);
VAR
   temp_pointer : stack;
BEGIN
    IF NOT empty(s) THEN
        temp_pointer:=s;
        character:=s^.data;
        s:=s^.link;
        DEALLOCATE(temp_pointer, SIZE(node));
    END;
END pop;

END StackIO.
```

The first worked example of this chapter imports from the definition module *StackIO* the abstract data type *stack*, and its operations *initialise*, *empty*, *push* and *pop*. The program builds a stack of characters, from data being input at the keyboard, then pops the contents of the stack displaying each character in turn on the screen. The characters output are displayed as the reverse of the characters that were input.

```
MODULE stack_ex;
(*
program to input and push single characters on to a stack, then
pop and display the characters from the stack in the reverse order
of input
*)

FROM StackIO IMPORT stack, initialise, empty, push, pop;
FROM STextIO IMPORT ReadChar, WriteChar, WriteString, WriteLn, SkipLine;

CONST
     terminator = '!';

VAR
     queue     : stack;
     character : CHAR;

BEGIN
     initialise(queue);

     WriteString('enter single characters on to the stack - ! to exit');
     WriteLn;
     ReadChar(character); SkipLine;
     WHILE character # terminator DO
           push(queue, character);
           ReadChar(character); SkipLine;
     END;

     WriteLn;
     WriteString('characters popped from the stack in reverse order of input')
     WriteLn;
     WHILE NOT empty(queue) DO
           pop(queue, character);
           WriteChar(character);
           WriteLn;
     END;
END stack_ex.
```

Results from program stack_ex being run

```
enter single characters on to the stack - ! to exit
a
b
c
!

characters popped from the stack in reverse order
c
b
a
```

15.2 Reverse Polish notation

In compiler writing it is more convenient to evaluate arithmetic expressions written in Reverse Polish notation than it is to evaluate arithmetic expressions written in infix notation. The following algorithm can be used to convert infix notations to reverse polish notations. For example, the expression a*(b+c/d) in infix notation is written as abcd/+* in Reverse Polish notation. The algorithm uses operator priorities as defined in figure 15.1. The operators [and] are used to delimit the infix expression. For example the expression a*(b+c/d) will be coded as [a*(b+c/d)].

operator	priority
^	4
*	3
/	3
+	2
-	2
(	1
[	0

figure 15.1 operator priorities

Using figure 15.2, if brackets [or (are encountered, each is pushed on to a stack. All operands that are encountered, for example a,b and c, are displayed on the screen. When an operator is encountered its priority is compared with that of the operator priority at the top of the stack. If when comparing priorities the operator encountered is not greater than the operator on the stack, the stack operator is popped and displayed. This process is repeated until the encountered operator has a higher priority than the stack top operator. The encountered operator is then pushed on to the stack. When a) is encountered all the operators up to, but not including (, are popped from the stack one at a time and displayed. The operator (is then deleted from the stack. When the operator] is encountered all the remaining operators, up to but not

313

including [, are popped from the stack one at a time and displayed. The string of characters that is displayed will be in Reverse Polish notation.

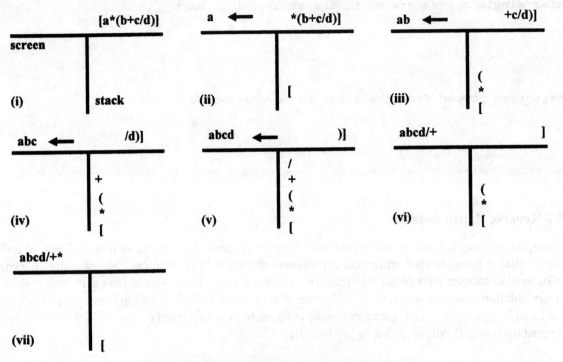

figure 15.2 conversion of infix to reverse Polish

The program that follows reads infix arithmetic expressions from a text file, converts each expression to Reverse Polish notation and displays the results on the screen of a monitor.

```
MODULE Polish;
(*
program to convert an infix expression into reverse Polish notation
*)

FROM StackIO IMPORT stack, initialise, push, pop;
FROM StreamFile IMPORT ChanId, Open, Close, read, OpenResults;
FROM IOResult IMPORT ReadResult, ReadResults;
FROM STextIO IMPORT WriteChar, WriteString, WriteLn;
FROM StringType IMPORT string;
FROM TextIO IMPORT ReadString;

CONST
    null = 0C;
```

```
TYPE
    symbol = RECORD
                    operator : CHAR;
                    priority : CARDINAL;
             END;

    array_type = ARRAY[1..7] OF symbol;

VAR
    operator_table    : array_type;
    operator_stack    : stack;
    datafile          : ChanId;
    results           : OpenResults;
    next_character    : CHAR;
    infix_expression  : string;
    index             : CARDINAL;

PROCEDURE initialisation(VAR operator_table : array_type;
                         VAR operator_stack : stack);
(* procedure to store the operators and their associated priorities in an
array and create an empty stack *)

BEGIN
    operator_table[1].operator := '['; operator_table[1].priority := 0;
    operator_table[2].operator := '('; operator_table[2].priority := 1;
    operator_table[3].operator := '-'; operator_table[3].priority := 2;
    operator_table[4].operator := '+'; operator_table[4].priority := 2;
    operator_table[5].operator := '/'; operator_table[5].priority := 3;
    operator_table[6].operator := '*'; operator_table[6].priority := 3;
    operator_table[7].operator := '^'; operator_table[7].priority := 4;

    initialise(operator_stack);
END initialisation;

PROCEDURE priority(operator_table : array_type; character : CHAR) : CARDINAL;
(* function to return the priority of an operator *)

VAR
  index : CARDINAL;

BEGIN
    FOR index := 1 TO 7 DO
        IF character = operator_table[index].operator THEN
            RETURN operator_table[index].priority;
        END;
    END;
END priority;
```

```
PROCEDURE stack_top_priority(operator_table : array_type;
                            VAR operator_stack : stack):CARDINAL;
(* function to return the priority of the operator at the top of the stack *)

VAR
   index : CARDINAL;
   character : CHAR;
BEGIN
    pop(operator_stack, character);
    push(operator_stack, character);
    RETURN priority(operator_table, character);
END stack_top_priority;

PROCEDURE analysis(VAR operator_stack : stack; next_character : CHAR);
(* procedure to perform the reverse Polish algorithm described in the text *)

VAR
   character : CHAR;
BEGIN
    IF next_character = ')' THEN
        pop(operator_stack, character);
        WHILE character # '(' DO
            WriteChar(character);
            pop(operator_stack, character);
        END;
    ELSIF next_character = ']' THEN
        pop(operator_stack, character);
        WHILE character # '[' DO
            WriteChar(character);
            pop(operator_stack, character);
        END;
    ELSIF (next_character ='(') OR
          (next_character = '[') THEN
            push(operator_stack, next_character);
    ELSIF (next_character = '^') OR
          (next_character = '*') OR
          (next_character = '/') OR
          (next_character = '+') OR
          (next_character = '-') THEN
            WHILE priority(operator_table, next_character)
                  <= stack_top_priority(operator_table, operator_stack) DO
                  pop(operator_stack, character);
                  WriteChar(character);
            END;
            push(operator_stack, next_character);
    ELSE
        WriteChar(next_character);
    END;
END analysis;
```

```
BEGIN
    Open (datafile, 'a:\infix.txt", read, results);
    IF results # opened THEN
      WriteString('file cannot be opened program abandoned');
      HALT;
    END;

    initialisation(operator_table, operator_stack);

    ReadString(datafile, infix_expression);
    WHILE ReadResult(datafile) # endOfInput DO
          index:=0;
          next_character := infix_expression[index];
          WHILE next_character # null DO
                analysis(operator_stack, next_character);
                INC(index);
                next_character := infix_expression[index];
          END;
          WriteLn;
          ReadString(datafile, infix_expression);
    END;

    Close(datafile);
END Polish.
```

Contents of text file infix.txt

```
[a*b+c]
[a*(b+c/d)]
[a*b+c/d]
[u+f*t]
[b^2-4*a*c]
[h*(a+4*b+c)/3]
[w*1-1/(w*c)]
```

Results from program Polish being run

```
ab*c+
abcd/+*
ab*cd/+
uft*+
b2^4a*c*-
ha4b*+c+*3/
w1*1wc*/-
```

317

15.3 Binary trees

The dynamic data structures that have been described had nodes that contained only one pointer which were used to point to the next node in either a linked list, queue or stack. It possible for a node to contain more than one pointer. However, in this section the reader will be introduced to nodes containing two pointers, left and right, such that the next node to be pointed at is dependent upon a condition related to the data being stored in the node. Figure 15.3 illustrates such a node.

figure 15.3 a single node with two pointer fields

If it is required to insert a second node, containing the fruit BANANA, such that the data is kept in an alphabetical order, then the reasoning would be:

```
IF 'BANANA' is less than ' LEMON' THEN
    branch to left
ELSE
    branch to right
END
```

The new node would be inserted as follows shown in figure 15.4.

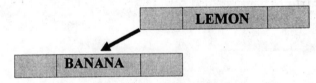

figure 15.4 attaching a node to the left branch

A third node containing ORANGE could be inserted using the same reasoning, as depicted in figure 15.5.

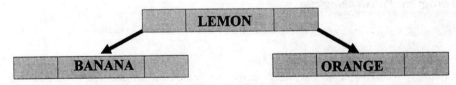

figure 15.5 attaching a node to the right branch

The data structure that is being formed is the basis of a binary tree. The term binary is used since there is the possibility of two paths at each node, pointing at the next node. If the following fruits are inserted into the binary tree - LEMON, BANANA, FIG, ORANGE, QUINCE, APPLE, PEAR, GRAPE, MELON - the data structure will appear as follows.

Those nodes that do not point to other nodes and have both pointers set at NIL are known as leaf nodes. The pointer at the top of the structure from which all nodes are descended is known as the *root*. The node containing LEMON is the parent to the nodes containing BANANA and ORANGE. Similarly, the node containing BANANA is the parent to the nodes containing APPLE and FIG. BANANA and ORANGE are children of the parent LEMON, and APPLE and FIG are children of the parent BANANA. Similar observations can be made about the relationships between other nodes as shown in figure 15.6.

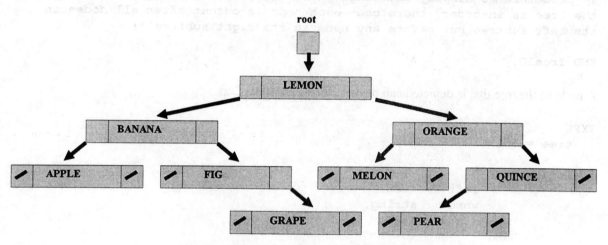

figure 15.6 an illustration of a binary tree

A binary tree can be defined as an abstract data type that has operations performed on it to initialise the tree, attach and remove nodes from the tree and display the contents of the tree. The definition module for such an abstract data structure follows.

```
DEFINITION MODULE TreeIO;

FROM StringType IMPORT string;

TYPE tree;

PROCEDURE initialise(VAR t:tree);
(* procedure to initialise the root of the tree *)

PROCEDURE empty(VAR t:tree):BOOLEAN;
(* function to return true if the tree is empty, otherwise false *)

PROCEDURE attach(VAR t:tree; new_word:string; VAR success:BOOLEAN);
(* procedure to insert a new word into the tree; success is true if
no duplicate is found, otherwise success is false and the new word is not
inserted *)
```

```
PROCEDURE remove(VAR t:tree; old_word:string; VAR success:BOOLEAN);
(* procedure to delete the node containing the word from the tree;
success is true if the word is found, otherwise success is false if the
word does not exist in the tree *)

PROCEDURE display(VAR t:tree);
(* procedure to display the contents of the tree - the order of traversing
the tree is in-order, therefore, each node is output after all nodes in
its left subtree but before any node in its right subtree *)

END TreeIO.
```

A node of the tree that is depicted can be described in Modula-2 as:

```
TYPE
   tree = POINTER TO node;

   node = RECORD
                left  : tree;
                word  : string;
                right : tree;
          END;
```

The following procedures are used to manipulate data in a binary tree. They are stored collectively in the IMPLEMENTATION MODULE TreeIO.

```
PROCEDURE initialise(VAR root:tree);
BEGIN
    root:=NIL;
END initialise;
```

The purpose behind the *initialise* procedure is to set the root pointer of a tree to NIL.

```
PROCEDURE empty(VAR parent:tree):BOOLEAN;
BEGIN
    IF parent = NIL THEN
        RETURN TRUE;
    ELSE
        RETURN FALSE;
    END;
END empty;
```

The procedure *empty* is identical to that described for the linked list, and its purpose is to allow the programmer to test for a tree structure that contains no nodes. This is particularly useful when attempting to display the contents of the tree or remove nodes from the tree.

The next procedure will allow a new node to be attached to a tree. The following code should be examined in conjunction with the illustration in figure 15.7, of attaching a new node containing the fruit 'DATE' to the binary tree depicted in figure 15.6.

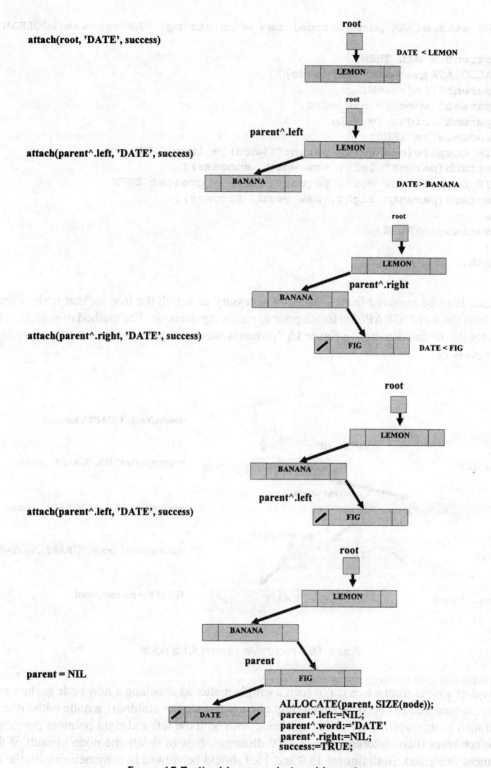

figure 15.7 attaching a node to a binary tree

```
PROCEDURE attach(VAR parent:tree; new_word:string; VAR success:BOOLEAN);
BEGIN
    IF parent = NIL THEN
        ALLOCATE(parent, SIZE(node));
        parent^.left :=NIL;
        parent^.word := new_word;
        parent^.right := NIL;
        success := TRUE;
    ELSIF Compare(new_word, parent^.word) = less THEN
        attach(parent^.left, new_word, success);
    ELSIF Compare(new_word, parent^.word) = greater THEN
        attach(parent^.right, new_word, success);
    ELSE
        success:=FALSE;
    END;
END attach;
```

When a node is to be removed from a tree it is necessary to search the tree for that node. Figure 15.8 illustrates how the word 'GRAPE' is found prior to removing the node. The method of searching through the tree is similar to that depicted in figure 15.7, when it was necessary to search for the correct place to insert the new node.

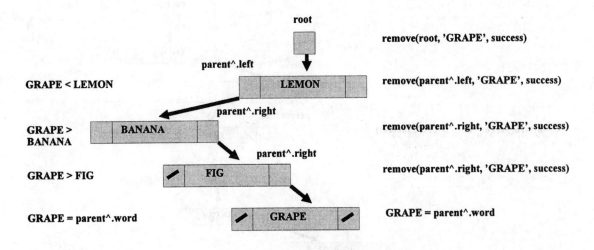

figure 15.8 recursive search for a node

The removal of a node from a tree is not such a simple matter as attaching a new node to the tree. When the node to be removed has been located it might be a leaf node (no children), a node with either the left or right branch pointers NIL (one child) or a node with both the left and right pointers pointing at two respective sub-trees (two children). Figure 15.9 illustrates how to delete the node in each of the three circumstances described. Both figures 15.8 and 15.9 should be viewed in conjunction with the code for the procedure to remove a node from the tree.

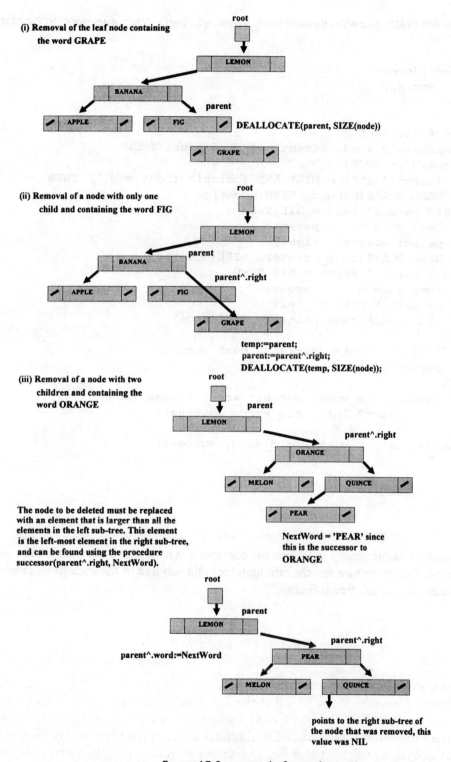

(i) Removal of the leaf node containing the word GRAPE

root

LEMON

BANANA

parent

APPLE   FIG

DEALLOCATE(parent, SIZE(node))

GRAPE

(ii) Removal of a node with only one child and containing the word FIG

root

LEMON

BANANA

parent

APPLE   FIG

parent^.right

GRAPE

temp:=parent;
parent:=parent^.right;
DEALLOCATE(temp, SIZE(node));

(iii) Removal of a node with two children and containing the word ORANGE

root

LEMON   parent

parent^.right

ORANGE

MELON   QUINCE

PEAR

The node to be deleted must be replaced with an element that is larger than all the elements in the left sub-tree. This element is the left-most element in the right sub-tree, and can be found using the procedure successor(parent^.right, NextWord).

NextWord = 'PEAR' since this is the successor to ORANGE

root

LEMON   parent

parent^.right

parent^.word:=NextWord

PEAR

MELON   QUINCE

points to the right sub-tree of the node that was removed, this value was NIL

figure 15.9 removal of a node

```
PROCEDURE remove(VAR parent:tree; old_word:string; VAR success:BOOLEAN);

VAR
   temp_pointer : tree;
   next_word : string;

BEGIN
     IF parent # NIL THEN
        IF Compare(old_word, parent^.word) = equal THEN
           success := TRUE;
           IF (parent^.left = NIL) AND (parent^.right = NIL) THEN
              DEALLOCATE(parent, SIZE(node));
           ELSIF parent^.left = NIL THEN
              temp_pointer := parent;
              parent:=parent^.right;
              DEALLOCATE(temp_pointer, SIZE(node));
           ELSIF parent^.right = NIL THEN
              temp_pointer := parent;
              parent := parent^.left;
              DEALLOCATE(temp_pointer, SIZE(node));
           ELSE
              successor(parent^.right, next_word);
              parent^.word := next_word;
           END;
        ELSIF Compare(old_word, parent^.word) = less THEN
           remove(parent^.left, old_word, success);
        ELSE
           remove(parent^.right, old_word, success);
        END;
     ELSE
        success:=FALSE;
     END;
END remove;
```

The procedure *successor* is necessary in finding the contents of a node that is the next in sequence to the node to be removed. The procedure searches through the right sub-tree of the node to be removed until the left-most element in this sub-tree is found.

```
PROCEDURE successor(VAR parent:tree; VAR next_word:string);
VAR
    temp_pointer : tree;

BEGIN
    IF parent # NIL THEN
        IF parent^.left = NIL THEN
            next_word := parent^.word;
            temp_pointer := parent;
            parent := parent^.right;
            DEALLOCATE(temp_pointer, SIZE(node));
        ELSE
            successor(parent^.left, next_word);
        END;
    END;
END successor;
```

The method of displaying the contents in sequential order, of the tree, uses as an in-order tree traversal. During an in-order traversal, the contents each node is displayed after all nodes in its left sub-tree, but before any node in its right subtree. Figure 15.10 illustrates the recursive execution of the procedure display, used to output the binary tree containing three nodes depicted in figure 15.3.

```
PROCEDURE display(VAR parent:tree);
BEGIN
    IF parent # NIL THEN
        display(parent^.left);
        WriteString(parent^.word);
        WriteLn;
        display(parent^.right);
    END;
END display;
```

To digress from the formation of the implementation module *TreeIO*. There are two other methods for traversing a binary tree - pre-order and post-order traversals. In a pre-order traversal a node is processed before the computer traverses either of the node's subtrees, however, with a post-order traversal both the subtrees of a node are traversed before processing the node. Figure 15.11 shows a binary tree containing numerical data and the results of performing pre-order and post-order traversals to output the data.

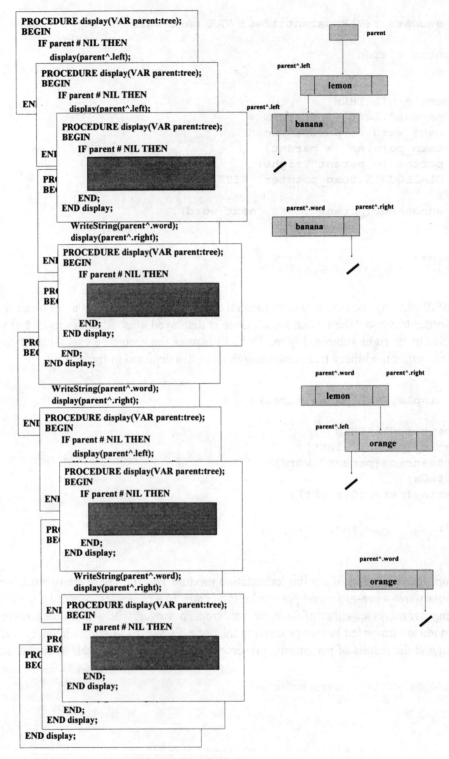

figure 15.10 recursive in-order traversal of tree

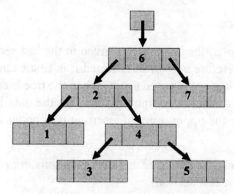

figure 15.11 binary tree of numbers

Pre-order

```
PROCEDURE pre-order(VAR parent : tree);
BEGIN
    IF parent # NIL THEN
        WriteCard(parent^.number, 2);
        pre-order(parent^.left);
        pre-order(parent^.right);
    END;
END pre-order;
```

Output from the pre-order traversal would be:

6 2 1 4 3 5 7

Post-order

```
PROCEDURE post-order(VAR parent : tree);
BEGIN
    IF parent # NIL THEN
        post-order(parent^.left);
        post-order(parent^.right);
        WriteCard(parent^.number, 2);
    END;
END post-order;
```

Output from the post-order traversal would be:

1 3 5 4 2 7 6

15.4 Binary tree maintenance

In the final program of this chapter, the list of fruits given in the last section, are each read from a text file and stored in a binary tree. Before each fruit is stored it is first examined to see whether it already exists in the tree. If it does exist it is not inserted again. When the tree is completely built it is recursively searched and the contents of each node is output. Notice that the data is now sorted into alphabetical sequence. The user is then given the opportunity of inserting new nodes or deleting existing nodes from the tree.

The program imports the abstract data type *tree* and the operations *initialise*, *empty*, *attach*, *remove* and *display* that were explained in the last section.

```
MODULE tree_ex;
(*
program to either insert, delete or display words in a binary tree
*)

FROM TreeIO IMPORT tree, initialise, empty, attach, remove, display;
FROM STextIO IMPORT ReadChar, ReadString, WriteString, WriteLn, SkipLine;
FROM StringType IMPORT string;

CONST
    insert = 'A';
    delete = 'R';
    show   = 'D';
    quit   = 'Q';

VAR
  binary_tree : tree;
  word        : string;
  success     : BOOLEAN;
  reply       : CHAR;

PROCEDURE menu():CHAR;
(*
function to return the choice made from the menu
*)

VAR
  reply : CHAR;

BEGIN
    WriteLn;
    WriteString('Do you want to:'); WriteLn;
    WriteString('[A]ttach a word to the tree'); WriteLn;
    WriteString('[R]emove a word from the tree'); WriteLn;
    WriteString('[D]isplay the contents of the tree'); WriteLn;
    WriteString('[Q]uit the program'); WriteLn;
```

```
    REPEAT
        WriteString('input A, R, D or Q ');
        ReadChar(reply);  SkipLine;
        reply := CAP(reply);
    UNTIL (reply = 'A') OR (reply = 'R') OR (reply = 'D') OR (reply = 'Q');
    WriteLn;
    RETURN reply;
END menu;

BEGIN
    initialise(binary_tree);
    reply := menu();
    WHILE reply # quit DO
        CASE reply OF

        insert : REPEAT
                    WriteString('word? ');
                    ReadString(word);
                    attach(binary_tree, word, success);
                 UNTIL success |

        delete : REPEAT
                    WriteString('word? ');
                    ReadString(word);
                    remove(binary_tree, word, success);
                 UNTIL success OR empty(binary_tree) |

        show   : WriteLn;
                 IF empty(binary_tree) THEN
                    WriteString('tree empty');
                    WriteLn;
                 ELSE
                    display(binary_tree);
                 END;
                 WriteLn;

        END;
        reply := menu();
    END;
END tree_ex.
```

Results from program tree_ex being run

```
Do you want to:
[A]ttach a word to the tree
[R]emove a word from the tree
[D]isplay the contents of the tree
[Q]uit the program
input A, R, D or Q A

word? apple

Do you want to:
[A]ttach a word to the tree
[R]emove a word from the tree
[D]isplay the contents of the tree
[Q]uit the program
input A, R, D or Q A

word? orange

Do you want to:
[A]ttach a word to the tree
[R]emove a word from the tree
[D]isplay the contents of the tree
[Q]uit the program
input A, R, D or Q A

word? banana

Do you want to:
[A]ttach a word to the tree
[R]emove a word from the tree
[D]isplay the contents of the tree
[Q]uit the program
input A, R, D or Q A

word? melon

Do you want to:
[A]ttach a word to the tree
[R]emove a word from the tree
[D]isplay the contents of the tree
[Q]uit the program
input A, R, D or Q A

word? fig
```

```
Do you want to:
[A]ttach a word to the tree
[R]emove a word from the tree
[D]isplay the contents of the tree
[Q]uit the program
input A, R, D or Q D


apple
banana
fig
melon
orange

Do you want to:
[A]ttach a word to the tree
[R]emove a word from the tree
[D]isplay the contents of the tree
[Q]uit the program
input A, R, D or Q R

word? lemon
word? orange

Do you want to:
[A]ttach a word to the tree
[R]emove a word from the tree
[D]isplay the contents of the tree
[Q]uit the program
input A, R, D or Q D


apple
banana
fig
melon

Do you want to:
[A]ttach a word to the tree
[R]emove a word from the tree
[D]isplay the contents of the tree
[Q]uit the program
input A, R, D or Q X
input A, R, D or Q Q
```

15.5 Summary

☐ Data abstraction is the technique of combining a data type with a set of operations on data of the same type.

☐ An abstract data type may appear in the definition module, but is implemented as a pointer to a type in the implementation module. Hence the type in the definition module is described as opaque.

☐ Since an abstract data type is opaque, the method of implementing the type is hidden from the user. This implies that provided the definition module remains unchanged, the method of implementing the type and operations upon that type can be changed without the user of the module being aware of the changes.

☐ A binary tree is a structure in which each node contains two pointers. If the data to be stored in the tree is less than the contents of the current node the data is stored in the node indicated by the left-hand pointer, otherwise, the data is stored in the node indicated by the right-hand pointer.

☐ Because of the manner in which data can be stored in a binary tree, an *in order* traversal of a tree will result in the *contents* of each node being accessed in sequence, therefore, the data can be accessed as if it was sorted.

15.6 Questions - *answers begin on page 418*

1. Include in the DEFINITION and IMPLEMENTATION modules of StackIO, a function that will return the size of a stack. Use this new function to modify procedure push, so that a test on the maximum size of the stack can be made before inserting a new record.

2. Write DEFINITION and IMPLEMENTATION modules for the abstract data structure FIFOq. This structure will be used in the next question. The format of the record structure for the node from the data required in the question is:

```
node =    RECORD
            CustomerNumber  : CARDINAL;
            TimeOfArrival   : CARDINAL;
            ServiceTime     : CARDINAL;
            link            : FIFOq;
          END;
```

where *CustomerNumber* is a value that identifies a particular customer; *TimeOfArrival* is the time in minutes when the customer enters the queue, if one exists; *ServiceTime* is the time in minutes for the customer, having left the queue, to be served; and *link* is a FIFOq is a pointer to *node*.

3. Write a program to simulate the arrival of customers at a single check-out in a supermarket. Your model should cater for the arrival of at least twenty customers. Use a random number generator to produce a number in the range 1-100, to represent a cumulative percentage. The appropriate time interval for the inter- arrival times and service times can then be obtained from the following tables.

Inter-arrival time distribution. (time between customers arriving)

time interval	cumulative %
0.1- 1.0	8
1.1- 2.0	25
2.1- 3.0	50
3.1- 4.0	70
4.1- 5.0	85
5.1- 6.0	89
6.1- 7.0	93
7.1- 8.0	95
8.1- 9.0	97
9.1-10.0	100

Thus given a random number of, say, 33 would yield an inter-arrival time of between 2.1 and 3.0 minutes. The mean value in this range can be taken giving an inter-arrival time of 2.55 minutes.

Service time distribution. (time spent at the check-out not in the queue)

time interval	cumulative %
1.0-1.5	15
1.5-2.0	40
2.0-2.5	60
2.5-3.0	75
3.0-3.5	85
3.5-4.0	90
4.0-4.5	95
4.5-5.0	100

The same method of generating a service time is used as for generating an inter-arrival time, a random number of 84 would yield a service-time of between 3.0 - 3.5 minutes. The mean value being 3.25 minutes. Use a FIFO queue to simulate the customers waiting to be served. In each node store the customer number, time of arrival and the time to be spent at the check-out. Each time a customer has completed a transaction at the check- out display the time elapsed since the customer joined the queue and the present size of the queue.

4. Modify TreeIO to store cardinal numbers and re-name the modules *BinTreeIO*. Generate a set of random numbers and store them in a binary tree. Output the numbers sorted into ascending order.

5. If the values of operands are stored in a linked list then using the following procedure evaluate a reverse polish string. Traverse the string from left to right and continue to push operands on the stack until an operator is encountered. For a unary operator pop an operand from the stack, evaluate it and push the

result back on the stack. For a binary operator pop two operands from the stack, evaluate the result and push the answer back on the stack. Continue traversing the reverse polish string until the end of the string, then pop the contents of the stack and display this value. You will need to modify StackIO to cater for storing real numbers and re-name it as *Stack*. Introduce the abstract data type *list* to represent a linked list and its associated operations.

6. A graph consists of nodes and edges. A node is a basic component, which usually contains some information. An edge connects two nodes. A directed graph, often called a digraph, is a graph whose edges have direction. Thus an edge not only relates two nodes, it also specifies a predecessor - successor relationship. Figure 15.12 illustrates a directed graph. The direction of each edge is denoted by an arrow. The predecessor - successor relationship between the nodes can be represented as characters in a file as follows.

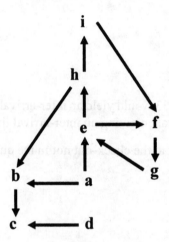

figure 15.12 an example of a directed graph

abe (implying that if a is the predecessor then b and e are its respective successors)
bc
c (implying that c has no successor)
dc
efh
fg
ge
hbi
if

This information can be stored in an array of linked lists as depicted by the array, direction, in figure 15.13. The array, visit, in the same diagram, is used to tag with TRUE or FALSE the nodes that have already been visited.

Write a procedure BuildGraph that reads the file of directed edges and places each direction in the node of a linked list as illustrated in figure 15.13. The head of each linked list is stored in the array named direction. Output the contents of this structure to verify that your program is correct.

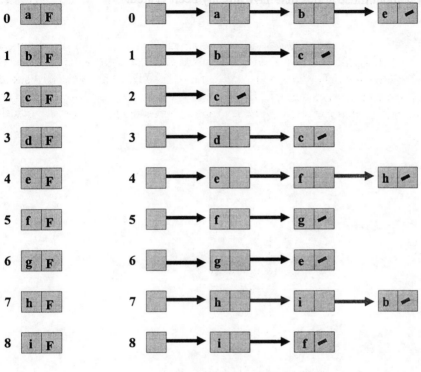

Array visit is used to tag a point when it has been visited

Array direction stores pointers to linked lists. Each linked list represents the points on the graph that can be visited from one starting point

figure 15.13 graph as an array of linked lists

7. Using the representation of the directed graph created in the last question, write a program to input start and finish nodes, then compute the series of nodes that must be visited to complete the journey. Alternatively, specify if the journey is not possible. For example, given the start node as (f) and the finish node as (b), the series of nodes that must be visited to travel from (f) to (b) is (fgehb). If the start node was (f) and the finish node was (a) then the journey is not possible since there is no connection in the direction (e) to (a) or (b) to (a).

Pay particular attention to:

   (i) backtracking from a dead-end, and
   (ii) not going around part of the graph in circles.

Hints. For every node visited push its value on to a stack. This will simplify re-tracing your steps, since backtracking would involve popping nodes from the stack.

Whenever a node in the linked list is visited, delete it from the list. Thus the head of each linked list will always point to the next possible node to visit. The structure depicted in figure 15.13 can always be rebuilt by reading the contents of the data file again. Keep the contents of the array named visit up-to-date since this contains the information about those nodes that have already been visited.

Chapter 16
Coroutines and quasi-concurrency

When Niklaus Wirth developed Modula-2, he intended the language to be used for many applications, including the programming of operating, control and simulation systems.

Up to now all the programs in this book have been written using a collection of instructions that are obeyed by the computer in a directed sequence. However, in the development of systems programs it is quite common for many different sequences of instructions to be executed in parallel, and together they cooperate towards the solution of the problem. A language suitable for systems programming must, therefore, have some form of provision for concurrent programming.

This final chapter explores the facilities in the language that simulate concurrent programming and interrupt handling through the use of coroutines. By the end of the chapter the reader should have an understanding of the following topics.

- [ ] The difference between a coroutine and a procedure.
- [ ] The creation of coroutines from procedures.
- [ ] The control of quasi-concurrent processes on a single processor machine.
- [ ] Use of coroutines as interrupt handlers.
- [ ] Scheduling of processes.
- [ ] Control and synchronisation of competing processes.

16.1 Coroutines

A *coroutine* can be used to simulate a process. A concurrent program is one that contains at least two sequential processes that are executed in parallel and cooperate towards the solution to a problem. On a single processor pseudo-concurrency is possible by interleaving the execution of each sequential process. Given two sequential processes A and B, the interleaving of the two processes implies that the processor executes part of process A, suspends A; executes part of process B, suspends B; resumes the execution of process A, and so on. Since the execution of coroutines can be organised in this way, they serve the purpose of simulating concurrency on a single processor.

By now the reader is all too familiar with the behaviour of a procedure. The computer executes the statements in the procedure from the first statement to a RETURN or to the last statement in the procedure. Upon entering the procedure all local variables are initialised and upon leaving the procedure the values of all local variables are lost. Their life-span is dependent upon the time spent in the procedure.

A coroutine differs from a procedure in several respects. The first call to a coroutine will result in the entry point being the first executable statement of the coroutine. The coroutine can be exited from any position within the body of the coroutine. However, the re-entry point will always be the statement after the last statement to be executed in the coroutine, when it was last visited. The values of all local variables are only initialised upon the first entry into the coroutine. Prior to an exit from the coroutine, the values of all local variables will be saved, therefore, upon re-entry into the code the values of the variables will indicate the state of the coroutine prior to the previous exit. Figure 16.1 contrasts the flow of control in one subroutine calling another subroutine, against control being passed between two coroutines.

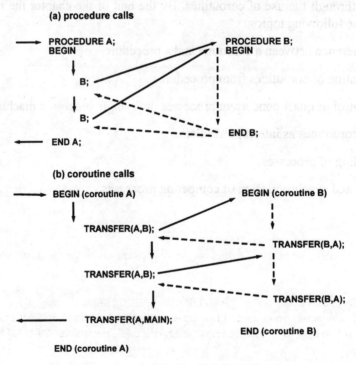

figure 16.1 procedure and coroutine calls

16.2 Coroutine creation

A coroutine is not explicitly declared, but created from a procedure. The creation and transfer of control between coroutines is controlled through procedures defined in the module COROUTINES.

```
DEFINITION MODULE COROUTINES;
(* facilities for coroutines and the handling of interrupts *)

IMPORT _SYSTEM;

TYPE
   COROUTINE;
   (* values of this type are created dynamically by NEWCOROUTINE
   and identify the coroutine in subsequent operations *)

PROCEDURE NEWCOROUTINE (procBody       : PROC;
                        workspace      : _SYSTEM.ADDRESS;
                        size           : CARDINAL;
                        VAR cr         : COROUTINE);
(* creates a new coroutine whose body is given by procBody, and returns
the identity of the coroutine in cr; workspace is a pointer to the work
space allocated to the coroutine; size specifies the size of this workspace
in terms of SYSTEM.LOC *)

PROCEDURE TRANSFER (VAR from : COROUTINE; to : COROUTINE);
(* returns the identity of the calling coroutine in from, and transfers
control to the coroutine specified by to *)

PROCEDURE IOTRANSFER (VAR from : COROUTINE; to : COROUTINE);
(* returns the identity of the calling coroutine in from and transfers
control to the coroutine specified by to; on occurrence of an interrupt,
associated with the caller, control is transferred back to the caller, and
the identity of the interrupted coroutine is returned in from. The calling
coroutine must be associated with a source of interrupts *)

PROCEDURE ATTACH (source : CARDINAL);
(* associates the specified source of interrupts with the calling
coroutine *)

PROCEDURE DETACH(source : CARDINAL);
(* dissociates the specified source of interrupts from the calling
coroutine *)

PROCEDURE IsATTACHED(source : CARDINAL) : BOOLEAN;
(* returns TRUE if and only if the specified source of interrupts is cur-
rently associated with a coroutine, otherwise returns FALSE *)
```

```
PROCEDURE HANDLER(source : CARDINAL) : COROUTINE;
(* returns the coroutine, if any, that is associated with the source of
interrupts; the result is undefined if IsATTACHED(source) = FALSE *)

PROCEDURE CURRENT() : COROUTINE;
(* returns the identity of the calling coroutine *)

END COROUTINES.
```

The _SYSTEM module imported by module COROUTINES provides low-level facilities for gaining access to the addresses and the underlying storage of variables, and for performing address arithmetic. **Notice that in the context of this chapter SYSTEM has been given an alias of _SYSTEM.** *TopSpeed* **Modula-2 also contains a module called SYSTEM, and without the alias there would be a duplication of names.**

The type ADDRESS imported from _SYSTEM refers to the address of a location in memory and is compatible with all pointer types. ADDRESS is defined within _SYSTEM as a POINTER TO LOC, where LOC refers to the smallest addressable unit of storage. The type LOC has been introduced into the *Draft Standard* as a mechanism to resolve the problem that, in many implementations of Modula-2, both BYTE and WORD occur in SYSTEM. Its introduction allows a consistent handling of both these types.

A function exported by _SYSTEM, that will be used later in the chapter is TSIZE which returns the number of LOCs used to store a value of specified type.

Procedures exported by COROUTINES include:

NEWCOROUTINE(procedure_name, work_space_address, work_space_size, coroutine_name) - creates a new coroutine and assigns the work space to it. Where **procedure_name** is a parameterless procedure of type PROC; **work_space_address** is a pointer to the work space of the coroutine; **work_space_size** is the size in LOCs of the work space allocated to the coroutine; and **coroutine_name** is a variable name that stores the address of the newly created coroutine. For example

NEWCOROUTINE(input_output, work_space1, TSIZE(work_space1), co_1);

work_space1 is the address of the workspace allocated by Storage.ALLOCATE(work_space1, work_space_size) where work_space_size is defined as a constant of 2 Kbytes.

Before a coroutine can be created it must be given an area of memory for workspace. The workspace is a fixed-size area in which to store the state of the coroutine when it becomes suspended. Data belonging to the coroutine's local variables and the coroutine's stack are stored in the workspace.

The workspace can be created from one of three different areas of memory, depending upon how permanent the coroutine is likely to be.

When a coroutine has the same life span as the program then the coroutine's workspace should be stored with the programs global variables.

If a coroutine only exists when a procedure is active then the workspace should be created with the procedure's local variables.

Finally, if the coroutines are created and destroyed in an arbitrary manner, then the workspace should be allocated from the system heap, in the same way as pointer variables are allocated space.

The effect of NEWCOROUTINE is to create a process out of an existing parameterless procedure. NEWCOROUTINE does not cause the process to execute.

16.3 Coroutine transfer

The COROUTINES module contains a further procedure, TRANSFER, which serves two purposes. Firstly, it causes a newly created coroutine to be executed.

```
NEWCOROUTINE(input_output, work_space1, TSIZE(work_space1), co_1);
TRANSFER(main, co_1);
```

Secondly, allows a previously suspended coroutine to resume execution.

```
TRANSFER(co_2, co_1);
```

In the example that follows, coroutine co_1 reads a string from the keyboard and stores it in a global string array. The first character is obtained from the string array and control then passes to a second coroutine co_2, which inspects the character for a vowel. If it is a vowel a vowel-counter is increased. Control returns to the first coroutine co_1, where the next character is obtained from the global string array.

Since control oscillates between the two coroutines, the only way to return back to the main program is when the end of the string is detected. Control then passes from the first coroutine co_1, back to the main program after the number of vowels in the string have been displayed.

Note that a coroutine should never be allowed to terminate, since the system cannot determine which coroutine should execute next, and the program will be prematurely terminated. Control should always be transferred to another coroutine or the main program.

```
MODULE co_ex1;
(* program to demonstrate change of control between coroutines *)

IMPORT Storage;
FROM _SYSTEM IMPORT TSIZE, ADDRESS;
FROM COROUTINES IMPORT NEWCOROUTINE, TRANSFER, COROUTINE;
FROM STextIO IMPORT ReadString, WriteString, WriteLn;
FROM SWholeIO IMPORT WriteCard;
FROM StringType IMPORT string;

CONST
    work_space_size = 2048;
    null            = 0C;

VAR
    work_space1, work_space2 : ADDRESS;
    main, co_1, co_2         : COROUTINE;
```

```
    character                    : CHAR;
    vowel_count, index           : CARDINAL;
    text                         : string;

PROCEDURE input_output;
(* procedure to input a line of text; transfer to another coroutine to
analyse the text character by character, and finally when the end of the
text is encountered, output the number of vowels in the text *)

BEGIN
    vowel_count := 0;
    WriteString('input a line of text'); WriteLn;
    ReadString(text);
    index:=0;
    character := text[index];
    WHILE character # null DO
        TRANSFER(co_1, co_2);
        INC(index);
        character := text[index];
    END;
    WriteString('number of vowels in text is ');
    WriteCard(vowel_count, 2);
    WriteLn;
    TRANSFER(co_1, main);
END input_output;

PROCEDURE  analysis;
(* procedure to test a character for a vowel, and increase vowel count if
test is true *)

BEGIN
    LOOP
        character := CAP(character);
        CASE character OF
        'A','E','I','O','U' : INC(vowel_count);
        ELSE
            (* no nothing *)
        END;
        TRANSFER(co_2, co_1);
    END;
END analysis;

BEGIN
    Storage.ALLOCATE(work_space1, work_space_size);
    Storage.ALLOCATE(work_space2, work_space_size);
    NEWCOROUTINE(input_output, work_space1, TSIZE(work_space1), co_1);
    NEWCOROUTINE(analysis, work_space2, TSIZE(work_space2), co_2);
    TRANSFER(main, co_1);
END co_ex1.
```

```
input a line of text
Under the bridges of Paris we roam.
number of vowels in text is 11
```

16.4 Timing

The ability to access time and measure the passing of time is often necessary in the production of systems programs. In the next example a simple round-robin scheduler is created that allocates a slice of time to each coroutine.

A circular linked list is built containing pointers to the coroutines that have been created in the program. This forms a directory of the coroutines that are to be executed. By transferring from the main program to any of the coroutines in the circular linked list, and allocating a fixed amount of time for that coroutine to be executed, it is possible to allocate a slice of time to a particular coroutine. Control may be transferred many times from the coroutine back to the main program and from the main program back to the coroutine, before the time slice expires.

After the time-slice expires control is transferred to the next coroutine in the circular linked list, and the process repeats itself again until the time-slice expires again. Using this technique it is possible to share the processor equally between several quasi-concurrent processes.

The module SysClock - see appendix III, provides facilities for accessing a system clock that records the date and time of day.

In the program that follows the function elapsed-time uses SysClock to return the elapsed time in hundredths of a second since midnight.

```
MODULE co_ex2;
(* program to demonstrate the use of a round-robin scheduling algorithm *)

IMPORT Lib;
IMPORT SysClock;
IMPORT Storage;
FROM _SYSTEM IMPORT TSIZE, ADDRESS;
FROM COROUTINES IMPORT CURRENT, COROUTINE, NEWCOROUTINE, TRANSFER;
FROM STextIO IMPORT WriteChar;

CONST
    work_space_size = 2048;
    time_slice      = LONGCARD(1);     (* 1/100th second *)
    running_time    = LONGCARD(500);   (* 5 seconds *)

TYPE
    pointer = POINTER TO node;
    node    = RECORD
```

```
                        id    : COROUTINE;
                        link : pointer;
                END;

VAR
   work_space1, work_space2, work_space3 : ADDRESS;
   main, co_1, co_2, co_3                : COROUTINE;
   coroutine_list, temp                  : pointer;
   start_time, clock_time                : LONGCARD;

PROCEDURE create_list(VAR head : pointer; co_id : COROUTINE);
VAR
   temp : pointer;
BEGIN
     Storage.ALLOCATE(temp, TSIZE(node));
     temp^.id := co_id;
     temp^.link := head;
     head := temp;
END create_list;

PROCEDURE proc_a;
BEGIN
     LOOP
        WriteChar('a'); Lib.Delay(100);
        TRANSFER(co_1, main);
     END;
END proc_a;

PROCEDURE proc_b;
BEGIN
     LOOP
        WriteChar('b'); Lib.Delay(100);
        TRANSFER(co_2, main);
     END;
END proc_b;

PROCEDURE proc_c;
BEGIN
     LOOP
        WriteChar('c'); Lib.Delay(100);
        TRANSFER(co_3, main);
     END;
END proc_c;

PROCEDURE elapsed_time():LONGCARD;
(* function to return the elapsed time in hundredths of seconds since mid-
night *)
VAR
   info : SysClock.DateTime;
```

```
BEGIN
    SysClock.GetClock(info);
    RETURN 100 * ((3600 * LONGCARD(info.hour))
        + (60 * LONGCARD(info.minute))
        + LONGCARD(info.second)) + LONGCARD(info.fractions);
END elapsed_time;

BEGIN
    (* create the coroutines *)
    Storage.ALLOCATE(work_space1, work_space_size);
    Storage.ALLOCATE(work_space2, work_space_size);
    Storage.ALLOCATE(work_space3, work_space_size);

    NEWCOROUTINE(proc_a, work_space1, TSIZE(work_space1), co_1);
    NEWCOROUTINE(proc_b, work_space2, TSIZE(work_space2), co_2);
    NEWCOROUTINE(proc_c, work_space3, TSIZE(work_space3), co_3);

    (* build a linked list of pointers to coroutines *)
    coroutine_list := NIL;
    create_list(coroutine_list, co_1);
    create_list(coroutine_list, co_2);
    create_list(coroutine_list, co_3);

    (* create a circular linked list from the linked list *)
    temp := coroutine_list;
    WHILE temp^.link # NIL DO
        temp := temp^.link;
    END;
    temp^.link := coroutine_list;

    (* enter round-robin scheduler in which each coroutine is given an
    allotted time in which to run *)

    clock_time := elapsed_time();
    LOOP
        start_time := elapsed_time();
        REPEAT
            TRANSFER(main, coroutine_list^.id);
        UNTIL elapsed_time() - start_time > time_slice;


        (* select next coroutine to run *)
        coroutine_list := coroutine_list^.link;
        IF elapsed_time() - clock_time > running_time THEN EXIT; END;
    END;
END co_ex2.
```

Results from program co_ex2 being run

cbacbacbacbacbacbacbacbacbacbacbacbacbacbacbacb

16.5 Interrupt handling

Many systems need to respond to external events, such as a key being pressed, or a signal that a period of time has just ended. The occurrence of such events may require the processor to be used to execute a program to service the event causing the interruption. This implies that the currently running program should be suspended; enough information about the state of the processor prior to the suspension of the program should be maintained; a program to service the requirements of the external event must be executed, and when such servicing is complete the suspended program may continue execution from the point at which it was interrupted. A language suitable for systems programming must, therefore, have some form of provision for interrupt handling.

In Modula-2 a coroutine can serve as an interrupt handler.

For a coroutine to serve as an interrupt handler it is necessary to use at least two further procedures from the module COROUTINES.

ATTACH connects the calling coroutine to the source of the interrupts. For example ATTACH(60H) would associate the calling coroutine with the software interrupt vector address 60H.

IsATTACHED is a function that returns TRUE if and only if the source of interrupts is connected to any coroutine, otherwise it returns FALSE.

For example after ATTACH(60H) had been executed IsATTACHED(60H) would return the value TRUE.

IOTRANSFER(coroutine_1, coroutine_2);

When the interrupt handling coroutine_1 executes IOTRANSFER for the first time it associates coroutine_1 with the interrupt vector, then transfers control to coroutine_2, effectively suspending itself. When the processor receives an interrupt, the current coroutine is suspended, its reference is stored in coroutine_2 and control is transferred to coroutine_1, the interrupt handler. After executing the necessary code for handling the interrupt, coroutine_1 executes IOTRANSFER again, thus transferring control to the interrupted coroutine_2, and effectively suspends itself.

In the example that follows, use will be made of a *TopSpeed* Modula-2 procedure from the library *Lib*. Lib.Intr permits a software interrupt through user interrupt vectors 60H to 66H inclusive. A software interrupt is generated by the call Lib.Intr(r,60H) where r is defined as a variable of type *Registers* imported from the *TopSpeed* Modula-2 module SYSTEM.

A coroutine can be coded to act as an interrupt handler for a software interrupt as follows.

```
MODULE interrupt_test;
   .
   .

PROCEDURE interrupt_handler;
BEGIN
   ATTACH(60H); (* interrupt vector associated with calling coroutine *)
   LOOP
      IOTRANSFER(handler, main);
      STextIO.WriteString(' INTERRUPT ');
   END;
END interrupt_handler;

(* main program *)
BEGIN
   .
   .

   NEWCOROUTINE(interrupt_handler, work_space, TSIZE(work_space),handler);

   TRANSFER(main, handler);
   .
   .

   LOOP
      .
      .
      Intr(r,60H); (* software interrupt to interrupt vector 60H *)
      .
      .
   END;
END interrupt_test.
```

The interrupt vector 60H is associated with the interrupt_handler coroutine. Initially control is transferred to the coroutine *handler* (interrupt_handler); *handler* then suspends itself and control is returned to the main program. Only when a software interrupt is generated will the main program be suspended, control will pass to the coroutine *handler* and the interrupt routine will be executed. The interrupt handler then suspends itself and control is returned back to main.

The next worked example demonstrates the use of an interrupt handler in the simulation of an alarm clock. The interrupt handler contains code that generates the sound of a wake-up alarm. The user is requested to set the wake-up time of the alarm. When the current time is the same as the wake-up time a software interrupt causes the interrupt handler to be repeatedly called for ten seconds.

In this example use is made of the Sound, Delay and NoSound procedures from the *TopSpeed* Modula-2 module *Lib*.

```
MODULE co_ex3;
(* program to demonstrate the use of software interrupts and IOTRANSFER *)


IMPORT Storage;
FROM _SYSTEM IMPORT TSIZE, ADDRESS;
FROM COROUTINES IMPORT COROUTINE, NEWCOROUTINE, IOTRANSFER,
     ATTACH, TRANSFER;
FROM STextIO IMPORT WriteChar, WriteLn, WriteString;
FROM SWholeIO IMPORT WriteCard, ReadCard;

IMPORT Lib;
IMPORT SysClock;
IMPORT SYSTEM;
IMPORT Window;

CONST
    work_space_size = 2048;

VAR
  handler, main                        : COROUTINE;
  work_space                           : ADDRESS;
  alarm_hrs, alarm_mins, hrs, mins, secs : CARDINAL;
  info                                 : SysClock.DateTime;
  r                                    : SYSTEM.Registers;

PROCEDURE interrupt_handler;
(* when a software interrupt occurs, this coroutine will be executed *)

BEGIN
    ATTACH(60H);
    LOOP
        IOTRANSFER(handler, main);
        Lib.Sound(1000); (* play a 1000 Hz sound *)
        Lib.Delay(250);  (* for 250 millisecs *)
        Lib.NoSound;     (* stop playing sound *)
    END;
END interrupt_handler;

PROCEDURE display_time(hours, minutes : CARDINAL);
BEGIN
    Window.Clear;
    WriteCard(hours,2); WriteChar(':');
    WriteCard(minutes,2); WriteLn;
END display_time;

BEGIN
    Storage.ALLOCATE(work_space, work_space_size);
    NEWCOROUTINE(interrupt_handler, work_space,
                 TSIZE(work_space), handler);
```

```
    TRANSFER(main, handler);
    (* transfer to interrupt handler to establish link *)

    SysClock.GetClock(info);
    mins:=info.minute;
    display_time(info.hour, info.minute);

    WriteString('set alarm - hours? ');   ReadCard(alarm_hrs);
    WriteString('            minutes? '); ReadCard(alarm_mins);

  LOOP
      SysClock.GetClock(info);
      IF info.minute # mins THEN
        display_time(info.hour, info.minute);
      END;

      WHILE (alarm_hrs = info.hour) AND (alarm_mins = info.minute) AND
      (info.second < 10) DO
            Lib.Intr(r,60H); (* generate a software interrupt *)
            SysClock.GetClock(info);
      END;

      mins:=info.minute;
    END;
END co_ex3.
```

Results from program co_ex3 being run

```
 9:17
set alarm - hours? 9
          minutes? 18

the screen is cleared leaving the time displayed in the top left-hand cor-
ner and the alarm bell sounds for ten seconds

 9:18
^C
```

When the current time reaches 9:18 the wake-up alarm sounds for ten seconds. After the wake-up period the time is displayed once every minute. The program is terminated by pressing the control and break keys simultaneously.

16.6 A scheduler

Earlier in the chapter a round-robin scheduler was developed to allow a ring of coroutines to share the processor on a regular basis with each being allocated a slice of time. This simplistic model assumed that every coroutine in the ring was always ready to use the processor. However, this is not always the case, and in concurrent programming it is possible to classify a process as being in at least one of the following three states:

ready eligible to use the processor but not actually doing so;
current using the processor;
waiting ineligible to use the processor until the occurrence of one of a set of events for which it is waiting.

It is possible to construct a scheduler for a single processor machine that uses coroutines to represent processes, and still take into account the state of a process.

The module Concurrent defines a set of procedures that permit the scheduling of quasi-concurrent processes. Concurrent is NOT defined in the *Draft Standard*.

```
DEFINITION MODULE Concurrent;

TYPE  CONDITION;

PROCEDURE CreateProcess(process : PROC);
(* activate procedure process as a process which runs concurrently with
the calling process *)

PROCEDURE EndProcess;
(* terminate the calling process *)

PROCEDURE StartScheduler;
(* the created processes become part of a non-pre-emptive round-robin
scheduler *)

PROCEDURE Initialise(VAR C:CONDITION);
(* create a condition queue C for use with Wait(C) and Signal(C) *)

PROCEDURE Wait(VAR C:CONDITION);
(* suspend currently running process and place on condition queue C *)

PROCEDURE Signal(VAR C:CONDITION);
(* resume the process waiting longest on condition queue C *)

PROCEDURE Awaited(C:CONDITION):BOOLEAN;
(* is any process awaiting a signal on condition queue C *)

END Concurrent.
```

A ring of processes can be constructed from the procedures that are identified as coroutines in a program. These processes are all eligible to run, and therefore, are in the ready state. Any one of the processes in this ring can be nominated as the current process and is using the processor.

If a current process calls to EndProcess, then the current process is removed from the ring and control passes to the next runnable process in the ring.

If a current process calls to Wait on a condition C, then the current process is removed from the ring and inserted into a FIFO queue of processes also waiting on the condition variable C. Control passes to the next eligible process in the ring.

If a current process calls to Signal on a condition C, then the process at the front of the FIFO queue of processes waiting on the condition variable C, is removed from the queue, and inserted back into the ring of runnable processes, in a position ahead of the currently running process. Control then passes to the process that has just been inserted back into the ring.

Notice that the scheduling of the change of control from one process to the next is not clock driven, as in the case of the simple round-robin scheduler given earlier, but event driven according to the procedures Wait, Signal, EndProcess and StartScheduler.

The program that follows is very similar to co_ex2, from section 16.4. The three processes proc_a, proc_b and proc_c are identical, however, the way in which the processes are scheduled differs from clock-driven to event driven.

```
MODULE co_ex4;
(* program to test procedures of Concurrent.MOD *)

IMPORT Lib;
FROM Concurrent IMPORT   CreateProcess,
                         StartScheduler,
                         Wait,
                         Signal,
                         Initialise,
                         CONDITION;

FROM STextIO IMPORT WriteChar;

VAR
  proc_a, proc_b : CONDITION;

PROCEDURE a;
BEGIN
  LOOP
    WriteChar('a'); Lib.Delay(250);
    Wait(proc_a);
    END;
END a;
```

```
PROCEDURE b;
BEGIN
  LOOP
    WriteChar('b'); Lib.Delay(250);
    Wait(proc_b);
  END;
END b;

PROCEDURE c;
BEGIN
  LOOP
    WriteChar('c'); Lib.Delay(250);
    Signal(proc_a);
    Signal(proc_b);
  END;
END c;

BEGIN
    CreateProcess(a);
    CreateProcess(b);
    CreateProcess(c);
    Initialise(proc_a);
    Initialise(proc_b);
    StartScheduler;
END co_ex4.
```

Results from program co_ex4 being run

abcabcabcabcabcabcabcabcabcabcabcabcabcabcabcabcabcabcabcabcabc^C

The characters ^C appear at the end of the output because the program was terminated by pressing the keys Ctrl and Break simultaneously.

In order to obtain a clearer understanding of the scheduler the listing of the implementation of Concurent is given here, and should be read in conjunction with together with figures 16.2 and 16.3.

```
IMPLEMENTATION MODULE Concurrent;

FROM Storage IMPORT ALLOCATE, DEALLOCATE;
FROM _SYSTEM IMPORT ADDRESS, TSIZE;
FROM COROUTINES IMPORT COROUTINE, NEWCOROUTINE, TRANSFER;

CONST
    workspace_size = 2048;
```

352

```
TYPE
    pointer = POINTER TO node;

    node = RECORD
                id   : COROUTINE;
                link : pointer;
           END;

    CONDITION = POINTER TO node;

VAR
    current                : pointer;
  (* pointer to current process in ready ring *)
    previous               : pointer;
  (* pointer to previous process in ready ring *)
    main                   : pointer;
  (* pointer to the main control program *)
    main_process           : COROUTINE;
  (* identification of the main control program *)
    number_of_processes : CARDINAL;
  (* number of processes in the ready ring *)

PROCEDURE CreateProcess(process : PROC);
VAR
  workspace : ADDRESS;

BEGIN
        (* insert a process into a ring of processes ready for activation *)

        INC(number_of_processes);
        previous := current;
        ALLOCATE(current, TSIZE(node));
        current^.link := previous^.link;
        previous^.link := current;
        ALLOCATE(workspace, workspace_size);
        NEWCOROUTINE(process, workspace, workspace_size, current^.id);
END CreateProcess;

PROCEDURE EndProcess;
VAR
  from, to : COROUTINE;

BEGIN
    (* delete a process from the ring of ready processes and activate the
    next process in the ring; if there are no further processes to run
    return to the main control program *)

    DEC(number_of_processes);
    IF number_of_processes = 0 THEN
```

```
            TRANSFER(current^.id, main^.id);
      ELSE
          from := current^.id;
          to   := current^.link^.id;
          previous^.link := current^.link;
          DEALLOCATE(current, TSIZE(node));
          current:=previous^.link;
          TRANSFER(from, to);
      END;
END EndProcess;

PROCEDURE StartScheduler;
BEGIN
      (* create a new ring of processes that are ready to be activated from
      the original ring of processes, but exclude the main process to avoid
      premature re-activation of the main control program *)

      current^.link := main^.link;
      previous := current;
      current := current^.link;
      TRANSFER(main^.id, current^.id);
END StartScheduler;

PROCEDURE Initialise(VAR C:CONDITION);
BEGIN
   (* set the head of a condition queue to nil, implying that it is empty *)
      C := NIL;
END Initialise;

PROCEDURE insert(VAR q : CONDITION; process : COROUTINE);
VAR
   temp : pointer;
   rear : pointer;

BEGIN
      (* find the rear of a condition queue *)
      temp:=pointer(q);
      WHILE temp # NIL DO
             rear := temp;
             temp := temp^.link;
      END;

      (* insert a node at the rear of the condition queue *)
      ALLOCATE(temp, TSIZE(node));
      temp^.id := process;
      temp^.link := NIL;
```

```
    IF q = NIL THEN
        q := CONDITION(temp);
    ELSE
        rear^.link := temp;
    END;
END insert;


PROCEDURE remove(VAR q : CONDITION; VAR process : COROUTINE);
VAR
    temp : pointer;

BEGIN
    (* remove information from the front of the condition queue and delete
    the node at the head of the queue *)

    temp := pointer(q);
    process := q^.id;
    q:=CONDITION(q^.link);
    DEALLOCATE(temp, TSIZE(node));
END remove;


PROCEDURE Wait(VAR C : CONDITION);
VAR
    from, to : COROUTINE;

BEGIN
    (* suspend the currently running process by removing it from the ring
    of ready processes and placing it at the rear of the condition queue;
    if there are no more processes to run return to the main program
    otherwise activate the next process in the ring of ready processes *)

    DEC(number_of_processes);
    IF number_of_processes = 0 THEN
        TRANSFER(current^.id, main^.id);
    ELSE
        from := current^.id;
        to   := current^.link^.id;
        previous^.link := current^.link;
        insert(C,current^.id);
        DEALLOCATE(current, TSIZE(node));
        current:=previous^.link;
        TRANSFER(from, to);
    END;
END Wait;
```

```
PROCEDURE Signal(VAR C:CONDITION);
VAR
  process  : COROUTINE;
  temp     : pointer;
  from, to : COROUTINE;

BEGIN
    (* remove the process that is currently suspended at the front of the
    condition queue; insert this process into the ring of ready processes
    and activate the process; if the condition queue is already empty then
    do nothing *)

    IF C # NIL THEN
        remove(C, process);
        ALLOCATE(temp, TSIZE(node));
        temp^.id := process;
        temp^.link := current^.link;
        current^.link := temp;
        from := current^.id;
        to   := current^.link^.id;
        previous := current;
        current:=current^.link;
        INC(number_of_processes);
        TRANSFER(from, to);
    END;
END Signal;

PROCEDURE Awaited(C:CONDITION):BOOLEAN;
BEGIN
    RETURN (C # NIL);
END Awaited;

BEGIN
    (* create an entry for the main program as the current process on
    a one-node ring *)
    ALLOCATE(current, TSIZE(node));
    current^.link        := current;
    current^.id          := main_process;
    main                 := current;
    number_of_processes  := 0;
END Concurrent.
```

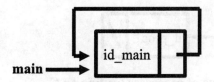

main program as the current process on a one-node ring

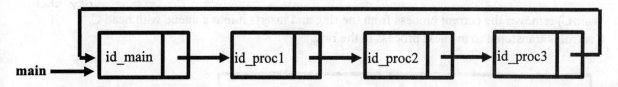

CreateProcess inserts new nodes into the ring of processes

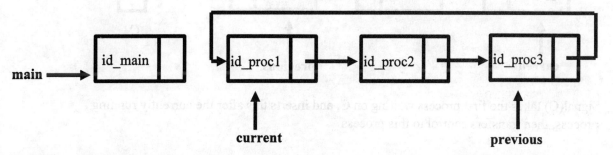

StartScheduler creates a ring of processes that excludes the main process, and transfers
control from the main process to the current process

figure 16.2

357

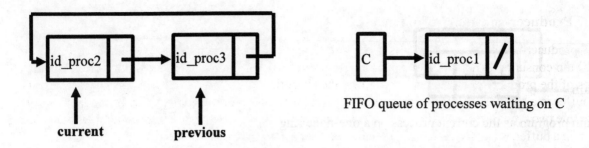

Wait(C) removes the current process from the ring and inserts it into a queue with head C. Control is transfered to the next process in the ring.

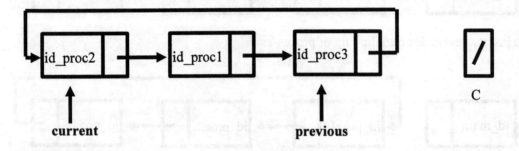

Signal(C) takes the first process waiting on C, and inserts this after the currently running process, then transfers control to this process

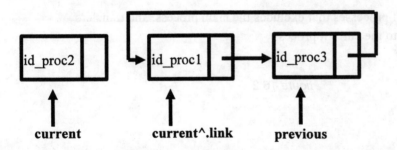

EndProcess will remove the current node from the ring and transfer control to current^.link. The current node then becomes previous^.link (the old value of current^.link)

figure 16.3

16.7 Producer-consumer problem

The producer-consumer problem arises because the producer of data must have somewhere to store it until the consumer is ready and the consumer must not try to consume data that is not there. If the data rates of the producer or consumer vary during the execution of the program then buffering is necessary. A buffer is a segment of memory common to both the producer and the consumer. In the next worked example two proceses execute in parallel, the first process *put_into*, generates random numbers and stores them in a buffer, ready for the second process *take_from*, to consume the random numbers from the buffer and display them on a screen.

A buffer is illustrated in figure 16.4 as an array of ten cells. A random number is stored in the buffer at the cell indexed by the variable *in*, and removed from the buffer at the cell indexed by the variable *out*. Initially, *in* and *out* are set at the first cell in the array. Every time a number is produced or consumed the appropriate index is moved along to the next cell in the array. When either index is at the tenth cell, the next cell to move to will be back to the first cell. This wrap-around effect is accomplished using modulo arithmetic. For example the statements *in := in MOD 10 + 1*; *out := out MOD 10 + 1*; manipulate the indices in the manner described.

The number of items that have not been consumed from the buffer is indicated by the variable *length*. The variable length is initally set at zero, whenever a number is stored in the buffer *length* is increased by 1, and whenever a number is consumed from the buffer *length* is decreased by 1.

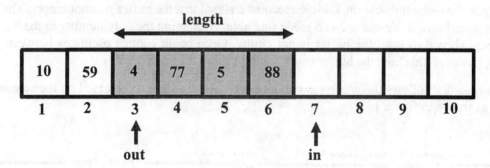

figure 16.4 A buffer

The production and consumption from the buffer must be regulated so that the process *put_into* cannot store numbers in a buffer that is already full, i.e. length = buffer_size. Similarly the process *take_from* cannot consume from an empty buffer, i.e. length = 0. This regulation can be achieved by using appropriate Wait and Signal statements within the two processes. For example,

PROCEDURE put_into;
.

  IF length = buffer_size THEN Wait(*until the buffer is not full*); END;
   .

   .
  Signal(*buffer not empty*);
END put_into;

PROCEDURE take_from;

   .

   IF length = 0 THEN Wait(*until buffer is not empty*); END;

   .

   .

   Signal(*buffer not full*);

   .

END take_from;

When these two processes run in a quasi-concurrent mode using the scheduler described in the previous section, the first runnable process *put_into* will run until the buffer is full. The process will then be queued on a suitable condition queue, waiting until the buffer is not full. The next process *take_from*, in the ring of runnable processes, will run until it signals that the buffer is not full. The process has in fact consumed just one number from the buffer, and has transferred control back to the process *put_into*. The process stores another random number in the buffer. The buffer is again full and since no process is waiting until the buffer is not empty, cannot signal and therefore must wait until the buffer is not full. Control continues to oscillate between the two processes, with the buffer never containing less than nine numbers to consume.

If the process *take_from* had been scheduled to run first it would have immediately been suspended and placed on a condition queue waiting until the buffer was not empty. The next runnable process in the ring would be *put_into* which would run until it executed a signal that the buffer was not empty. The process *take_from* would then be de-queued and made runnable, consuming the only number in the buffer. The process must then wait until the buffer is not empty. Once again control oscillates between the two processes, however, this time the buffer never contains more than one item!

In the example that follows the processes *put_into* and *take_from* are represented on the screen by two windows as shown in figure 16.5.

```
┌──────── put_into ─────────┐ ┌──────── take_from ────────┐
│   10   59    4   77    5  88  57  70  26  │ │   10   59    4   77    5  88  57  70  26  │
│ 90    7   26   89   80   17   86   54   13   36 │ │ 90    7   26   89   80   17   86   54   13   36 │
│   76   72    7   28   29   33   27   95   92   │ │   76   72    7   28   29   33   27   95   92   │
│ 30   58   92   44   32   93   54   10   80    6 │ │ 30   58   92   44   32   93   54   10   80    6 │
│    8   36   71   37   99   73   78   69    9  │ │                                           │
│ 57                                        │ │                                           │
│                                           │ │                                           │
│                                           │ │                                           │
│                                           │ │                                           │
└───────────────────────────┘ └───────────────────────────┘
```

figure 16.5

360

To provide the reader with the necessary background information to program these windows in *TopSpeed* Modula-2 it will be necessary to digress from the producer consumer problem.

TopSpeed Modula-2 provides a module called Window that will allow the screen to be divided up into several separate input and output areas.

A window is defined using the following record.

```
WinDef  = RECORD
                X1,Y1,X2,Y2               : AbsCoord; (* outer coordinates of opposite corners *)
                Foreground, Background : Color;
                CursorOn                  : BOOLEAN;
                WrapOn                    : BOOLEAN;
                Hidden                    : BOOLEAN;
                FrameOn                   : BOOLEAN;
                FrameDef                  : FrameStr;
                FrameFore, FrameBack   : Color;
            END;
```

For example,

```
CONST
    window_1 = Window.WinDef ( 0,0,39,15,
                          Window.White, Window.Black,
                          TRUE,
                          TRUE,
                          FALSE,
                          TRUE,
                          Window.SingleFrame,
                          Window.White, Window.Black);
```

A window can be opened for use by w1 := Window.Open(window_1) where w1 is declared as a variable of type Window.WinType. Similarly a window can be closed when no longer required by the statement Window.Close(w1).

A title may be inserted into the frame of a window by the statement:

Window.SetTitle(w1, 'put_into', Window.CentreUpperTitle);

Input or output may be directed to a particular window by the statement Window.Use(w1).

In the program that follows the process *put_into* generates a random number, displays it in window w1, and stores the number in a buffer. The process *take_from* consumes random numbers from the buffer and displays them in window w2. When this program runs, window w2 remains empty until ten random numbers have been generated and the buffer is full. Notice that process take_from has been allocated a time-slice in which to operate. When the time slice expires the process is terminated. At this point if the process *put_into* is waiting until the buffer is not full, then control returns to the main program.

```
MODULE co_ex5;

FROM Concurrent IMPORT   CreateProcess,
                         StartScheduler,
                         Wait,
                         Signal,
                         Initialise,
                         CONDITION,
                         EndProcess,
                         Awaited;

IMPORT Random;
IMPORT SWholeIO;
IMPORT Window;
IMPORT Lib;
IMPORT SysClock;

CONST
    time_slice  = 1000; (* units hundredths of a second *)
    buffer_size = 10;

    window_1 = Window.WinDef(
                             0,0,39,15,Window.White, Window.Black,
                             TRUE,TRUE,FALSE,TRUE,Window.SingleFrame,
                             Window.White, Window.Black
                          );

    window_2 = Window.WinDef(
                             40,0,79,15,Window.White, Window.Black,
                             TRUE,TRUE,FALSE,TRUE,Window.SingleFrame,
                             Window.White, Window.Black
                          );


VAR
    buffer              : ARRAY[1..buffer_size] OF CARDINAL;
    front, rear         : CARDINAL;
    length              : CARDINAL;
    not_full            : CONDITION;
    not_empty           : CONDITION;
    w1, w2              : Window.WinType;
    start_time          : LONGCARD;

PROCEDURE elapsed_time():LONGCARD;
VAR
    info : SysClock.DateTime;
```

```
BEGIN
    SysClock.GetClock(info);
    RETURN 100 * ((3600 * LONGCARD(info.hour))
    + (60 * LONGCARD(info.minute))
    + LONGCARD(info.second)) + LONGCARD(info.fractions);
END elapsed_time;

PROCEDURE put_into;
BEGIN
  LOOP
    IF length = buffer_size THEN Wait(not_full); END;
    Window.Use(w1);
    buffer[front]:=TRUNC(10000.0*Random.RND()) MOD 100 + 1;
    SWholeIO.WriteCard(buffer[front],4);
    front := front MOD buffer_size + 1;
    INC(length);
    IF Awaited(not_empty) THEN Signal(not_empty); END;
    Lib.Delay(250);
  END;
END put_into;

PROCEDURE take_from;
BEGIN
    start_time := elapsed_time();
    LOOP
        IF length = 0 THEN Wait(not_empty); END;
        Window.Use(w2);
        SWholeIO.WriteCard(buffer[rear],4);
        rear := rear MOD buffer_size + 1;
        DEC(length);
        IF Awaited(not_full) THEN Signal(not_full); END;
        IF elapsed_time() - start_time > time_slice THEN EXIT; END;
    END;
    EndProcess;
END take_from;

BEGIN
    (* open windows *)
    w1 := Window.Open(window_1);
    w2 := Window.Open(window_2);

    (* title each window *)
    Window.SetTitle(w1, 'put_into', Window.CenterUpperTitle);
    Window.SetTitle(w2, 'take_from', Window.CenterUpperTitle);

    front  := 1;
    rear   := 1;
    length := 0;
```

```
        CreateProcess(put_into);
        CreateProcess(take_from);
        Initialise(not_full);
        Initialise(not_empty);
        StartScheduler;

        (* close windows *)
        Window.Close(w1);
        Window.Close(w2);
END co_ex5.
```

The results from program co_ex5 being run are identical to those shown in figure 16.5

16.8 Monitors

In a concurrent environment, if two producer processes attempted to access a buffer at the same time, it could lead to disasterous circumstances. There would be a need to enforce a mutual exclusion between the competing processes such that only one process was allowed access to the buffer at any one time. A module which enforces the mutual exclusion property on the use of its exported procedures is called a *monitor*. Any process calling an exported procedure of such a module while another process is currently executing any exported procedure of the same module is forced to wait until either the other process has completed its execution of the exported procedure concerned, or has relinquished its exclusive access by executing either a Wait or Signal operation.

In Modula-2 a monitor can be represented by a local module (refer to section 14.9). A monitor is written as a set of variable declarations (global to the monitor), followed by a set of procedures, which may be have parameters. The monitor has a body which contains a sequence of statements that are executed immediately when the program is initialised.

The variables in a monitor are directly accessible only within the monitor procedures. Communication between a monitor and the outside world is through the parameters of the procedures. Since a monitor exists only as a package of data and procedures, the only way to execute the monitor is for a process to call a monitor procedure.

Access to the buffer described in the previous section can be guarded by the introduction of the monitor *buffer_io*. Random numbers are input to the buffer by calling *buffer_io.input(random_number)* and are consumed from the buffer by calling *buffer_io.output(random_number)*.

PROCEDURE put_into;
    .
    LOOP
        random_number := TRUNC(10000.0*Random.RND()) MOD 100 + 1;
        buffer_io.input(random_number);
    .
    END
END put_into;

```
PROCEDURE take_from;
    .
    LOOP
        .
        buffer_io.output(random_number);
        .
    END;
END take_from;

MODULE buffer_io;

IMPORT CONDITION, Wait, Signal, Awaited, Initialise, SWholeIO;
EXPORT QUALIFIED input, output;

CONST
    buffer_size = 10;

VAR
    buffer              : ARRAY[1..buffer_size] OF CARDINAL;
    in, out             : CARDINAL;
    length              : CARDINAL;
    not_full, not_empty : CONDITION;

PROCEDURE input(value : CARDINAL);
BEGIN
    IF length = buffer_size THEN Wait(not_full); END;
    buffer[in]:=value;
    in:=in MOD buffer_size + 1;
    INC(length);
    IF Awaited(not_empty) THEN Signal(not_empty); END;
END input;

PROCEDURE output(VAR value : CARDINAL);
BEGIN
    IF length = 0 THEN Wait(not_empty); END;
    value := buffer[out];
    out:=out MOD buffer_size + 1;
    DEC(length);
    IF Awaited(not_full) THEN Signal(not_full); END;
END output;

BEGIN
    length  := 0;
    in      := 1;
    out     := 1;
    Initialise(not_full);
    Initialise(not_empty);
END buffer_io;
```

16.9 Module priorities

An interrupt handler should not be interrupted by interrupts of equal or lower priority. Modula-2 allows the programmer to disable interrupts within a module by specifying a priority in the heading of that module, for example MODULE IRQ[5]; This priority is a command to disable interrupts of equal or lower priority.

When control enters a module whose heading specifies a priority value of 5, say, interrupts with a priority of 5 or less are disabled. Only when control leaves the module will the previous priority be restored.

Procedures within a module of fixed priority p, say, may call procedures outside that module, provided they are of a priority not less than p. If the called procedure is a higher priority, all interrupts with that priority are temporarily disabled until control returns back to the calling procedure. The priority then returns to that of the calling procedure.

16.10 Summary

☐ A coroutine may be regarded as re-entrant code. The re-entry point is always the next executable statement after the transfer statement that caused the previous exit from the coroutine.

☐ The local variables of a coroutine are only initialised once. These values are preserved upon transferring from the coroutine and are not initialised by re-entry to the coroutine.

☐ A coroutine can act as the service routine for an interrupt.

☐ Coroutines can be used to provide quasi-concurrency on a single processor computer.

☐ It is possible to organise a quasi-concurrent environment under which processes can either be currently active, ready to use the processor or suspended waiting on a queue for an event to happen.

☐ Coroutines can tranfer data between themselves by using global variables. Multiple access to shared variables in a quasi-concurrent environment does not present itself as a problem, since there can be only one process using the processor at any one time.

☐ In a concurrent environment, processes competing for the same shared variables must be controlled. In such circumstances it is necessary to allow one process to mutually exclude another process from accessing the same shared variables.

☐ A mechanism for protecting shared variables from multiple access at the same time is the monitor. In Modula-2 this is implemented as a local module. Access to the shared variables can only be gained through the access procedures of the monitor. Direct manipulation of the shared variables from competing processes is forbidden.

☐ A monitor will provide mutual exclusion between calls from different processes to the same access procedure, and deal with each process one at a time.

☐ Modules can be given priorities to prevent interruption from processes of a lower priority.

16.11 Questions - *answers begin on page 424*

1. Three processes A, B and C are to run on a single processor in a quasi-concurrent mode. Process A will read a stream of characters from a text data file and write this stream to a screen; process B will format the data stream into lines containing line numbers with no more than fifty characters to a line (excluding the line numbers); process C will write the formatted data stream to a new file. Write a program to implement the behaviour of the processes.

2. Write a software interrupt handler, that when called, displays the next value in a three digit octal number. Assume that a software interrupt is generated once every second, and that the octal numbers cycle through the range 000..777.

3. Write a process to read lines of text from a file and display these lines in a window. Write a second process that inserts a line number before each line read from the text file and displays the numbered line at a second window. Use the procedures *wait* and *signal* from the module *Concurrent* to alternate between the two processes.

4. A definition of the module *Semaphores* is listed below. Using many of the procedures available to you from the module Concurrent, write code to implement this definition.

```
DEFINITION MODULE Semaphores;

TYPE
    SEMAPHORE;

PROCEDURE Create(VAR s : SEMAPHORE; initialCount : CARDINAL);
(* creates and returns s as the identity of a new semaphore that has its
associated count initialised to initialCount, and has no processes yet
waiting on it *)

PROCEDURE Claim(s : SEMAPHORE);
(* if the count associated with the semaphore s is non-zero, decrements
this count and allows the calling process to continue; otherwise suspends
the calling process until s is released *)

PROCEDURE Release(s : SEMAPHORE);
(* if there are any processes waiting on the semaphore s, allows one of
them to enter the ready state; otherwise increments the count associated
with s *)

PROCEDURE CondClaim(s : SEMAPHORE):BOOLEAN;
(* if the call Claim(s) would cause the calling process to be suspended,
the count associated with s is not changed, and the procedure returns
FALSE; otherwise the associated count is decremented, and the procedure re-
turns TRUE *)

END Semaphores.
```

5. Modify the program *co_ex5*, from section 16.7, such that the condition variables are replaced by a single semaphore.

The semaphore is initialised to the size of the buffer, so that provided process *put_into* is executed first, the buffer will be filled. When the buffer becomes full process *put_into* is suspended and control passes to process *take_from*. After one cardinal number has been consumed from the buffer, the process *take_from* is suspended and control passes back to process *put_into*. This in turn replenishes the buffer with a single cardinal number, the process *put_into* becomes suspended and control passes to *take_from* to consume a second cardinal number from the buffer. Control continues to alternate between the two processes until a time out occurs.

Use the type SEMAPHORE and the procedures Create, Claim and Release from the module Semaphores in the implementation of your solution.

Appendices

Appendix I

Chapter 1

1. The activities associated with programming include:

Designing and testing an algorithm as a solution to a problem.
Coding the algorithm into a computer program using an appropriate language.
Testing the computer program to prove that it solves the problem.
Documenting the computer program so that it can be maintained by others at a later time.

2. Central processing unit, main memory, secondary storage units, input and output units.

In a personal computer the CPU and main memory are represented by silicon chips. Typical secondary storage units are the internal hard disk, and floppy drives. A common input unit is a keyboard with a pointing device known as a mouse. A common output unit would be a printer.

Main memory storage capacity is typically of the order of Mbytes, for example 8 Mb.
Hard disk storage capacity varies from say 100 Mb to 1000 Mb.
Floppy disk storage is typically small in comparison to a hard disk, for example 1.4 Mb is common.

3. Input units: keyboard, mouse, magnetic tape or disk, light pen.
Output units: screen, printer, plotter. Common input/ output units in a Modula-2 development environment are the keyboard, monitor (screen) and printer.

4. The advantages of networking computers together is to enable software to be distributed over the network without the need for each user to possess an individual copy of the software. Similarly common hardware resources such as printers and plotters can be accessed by all users of the network, without the need to provide each user with a separate item of hardware.

5. Modula-2 is a high-level language, therefore, the instructions are not in a machine recognisable form (machine code). A Modula-2 program must be translated into machine code using a compiler.

6. Phase 1 - creation of a Modula-2 program, in text mode, using an editor.
Phase 2 - translation of the program into a machine recognisable form using a compiler. Phase 3 - linking extra routines to allow the program to run (for example routines that permit input and output), and loading the program into the main memory of the computer. Phase 4 - program running on a computer (program execution).

7. The same program written in a high-level language for one dialect of Modula-2, can be compiled without modification using a compiler from a different dialect of Modula-2 and a different computer. The program when executed on both computers must produce the same results. Note that in Modula-2, incompatibility between dialects is most likely to be caused through the variation in libraries between different compiler writers, and the different word sizes between computers.

Low-level language statements are not portable between computers since the language statements relate to the specific architecture of the CPU.

Chapter 2

1. The data in the 'Used Cars for Sale', figure 2.13, are the details about each car and the price of each car. In Modula-2 this might be described as:

```
VAR
    details : string;
    price   : CARDINAL ;
```

In declaring the price of the car as being type CARDINAL it is assumed that there will be no price greater than £65535.

The data in the 'Statement of Account', figure 2.14, will cover such items as the name of the account, the year, the sheet number, the account number, the date of the transaction, the description of the transaction, the amount of the transaction, the balance and whether the balance is in credit or debit.

```
VAR
    name_of_account : string;
    year            : CARDINAL;
    sheet           : CARDINAL;
    account_number  : string;
    date            : string;
    transaction     : string;
    amount          : REAL;
    balance         : REAL;
    credit_debit    : CHAR;
```

The data in the 'Gas Bill', figure 2.15, will cover such items as the name and address of the consumer, the date of the bill, the date of the meter reading, the present and previous meter readings, the amount of gas supplied, the power consumed, the charge for using the amount of gas, the dates of the billing perios, the number of days in that period, the standing charge and the final amount due.

```
VAR
  customer_name    : string;
  address          : string;
  town             : string;
  postcode         : string;
  date_of_bill     : string;
  date_of_reading  : string;
  present_reading  : CARDINAL;
  estimate         : CHAR;
  previous reading : CARDINAL;
  gas supplied     : REAL;
  power consumed   : CARDINAL;
  gas charge       : REAL;
  previous_date_DD : CARDINAL;
  previous_date_MM : CARDINAL;
  previous_date_YY : CARDINAL;
  current_date_DD  : CARDINAL;
  current_date_MM  : CARDINAL;
  current_date_YY  : CARDINAL;
  days             : CARDINAL;
  standing_charge  : REAL;
  amount_due       : REAL;
```

Note - whenever a date is required in a calculation it is recommended to store the date as three separate cardinal values that represent DD MM YY.

2. Illegal names   reason for illegaility
   (b) net-pay   hyphen
   (d) cost of paper   embedded spaces
   (e) INTEGER   reserved word (pervasive identifier)
   (f) ?X?Y   question marks
   (g) 1856AD   variable name must start with a letter
                         or underscore

Note - Modula-2 identifiers are case sensative, for example the identifier cardinal is different from the reserved word CARDINAL

3.
(a) string
(b) REAL
(c) INTEGER or CARDINAL
(d) CHAR

Appendix I

(e) CARDINAL
(f) REAL
(g) INTEGER
(h) INTEGER
(i) INTEGER or CARDINAL
(j) CARDINAL (can also be a long integer)
(k) REAL

4.

	character	ASCII code
(a)	A	65
(b)	M	77
(c)	*	42
(d)	a	97
(e)	m	109
(f)	NUL	0
(g)	9	57

5.
(a) -8.74458E+02
(b) 1.23456E-03
(c) 1.23456789E+08

6.
(a) Exponent too large - overflow. Note 3.016E+39 is too large to store.
(b) Accuracy of the number will be lost, however, the approximation can be stored 1.23456789010E+09
(c) Exponent too small - underflow. Note -4.56E-43 is too small to store.

7.
+7384 = 0001100110011011000
-7384 = 1110011001101010001000 (2's complement)

8.
(a) 0.37948E17
(b) -0.26394782E1
(c) 0.739462134E3   truncation of digit 8
(d) -0.17694327E40 overflow
(e) 0.471E-40   underflow

9.
* ASCII code 42 = 00101010
7 ASCII code 55 = 00110111
z ASCII code 122 = 01111010

Appendix I

Chapter 3

1.

(a)
A	B	C	D
36	36	36	36

(b)
A	B	C	D
10	14	29	89

(c)
A	B
48	50

(d)
X	Y
-19	-13

(e)
X	Y	Z
18	3	54

(f)
A	B
12.5	2.0

(g)
A	B	X
16	3	5

(h)
C	D	Y
18	5	3

(i)
D	E
-16	-16.9

2.

(a) (A+B)/C
(b) (W-X)/(Y+Z)
(c) (D-B)/(2*A)
(d) (A*A+B*B)/2
(e) (A-B)*(C-D)
(f) B*B-4*A*C
(g) X*X*(A+B)+C

3.

(a) A B
      ^ no operator

(b) A*-Y
      ^ combined operators

(c) (64+B2)/-6
              ^ combined operators

(d) (A-B) (A+B)
         ^ no operator between parenthesis

(e) -2/A+-6
         ^ combined operators

(f) 1*(X-Y)
     -
     2
     ^ illegal division operator

4.

(a) $X + 2 + \dfrac{4}{Y}$

(b) $\dfrac{A.B}{C+2}$

(c) $\dfrac{U.W}{V.X}$

(d) $B^2 - 4.A.C$

(e) $\dfrac{A}{B} + \dfrac{C}{D} + \dfrac{E}{F}$

5.

```
MODULE C3Q5a;
FROM STextIO IMPORT WriteString, WriteLn;
BEGIN
    WriteString('Hello World');
    WriteLn;
END C3Q5a.

MODULE C3Q5b;
FROM STextIO IMPORT WriteString, ReadString, WriteLn;
FROM StringType IMPORT string;
VAR
    message : string;
BEGIN
    WriteString('input message ');
    ReadString(message);
    WriteString('My message to the World is ');
    WriteString(message);
    WriteLn;
END C3Q5b.
```

```
6.
MODULE C3Q6;
FROM SWholeIO IMPORT WriteInt;
FROM STextIO IMPORT WriteString, WriteLn;
VAR
   A, B   : INTEGER;
BEGIN
   A:=5;
   B:=9;
   WriteString('sum = ');              WriteInt(A+B, 6); WriteLn;
   WriteString('difference = ');       WriteInt(A-B, 6); WriteLn;
   WriteString('product = ');          WriteInt(A*B, 6); WriteLn;
   WriteString('integer division = '); WriteInt(A DIV B, 6);
   WriteLn;
   WriteString('remainder after integer division = ');
   WriteInt(A MOD B, 6); WriteLn;
END C3Q6.
```

```
7.
MODULE C3Q7;
FROM STextIO IMPORT WriteString, ReadString, WriteLn;
FROM SRealIO IMPORT ReadReal, WriteFixed;
FROM StringType IMPORT string;
CONST
   InchCm = 2.54;  (* 1 inch = 2.54 cm *)
   StoneKg = 6.364;(* 1 stone = 6.364 Kg *)
VAR
   name                    : string;
   HeightInch, WeightStone : REAL;  (* input values *)
   HeightCm, WeightKg      : REAL;  (* output values *)
BEGIN
   WriteString('input your name ');
   ReadString(name);
   WriteString('input your height in inches ');
   ReadReal(HeightInch);
   WriteString('input your weight in stones ');
   ReadReal(WeightStone);
   HeightCm:=HeightInch*InchCm;
   WeightKg:=WeightStone*StoneKg;
   WriteLn;
   WriteString('PERSONAL DETAILS'); WriteLn;
   WriteString('NAME: ');
   WriteString(name); WriteLn;
   WriteString('HEIGHT (cm):'); WriteFixed(HeightCm,0,6);
   WriteLn;
   WriteString('WEIGHT (Kg): '); WriteFixed(WeightKg,0,6);
   WriteLn;
END C3Q7.
```

```
8.
MODULE C3Q8;
FROM STextIO IMPORT WriteString, WriteLn;
FROM SRealIO IMPORT ReadReal, WriteFixed;
VAR
   Fahrenheit, Centigrade : REAL;
BEGIN
   WriteString('input temperature in degrees Fahrenheit ');
   ReadReal(Fahrenheit);
   Centigrade := (Fahrenheit - 32.0) * (5.0/9.0);
   WriteString('temperature in degrees Centigrade ');
   WriteFixed(Centigrade,1,6); WriteLn;
END C3Q8.
```

```
9.
MODULE C3Q9;
FROM SRealIO IMPORT ReadReal, WriteFixed;
FROM STextIO IMPORT WriteString, WriteLn;
CONST
   border=0.5;  (* width of border *)
   turf=0.75;   (* cost of turfin £ *)
VAR
   length, width, GardenArea, LawnArea, cost : REAL;
BEGIN
   WriteString('input the length and width of the garden ');
   ReadReal(length); ReadReal(width);
   GardenArea:=length*width;
   LawnArea:=(length-(2.0*border))*(width-(2.0*border));
   cost:=turf*LawnArea;
   WriteString('Area of garden ');
   WriteFixed(GardenArea,1,6);
   WriteString(' Area of lawn '); WriteFixed(LawnArea,1,6);
   WriteLn;
   WriteString('cost of turfing lawn £');
   WriteFixed(cost,2,7);
   WriteLn;
END C3Q9.
```

```
10.
MODULE C3Q10;
FROM STextIO IMPORT WriteString, WriteLn;
FROM SWholeIO IMPORT ReadCard, WriteCard;
VAR
   money, twenty, ten, five, one : CARDINAL;
BEGIN
   WriteString('input an amount of money in £ ');
   ReadCard(money);
   twenty:=money DIV 20; money:=money MOD 20;
   ten:=money DIV 10; money:=money MOD 10;
   five:=money DIV 5; one:=money MOD 5;
```

```
  WriteString('Breakdown of notes into denominations');
  WriteLn;
  WriteString('£20 notes '); WriteCard(twenty, 6); WriteLn;
  WriteString('£10 notes '); WriteCard(ten,6); WriteLn;
  WriteString('£ 5 notes '); WriteCard(five,6); WriteLn;
  WriteString('£ 1 coins '); WriteCard(one, 6); WriteLn;
END C3Q10.

11.

MODULE C3Q11;
FROM STextIO IMPORT WriteString, WriteLn;
FROM SRealIO IMPORT ReadReal, WriteFixed;
VAR
  length, width, shallow, deep, volume : REAL;
BEGIN
  WriteString('input length '); ReadReal(length);
  WriteString('input width '); ReadReal(width);
  WriteString('input depth of shallow end ');
  ReadReal(shallow);
  WriteString('input depth of deep end '); ReadReal(deep);
  volume:=(length*width)*(shallow+deep)/2.0);
  WriteString('volume of water required to fill the pool ');
  WriteFixed(volume,1,10); WriteString(' cubic units');
  WriteLn;
END C3Q11.

12.

MODULE C3Q12;
FROM STextIO IMPORT WriteString, ReadChar, WriteLn;
FROM SRealIO IMPORT WriteFixed;
CONST
  pi = 3.14159;
  base_value = 48;
VAR
  character      : CHAR;
  decimal_number : REAL;
BEGIN
  WriteString('input a character in the range 0..9 ');
  ReadChar(character);
  decimal_number := pi * FLOAT(ORD(character) - base_value);
  WriteString('result of computation is ');
  WriteFixed(decimal_number,4,10); WriteLn;
END C3Q12.
```

13.

```
MODULE C3Q13a;
FROM STextIO IMPORT WriteString, WriteLn;
FROM SWholeIO IMPORT ReadInt;
FROM SRealIO IMPORT WriteFixed;
VAR
  x, y, z  : INTEGER;
  mean     : REAL;
BEGIN
  WriteString('input three integers separated by spaces
              e.g. 2 5 7 ');
  WriteString('then press the RETURN key'); WriteLn;
  ReadInt(x); ReadInt(y); ReadInt(z);
  mean:=FLOAT(x+y+z)/3.0;
  WriteString('arithmetic mean of integers = ');
  WriteFixed(mean, 2, 10); WriteLn;
END C3Q13a.

MODULE C3Q13b;
FROM STextIO IMPORT WriteString, WriteLn;
FROM SWholeIO IMPORT ReadCard;
FROM SRealIO IMPORT WriteFixed;
CONST
  pi = 3.14159;
VAR
  radius              : CARDINAL;
  SurfaceArea, volume : REAL;
BEGIN
  WriteString('input cardinal value for radius of sphere ');
  ReadCard(radius);
  SurfaceArea := 4.0 * pi * FLOAT(radius * radius);
  volume := SurfaceArea * FLOAT(radius) / 3.0;
  WriteString('surface area of sphere = ');
  WriteFixed(SurfaceArea,2,10); WriteLn;
  WriteString('volume of sphere = ');
  WriteFixed(volume,2,10); WriteLn;
END C3Q13b.

MODULE C3Q13c;
FROM STextIO IMPORT WriteString, WriteLn;
FROM SRealIO IMPORT ReadReal, WriteFixed;
CONST
  VAT = 0.175;
VAR
  item1, item2, item3 : REAL;
  SubTotal, Tax, total : REAL;
BEGIN
  WriteString('    S A L E S    I N V O I C E');
  WriteLn; WriteLn;
  WriteString('input cost of item 1 '); ReadReal(item1);
```

```
    WriteString('input cost of item 2 '); ReadReal(item2);
    WriteString('input cost of item 3 '); ReadReal(item3);
    SubTotal:=item1+item2+item3;
    Tax:=SubTotal*VAT;
    total:=SubTotal+Tax;
    WriteString('Sub Total          ');
    WriteFixed(SubTotal,2,10); WriteLn;
    WriteString('VAT @ 17.5%        ');
    WriteFixed(Tax,2,10); WriteLn;
    WriteString('Total              ');
    WriteFixed(total,2,10); WriteLn;
END C3Q13c.
```

14.
```
MODULE C3Q14;
FROM SRealIO IMPORT ReadReal, WriteFixed;
FROM STextIO IMPORT WriteString, WriteLn;
CONST
    pi=3.14159;

VAR radius, height, SlantHeight     : REAL;
    CylArea, CylVol, ConeArea, ConeVol : REAL;

BEGIN
    (* process cylinder *)
    WriteString('input perpendicular height and base radius
                 of cylinder ');
    ReadReal(height); ReadReal(radius);
    CylArea:=2.0*pi*radius*(height+radius);
    CylVol:=pi*radius*radius*height;
    WriteString('CYLINDER area = '); WriteFixed(CylArea,1,6);
    WriteString(' volume = '); WriteFixed(CylVol,1,6);
    WriteLn;

    (* process cone *)
    WriteString('input slant height of cone ');
    ReadReal(SlantHeight);
    WriteString('input perpendicular height and base radius
                 of cone ');
    ReadReal(height); ReadReal(radius);
    ConeArea:=pi*radius*SlantHeight;
    ConeVol:=(1.0/3.0)*(pi*radius*radius)*height;
    WriteString('CONE area of curved surface = ');
    WriteFixed(ConeArea,1,6);
    WriteString(' volume = '); WriteFixed(ConeVol,1,6);
    WriteLn;
END C3Q14.
```

Chapter 4

1.
(a) false
(b) true
(c) true
(d) false
(e) true
(f) true
(g) true

2.
(a) X=Y
(b) X#Y
(c) A<=B
(d) Q<=T
(e) X>=Y
(f) (X<=Y) AND (A#B)
(g) (A>18) AND (H>68) AND (W>75)
(h) (G<100) AND (G>50)
(i) (H<50) OR   (H>100)

3.

	A	B	C	output
(a)	16	16	32	y
(b)	16	-18	32	x
(c)	-2	-4	16	z

4.
```
MODULE C4Q4;
FROM StringType IMPORT string;
FROM STextIO IMPORT ReadString, WriteString, ReadChar,
                    WriteLn, SkipLine;
FROM SWholeIO IMPORT ReadCard;
CONST
    male = 'M';

VAR
    name     : string;
    age      : CARDINAL;
    height   : CARDINAL;
    sex      : CHAR;
    sex_male : BOOLEAN;

BEGIN
    WriteString('input name of suspect '); ReadString(name);
    WriteString('age? ');    ReadCard(age);
    WriteString('height? '); ReadCard(height);
    SkipLine;
```

Appendix I

```modula2
    WriteString('sex? ');        ReadChar(sex);
    sex := CAP(sex);

    IF sex = male THEN
        sex_male := TRUE;
    ELSE
        sex_male := FALSE;
    END;

    IF (age >= 20) AND (age <= 25) AND (height >= 66) AND
    (height <= 70) AND sex_male THEN
        WriteString(name);
        WriteString(' is a suspect and should be held for
                    interrogation'); WriteLn;

    END;
END C4Q4.

5.
MODULE C4Q5;
FROM STextIO IMPORT WriteString, WriteLn;
FROM SRealIO IMPORT ReadReal, WriteFixed;
CONST
    FlatRate    = 8.0;
    NormalHours = 35.0;
    threshold   = 60.0;
    rate1       = 12.0;
    rate2       = 16.0;
VAR
    HoursWorked, OvertimePay : REAL;
BEGIN
    WriteString('input number of hours worked ');
    ReadReal(HoursWorked);
    IF HoursWorked > threshold THEN
        OvertimePay:=(threshold-NormalHours) * rate1
                    +(HoursWorked-threshold) * rate2;
    ELSE
        IF HoursWorked > NormalHours THEN
            OvertimePay:=(HoursWorked-NormalHours) * rate1;
        ELSE
            OvertimePay:=0.0;
        END;
    END;
    WriteString('overtime pay is £');
    WriteFixed(OvertimePay,2,7);
END C4Q5.

6.
MODULE C4Q6;
FROM STextIO IMPORT WriteString, WriteLn;
FROM SRealIO IMPORT ReadReal, WriteFixed;
CONST
    band1=999.0;
    band2=9999.0;
    band3=99999.0;
    comm1=0.01;
    comm2=0.05;
    comm3=0.1;
VAR
    sales, commission:REAL;
BEGIN
    WriteString('input sales figure ');
    ReadReal(sales);
    IF (sales > band2) AND (sales <= band3) THEN
        commission:=sales*comm3;
    ELSE
        IF (sales > band1) AND (sales <=band2) THEN
            commission:=sales*comm2;
        ELSE
            commission:=sales*comm1;
        END;
    END;
    WriteString('commission on sales is £');
    WriteFixed(commission,2,8);
END C4Q6.

7.
MODULE C4Q7;
FROM STextIO IMPORT WriteString, ReadChar, WriteLn, SkipLine;
CONST
    yes = 'Y';
VAR
    reading : CHAR;
    reply   : CHAR;
BEGIN
    WriteString('input first letter of barometer reading');
    WriteLn;
    WriteString(' [S]TORM, [R]AIN, [C]HANGE, [F]AIR,
                [V]ERY DRY ');

    ReadChar(reading); SkipLine;
    reading := CAP(reading);

    CASE reading OF
    'S': WriteString('wear overcoat and hat')  |
    'R': WriteString('wear raincoat and take umbrella'  |
    'C': WriteString('did it rain yesterday? answer y[es]
                    or n[o] ');

        ReadChar(reply); reply := CAP(reply);
        IF reply = yes THEN
            WriteString('wear jacket and take umbrella');
        ELSE
            WriteString('wear raincoat and take umbrella');
        END |
    'F': WriteString('wear jacket and take umbrella')  |
    'V': WriteString('wear jacket');
```

```
    ELSE
        WriteString('DATA ERROR - code for barometer
                    reading incorrect');
    END;
END C4Q7.


8.
MODULE C4Q8;
FROM STextIO IMPORT WriteString, ReadChar, WriteLn, SkipLine;
FROM SWholeIO IMPORT ReadCard;
FROM SRealIO IMPORT WriteFixed;
CONST
    Spring = 5.0;
    Summer = 7.5;
    Autumn = 3.75;
    Winter = 2.5;
    period = 7;
    discount = 0.25;
    deposit = 50.0;
VAR
    season : CHAR;
    days : CARDINAL;
    charge : REAL;
    error : BOOLEAN;
BEGIN
    error := FALSE;
    WriteString('input season code A - Spring, B - Summer,
                 C - Autumn, D - Winter ');
    ReadChar(season); SkipLine;
    season := CAP(season);
    WriteString('input number of days hire ');
    ReadCard(days);
    CASE season OF
    'A' : charge := FLOAT(days) * Spring |
    'B' : charge := FLOAT(days) * Summer |
    'C' : charge := FLOAT(days) * Autumn |
    'D' : charge := FLOAT(days) * Winter;
    ELSE
        WriteString('ERROR - wrong seasonal code - use A,B,C
                     or D only');
        WriteLn; WriteString('re-run program');
        error := TRUE;
    END;
    IF NOT error THEN
        IF days > period THEN
            charge := charge * (1.0 - discount);
        END;
        charge := charge + deposit;
        WriteString('cost of hiring bicycle is ');
        WriteFixed(charge,2,10);
    END;
END C4Q8.
```

Chapter 5

```
1.
MODULE C5Q1;
FROM STextIO IMPORT WriteString, WriteLn;
VAR
    counter : CARDINAL;
BEGIN
    counter := 0;
    REPEAT
        WriteString('HELLO WORLD'); WriteLn;
        counter := counter + 1;
    UNTIL counter = 10;
END C5Q1.


2.
MODULE C5Q2; IMPORT WriteString, ReadString, WriteLn;
FROM StringType IMPORT string;
FROM SWholeIO IMPORT ReadCard;
VAR
    counter : CARDINAL;
    times : CARDINAL;
    message : string;
BEGIN
    WriteString('what is your message? ');
    ReadString(message);
    WriteString('how many times do you want it repeated? ');
    ReadCard(times);
    counter := 0;
    REPEAT
        WriteString(message); WriteLn;
        counter := counter + 1;
    UNTIL counter = times;
END C5Q2.


3.
MODULE C5Q3;
FROM STextIO IMPORT WriteString, WriteLn;
FROM SRealIO IMPORT WriteFixed;
VAR Fahrenheit, Centigrade : REAL;
BEGIN
    WriteString('Fahrenheit Centigrade'); WriteLn;
    Fahrenheit:=32.0;
    WHILE Fahrenheit <= 212.0 DO
        Centigrade := (Fahrenheit - 32.0) * (5.0/9.0);
        WriteFixed(Fahrenheit,1,10);
        WriteFixed(Centigrade,1,10);
        WriteLn;
        Fahrenheit:=Fahrenheit + 10.0;
    END;
END C5Q3.
```

```
4.
MODULE C5Q4;
FROM STextIO IMPORT WriteString, WriteLn;
FROM SRealIO IMPORT WriteFixed;
FROM SWholeIO IMPORT WriteCard;
CONST
    conversion_factor = 1.609344;

VAR
    miles      : CARDINAL;
    kilometres : REAL;
BEGIN
    WriteString('MILES       KILOMETRES'); WriteLn;
    miles :=1;
    WHILE miles <= 50 DO
        IF miles MOD 20 = 0 THEN
            WriteLn; WriteString('MILES       KILOMETRES');
            WriteLn;
        END;
        kilometres := FLOAT(miles) * conversion_factor;
        WriteCard(miles,5);
        WriteFixed(kilometres,2,12);
        WriteLn;
        miles := miles + 1;
    END;
END C5Q4.

5.
MODULE C5Q5;
FROM SWholeIO IMPORT WriteCard;
FROM STextIO IMPORT WriteChar, WriteString, WriteLn;
VAR
    counter : CARDINAL;
    result  : CARDINAL;
BEGIN
(* a *)
    counter := 1;
    REPEAT
        WriteCard(counter,4);
        counter := counter+2;
    UNTIL counter > 29;
    WriteLn;
(* b *)
    counter := 2;
    REPEAT
        WriteCard(counter, 4);
        counter := counter+2;
    UNTIL counter > 20;
    WriteLn;
(* c *)
    result := 0;
    counter := 1;
    REPEAT
        result := result + (counter * counter);
        counter := counter+2;
    UNTIL counter > 13;
    WriteString('sum of squares '); WriteCard(result,6);
    WriteLn;
(* d *)
    WriteString('UPPER CASE'); WriteLn;
    counter := 65;
    REPEAT
        WriteChar(CHR(counter));
        counter := counter + 1;
    UNTIL counter > 90;
    WriteLn;
    WriteString('lower case'); WriteLn;
    counter := 97;
    REPEAT
        WriteChar(CHR(counter));
        counter := counter + 1;
    UNTIL counter > 122;
    WriteLn;
END C5Q5.

6.
MODULE C5Q6;
FROM STextIO IMPORT WriteString, WriteLn;
FROM SWholeIO IMPORT ReadCard, WriteCard;
FROM SRealIO IMPORT WriteFixed;
CONST    sentinel=0;

VAR
    sum, number, counter : CARDINAL;
    mean                 : REAL;

BEGIN
    sum:=0;
    counter:=0;
    REPEAT
        WriteString('input cardinal number ');
        ReadCard(number);
        sum:=sum+number;
        counter:=counter+1;
    UNTIL number=sentinel;

    IF counter # 1 THEN
        mean:=FLOAT(sum)/FLOAT(counter-1);
        WriteString('arithmetic mean of ');
        WriteCard(counter-1, 3);
        WriteString(' positive numbers is ');
        WriteFixed(mean,1,7);
    END;
END C5Q6.
```

```
7.
MODULE C5Q7; IMPORT WriteString, WriteLn;
FROM STextIO IMPORT WriteString, WriteLn;
FROM SWholeIO IMPORT ReadCard, WriteCard;
FROM SRealIO IMPORT WriteFixed;
CONST
      OvertimeRate = 12.0;
      NormalHours  = 40;
      MaxEmployees = 10;

VAR   HoursWorked   : CARDINAL;
      OvertimePay   : REAL;
      employee      : CARDINAL;
      TotalOvertime : REAL;

BEGIN
      TotalOvertime := 0.0;
      FOR employee:=1 TO MaxEmployees DO
         WriteString('input hours worked for employee ');
         WriteCard(employee,3); WriteString(' ');
         ReadCard(HoursWorked);
         IF HoursWorked > NormalHours THEN
            OvertimePay:=
               FLOAT(HoursWorked-NormalHours)*OvertimeRate;
            TotalOvertime := TotalOvertime + OvertimePay;

         ELSE  OvertimePay:=0.0;

         END;
         WriteString('overtime due is ');
         WriteFixed(OvertimePay,2,6); WriteLn;
      END;
      WriteString('Total Overtime paid ');
      WriteFixed(TotalOvertime,2,8);
      WriteLn;
END C5Q7.

8.
MODULE C5Q8; IMPORT WriteString, ReadChar, WriteChar, WriteLn;
FROM STextIO IMPORT WriteString, ReadChar, WriteChar, WriteLn;
FROM SWholeIO IMPORT WriteCard;
CONST return = 15C;
VAR character : CHAR;
BEGIN
      WriteString('input phrase ');
      ReadChar(character);
      WHILE character # return DO
         WriteString('ASCII code for ');
         WriteChar(character);
         WriteString(' is ');
         WriteCard(ORD(character),3);
         WriteLn;
         ReadChar(character);

      END;
END C5Q8.
```

```
9.
MODULE C5Q9; IMPORT WriteString, WriteLn;
FROM STextIO IMPORT WriteString, WriteLn;
FROM SWholeIO IMPORT ReadInt, WriteInt;
VAR
      largest : INTEGER;
      number  : INTEGER;
      counter : CARDINAL;
BEGIN
      WriteString('integer? '); ReadInt(number);
      largest := number;
      counter := 1;
      WHILE counter # 10 DO
         WriteString('integer? '); ReadInt(number);
         IF number > largest THEN
            largest := number;
         END;
         counter := counter + 1;

      END;
      WriteString('largest integer input was ');
      WriteInt(largest,6);
      WriteLn;
END C5Q9.

10.
MODULE C5Q10; IMPORT ReadChar, WriteChar, WriteString, WriteLn;
FROM STextIO IMPORT ReadChar, WriteChar, WriteString, WriteLn;
CONST
      EndOfLine = 15C;

VAR
      character : CHAR;

BEGIN
      WriteString('input one line of text'); WriteLn;
      ReadChar(character);
      WHILE character # '(' DO
         ReadChar(character);

      END;
      ReadChar(character);
      WHILE character # ')' DO
         WriteChar(character);
         ReadChar(character);

      END;
END C5Q10.
```

Appendix I

Chapter 6.

1.

(a) Actual parameter list is missing in the call to procedure alpha.

(b) Formal parameter list of procedure beta is missing.

(c) The corresponding variables between the actual and formal parameter lists are inconsistent. C has been defined as a variable yet appears as a constant in the actual parameter list - this is an error. Since Z has not been defined as a variable whose value will be passed back to the calling program, it is permissible to pass the constant * to Z in the procedure delta.

(d) There is a data type mis-match between the actual and formal parameter lists. X and Y are of type CHAR, yet i,j and k are of type INTEGER. Furthermore, the number of parameters in both lists is not the same, hence the syntax error.

2. The value of the variable result after each call to procedure test is FALSE, TRUE, FALSE respectively.

```
3.
MODULE C6Q3; IMPORT WriteString, WriteLn;
FROM STextIO IMPORT WriteString, WriteLn;
FROM SRealIO IMPORT ReadReal, WriteFixed;
VAR
    radius, diameter, circumference, area : REAL;

PROCEDURE DataIn(VAR radius : REAL);
BEGIN
    WriteString('terminate with zero'); WriteLn;
    REPEAT
        WriteString('input radius ');
        ReadReal(radius);
    UNTIL radius >= 0.0;
END DataIn;

PROCEDURE calculate(radius:REAL; VAR diameter, circumference,
                    area : REAL);
CONST    pi=3.14159;
BEGIN
    diameter:=2.0*radius;
    circumference:=2.0*pi*radius;
    area:=pi*radius*radius;
END calculate;
```

```
PROCEDURE results(diameter, circumference, area : REAL);
BEGIN
    WriteLn;WriteLn;
    WriteString('diameter:      ');  WriteLn;
    WriteFixed(diameter,2,10);  WriteLn;
    WriteString('circumference:');
    WriteFixed(circumference,2,10);WriteLn;
    WriteString('area:          ');
    WriteFixed(area,2,10);WriteLn;WriteLn;
END results;

BEGIN
    DataIn(radius);
    WHILE radius # 0.0 DO
        calculate(radius, diameter, circumference, area);
        results(diameter, circumference, area);
        DataIn(radius);
    END;
END C6Q3.
```

```
4.
MODULE C6Q4;
FROM STextIO IMPORT WriteString, WriteLn, ReadChar,
                    WriteChar, SkipLine;

FROM StringType IMPORT string;
CONST
    bell = CHR(7);

VAR
    character : CHAR;
    value     : string;
    success   : BOOLEAN;

PROCEDURE convert(OctalDigit : CHAR; VAR value : string;
                  VAR success : BOOLEAN);
BEGIN
    success := TRUE;
    CASE OctalDigit OF
        '0' : value := 'zero'  |
        '1' : value := 'one'   |
        '2' : value := 'two'   |
        '3' : value := 'three' |
        '4' : value := 'four'  |
        '5' : value := 'five'  |
        '6' : value := 'six'   |
        '7' : value := 'seven' ;
    ELSE
        success := FALSE;
    END;
END convert;
```

```
PROCEDURE WhereTo(JuncNo : CARDINAL; VAR destination : string;
                  VAR error : BOOLEAN);
BEGIN
  error := FALSE;
  CASE JuncNo OF
  1:destination :=  'A2 only'                       |
  2:destination :=  'A228 Snodland Rochester'       |
  3:destination :=  'A229 Maidstone Chatham'        |
  4:destination :=  'A278 Gillingham'               |
  5:destination :=  'A249 Sittingbourne Sheerness'  |
  6:destination :=  'A251 Ashford Faversham'        |
  7:destination :=  'A2 Canterbury Dover/
                     A299 Margate Ramsgate';
  ELSE
    error := TRUE;
  END;
END WhereTo;

BEGIN
  REPEAT
    WriteString('input junction number on the M2 ');
    ReadCard(junction);
    WhereTo(junction, signpost, error);
    IF NOT error THEN
      WriteString(signpost);
    ELSE
      WriteString('ERROR - junction number does
                   not exist');
    END;
    WriteLn;
  UNTIL error;
END C6Q6.
```

Chapter 7

1.

```
MODULE C7Q1;
FROM STextIO IMPORT WriteString, WriteLn, WriteCard;
FROM SWholeIO IMPORT ReadCard, WriteCard;
FROM SRealIO IMPORT ReadReal;

VAR
  A,B,C,D            : CARDINAL;   (* categories *)
  counter, ClassSize : CARDINAL;
  dist               : REAL;   (* distance to school *)

PROCEDURE initialise(VAR category_A, category_B, category_C,
                         category_D : CARDINAL;
                     VAR pupil_counter : CARDINAL);
```

```
BEGIN
  WriteString('octal digit? '); ReadChar(character);
  SkipLine;
  convert(character, value, success);
  IF success THEN
    WriteString(value);
    WriteLn;
  ELSE
    WriteString('DATA ERROR - character not in range
                 0..7');
    WriteChar(bell);
  END;
END C6Q4.

5.
MODULE C6Q5;
FROM STextIO IMPORT WriteString, WriteLn, ReadChar;
VAR
  character : CHAR;
  success   : BOOLEAN;

PROCEDURE vowel(letter : CHAR; VAR success : BOOLEAN);
BEGIN
  CASE letter OF
  'a','A','e','E','i','I','o','O','u','U' : success := TRUE;
  ELSE
    success := FALSE;
  END;
END vowel;

BEGIN
  WriteString('character? '); ReadChar(character);
  vowel(character, success);
  IF success THEN
    WriteString('character is a vowel');
  ELSE
    WriteString('character is NOT a vowel');
  END;
END C6Q5.

6.
MODULE C6Q6;
FROM STextIO IMPORT WriteString, WriteLn;
FROM StringType IMPORT string;
FROM SWholeIO IMPORT ReadCard;

VAR
  junction : CARDINAL;
  signpost : string;
  error    : BOOLEAN;
```

```
BEGIN
    category_A:=0;
    category_B:=0;
    category_C:=0;
    category_D:=0;
    pupil_counter:=0;
END initialise;

PROCEDURE InputClassSize(VAR size : CARDINAL);
BEGIN
    REPEAT
        WriteString('input size of class ');
        ReadCard(size);
    UNTIL size > 0;
END InputClassSize;

PROCEDURE InputDistance(VAR distance : REAL);
BEGIN
    REPEAT
        WriteString('input distance of pupil from school ');
        ReadReal(distance);
    UNTIL distance > 0.0;
END InputDistance;

PROCEDURE analysis(distance : REAL; VAR category_A, category_B, category_C,
                   category_B, category_C, category_D : CARDINAL);
BEGIN
    IF distance < 1.0 THEN
        category_A := category_A + 1;
    ELSIF distance < 5.0 THEN
        category_B := category_B + 1;
    ELSIF distance < 10.0 THEN
        category_C := category_C + 1;
    ELSE
        category_D := category_D + 1;
    END;
END analysis;

PROCEDURE results(category_A, category_B, category_C,
                  category_D : CARDINAL;
BEGIN
    WriteString('category pupils'); WriteLn;
    WriteString('A'); WriteCard(category_A,14); WriteLn;
    WriteString('B'); WriteCard(category_B,14); WriteLn;
    WriteString('C'); WriteCard(category_C,14); WriteLn;
    WriteString('D'); WriteCard(category_D,14); WriteLn;
END results;

BEGIN
    initialise(A,B,C,D,counter);
    InputClassSize(ClassSize);
    WHILE counter # ClassSize DO
        InputDistance(dist);
        analysis(dist,A,B,C,D);
        counter := counter + 1;
    END;
    results(A,B,C,D);
END C7Q1.

2.
MODULE C7Q2;
FROM STextIO IMPORT WriteString, WriteLn, ReadChar, SkipLine;
FROM StringType IMPORT string;
FROM SWholeIO IMPORT ReadCard;
FROM SRealIO IMPORT ReadReal;
VAR
    angle       : CARDINAL;
    s1,s2,s3,s4 : REAL;  (* lengths of sides *)
    NoMoreData  : BOOLEAN;
    shape       : string;

PROCEDURE InputData(VAR angle : CARDINAL;
                    VAR side1, side2, side3, side4 : REAL);
BEGIN
    REPEAT
        WriteString('input size of one internal angle ');
        ReadCard(angle);
    UNTIL (angle > 0) AND (angle < 180);

    REPEAT
        WriteString('input lengths of the four sides ');
        ReadReal(side1); ReadReal(side2); ReadReal(side3);
        ReadReal(side4);
    UNTIL (side1 > 0.0) AND (side2 > 0.0) AND (side3 > 0.0)
    AND (side4 > 0.0);
    SkipLine;
END InputData;

PROCEDURE AnalyseShape( angle : CARDINAL; sideA, sideB, sideC,
                        sideD : REAL; VAR name : string);
BEGIN
    IF (sideA = sideB) AND (sideB = sideC) AND
       (sideC = sideD) THEN
        IF angle = 90 THEN
            name := 'SQUARE';
        ELSE
            name := 'RHOMBUS';
        END;
    ELSE
        IF (sideA = sideC) AND (sideB = sideD) THEN
            IF angle = 90 THEN
                name := 'RECTANGLE';
            ELSE
                name := 'PARALLELOGRAM';
```

PROCEDURE DataIn(VAR code : CARDINAL; VAR value : CARDINAL);
VAR
```
PROCEDURE DataIn(VAR code : CARDINAL; VAR value : CARDINAL);
VAR
  age      : CARDINAL;
  foreign  : CHAR;
  accident : CHAR;
  bit0, bit1, bit2 : CARDINAL;

BEGIN
  REPEAT
    WriteString('input age of driver '); ReadCard(age);
  UNTIL (age >= 17) AND (age <= 100);
  SkipLine;
  IF age >= 25 THEN bit2 := 0; ELSE bit2 := 4; END;

  WriteString(' answer Y[es] or N[o] to the next two
                 questions'); WriteLn;
  REPEAT
    WriteString('is the car foreign? ');
    ReadChar(foreign); SkipLine;
  UNTIL (foreign = 'Y') OR (foreign = 'N');

  IF foreign = 'N' THEN bit1 := 0; ELSE bit1:=2; END;
  REPEAT
    WriteString('accident in the last three years? ');
    ReadChar(accident); SkipLine;
  UNTIL (accident = 'Y') OR (accident = 'N');
  IF accident = 'N' THEN bit0:=0; ELSE bit0:=1; END;
  code := bit2 + bit1 + bit0;
  REPEAT
    WriteString('input insured value of car ');
    ReadCard(value); SkipLine;
  UNTIL value > 0;
END DataIn;

PROCEDURE analysis(code:CARDINAL; VAR policy:string;
                   VAR percent : REAL);
BEGIN
  CASE code OF
  0  : policy := '10% comprehensive'; percent := 10.0 |
  1  : policy := '10% comprehensive + £50 excess';
       percent := 10.0 |
  2, 4 : policy := '15% comprehensive'; percent := 15.0 |
  3  : policy := '15% comprehensive + £50 excess';
       percent := 15.0 |
  5  : policy := '7.5% third party only'; percent := 7.5 |
  6  : policy := '20% comprehensive'; percent := 20.0 |
  7  : policy := 'decline to issue policy'; percent := 0.0;
  END;
END analysis;

PROCEDURE display(policy : string; percent : REAL;
                  value : CARDINAL);
VAR
```

```
      END;
    ELSE
      name := 'IRREGULAR';
    END;
  END;
END AnalyseShape;

PROCEDURE display(name : string);
BEGIN
  WriteString('from the size of the internal angle and the
              lengths '); WriteLn;
  WriteString('of the four sides, the figure would appear
              to be a ');
  WriteLn; WriteString(name); WriteLn;
END display;

PROCEDURE MoreData(VAR NoMoreData : BOOLEAN);
VAR
  reply : CHAR;
BEGIN
  WriteString('continue? - answer [Y]es or [N]o ');
  ReadChar(reply); SkipLine;
  IF (reply = 'N') OR (reply = 'n') THEN
    NoMoreData := TRUE;
  ELSE
    NoMoreData := FALSE;
  END;
END MoreData;

BEGIN
  REPEAT
    InputData(angle, s1,s2,s3,s4);
    AnalyseShape(angle, s1,s2,s3,s4, shape);
    display(shape);
    MoreData(NoMoreData);
  UNTIL NoMoreData;
END C7Q2.


3.
MODULE C7Q3;
FROM STextIO IMPORT WriteString, WriteLn, ReadChar, SkipLine;
FROM StringType IMPORT string;
FROM SWholeIO IMPORT ReadCard, WriteCard;
FROM SRealIO IMPORT ReadReal, WriteFixed;
CONST
  finish = 'Y';

VAR
  code       : CARDINAL;
  reply      : CHAR;
  CostOfCar  : CARDINAL;
  percentage : REAL;
  PolicyType : string;
```

Appendix I

```
    premium : REAL;
BEGIN
    WriteString('insurance policy: '); WriteString(policy);
    WriteLn;
    IF percent > 0.0 THEN
      WriteString('car insured for £'); WriteCard(value,6);
      WriteLn;
      premium := FLOAT(value) * percent / 100.00;
      WriteString('Premium due £'); WriteFixed(premium,2,6);
      WriteLn;
    END;
END display;

PROCEDURE request(VAR reply : CHAR);
BEGIN
    REPEAT
      WriteString('do you want to finish? -
                   ANSWER [Y]es or N[o] ');
      ReadChar(reply);  SkipLine;
    UNTIL (reply = 'Y') OR (reply = 'N');
END request;

BEGIN
    REPEAT
      DataIn(code, CostOfCar);
      analysis(code, PolicyType, percentage);
      display(PolicyType, percentage, CostOfCar);
      request(reply);
    UNTIL reply = finish;
END C7Q3.


4.
MODULE C7Q4;

FROM STextIO IMPORT WriteString, WriteLn;
FROM SWholeIO IMPORT WriteCard;
FROM SRealIO IMPORT ReadReal, WriteFixed;
CONST
    ErrorFactor = 1.0E-6;
    (* required to compensate for machine inaccuracy *)

VAR
    length, TotalWaste, waste : REAL;
    L5, L2, TotalL5, TotalL2 : INTEGER;
    (* L5 and L2 are the number of 0.5m and 0.2m strips from
       one length;
       TotalL5 and TotalL2 are the total number of 0.5m and 0.2m
       strips *)

PROCEDURE initialise;
BEGIN
    TotalL5 := 0;
```

```
    TotalL2 := 0;
    TotalWaste := 0.0;
END initialise;

PROCEDURE DataIn(VAR length : REAL);
BEGIN
    REPEAT
      WriteString('input length of moulding
                   (max 2 dec. pl.) ');
      ReadReal(length);
    UNTIL length >= 0.0;
END DataIn;

PROCEDURE calculate(length, size : REAL;
                    VAR pieces : INTEGER; VAR waste : REAL);
BEGIN
    pieces := 0;
    waste := 0.0;
    WHILE (length+ErrorFactor) >= size DO
      length := length - size;
      pieces := pieces + 1;

    END;
    waste := length;
END calculate;

PROCEDURE Results(L5, L2 : CARDINAL; waste : REAL);
BEGIN
    WriteString('0.5m           0.2m         waste'); WriteLn;
    WriteCard(L5,3); WriteCard(L2,11);
    WriteFixed(waste,2,12); WriteLn;
END Results;

BEGIN
    initialise;
    DataIn(length);
    WHILE length > 0.0 DO
      calculate(length, 0.5, L5, waste);
      TotalL5:=TotalL5+L5;
      calculate(waste, 0.2, L2, waste);
      TotalL2:=TotalL2+L2;
      TotalWaste:=TotalWaste+waste;
      Results(L5,L2,waste);
      DataIn(length);

    END;
    WriteLn;
    WriteString('totals'); WriteLn;
    WriteString('0.5m    '); WriteCard(TotalL5,3); WriteLn;
    WriteString('0.2m    '); WriteCard(TotalL2,3); WriteLn;
    WriteString('waste   '); WriteFixed(TotalWaste,2,6);
    WriteLn;
END C7Q4.
```

```
5.
MODULE C7Q5;
FROM STextIO IMPORT WriteString, WriteLn, ReadChar, SkipLine;
FROM SWholeIO IMPORT ReadCard;
FROM SRealIO IMPORT ReadReal, WriteFixed;
CONST
   SingleAllowance  = 1200.0;
   MarriedAllowance = 2300.0;
   ChildAllowance   = 100.0;
   Band1 = 1000.0; Band2 = 2000.0; Band3 = 4000.0;
   Rate1 = 0.0; Rate2 = 0.2; Rate3 = 0.3; Rate4 = 0.4;
   yes = 'Y';

VAR
   GrossSalary      : REAL;
   PersonalStatus   : CHAR;
   NumberOfChildren : CARDINAL;
   TaxableIncome    : REAL;
   tax              : REAL;
   reply            : CHAR;

PROCEDURE DataIn( VAR GrossSalary : REAL;
                 VAR PersonalStatus : CHAR;
                 VAR NumberOfChildren : CARDINAL);

BEGIN
   REPEAT
      WriteString('input gross salary ');
      ReadReal(GrossSalary);
   UNTIL GrossSalary > 0.0;
   SkipLine;
   REPEAT
      WriteString('input personal status
                   [M]arried or [S]ingle ');
      ReadChar(PersonalStatus);
   UNTIL (PersonalStatus = 'M') OR (PersonalStatus = 'S');
   SkipLine;

   REPEAT
      WriteString('input number of children ');
      ReadCard(NumberOfChildren);
   UNTIL (NumberOfChildren >= 0) AND (NumberOfChildren < 15);
   SkipLine;
END DataIn;

PROCEDURE analysis(GrossSalary : REAL; PersonalStatus :
     CHAR; NumberOfChildren : CARDINAL; VAR tax : REAL);

BEGIN
   IF PersonalStatus = 'S' THEN
      TaxableIncome := GrossSalary - SingleAllowance;
   ELSE
      TaxableIncome := GrossSalary - MarriedAllowance;
   END;

   TaxableIncome := TaxableIncome -
                    (ChildAllowance * FLOAT(NumberOfChildren));
   IF  TaxableIncome <=Band1 THEN
      tax := Rate1 * TaxableIncome;
   ELSIF TaxableIncome <= Band2 THEN
      tax := Rate2 * (TaxableIncome - Band1) +
                     (Band1 * Rate1);
   ELSIF TaxableIncome <= Band3 THEN
      tax := Rate3 * (TaxableIncome - Band2) +
             Rate2 * (Band2-Band1)+ (Band1 * Rate1);
   ELSE
      tax := Rate4 * (TaxableIncome - Band3) +
             Rate3 * (Band3-Band2)
             +Rate2 * (Band2-Band1) + (Band1 * Rate1);
   END;
END analysis;

PROCEDURE Result(tax : REAL);
BEGIN
   WriteString('amount of tax to pay £');
   WriteFixed(tax,2,8);
   WriteLn;
END Result;

PROCEDURE Request(VAR reply : CHAR);
BEGIN
   WriteString('do you want to finish [Y]es or [N]o ');
   ReadChar(reply);
   SkipLine;
END Request;

BEGIN
   REPEAT
      DataIn(GrossSalary, PersonalStatus,
             NumberOfChildren);
      analysis(GrossSalary, PersonalStatus,
               NumberOfChildren, tax);
      Result(tax);
      Request(reply);
   UNTIL reply = yes;
END C7Q5.
```

Appendix I

Chapter 8

```
1.
MODULE C8Q1;
(*$R+*)
FROM STextIO IMPORT WriteString, WriteLn;
FROM SWholeIO IMPORT ReadCard, WriteCard;

TYPE
  range=CARDINAL[1..31];

VAR
  number : CARDINAL;
  result : range;

BEGIN
  WriteString('input number in excess of 15 ');
  ReadCard(number);
  result:=2*number;
  WriteString('twice the value is '); WriteCard(result,6);
  WriteLn;
END C8Q1.
```

```
2.

(a) DecimalDigit = [0..9];
(b) week = [1..52];
(c) compass = [1..360];
(d) IdCode = [100..999];
(e) alphabet = ['A'..'Z'];
```

```
3.

(a) operator = (+, -, *, /);
(b) CardSuits = (Clubs, Diamonds, Hearts, Spades);
(c) CardValue = (Deuce, Three, Four, Five, Six, Seven, Eight,
                 Nine, Ten, Jack, Queen, King, Ace);
(d) points = (North, South, East, West);
```

4.   (a) >   (b) 1   (c) 58   (d) Q

```
5.

(a) violet, 6
(b) orange, 6
(c) No. The ordinal value of the first object (red) is 0.
(d) indigo, INC(colour,2);
```

(e) Will result in an error, since no object has an ordinal value of (-2).

```
6.
MODULE C8Q6;
FROM SRealIO IMPORT WriteFixed;
FROM STextIO IMPORT WriteString, WriteLn;
FROM RealMath IMPORT ln;
VAR
         number : REAL;
         base   : CARDINAL;
         index  : CARDINAL;

PROCEDURE logarithm(base:CARDINAL; X:REAL):REAL;
BEGIN
         RETURN ln(X)/ln(FLOAT(base));
END logarithm;

BEGIN
         WriteString('Number                              Bases');
         WriteLn;
         WriteString('       2          4          6          8
         10');
         WriteLn;

         WriteLn; WriteLn;
         number:=2.0;
         WHILE number <=10.0 DO
           WriteFixed(number,1,4);
             FOR index:=1 TO 5 DO
               base:=2*index;
               WriteFixed(logarithm(base, number),4,10);

             END;
             WriteLn;
             number:=number+0.5;

         END;

END C8Q6.
```

```
7.
MODULE C8Q7;
FROM RealMath IMPORT sin, exp;
FROM STextIO IMPORT WriteChar, WriteLn;
CONST
         scale=30.0;
         centre=40.0;
         increment=0.1;
         pi=3.14159;
         point='.';
         space=40C;

VAR      index:INTEGER;
         angle:REAL;
```

```
PROCEDURE trace():INTEGER;
BEGIN
    RETURN TRUNC(centre-scale*exp(-angle)*sin(2.0*pi*angle));
END trace;

BEGIN
    angle:=0.0;
    WHILE angle<=2.5 DO
        FOR index:=1 TO trace() DO
            WriteChar(space);
        END;
        WriteChar(point); WriteLn;
        angle:=angle+increment;
    END;
END C8Q7.

8.
MODULE C8Q8;
FROM RealMath IMPORT sqrt, exp, ln, arctan, sin, cos;
FROM SRealIO IMPORT WriteFixed;
FROM STextIO IMPORT WriteLn, WriteString, WriteChar,
                    ReadChar, SkipLine;

VAR
    x,y   :REAL;
    return : CHAR;

PROCEDURE display(x,y:REAL);
CONST   space=40C;
BEGIN
    WriteString('x=');
    WriteFixed(x,6,2);
    WriteChar(space); WriteString('y=');
    WriteFixed(y,15,10);
    WriteLn;
END display;

BEGIN
(* a *)
    x:=0.0;
    REPEAT
        y:=sqrt(x)*sqrt(x)-x;
        display(x,y);
        x:=x+0.05;
    UNTIL x>1.0;
    WriteString('press <RETURN> to continue');
    ReadChar(return); SkipLine;
(* b *)
    x:=1.0;
    REPEAT
        y:=exp(ln(x))-x;
        display(x,y);
        x:=x+1.0;
    UNTIL x>10.0;
    WriteString('press <RETURN> to continue');
    ReadChar(return); SkipLine;
(* c *)
    x:=-100.0;
    REPEAT
        y:=arctan(x);
        y:=(sin(y)/cos(y))-x;
        display(x,y);
        x:=x+10.0;
    UNTIL x>100.0;

END C8Q8.

9.
MODULE C8Q9a;
FROM STextIO IMPORT WriteString;
FROM SWholeIO IMPORT WriteCard;
TYPE
    SquareFunc=PROCEDURE(CARDINAL):CARDINAL;

PROCEDURE Square(X:CARDINAL):CARDINAL;
BEGIN
    RETURN X*X;
END Square;

PROCEDURE sum(Function:SquareFunc;limit:CARDINAL):CARDINAL;
VAR
    index, total:CARDINAL;
BEGIN
    total:=0;
    FOR index:=1 TO limit DO
        total:=total+Function(index);
    END;
    RETURN total;
END sum;

BEGIN
    WriteString('sum of squares of first twenty cardinal
                 numbers is');
    WriteCard(sum(Square, 20),6);
END C8Q9a.

MODULE C8Q9b;
FROM STextIO IMPORT WriteString, WriteChar, WriteLn;
FROM SWholeIO IMPORT ReadCard;
TYPE
    error=PROCEDURE;
VAR
    digit1, digit2:CARDINAL;
```

Appendix I

```
PROCEDURE abandon;
BEGIN
    WriteString('second digit zero program abandoned');
    HALT;
END abandon;

PROCEDURE warning;
CONST
    bell=7C;
BEGIN
    WriteChar(bell); WriteLn;
    WriteString('WARNING input value not in range 0-9');
    WriteLn; WriteString('input digit again ');
END warning;

PROCEDURE ErrorHandler(ErrorProc:error);
BEGIN
    ErrorProc;
END ErrorHandler;

PROCEDURE RepeatInput(VAR digit:CARDINAL);
BEGIN
    WHILE (digit < 0) OR (digit > 9) DO
        ErrorHandler(warning);
        ReadCard(digit);
    END;
END RepeatInput;

BEGIN
    WriteString('input first decimal digit ');
    ReadCard(digit1);
    RepeatInput(digit1);
    WriteString('input second decimal digit ');
    ReadCard(digit2);
    IF digit2 = 0 THEN ErrorHandler(abandon);END;
    RepeatInput(digit2);
    IF digit2 = 0 THEN ErrorHandler(abandon);END;
    WriteString('digits verified and are in range');
END C8Q9b.

10.
MODULE C8Q10;
FROM STextIO IMPORT WriteString, WriteLn, WriteChar;
FROM SWholeIO IMPORT ReadInt, WriteInt;

CONST
    WordLength=16;
    LeastSigBit=0;

VAR
    word1, word2 : INTEGER;

PROCEDURE add(word1, word2:INTEGER) :BITSET;
VAR
    sum, carry : BITSET;
    i:CARDINAL;
    CarryValue, word1Value, word2Value : CARDINAL;
BEGIN
    (* clear bits in sum and carry *)
    FOR i:=WordLength-1 TO 0 BY -1 DO
        EXCL(sum, i); EXCL(carry, i);
    END;
    FOR i:=0 TO WordLength-1 DO
        CarryValue:=0; word1Value:=0; word2Value:=0;
        IF LeastSigBit IN carry THEN CarryValue:=1; END;
        IF i IN BITSET(word1) THEN word1Value:=2; END;
        IF i IN BITSET(word2) THEN word2Value:=4; END;

        CASE (CarryValue+word1Value+word2Value) OF
        0     : EXCL(sum,i); EXCL(carry, LeastSigBit)|
        1,2,4 : INCL(sum,i); EXCL(carry, LeastSigBit)|
        3,5,6 : EXCL(sum,i); INCL(carry, LeastSigBit)|
        7     : INCL(sum,i); INCL(carry, LeastSigBit);
        END;

    END;
    RETURN sum;
END add;

PROCEDURE TwosComp(word2:INTEGER):BITSET;
BEGIN
    (* perform two's complement of word2 *)
    RETURN add(INTEGER({0..15} - BITSET(word2)),1);
END TwosComp;

PROCEDURE display(word:BITSET);
VAR
    i:CARDINAL;
BEGIN
    FOR i:=WordLength-1 TO 0 BY -1 DO
        IF i IN word THEN
            WriteChar('1');
        ELSE
            WriteChar('0');
        END;
    END;
    WriteLn; WriteLn;
END display;

BEGIN
    WriteString('input integer (word1 '); ReadInt(word1);
    WriteString('input integer (word2 '); ReadInt(word2);
    WriteString('bit representation of ');
    WriteInt(word,6); WriteLn;
    display(BITSET(word1));
```

```
      WriteString('bit representation of ');
      WriteInt(word2,6); WriteLn;
      display(BITSET(word2));
      WriteString('sum of numbers'); WriteLn;
      display(add(word1, word2));
      WriteString('difference of numbers'); WriteLn;
      display(add(word1,INTEGER(TwosComp(word2))));
    END C8Q10.

    11.
    MODULE C8Q11; IMPORT WriteString, WriteLn, WriteChar,
                         ReadChar, SkipLine;
    FROM SWholeIO IMPORT ReadInt, ReadCard;

    CONST
      WordLength=16;
      left='L';
      right='R';

    VAR
      word:INTEGER;
      places:CARDINAL;
      reply:CHAR;

    PROCEDURE LeftShift(word:INTEGER; places:CARDINAL):BITSET;
    VAR
      temp:BITSET;
      i :CARDINAL;
    BEGIN
      FOR  i:=0 TO places-1 DO
        EXCL(temp,i);
      END;
      FOR i:=places TO WordLength-1 DO
        IF i-places IN BITSET(word) THEN
          INCL(temp,i);
        ELSE
          EXCL(temp,i);
        END;
      END;
      RETURN temp;
    END LeftShift;

    PROCEDURE RightShift(word:INTEGER; places:CARDINAL):BITSET;
    VAR
      temp:BITSET;
      i :CARDINAL;
    BEGIN
      FOR  i:=places TO WordLength-1 DO
        IF i IN BITSET(word) THEN
          INCL(temp,i-places);
        ELSE
          EXCL(temp,i-places);
        END;
      END;
      FOR i:=WordLength-places TO WordLength-1 DO
        EXCL(temp,i);
      END;
      RETURN temp;
    END RightShift;

    PROCEDURE display(word:BITSET);
    VAR
      i:CARDINAL;
    BEGIN
      FOR i:=WordLength-1 TO 0 BY -1 DO
        IF i IN word THEN
          WriteChar('1');
        ELSE
          WriteChar('0');
        END;
      END;
      WriteLn; WriteLn;
    END display;

    BEGIN
      WriteString('input integer (word) ');
      ReadInt(word); SkipLine;
      WriteString('bit representation of integer'); WriteLn;
      display(BITSET(word)); WriteLn;

      REPEAT
        WriteString('shift (L)eft or (R)ight ');
        ReadChar(reply); SkipLine;
        reply:=CAP(reply);
      UNTIL (reply=left) OR (reply=right);

      WriteString('input number of bits to shift ');
      ReadCard(places); SkipLine;
      WriteString('bit representation of shifted integer');
      WriteLn;

      IF reply=left THEN
        display(LeftShift(word, places));
      ELSE
        display(RightShift(word, places));
      END;
    END C8Q11.
```

Appendix I

Chapter 9

1. The redirection file called food.TXT would contain the following data

```
soup
0.50
cold meat salad
2.50
coffee
0.35
```

Input is taken from the file by using the command line

```
meal <a:\food.TXT >a:output.TXT
```

This assumes that the file can be found on drive a. Output will be redirected to the file output.TXT that can also be found on drive a.

2.
```
MODULE C9Q2;
FROM StreamFile IMPORT ChanId, Open, Close, read, OpenResults;
FROM IOResult IMPORT ReadResult, ReadResults;
FROM StringType IMPORT string;
IMPORT TextIO;
IMPORT STextIO;
VAR
  filename : string;
  line     : string;
  channel  : ChanId;
  results  : OpenResults;
BEGIN
  STextIO.WriteString('input name of file ');
  STextIO.ReadString(filename);
  Open(channel, filename, read, results);
  IF results # opened THEN
    STextIO.WriteString('file cannot be opened ');
    STextIO.WriteString('program abandoned');
    HALT;
  END;

  TextIO.ReadString(channel, line);
  WHILE ReadResult(channel) # endOfInput DO
    STextIO.WriteString(line);
    STextIO.WriteLn;
    TextIO.ReadString(channel, line);

  END;
  Close(channel);
END C9Q2.
```

3.
```
MODULE C9Q3;
FROM StreamFile IMPORT ChanId, Open, Close, read, write,
                       OpenResults, FlagSet;
FROM IOResult IMPORT ReadResult, ReadResults;
FROM StringType IMPORT string;
IMPORT TextIO;
IMPORT STextIO;
VAR
  filename_1, filename_2, filename_3 : string;
  line                               : string;
  channel_1, channel_2, channel_3    : ChanId;
  results                            : OpenResults;

PROCEDURE OpenFile(VAR channel : ChanId; filename : string;
                       mode : FlagSet) : BOOLEAN;

BEGIN
  Open(channel, filename, mode, results);
  IF results # opened THEN
    RETURN FALSE;
  ELSE
    RETURN TRUE;
  END;
END OpenFile;

PROCEDURE input(VAR filename : string);
BEGIN
  STextIO.WriteString('input name of file ');
  STextIO.ReadString(filename);
END input;

PROCEDURE error(filename : string);
BEGIN
  STextIO.WriteString(filename);
  STextIO.WriteString(' cannot be opened -
                       program terminated');

  HALT;
END error;

PROCEDURE copy(VAR from, to : ChanId);
BEGIN
  TextIO.ReadString(from, line);
  WHILE ReadResult(from) # endOfInput DO
    TextIO.WriteString(to, line);
    TextIO.WriteLn(to);
    TextIO.ReadString(from, line);

  END;
END copy;

BEGIN
  input(filename_1);
  IF NOT OpenFile(channel_1, filename_1, read) THEN
```

```
        error(filename_1); END;
input(filename_2);
IF NOT OpenFile(channel_2, filename_2, read) THEN
    error(filename_2); END;
input(filename_3);
IF NOT OpenFile(channel_3, filename_3, write) THEN
    error(filename_3); END;
copy(channel_1, channel_3);
copy(channel_2, channel_3);
Close(channel_1); Close(channel_2); Close(channel_3);
END C9Q3.

4.
MODULE C9Q4;
FROM StreamFile IMPORT ChanId, Open, Close, read, write,
                OpenResults;
FROM IOResult IMPORT ReadResult, ReadResults;
FROM StringType IMPORT ReadString;
FROM TextIO IMPORT ReadString, WriteString, WriteLn;
FROM RealIO IMPORT WriteFixed;
FROM WholeIO IMPORT ReadCard, WriteCard;
CONST
    UnitCost = 0.04;

VAR
    input, output      : ChanId;
    results            : OpenResults;
    previous_reading   : CARDINAL;
    current_reading    : CARDINAL;
    units_used         : CARDINAL;
    details            : string;
    charge             : REAL;

BEGIN
    Open(input, "a:\subscr.TXT", read, results);
    IF results # opened THEN HALT; END;
    Open(output, "a:\telerept.TXT", write, results);
    IF results # opened THEN HALT; END;

    WriteString(output,
                '        TELEPHONE SUBSCRIBERS');
    WriteLn(output); WriteLn(output);
    WriteString(output,
        'NAME        NUMBER        UNITS        CHARGE');
    WriteLn(output);
    WriteString(output,
                        '        USED        £');
    WriteLn(output);

    ReadCard(input, previous_reading);
    WHILE ReadResult(input) # endOfInput DO
        ReadCard(input, current_reading);
        ReadString(input, details);
        units_used := current_reading - previous_reading;
```

```
        charge := UnitCost * FLOAT(units_used);
        WriteString(output, details);
        WriteCard(output, units_used, 8);
        WriteFixed(output, charge, 2, 8);
        WriteLn(output);
        ReadCard(input, previous_reading);
    END;
    Close(input); Close(output);
END C9Q4.

5.
MODULE C9Q5;
FROM StreamFile IMPORT ChanId, Open, Close, read, write,
                OpenResults;
FROM IOResult IMPORT ReadResult, ReadResults;
FROM StringType IMPORT ReadString;
FROM TextIO IMPORT ReadString, WriteString, WriteLn;
FROM RealIO IMPORT ReadReal, WriteFixed;
FROM WholeIO IMPORT ReadCard, WriteCard;
CONST
    UnitCost = 0.04;

VAR
    input, output      : ChanId;
    results            : OpenResults;
    stock_quantity     : CARDINAL;
    unit_cost          : REAL;
    details            : string;
    value              : REAL;
    total              : REAL;

BEGIN
    Open(input, "a:\beer.TXT", read, results);
    IF results # opened THEN HALT; END;
    Open(output, "a:\stock.TXT", write, results);
    IF results # opened THEN HALT; END;

    WriteString(output, '                   STOCK REPORT');
    WriteLn(output); WriteLn(output);
    WriteString(output,
        'STOCK DESCRIPTION        UNIT    LEVEL    VALUE');
    WriteLn(output);
    WriteString(output, 'NUMBER                          COST');
    WriteLn(output);

    total := 0.0;
    ReadCard(input, stock_quantity);
    WHILE ReadResult(input) # endOfInput DO
        ReadReal(input, unit_cost);
        ReadString(input, details);
        value := unit_cost * FLOAT(stock_quantity);
        WriteString(output, details);
        WriteFixed(output, unit_cost, 2, 6);
```

```
      WriteCard(output, stock_quantity, 7);
      WriteFixed(output, value, 2, 8);
      total := total + value;
      WriteLn(output);
      ReadCard(input, stock_quantity);

   END;
   WriteLn(output);
   WriteString(output,                   TOTAL £');
   WriteFixed(output, total, 2, 8);
   WriteLn(output); Close(output);
   Close(input); Close(output);
END C9Q5.

6.
MODULE C9Q6;
FROM StreamFile IMPORT ChanId, Open, Close, read, OpenResults;
FROM IOResult IMPORT ReadResult, ReadResults;
FROM StringType IMPORT string;
IMPORT TextIO;
IMPORT RealIO;
FROM STextIO IMPORT WriteString, WriteLn, ReadChar, WriteChar;
FROM SRealIO IMPORT WriteFixed;

VAR
   data      : ChanId;
   category  : CHAR;
   audience  : REAL;
   total     : REAL;
   programme : string;
   results   : OpenResults;
   choice    : CHAR;
   exit      : BOOLEAN;
   LF        : CHAR; (* remove this line for version 3.0 *)

BEGIN
   Open(data, "a:\viewers.TXT", read, results);
   IF results # opened THEN HALT; END;

   total := 0.0;
   exit := FALSE;
   WriteString('input category D, L, N or S ');
   ReadChar(choice);  choice := CAP(choice);

   CASE choice OF
   'D' : WriteString('DRAMA') |
   'L' : WriteString('LIGHT ENTERTAINMENT') |
   'N' : WriteString('NATURAL HISTORY') |
   'S' : WriteString('SPORT');
   END;
   WriteLn;
   TextIO.ReadChar(data, category);
```

```
   WHILE (ReadResult(data) # endOfInput) AND NOT exit DO
      RealIO.ReadReal(data, audience);
      TextIO.ReadString(data, programme);
      IF choice = category THEN
         total := total + audience;
         WriteString(programme);
         WriteFixed(audience,2,8);
         WriteLn;
      ELSIF choice < category THEN
         exit := TRUE;

      END;
      TextIO.ReadChar(data, LF); (* remove for ver 3.0 *)
      TextIO.ReadChar(data, category);

   END;
   WriteLn;
   WriteString('total audience viewing figure ');
   WriteFixed(total,2,8);
   Close(data);
END C9Q6.

7.
MODULE C9Q7;
FROM StreamFile IMPORT ChanId, Open, Close, read, write,
                       OpenResults;
FROM IOResult IMPORT ReadResult, ReadResults;
FROM StringType IMPORT string;
FROM STextIO IMPORT ReadString, WriteString, WriteLn, ReadChar,
                    WriteChar, WriteLn;
FROM TextIO IMPORT ReadString, WriteString, WriteLn,
                   WriteChar, WriteLn;
FROM RealIO IMPORT ReadReal, WriteFixed;

VAR
   account, report  : ChanId;
   results          : OpenResults;
   amount           : REAL;
   c_d              : CHAR;
   transaction      : string;
   balance          : REAL;
   LF               : CHAR;

BEGIN
   Open(account, 'a:\bank.TXT', read, results);
   IF results # opened THEN HALT; END;
   Open(report, 'a:\statement.TXT', write, results);
   IF results # opened THEN HALT; END;
   WriteString(report,                   XYZ Bank plc');
   WriteLn(report);
   WriteString(report,
               'Mr A.N.Other                 Market Place,
               Anytown, B1 6PT');
   WriteLn(report);
```

```
    WriteString(report,                    Statement of
    Account');
    WriteLn(report); WriteLn(report);
    WriteString(report,                    DEBIT     CREDIT
    ',
    BALANCE');
    WriteLn(report);
    WriteString(report,'1993 sheet 90     Account No. 5678910
    Credit C Debit D');
    WriteLn(report); WriteLn(report);

    balance := 0.0;
    ReadChar(account, c_d);
    WHILE ReadResult(account) # endOfInput DO
        ReadReal(account, amount);
        ReadString(account, transaction);
        ReadChar(account, LF); (* remove for ver 3.0 *)
        WriteString(report, transaction);
        IF c_d = 'C' THEN
            balance := balance + amount;
            WriteFixed(report, amount, 2, 22);
        ELSE
            balance := balance - amount;
            WriteFixed(report, amount, 2, 13);
            WriteString(report, '          ');
        END;
        WriteFixed(report, balance, 2, 9);
        IF balance > 0.0 THEN
            WriteString(report, ' C');
        ELSE
            WriteString(report, ' D');
        END;
        WriteLn(report);

        ReadChar(account, c_d);
    END;

    WriteLn(report);
    WriteString(report, '          BALANCE CARRIED FORWARD ');
    WriteFixed(report, balance, 2, 30);
    IF balance > 0.0 THEN
        WriteString(report, ' C');
    ELSE
        WriteString(report, ' D');
    END;

    Close(account); Close(report);
END C9Q7.
```

Chapter 10

```
1.
MODULE C10Q1;
FROM STextIO IMPORT WriteChar, WriteLn;
FROM SWholeIO IMPORT WriteCard;
VAR
    counter : CARDINAL;
    sum     : CARDINAL;
    letter  : CHAR;

BEGIN
    (* a *)
    FOR counter := 50 TO 75 DO
        WriteCard(counter, 3);
    END;
    WriteLn;
    (* b *)
    FOR counter := 20 TO 5 BY -1 DO
        WriteCard(counter,3);
    END;
    WriteLn;
    (* c *)
    FOR counter := 1 TO 29 DO
        IF counter MOD 2 # 0 THEN
            WriteCard(counter, 3);
        END;
    END;
    WriteLn;
    (* d *)
    FOR counter := 2 TO 20 DO
        IF counter MOD 2 = 0 THEN
            WriteCard(counter * counter, 5);
        END;
    END;
    WriteLn;
    (* e *)
    sum := 0;
    FOR counter := 1 TO 13 DO
        IF counter MOD 2 # 0 THEN
            sum := sum + counter * counter;
        END;
    END;
    WriteCard(sum, 5);
    WriteLn;
    (* f *)
    FOR letter := 'Z' TO 'A' BY -1 DO
        WriteChar(letter);
    END;
    WriteLn;
END C10Q1.
```

```
2.
MODULE C10Q2;
FROM STextIO IMPORT WriteString, WriteChar, WriteLn;
CONST
  alphabet = 'ABCDEFGHIJKLMNOPQRSTUVWXYZ';

VAR
  alpha_string : ARRAY[1..26] OF CHAR;
  index        : CARDINAL;

BEGIN
  alpha_string := alphabet;

  (* a *)
  WriteString(alpha_string); WriteLn;
  (* b *)
  FOR index := 1 TO 6 DO
    WriteChar(alpha_string[index]);
  END;
  WriteLn;
  (* c *)
  FOR index := 17 TO 26 DO
    WriteChar(alpha_string[index]);
  END;
  WriteLn;
  (* d *)
  WriteChar(alpha_string[10]);
  WriteLn;
END C10Q2.
```

```
3.
MODULE C10Q3;
FROM STextIO IMPORT WriteString, WriteLn;
FROM SWholeIO IMPORT WriteInt, ReadInt;
VAR
  X, Y : ARRAY[1..8] OF INTEGER;
  index : CARDINAL;
BEGIN
  WriteString('input eight integers in ascending order ');
  WriteLn;
  FOR index := 1 TO 8 DO
    ReadInt(X[index]);
  END;
  FOR index := 8 TO 1 BY -1 DO
    Y[8-index+1] := X[index];
  END;
  WriteString('numbers in descending order are');
  WriteLn;
  FOR index := 1 TO 8 DO
    WriteInt(Y[index],6);
  END;
  WriteLn;
END C10Q3.
```

```
4.
MODULE C10Q4;
FROM STextIO IMPORT ReadString, WriteString, WriteLn;
FROM StringType IMPORT string;
FROM Strings IMPORT Equal;
CONST
  size = 10; (* size of array *)
TYPE
  entry = RECORD
            exchange : string;
            STDcode  : string;
          END;

  data = ARRAY[1..size] OF entry;

VAR
  DataArray : data;
  STDkey    : string;
  found     : BOOLEAN;
  position  : CARDINAL;

PROCEDURE DataInput(VAR DataArray : data);
VAR
  index : CARDINAL;
BEGIN
  FOR index := 1 TO size DO
    WriteString('input exchange ');
    ReadString(DataArray[index].exchange);
    WriteString('input STD code ');
    ReadString(DataArray[index].STDcode);
  END;
END DataInput;

PROCEDURE search(VAR DataArray : data; key : string;
                 VAR found :BOOLEAN; VAR location : CARDINAL);
BEGIN
  location := 1;
  found := FALSE;
  WHILE (location <= size) AND NOT found DO
    IF Equal(key, DataArray[location].STDcode) THEN
      found := TRUE;
    ELSE
      INC(location);
    END;
  END;
END search;

BEGIN
  DataInput(DataArray);
  REPEAT
    WriteString('STD code? '); ReadString(STDkey);
    search(DataArray, STDkey, found, position);
    IF found THEN
      WriteString(DataArray[position].exchange);
```

```
        ELSE
            WriteString('key not found - try again');
            WriteLn;
        END;
    UNTIL found;
END C10Q4.

5.
MODULE C10Q5;
FROM STextIO IMPORT WriteString, WriteLn;
FROM SWholeIO IMPORT WriteCard, ReadCard;
TYPE
    matches  = ARRAY[1..58] OF BOOLEAN;
    forecast = ARRAY[1..12] OF CARDINAL;

VAR
    score_draws : matches;
    coupon      : forecast;
    draws       : CARDINAL;
    index       : CARDINAL;

PROCEDURE initialise_draws(VAR score_draws : matches);
VAR
    index : CARDINAL;
BEGIN
    FOR index := 1 TO 58 DO
        score_draws[index] := FALSE;
    END;

    WriteString('input the score draw results in the range
                 1..58 - zero to exit');
    WriteLn;
    WriteString('? '); ReadCard(index);
    WHILE index # 0 DO
        score_draws[index] := TRUE;
        WriteString('? '); ReadCard(index);
    END;

    WriteLn;
END initialise_draws;

PROCEDURE initialise_coupon(VAR coupon : forecast);
VAR
    index : CARDINAL;
BEGIN
    WriteString('input your forecast for matches resulting in
                 a score-draw only');
    WriteLn; WriteString('using match numbers from 1..58
             inclusive');
    WriteLn;
    FOR index := 1 TO 12 DO
        WriteString('selection '); WriteCard(index,3);
        WriteString(' ? ');
        ReadCard(coupon[index]);
    END;

END initialise_coupon;

BEGIN
    initialise_draws(score_draws);
    initialise_coupon(coupon);
    draws := 0;
    FOR index := 1 TO 12 DO
        IF score_draws[coupon[index]] THEN
            INC(draws);
        END;
    END;
    WriteString('number of draws on your coupon
                 this week are ');
    WriteCard(draws,2);
END C10Q5.

6.
MODULE C10Q6;
FROM StringType IMPORT string;
FROM Strings IMPORT Equal;
FROM STextIO IMPORT ReadString, WriteString, WriteLn;
FROM SRealIO IMPORT ReadReal, WriteFixed;
TYPE
    food = RECORD
               name  : string;
               price : REAL;
           END;
    food_prices = ARRAY[1..10] OF food;

VAR
    menu : food_prices;
    cost : REAL;
    item : string;

PROCEDURE initialise(VAR menu : food_prices);
BEGIN
    menu[1].name  := 'fruit juice';       menu[1].price  := 0.30;
    menu[2].name  := 'soup';              menu[2].price  := 0.50;
    menu[3].name  := 'cold meat salad';   menu[3].price  := 2.50;
    menu[4].name  := 'sausages (2)';      menu[4].price  := 1.00;
    menu[5].name  := 'bacon & egg';       menu[5].price  := 1.00;
    menu[6].name  := 'cod';               menu[6].price  := 1.50;
    menu[7].name  := 'plaice';            menu[7].price  := 2.00;
    menu[8].name  := 'portion of chips';  menu[8].price  := 0.75;
    menu[9].name  := 'tea';               menu[9].price  := 0.25;
    menu[10].name := 'coffee';            menu[10].price :=0.35;
END initialise;

(* a *)
PROCEDURE part_a(VAR menu : food_prices; food_name : string;
                 VAR cost : REAL);

VAR
    index : CARDINAL;
    found : BOOLEAN;
```

Appendix I

```
BEGIN
  index := 1;
  found := FALSE;
  WHILE (index <= 10) AND NOT found DO
    IF Equal(food_name, menu[index].name) THEN
      found := TRUE;
    ELSE
      INC(index);
    END;
  END;
  IF found THEN
    cost := menu[index].price;
  ELSE
    cost := 0.0;
  END;
END part_a;

(* b *)
PROCEDURE part_b(VAR menu : food_prices);
VAR
  index : CARDINAL;
  money : REAL;
BEGIN
  WriteString('How much do you have to spend? ');
  ReadReal(money);
  FOR index := 1 TO 10 DO
    IF menu[index].price <= money THEN
      WriteString(menu[index].name);
      WriteLn;
    END;
  END;
END part_b;

(* c *)
PROCEDURE part_c(VAR menu : food_prices);
CONST
  VATrate = 0.175;
VAR
  starter, main, beverage : string;
  cost, vat, total        : REAL;
BEGIN
  total:=0.0;
  WriteString('starter? ');      ReadString(starter);
  WriteString('main course? ');  ReadString(main);
  WriteString('beverage? ');     ReadString(beverage);
  WriteLn; WriteLn;
  WriteString('Greasy Spoon Cafe'); WriteLn; WriteLn;
  WriteString(starter); WriteLn;
  part_a(menu, starter, cost);
  total:=total+cost;
  WriteFixed(cost,2,20); WriteLn;
```

```
  WriteString(main); WriteLn;
  part_a(menu,main,cost);
  total:=total+cost;
  WriteFixed(cost,2,20); WriteLn;
  WriteString('portion of chips'); WriteLn;
  part_a(menu, 'portion of chips', cost);
  total:=total+cost;
  WriteFixed(cost,2,20); WriteLn;
  WriteString(beverage); WriteLn;
  part_a(menu, beverage, cost);
  total:=total+cost;
  WriteFixed(cost,2,20); WriteLn;
  WriteString('SUBTOTAL   ');
  WriteFixed(total,2,6); WriteLn;
  vat:=VATrate*total;
  WriteString('VAT   ');
  WriteFixed(vat,2,6); WriteLn;
  total:=total+vat;
  WriteString('TOTAL   ');
  WriteFixed(total,2,6); WriteLn;
END part_c;

BEGIN
  initialise(menu);
  WriteString('input name of food '); ReadString(item);
  part_a(menu, item, cost); WriteString(item);
  WriteString('cost of '); WriteString(item);
  WriteString(' is ');
  WriteFixed(cost,2,6); WriteLn;
  part_b(menu); WriteLn;
  part_c(menu);
END C10Q6.

7.
MODULE C10Q7;
FROM StringType IMPORT string;
FROM STextIO IMPORT WriteString, WriteLn;
FROM SWholeIO IMPORT ReadCard, WriteCard;
TYPE
  months = RECORD
             name : string;
             days : CARDINAL;
           END;
  days_in_months = ARRAY[1..12] OF months;

VAR
  month_array : days_in_months;
  MM          : CARDINAL;
  year        : CARDINAL;
  day         : CARDINAL;
```

```
PROCEDURE initialise(VAR dim : days_in_months;
                     year : CARDINAL);
VAR
    MM : CARDINAL;

BEGIN
    dim[1].name  := 'January';
    dim[2].name  := 'February';
    dim[3].name  := 'March';
    dim[4].name  := 'April';
    dim[5].name  := 'May';
    dim[6].name  := 'June';
    dim[7].name  := 'July';
    dim[8].name  := 'August';
    dim[9].name  := 'September';
    dim[10].name := 'October';
    dim[11].name := 'November';
    dim[12].name := 'December';

    FOR MM := 1 TO 12 DO
        CASE MM OF
        2        : IF year MOD 4 = 0 THEN dim[2].days:=29;
                   ELSE                   dim[2].days:=28;
                   END |

        4,6,9,11 : dim[MM].days:=30;
        ELSE       dim[MM].days:=31;    END;

        END;

END initialise;

PROCEDURE NewYearsDay(year:CARDINAL; VAR day : CARDINAL);
VAR
    LeapDays : CARDINAL;
BEGIN
    day := year - 1993;
    LeapDays := day DIV 4;
    day := (day+LeapDays+6) MOD 7;
    IF day = 0 THEN day:=7; END;
END NewYearsDay;

PROCEDURE PrintCalendar(year:CARDINAL;
                        calendar:days_in_months);
VAR
    MM, DD : CARDINAL;
    day    : CARDINAL;
BEGIN
    WriteCard(year,15); WriteLn; WriteLn;
    NewYearsDay(year, day);
    FOR MM := 1 TO 12 DO
        WriteString('  ');
        WriteString(calendar[MM].name);
        WriteLn; WriteLn;

        (* adjust spacing for first day of month *)
        WriteString(' SUN MON TUE WED THU FRI SAT'); WriteLn;
        FOR DD := 1 TO day-1 DO
            WriteString('    ');
        END;

        FOR DD:=1 TO calendar[MM].days DO
            WriteCard(DD,4);
            IF day MOD 7 = 0 THEN
                WriteLn;
                day := 1;
            ELSE
                INC(day);
            END;

        END;
        WriteLn; WriteLn;
    END;

END PrintCalendar;

BEGIN
    WriteString('input year of calendar '); ReadCard(year);
    initialise(month_array, year);
    NewYearsDay(year, day);
    PrintCalendar(year, month_array);
END C10Q7.

8.
MODULE C10Q8;
FROM STextIO IMPORT ReadString, WriteString, WriteLn;
CONST zero='00000000000000000000';
TYPE
    LongNumber=ARRAY[0..19] OF CHAR;
VAR
    (* arrays used to store two numbers and answer *)
    x,y,z:LongNumber;
    carry : INTEGER;

PROCEDURE DataIn(VAR number:LongNumber);
BEGIN
    WriteString('input a twenty digit number => ');
    ReadString(number);
END DataIn;

PROCEDURE addition(x,y:LongNumber; VAR z:LongNumber;
                                   VAR carry:INTEGER);
VAR
    index:CARDINAL;
    sum : INTEGER;
BEGIN
    carry:=0;
    FOR index:=19 TO 0 BY -1 DO
```

Appendix I

```
    sum:=INTEGER(ORD(x[index])-48)+
         INTEGER(ORD(y[index])-48)+carry;
    IF sum > 9 THEN
      z[index]:=CHR(sum-10+48);
      carry:=1;
    ELSE
      z[index]:=CHR(sum+48);
      carry:=0;
    END;
  END;
  IF carry = 1 THEN
    WriteString('overflow'); WriteLn;
  END;
END addition;

PROCEDURE subtraction(x,y:LongNumber; VAR z:LongNumber;
                      VAR carry:INTEGER);
VAR
  index:CARDINAL;
  difference : INTEGER;
BEGIN
  carry:=0;
  FOR index:=19 TO 0 BY -1 DO
    difference:=INTEGER(ORD(x[index])-48)-
                INTEGER(ORD(y[index])-48)-carry;
    IF difference < 0 THEN
      z[index]:=CHR(10-ABS(difference)+48);
      carry:=1;
    ELSE
      z[index]:=CHR(difference+48);
      carry:=0;
    END;
  END;
END subtraction;

BEGIN
  DataIn(x); DataIn(y);
  addition(x,y,z,carry);
  IF carry = 0 THEN
    WriteString('sum = '); WriteString(z);
  ELSE
    WriteString('overflow');
  END;
  WriteLn;
  subtraction(x,y,z,carry);
  IF carry = 0 THEN
    WriteString('difference = +'); WriteString(z);
  ELSE
    subtraction(zero,z,z,carry);
    WriteString('difference = -'); WriteString(z);
  END;
END C10Q8.
```

```
9.
MODULE C10Q9;
FROM STextIO IMPORT WriteString, WriteLn;
FROM SWholeIO IMPORT WriteCard;
FROM StringType IMPORT string;
CONST
  null = 0C;
  S1='abcdef'; S2='xyzabcdefghijkl';
VAR
  p,q: string;

PROCEDURE LENGTH(S:string):CARDINAL;
VAR
  index:CARDINAL;
BEGIN
  index:=0;
  WHILE S[index] # null DO
    index:=index+1;
  END;
  RETURN index;
END LENGTH;

PROCEDURE DELETE(VAR S:string; I,N:CARDINAL);
VAR
  index, count:CARDINAL;
  temp:string;
BEGIN
  FOR index:=0 TO I-2 DO
    temp[index]:=s[index];
  END;
  count:=I+N-1; index:=I-1;
  WHILE S[index] # null DO
    temp[index]:=S[count];
    INC(count); INC(index);
  END;
  temp[index]:=null;
  S:=temp;
END DELETE;

PROCEDURE INSERT(S1:string; VAR S2:string; I:CARDINAL);
VAR
  index, count : CARDINAL;
  temp:string;
BEGIN
  IF I=1 THEN
    FOR index:=0 TO LENGTH(S1)-1 DO
      temp[index]:=S1[index];
    END;
    FOR index:=LENGTH(S1) TO LENGTH(S2)+LENGTH(S1)-1 DO
      temp[index]:=S2[index-LENGTH(S1)];
    END;
  ELSE
```

```
          FOR index:=0 TO I-2 DO
             temp[index]:=S2[index]
          END;
          FOR index:=I-1 TO I+LENGTH(S1)-2 DO
             temp[index]:=S1[index-I+1];
          END;
          FOR index:=
             LENGTH(S1)+I-1 TO LENGTH(S1)+LENGTH(S2)-1 DO;
             temp[index]:=S2[index-LENGTH(S1)];
          END;
       temp[LENGTH(S1)+LENGTH(S2)]:=null;
       S2:=temp;
END INSERT;

PROCEDURE COPY(S:string; I,N:CARDINAL):string;
VAR
   index, count:CARDINAL;
   temp:string;
BEGIN
   count:=0;
   FOR index:=I-1 TO I+N-2 DO
      temp[count]:=s[index];
      INC(count);
   END;
   temp[N]:=null;
   RETURN temp;
END COPY;

PROCEDURE CONCAT(S1,S2:string):string;
VAR
   index:CARDINAL;
   temp:string;
BEGIN
   FOR index:=0 TO LENGTH(S1)-1 DO
      temp[index]:=S1[index]
   END;
   FOR index:=LENGTH(S1) TO LENGTH(S1)+LENGTH(S2)-1 DO
      temp[index]:=S2[index-LENGTH(S1)];
   END;
   temp[LENGTH(S1)+LENGTH(S2)]:=null;
   RETURN temp;
END CONCAT;

PROCEDURE POS(S1,S2:string):CARDINAL;
VAR
   found:BOOLEAN;
   index, marker, count : CARDINAL;
BEGIN
   found:=FALSE; index:=0;
   REPEAT
      WHILE (S2[index] # null) AND (NOT found) DO
         IF S1[0]=S2[index] THEN
             found:=TRUE;
          END;
          index:=index+1;
      END;
      IF found THEN
         marker:=index-1;
         count:=1;
         FOR index:=1 TO LENGTH(S1)-1 DO
            IF S1[index]=S2[index+marker] THEN
               count:=count+1;
            END;
          END;

         IF count=LENGTH(S1) THEN
            found:=TRUE;
            RETURN marker;
         ELSE
            found:=FALSE;
            index:=marker+1;
          END;
      END;
   UNTIL found OR (S2[index]=null);
END POS;

BEGIN
   p:=S1; q:=S2;
   DELETE(p,3,4);
   WriteString(p); WriteLn;
   p:=S1;
   INSERT(p,q,1);
   WriteString(q); WriteLn;
   p:=S1;
   WriteString(COPY(p,3,2)); WriteLn;
   q:=S2;
   WriteString(CONCAT(p,q)); WriteLn;
   WriteCard(LENGTH(p),3); WriteLn;
   WriteCard(POS(p,q),3); WriteLn;
END C10Q9.

10.
MODULE C10Q10;
FROM STextIO IMPORT ReadString, WriteString, WriteLn,
                    ReadChar, SkipLine;
FROM SRealIO IMPORT ReadReal, WriteFixed;
FROM StringType IMPORT string;
FROM Strings IMPORT Equal;
CONST
   no='N';
VAR
   county : ARRAY[1..3] OF string;          (* array of counties *)
   town   : ARRAY[1..3], [1..3] OF string;  (* array of towns *)
   pop    : ARRAY[1..3], [1..3] OF REAL;    (* array of populations
                                               of towns *)
```

```
    reply  : CHAR;
    name   : string;
    TotalPopulation:REAL;

PROCEDURE initialise;
VAR
    CountyIndex, TownIndex:CARDINAL;
BEGIN
    county[1]:='Cornwall';
    county[2]:='Dorset';
    county[3]:='Hampshire';

    town[1,1]:='Penzance';
    town[1,2]:='Truro';town[1,3]:='Newquay';
    town[2,1]:='Poole';
    town[2,2]:='Dorchester';town[2,3]:='Shaftesbury';
    town[3,1]:='Southampton';
    town[3,2]:='Basingstoke';town[3,3]:='Winchester';

    pop[1,1]:=19210.0; pop[1,2]:=18557.0; pop[1,3]:=15209.0;
    pop[2,1]:=124974.0;pop[2,2]:=14225.0; pop[2,3]:=4951.0;
    pop[3,1]:=214802.0;pop[3,2]:=73492.0; pop[3,3]:=35664.0;

    TotalPopulation:=0.0;
    FOR CountyIndex:=1 TO 3 DO
      FOR TownIndex:=1 TO 3 DO
        TotalPopulation:=TotalPopulation+
                         pop[CountyIndex,TownIndex];
      END;
    END;
END initialise;

PROCEDURE search;
VAR
    row, column, index:CARDINAL;
    found:BOOLEAN;
BEGIN
    WriteString('input name of county ');
    ReadString(name);
    found:=FALSE;
    FOR index:=1 TO 3 DO
      IF Equal(name, county[index]) THEN
        found:=TRUE;
        row:=index;
      END;
    END;
    IF found THEN
      WriteString('input name of town ');
      ReadString(name);
      found:=FALSE;
      FOR index:=1 TO 3 DO
        IF Equal(name, town[row, index]) THEN
          found:=TRUE;
          column:=index;
        END;
      END;
      IF found THEN
        WriteString('population is ');
        WriteFixed(pop[row, column],0,10);
      ELSE
        WriteString('*** town not known ***');
      END;
    ELSE
      WriteString('*** county not known ***');
    END;
    WriteLn;
END search;

PROCEDURE PopSize;
VAR
    row, column, index:INTEGER;
    sum:REAL;
    found:BOOLEAN;
BEGIN
    WriteString('input name of county ');
    ReadString(name);
    found:=FALSE;
    FOR index:=1 TO 3 DO
      IF Equal(name, county[index]) THEN
        found:=TRUE;
        row:=index;
      END;
    END;
    IF found THEN
      sum:=0.0;
      FOR column:=1 TO 3 DO
        sum:=sum+pop[row, column];
      END;
      WriteString('total population of all towns listed in ');
      WriteString(name); WriteFixed(sum,0,12);
      WriteLn;  WriteString('% population');
      WriteFixed(100.0*(sum/TotalPopulation),2,5);
    ELSE
      WriteString('*** county not found ***');
    END;
END PopSize;

PROCEDURE request;
BEGIN
    WriteLn; WriteString('continue? answer (Y)es or N(o) ');
    ReadChar(reply); reply:=CAP(reply); SkipLine;
END request;
```

```
(* main program *)
BEGIN
  initialise;
  REPEAT
    search;
    request;
  UNTIL reply=no;

  REPEAT
    PopSize;
    request;
  UNTIL reply=no;
END C10Q10.


11.
MODULE C10Q11;
FROM STextIO IMPORT ReadChar, WriteChar, WriteString, WriteLn,
                    SkipLine, WriteLn;
FROM SWholeIO IMPORT ReadCard;

CONST
  nought = 'O';
  cross  = 'X';
  space  = 40C;
  no     = 'N';

TYPE
  player = (computer, you);

VAR
  board   : ARRAY[1..3], [1..3] OF CHAR;
  who     : player;
  success : BOOLEAN;
  reply   : CHAR;
  moves   : CARDINAL;

PROCEDURE initialise;
VAR row, column : CARDINAL;
BEGIN
  FOR row := 1 TO 3 DO
    FOR column := 1 TO 3 DO
      board[row, column] := space;
    END;
  END;
  moves := 0;
END initialise;

PROCEDURE CheckPosition(row, column : CARDINAL;
                        VAR success : BOOLEAN);
BEGIN
  IF board[row, column] = space THEN
    success := TRUE;
  ELSE
    success := FALSE;
  END;
END CheckPosition;
```

```
PROCEDURE CheckWinner(who : player; VAR success : BOOLEAN) ;
VAR
  character    : CHAR;
  row, column : CARDINAL;
BEGIN
  success := FALSE;
  IF who = you THEN
    character := cross;
  ELSE
    character := nought;
  END;
  (* check for rows *)
  FOR row := 1 TO 3 DO
    IF (board[row,1] = character)
       AND (board[row,2] = character)
       AND (board[row,3] = character) THEN
      success := TRUE;
    END;
  END;
  (* check for columns *)
  IF NOT success THEN
    FOR column := 1 TO 3 DO
      IF (board[1,column] = character)
         AND (board[2,column] = character)
         AND (board[3,column] = character) THEN
        success := TRUE;
      END;
    END;
  END;
  (* check diagonals *)
  IF NOT success THEN
    IF (board[1,1] = character)
       AND (board[2,2] = character)
       AND (board[3,3] = character) THEN
      success := TRUE;
    END;
  END;
  IF NOT success THEN
    IF (board[1,3] = character)
       AND (board[2,2] = character)
       AND (board[3,1] = character) THEN
      success := TRUE;
    END;
  END;
END CheckWinner;

PROCEDURE display;
VAR
  row, column : CARDINAL;
BEGIN
  WriteLn; WriteLn;
  FOR row := 1 TO 3 DO
    FOR column := 1 TO 3 DO
```

```
        WriteChar(board[row, column]);
        IF column # 3 THEN WriteString(' | '); END;
      END;
      WriteLn;
      IF row # 3 THEN WriteString('--------'); WriteLn; END;
    END;
    WriteLn; WriteLn;
END display;

PROCEDURE play(who:player);
VAR
    row, column : CARDINAL;
    Xrow, Xcol  : CARDINAL;
    success     : BOOLEAN;
BEGIN
    IF who = you THEN
      REPEAT
        WriteString('input position of play ');
        ReadCard(row);ReadCard(column); SkipLine;
      UNTIL (row >=1) AND (row <=3) AND (column >=1)
                      AND (column <=3);
        CheckPosition(row, column, success);
      UNTIL success;
      board[row, column] := cross;
      Xrow := row;
      Xcol := column;
    ELSE
      row    := (4-Xrow) MOD 4;
      column := (4-Xcol) MOD 4;
      REPEAT
        CheckPosition(row, column, success);
        IF NOT success THEN
          INC(column);
          IF column > 3 THEN
            column := 1;
            INC(row);
            IF row > 3 THEN
              row := 1;
            END;
          END;
        END;
      UNTIL success;
      board[row, column] := nought;
    END;
END play;

BEGIN
    initialise;
    REPEAT
      who := you;
```

```
        play(who); display; INC(moves);
        CheckWinner(who, success);
        IF success THEN WriteString('player wins'); END;
        IF NOT success AND (moves < 9) THEN
          who := computer;
          play(who); display; INC(moves);
          CheckWinner(who, success);
          IF success THEN
            WriteString('computer wins');
          END;
        END;
      UNTIL success OR (moves = 9);
      IF NOT success AND (moves = 9) THEN
        WriteString('stale mate');
      END;
      WriteLn; WriteLn;
      WriteString('another game - Y[es] or N[o] ');
      ReadChar(reply);
    UNTIL CAP(reply) = no;
END C10Q11.

12.
MODULE C10Q12;
FROM StreamFile IMPORT ChanId, Open, Close, read, OpenResults;
FROM IOResult IMPORT ReadResult, ReadResults;
FROM TextIO IMPORT ReadString, ReadResults;
FROM WholeIO IMPORT ReadCard;
FROM STextIO IMPORT WriteString, WriteChar, WriteLn;
FROM SWholeIO IMPORT WriteCard;
FROM StringType IMPORT string;
CONST
    space = 40C;
TYPE
    data =   RECORD
               name : string;
               CASE tag : CHAR OF
                 'F' : habitat    : string|
                 'B' : fly        : BOOLEAN|
                 'I' : wings      : CARDINAL|
                 'R' : description: string;
               END;
               CASE Amble : BOOLEAN OF |
                 TRUE  : legs : CARDINAL;
                         AmbleMode: string|

                 FALSE:
               END;
               CASE LivesInWater : BOOLEAN OF |
                 TRUE  : SwimmingMode : string|
                 FALSE : FearsWater   : BOOLEAN;
               END;

             END;
```

```modula-2
VAR
  animal : data;  DataFile : ChanId;  results : OpenResults;
  LF : CHAR;

PROCEDURE ReadBoolean(VAR value:BOOLEAN);
VAR
  truth : string;  character : CHAR;
BEGIN
  ReadString(DataFile, truth);
  character:=CAP(truth[0]);
  CASE character OF
    'T' : value:= TRUE |
    'F' : value:= FALSE;
  END;
END ReadBoolean;

PROCEDURE ReadRecord(VAR animal : data);
VAR
  tags :string;
BEGIN
  WITH animal DO
    ReadString(DataFile, name);
    ReadString(DataFile, tags);
    tag:=CAP(tags[0]);
    CASE tag OF
      'F' : ReadString(DataFile, habitat) |
      'B' : ReadBoolean(fly) |
      'I' : ReadCard(DataFile, wings);
            ReadChar(DataFile, LF);
      'R' : ReadString(DataFile, description);
    END;
    ReadBoolean(Amble);
    IF Amble THEN
      ReadCard(DataFile, legs);
      ReadChar(DataFile, LF);
      ReadString(DataFile, AmbleMode);
    END;
    ReadBoolean(LivesInWater);
    IF LivesInWater THEN
      ReadString(DataFile, SwimmingMode);
    ELSE
      ReadBoolean(FearsWater);
    END;
  END;
END ReadRecord;

PROCEDURE WriteRecord(animal : data);
BEGIN
  WITH animal DO
    WriteLn;
    WriteString('The '); WriteString(name);
    CASE tag OF
      'F' : WriteString(' is a '); WriteString(habitat);
            WriteString(' fish.'); WriteLn|
      'B' : WriteString(' is a ');
            IF NOT fly THEN WriteString(' flightless ');
            END;
            WriteString(' bird '); WriteLn|
      'I' : WriteString(' is an insect with ');
            WriteCard(wings, 2);
            WriteString(' wings.'); WriteLn|
      'R' : WriteString(' is a reptile ');
            WriteString(description);
            WriteLn;
    ELSE
            WriteString('is neither a fish, bird,
                        insect or reptile ');
            WriteLn;
    END;

    IF Amble THEN
      WriteString('it can ');
      WriteString(AmbleMode);
      WriteString(' on '); WriteCard(legs, 2);
      WriteString(' legs.');
    ELSE
      WriteString('it has no legs.');
    END;
    WriteLn;
    IF LivesInWater THEN
      WriteString('It lives in water and swims using its ');
      WriteString(SwimmingMode);
    ELSE
      WriteString('It lives on land ');
      IF FearsWater THEN
        WriteString(' and fears water ');
      ELSE
        WriteString(' but likes water');
      END;
    END;
    WriteLn; WriteLn;
  END;
END WriteRecord;

BEGIN
  Open(DataFile, "a:animal.txt", read, results);
  IF results # opened THEN HALT; END;
  ReadRecord(animal);
  WHILE ReadResult(DataFile) # endOfInput DO
    WriteRecord(animal);
    WriteLn;
    ReadRecord(animal);
  END;
  Close(DataFile);
END C10Q12.
```

Appendix I

Appendix I

Chapter 11

```
1.
MODULE C11Q1;
FROM STextIO IMPORT WriteString, WriteLn;
FROM SWholeIO IMPORT ReadCard, WriteCard;
VAR
   table:ARRAY [1..100] OF CARDINAL;

PROCEDURE initialise;
VAR
   index:CARDINAL;
BEGIN
   FOR index:=1 TO 100 DO
      table[index]:=0;
   END;
END initialise;

PROCEDURE DataIn;
VAR
   index:CARDINAL;
   datum:CARDINAL;
BEGIN
   WriteString('input ten different numbers, unsorted,
               in the range 1..100 ');
   WriteLn;
   FOR index:=1 TO 10 DO
      REPEAT          (* validate numbers being different *)
         WriteString('? ');
         ReadCard(datum);
      UNTIL datum # table[datum];
      table[datum]:=datum;
   END;
END DataIn;

PROCEDURE display;
VAR
   index:CARDINAL;
BEGIN
   FOR index:=1 TO 100 DO
      IF table[index] # 0 THEN
         WriteCard(table[index],4);
      END;
   END;
END display;

BEGIN
   initialise;
   DataIn;
   display;
END C11Q1.
```

```
2.
MODULE C11Q2;
FROM STextIO IMPORT WriteString, WriteLn;
FROM SWholeIO IMPORT ReadCard;
FROM SRealIO IMPORT WriteFixed;

CONST
   MaxNumb=40; (*cater for a maximum of 40 numbers in the set*)

VAR
   table:ARRAY [0..MaxNumb-1] OF CARDINAL;
   size:CARDINAL;

PROCEDURE DataIn(VAR size:CARDINAL);
VAR
   datum:CARDINAL;
BEGIN
   WriteString('input set of numbers one per line terminate
               with 0 ');
   WriteLn;
   size:=0;
   ReadCard(datum);
   WHILE datum # 0 DO
      table[size]:=datum;
      ReadCard(datum);
      INC(size);
   END;
END DataIn;

PROCEDURE insertion_sort(VAR numbers : ARRAY OF CARDINAL;
                             size : CARDINAL);
VAR
   current, location, index : CARDINAL;
BEGIN
   FOR index:=1 TO size-1 DO
      current := numbers[index]; location := index;
      WHILE (location > 0)
         AND (numbers[location-1] > current) DO
         numbers[location] := numbers[location-1];
         DEC(location);
      END;
      numbers[location]:=current;
   END;
END insertion_sort;

PROCEDURE median(size:CARDINAL):REAL;
VAR
   MidPoint:REAL;
BEGIN
   insertion_sort;
   MidPoint:=(FLOAT(size))/2.0;
   IF ODD(size) THEN
      RETURN FLOAT(table[TRUNC(MidPoint)]);
   ELSE
```

```
        RETURN FLOAT(table[TRUNC(MidPoint)]
                    +table[TRUNC(MidPoint)-1])/2.0;

    END;
END median;

BEGIN
    DataIn(size);
    insertion_sort(table, size);
    WriteString('median of set of numbers is ');
    WriteFixed(median(size),1,5);
END C11Q2.

3.
MODULE C11Q3;
FROM STextIO IMPORT WriteString, WriteLn;
FROM SWholeIO IMPORT ReadCard, WriteCard;
VAR
    table:ARRAY [1..20] OF CARDINAL;

PROCEDURE DataIn;
VAR
    index : CARDINAL;
BEGIN
    WriteString('input twenty cardinal numbers'); WriteLn;
    FOR index := 1 TO 20 DO
        ReadCard(table[index]);
    END;
END DataIn;

PROCEDURE sort;
VAR
    swap             : BOOLEAN;
    index, last_index : CARDINAL;
    temp             : CARDINAL;
BEGIN
    last_index := 19;
    REPEAT
        swap := FALSE;
        (* compare adjacent numbers *)
        FOR index:=1 TO last_index DO
            IF table[index] > table[index+1] THEN
                (* swap numbers *)
                temp            := table[index+1];
                table[index+1]  := table[index];
                table[index]    := temp;
                swap            := TRUE;
            END;
        END;
        DEC(last_index);
    UNTIL NOT swap;
END sort;
```

```
PROCEDURE display;
VAR
    index : CARDINAL;
BEGIN
    FOR index := 1 TO 20 DO
        WriteCard(table[index], 4);
    END;
    WriteLn;
END display;

BEGIN
    DataIn;
    sort;
    display;
END C11Q3.

4.
MODULE C11Q4;
(* program to merge the contents of three ordered files into
a fourth ordered file *)

FROM StreamFile IMPORT ChanId, Open, Close, read, write,
                       OpenResults;
FROM IOResult IMPORT ReadResult, ReadResults;
FROM StringType IMPORT string;
FROM Strings IMPORT Compare, less;
FROM TextIO IMPORT ReadString, WriteString, WriteLn;

CONST
    high_key = "~";

VAR
    file_a, file_b, file_c, file_d : ChanId;
    results                        : OpenResults;
    key_a, key_b, key_c            : string;
    eof_a, eof_b, eof_c            : ReadResults;

BEGIN
    Open (file_a, "a:file_a.txt", read, results);
    IF results # opened THEN HALT; END;
    Open (file_b, "a:file_b.txt", read, results);
    IF results # opened THEN HALT; END;
    Open (file_c, "a:file_c.txt", read, results);
    IF results # opened THEN HALT; END;
    Open (file_d, "a:file_d.txt", write, results);
    IF results # opened THEN HALT; END;

    ReadString(file_a, key_a);
    eof_a := ReadResult(file_a);
    ReadString(file_b, key_b);
    eof_b := ReadResult(file_b);
    ReadString(file_c, key_c);
    eof_c := ReadResult(file_c);
```

```
    WHILE (eof_a # endofInput)   OR  (eof_b # endofInput)
                     OR  (eof_c # endofInput) DO
      IF (Compare(key_a, key_b) = less)
      AND (Compare(key_a, key_c) = less) THEN
          WriteString(file_d, key_a);
          WriteLn(file_d);
          ReadString(file_a, key_a);
          eof_a := ReadResult(file_a);
          IF eof_a = endofInput THEN
             key_a := high_key; END;
      ELSIF (Compare(key_b, key_a) = less)
      AND (Compare(key_b, key_c) = less) THEN
          WriteString(file_d, key_b);
          WriteLn(file_d);
          ReadString(file_b, key_b);
          eof_b := ReadResult(file_b);
          IF eof_b = endofInput THEN
             key_b := high_key; END;
      ELSE    WriteString(file_d, key_c);
          WriteLn(file_d);
          ReadString(file_c, key_c);
          eof_c := ReadResult(file_c);
          IF eof_c = endofInput THEN
             key_c := high_key; END;
      END;
    END;
    Close(file_a); Close(file_b); Close(file_c);Close(file_d);
END C11Q4.

5.
MODULE C11Q5;
(* program to demonstrate a sequential search for information
that is ordered on a particular key *)

FROM StreamFile IMPORT ChanId, Open, Close, read, OpenResults;
FROM IOResult IMPORT ReadResult, ReadResults;
FROM StringType IMPORT string;
FROM Strings IMPORT Equal, Compare, less, Capitalize;
FROM TextIO IMPORT ReadString;
IMPORT STextIO;

CONST
NO = 'NO';

VAR
    datafile  : ChanId;
    line      : string;
    surname   : string;
    found     : BOOLEAN;
    reply     : string;
```

```
PROCEDURE IsolateKey(VAR surname : string; line : string);
(* procedure to isolate the surname as a key from a line in
the text file *)
CONST
    null = 0C;
    comma = 54C;

VAR index : CARDINAL;

BEGIN
    index := 0;
    WHILE line[index] # comma DO
       surname[index]:=line[index];
       INC(index);
    END;
    surname[index]:=null;
END IsolateKey;

PROCEDURE OpenFile(VAR datafile : ChanId; filename : string);
VAR
    results : OpenResults;
BEGIN
    Open (datafile, filename, read, results);
    IF results # opened THEN
       STextIO.WriteString(filename);
       STextIO.WriteString(' cannot be opened ');
       STextIO.WriteString('program abandoned');
       STextIO.WriteLn;
       HALT;
    END;
END OpenFile;

PROCEDURE sequential_search      (key : string; VAR line : string;
                                 VAR found : BOOLEAN) ;
(* procedure to search an ordered array for a key *)

VAR surname : string;
BEGIN
    found := FALSE;
    ReadString(datafile, line);
    WHILE (ReadResult(datafile) # endofInput) AND NOT found DO
       IsolateKey(surname, line);
       IF Equal(key, surname) THEN
          found := TRUE;
       ELSE
          IF Compare(key, surname) = less THEN
             RETURN;
          ELSE
             ReadString(datafile, line);
          END;
       END;
    END;
END sequential_search;
```

```
BEGIN
    REPEAT
        OpenFile(datafile, "a:datafile.txt");
        STextIO.WriteString('input a surname ');
        STextIO.ReadString(surname);
        sequential search(surname, line, found);
        IF found THEN
            STextIO.WriteString(line);
        ELSE
            STextIO.WriteString(surname);
            STextIO.WriteString(' not listed');
        END;
        STextIO.WriteLn; STextIO.WriteLn;
        STextIO.WriteString('continue search - yes or no? ');
        STextIO.ReadString(reply);
        Capitalize(reply);
        Close(datafile);
    UNTIL Equal(reply, NO);
END C11Q5.
```

Chapter 12

```
1.
MODULE C12Q1;
FROM STextIO IMPORT WriteString, WriteLn;
FROM SWholeIO IMPORT WriteCard, ReadCard;
CONST
    MaxNumber=10;
VAR
    table:ARRAY [0..MaxNumber-1] OF CARDINAL;

PROCEDURE DataIn;
VAR
    index:INTEGER;
BEGIN
    WriteString('input 10 non-zero cardinal values ');WriteLn;
    FOR index:=0 TO MaxNumber-1 DO
        ReadCard(table[index]);
    END;
END DataIn;

PROCEDURE sum(table:ARRAY OF CARDINAL; size:INTEGER):CARDINAL;
BEGIN
    IF size < 0 THEN
        RETURN 0;
    ELSE
        RETURN table[size]+sum(table, size-1);
    END;
END sum;
```

```
BEGIN
    DataIn;
    WriteString('sum of numbers in array is ');
    WriteCard(sum(table,MaxNumber-1),6); WriteLn;
END C12Q1.

2.
MODULE C12Q2;
FROM STextIO IMPORT WriteString, WriteLn;
FROM SWholeIO IMPORT ReadCard, WriteCard;
VAR
    X,n : CARDINAL;

PROCEDURE power(X,n:CARDINAL):CARDINAL;
BEGIN
    IF n=0 THEN
        RETURN 1;
    ELSE
        RETURN X*power(X,n-1);
    END;
END power;

BEGIN
    WriteString('input a value for X '); ReadCard(X);
    WriteString('input a value for n '); ReadCard(n);
    WriteString('X raised to the power of n is ');
    WriteCard(power(X,n),6);
END C12Q2.

3.
MODULE C12Q3;
FROM SWholeIO IMPORT WriteCard;
VAR
    n:CARDINAL;

PROCEDURE Fibonacci(n:CARDINAL):CARDINAL;
BEGIN
    IF (n=1) OR (n=2) THEN
        RETURN 1;
    ELSE
        RETURN Fibonacci(n-2)+Fibonacci(n-1);
    END;
END Fibonacci;

BEGIN
    FOR n:=1 TO 15 DO
        WriteCard(Fibonacci(n),4);
    END;
END C12Q3.
```

Appendix I

```
4.
MODULE C12Q4;
FROM STextIO IMPORT WriteString, WriteLn;
FROM SWholeIO IMPORT WriteCard, ReadCard;
CONST
    MaxNumber=10;
VAR
    table:ARRAY [0..MaxNumber-1] OF CARDINAL;
    big:CARDINAL;

PROCEDURE DataIn;
VAR
    index:INTEGER;
BEGIN
    WriteString('input 10 non-zero cardinal values ');WriteLn;
    FOR index:=0 TO MaxNumber-1 DO
        ReadCard(table[index]);
    END;

END DataIn;

PROCEDURE largest(table:ARRAY OF CARDINAL; size:INTEGER);
BEGIN
    IF size = 0 THEN
        RETURN;
    ELSE
        IF table[size] > big THEN
            big:=table[size];
        END;
        largest(table, size-1);

    END;
END largest;

BEGIN
    DataIn;
    big:=table[0];
    largest(table, MaxNumber-1);
    WriteString('largest number in list is ');
    WriteCard(big,5);
END C12Q4.

5.
MODULE C12Q5;
FROM STextIO IMPORT WriteString, WriteLn;
FROM SWholeIO IMPORT WriteInt;
FROM WholeIO IMPORT ReadInt;
FROM StreamFile IMPORT ChanId, Open, Close, read, OpenResults;
FROM IOResult IMPORT ReadResult, ReadResults;
CONST
    MaxNumbers=100;
TYPE
    table = ARRAY[0..MaxNumbers-1] OF INTEGER;
VAR
    numbers: table;
    size   : CARDINAL;

PROCEDURE DataInput (VAR numbers:ARRAY OF INTEGER;
                     VAR size:CARDINAL);
VAR
    file   : ChanId;
    results : OpenResults;
BEGIN
    Open(file, 'a:\file.txt', read, results);
    IF results # opened THEN HALT; END;
    size := 0;
    ReadInt(file, numbers[size]);
    WHILE ReadResult(file) # endOfInput DO
        INC(size);
        ReadInt(file, numbers[size]);

    END;
    Close(file);
END DataInput;

PROCEDURE DataOut(numbers : ARRAY OF INTEGER;
                  size : CARDINAL);
VAR index : CARDINAL;
BEGIN
    FOR index := 0 TO size-1 DO
        IF index MOD 10 = 0 THEN
            WriteLn;
        END;
        WriteInt(numbers[index], 6);

    END;
    WriteLn;
END DataOut;

PROCEDURE selection_sort(VAR numbers:ARRAY OF INTEGER;
                         size:CARDINAL);
VAR
    index, position : CARDINAL;
    temp, largest   : INTEGER;
BEGIN
    IF size=0 THEN RETURN; END;
    largest:=MIN(INTEGER);
    FOR index:=0 TO size-1 DO
        IF numbers[index] > largest THEN
            largest:=numbers[index];
            position:=index;
        END;

    END;
    temp:=numbers[index];
    numbers[index]:=largest;
    numbers[position]:=temp;
    selection_sort(numbers, size-1);
END selection_sort;
```

```
BEGIN
  DataInput(numbers, size);
  DataOut(numbers, size);
  selection sort(numbers, size);
  DataOut(numbers, size);
END C12Q5.
```

Chapter 13

```
1.
MODULE C13Q1;
FROM STextIO IMPORT WriteLn, WriteString;
FROM SWholeIO IMPORT ReadInt, WriteInt;
FROM Storage IMPORT ALLOCATE, DEALLOCATE;
CONST
  terminator=0; (* input terminator *)
TYPE
  pointer=POINTER TO node;
  node=RECORD
    number:INTEGER;
    link  :pointer;
    END;
VAR
  head1, head2 :pointer;    (* heads of two linked lists *)
  last: pointer;
  max:INTEGER;

PROCEDURE CreateList(VAR head:pointer);
(* build first linked list *)
VAR
  last : pointer; value : INTEGER;

PROCEDURE CreateNode(VAR next:pointer; value : INTEGER);
BEGIN
  ALLOCATE(next,SIZE(node));
  next^.number := value;
  next^.link:=NIL;
END CreateNode;

BEGIN
  head := NIL;
  WriteString('input integers - terminate with 0'); WriteLn;
  WriteString('? ');
  ReadInt(value);
  WHILE value # terminator DO
    IF head = NIL THEN
      CreateNode(head, value);
      last:=head;
    ELSE
      CreateNode(last^.link, value);
      last := last^.link;
```

```
  END;
  WriteString('? ');
  ReadInt(value);
END;
END CreateList;

PROCEDURE ListOut(head:pointer);
(* display the contents of a linked list *)
VAR
  current:pointer;
BEGIN
  current:=head;
  WHILE current # NIL DO
    WriteInt(current^.number,4); WriteLn;
    current:=current^.link;
  END;
END ListOut;

PROCEDURE DeleteNode(VAR head :pointer; max:INTEGER);
(* search for the largest item in the list and delete the node
containing this item *)
VAR
  temp, last, current : pointer;
BEGIN
  current:=head;
  last:=head;
  WHILE current^.number # max DO
    last:=current;
    current:=current^.link;
  END;
  IF head=current THEN
    head:=head^.link;
    DEALLOCATE(current,SIZE(node));
  ELSE
    last^.link:=current^.link;
    DEALLOCATE(current, SIZE(node));
  END;
END DeleteNode;

PROCEDURE largest(VAR head:pointer):INTEGER;
(* function that returns the largest integer in the linked
list *)
VAR
  max:INTEGER;
  current:pointer;
BEGIN
  current:=head;
  max:=MIN(INTEGER);
  WHILE current # NIL DO
    IF current^.number > max THEN
      max:=current^.number;
    END;
```

Appendix I

```
            current:=current^.link;
    END;
    RETURN max;
END largest;

PROCEDURE build(VAR next:pointer; value:INTEGER);
(* procedure to build the second linked list containing
integers sorted into descending order *)
BEGIN
    ALLOCATE(next,SIZE(node));
    next^.number:=value;
    next^.link:=NIL;
END build;

BEGIN
    CreateList(head1);
    max:=largest(head1);
    build(head2, max);
    last:=head2;
    DeleteNode(head1, max);
    WHILE head1 # NIL DO
        max:=largest(head1);
        build(last^.link, max);
        last:=last^.link;
        DeleteNode(head1, max);
    END;
    ListOut(head2);
END C13Q1.

2.
MODULE C13Q2;
FROM STextIO IMPORT ReadChar, WriteChar, WriteString,
                    WriteLn, SkipLine;
FROM Storage IMPORT ALLOCATE, DEALLOCATE;
CONST
    terminator = 40C;
TYPE
    stack = POINTER TO node;
    node  = RECORD
               data : CHAR;
               link : stack;
            END;
VAR
    character : CHAR;
    lifo : stack;

PROCEDURE initialise(VAR s : stack);
BEGIN
    s:=NIL;
END initialise;
```

```
PROCEDURE empty(s : stack) : BOOLEAN;
BEGIN
    IF s = NIL THEN
        RETURN TRUE;
    ELSE
        RETURN FALSE;
    END;
END empty;

PROCEDURE push(VAR s : stack; character : CHAR);
VAR
    temp : stack;
BEGIN
    ALLOCATE(temp, SIZE(node));
    temp^.data := character;
    temp^.link := s;
    s :=temp;
END push;

PROCEDURE pop(VAR s : stack; VAR character : CHAR);
VAR
    temp : stack;
BEGIN
    IF NOT empty(s) THEN
        temp := s;
        character := s^.data;
        s := s^.link;
        DEALLOCATE(temp, SIZE(node));
    END;
END pop;

BEGIN
    initialise(lifo);
    WriteString('enter single characters on to a stack');
    WriteLn;
    WriteString('press SPACE RETURN to exit'); WriteLn;
    ReadChar(character); SkipLine;
    WHILE character # terminator DO
        push(lifo, character);
        ReadChar(character); SkipLine;
    END;
    WriteString('reverse order of characters input'); WriteLn;
    WHILE NOT empty(lifo) DO
        pop(lifo, character);
        WriteChar(character);
    END;
    WriteLn;
END C13Q2.
```

```
3. (a)
PROCEDURE ListOut(head : pointer);
VAR
    current : pointer;
BEGIN
    current:=head;
    IF current=NIL THEN RETURN; END;
    STextIO.WriteString(current^.text);
    STextIO.WriteLn;
    ListOut(current^.link);
END ListOut;

(b)
```

the following three assignments are inserted after LOOP in the main program
found := FALSE; current:=head; last:=current;

```
PROCEDURE search(VAR last, current : pointer; key : string;
                 VAR found : BOOLEAN);
VAR word : string;
BEGIN
    IF current=NIL THEN RETURN;
    ELSE
        IsolateKey(word, current^.text);
        IF Equal(key, word) THEN
            found := TRUE;
            RETURN;
        ELSIF Compare(key, word) = less THEN
            RETURN;
        ELSE
            last:=current;
            current:=current^.link;
        END;
        search(last,current,key,found);
    END;
END search;

4.
MODULE C13Q4;
FROM STextIO IMPORT WriteLn, WriteString;
FROM SWholeIO IMPORT ReadInt, WriteInt;
FROM Storage IMPORT ALLOCATE, DEALLOCATE;
CONST
    terminator=0; (* input terminator *)
TYPE
    pointer=POINTER TO node;
    node=RECORD
        number:INTEGER;
        link  :pointer;
    END;
VAR
    head :pointer;

PROCEDURE CreateList(VAR head:pointer);
(* build circular linked list *)
VAR last:pointer;

PROCEDURE CreateNode(VAR next:pointer; head:pointer);
BEGIN
    ALLOCATE(next,SIZE(node));
    WriteString('? ');
    ReadInt(next^.number);
    IF head=NIL THEN
        next^.link:=next;
    ELSE
        next^.link:=head;
    END;
END CreateNode;

BEGIN
    WriteString('input integers - terminate with 0'); WriteLn;
    CreateNode(head,NIL);
    last:=head;
    WHILE last^.number # terminator DO
        CreateNode(last^.link, head);
        last:=last^.link;
    END;
END CreateList;

PROCEDURE ListOut(head:pointer);
(* display the contents of a circular linked list *)
VAR
    current:pointer;
    counter:CARDINAL;
BEGIN
    current:=head;
    counter:=0;
    WHILE counter # 1 DO
        WriteInt(current^.number,4); WriteLn;
        current:=current^.link;
        IF current = head THEN INC(counter); END;
    END;
END ListOut;

PROCEDURE ReverseLinks(head:pointer);
VAR current, last, temporary : pointer;
BEGIN
    (* initialise current to node after head *)
    current:=head^.link;
    last:=head; (* initialise last to head *)
    WHILE current^.link # last DO
        (* save addres of next node in list *)
        temporary:=current^.link;
        (* reverse pointer to point to previous node *)
        current^.link:=last;
        last:=current; (* move last to next node *)
```

```
    (* move current to next node to change *)
        current:=temporary;
    END END;
END ReverseLinks;

BEGIN
    head:=NIL;
    CreateList(head);
    WriteString('contents of circular linked list '); WriteLn;
    ListOut(head);
    WriteLn;
    WriteString('contents with links reversed '); WriteLn;
    ReverseLinks(head);
    ListOut(head);
    WriteLn;
END C13Q4.

5.
MODULE C13Q5; IMPORT ALLOCATE, DEALLOCATE;
FROM Storage IMPORT ALLOCATE, DEALLOCATE;
FROM STextIO IMPORT ReadString, WriteString, WriteLn,
        ReadChar, SkipLine;
FROM SRealIO IMPORT ReadReal, WriteFixed;
FROM StringType IMPORT string;

CONST
    exit='E';

TYPE
    pointer = POINTER TO node;
    node = RECORD
            time  : REAL;
            number : string;
            name  : string;
            message: string;
            link  : pointer;
          END;

VAR
    head, last, current : pointer;
    MenuCode           : CHAR;
    key                : REAL;
    NotFound           : BOOLEAN;
    name, number, message : string;

PROCEDURE InputTime(VAR TimeOfDay:REAL);
VAR
    hours, minutes : CARDINAL;

BEGIN
    REPEAT
        WriteString('input time of call (24 hour clock) ');
        ReadReal(TimeOfDay);
        hours:=TRUNC(TimeOfDay);
        minutes:=TRUNC(100.0*(TimeOfDay-FLOAT(hours))+0.5);
    UNTIL (hours>=0) AND (hours<=23) AND (minutes>=0)
                       AND (minutes<=59);

    (* adjust time from noon to noon *)
    IF TimeOfDay >= 12.00 THEN
        TimeOfDay:=TimeOfDay-12.00;
    ELSE
        TimeOfDay:=TimeOfDay+12.00;
    END;
END InputTime;

PROCEDURE InputData(VAR name, number, message : string);
BEGIN
    WriteString('input name of customer '); ReadString(name);
    WriteString('input telephone number ');
    ReadString(number);
    WriteString('input message             ');
    ReadString(message);
END InputData;

PROCEDURE display(head:pointer);
VAR
    TimeOfDay:REAL;
BEGIN
    IF head = NIL THEN RETURN; END;
    WriteLn; WriteLn;
    WriteString('EARLY BIRD ALARM CALL'); WriteLn;
    WriteString('next customer');WriteLn;
    WriteString('time of call is      ');
    TimeOfDay:=head^.time;
    IF (TimeOfDay>=0.0) AND (TimeOfDay<=11.59) THEN
        TimeOfDay:=TimeOfDay-12.0;
    ELSE
        TimeOfDay:=TimeOfDay-12.00;
    END;
    WriteFixed(TimeOfDay,2,5); WriteLn;
    WriteString('telephone number      ');
    WriteString(head^.number); WriteLn;
    WriteString('name                  ');
    WriteString(head^.name); WriteLn;
    WriteString('special message is ');
    WriteString(head^.message); WriteLn;
    WriteLn;
END display;

PROCEDURE menu(VAR MenuCode:CHAR);
BEGIN
    SkipLine;
    WriteLn;
    WriteString('select code to'); WriteLn; WriteLn;
    WriteString('(I)nsert'); WriteLn;
```

```
      WriteString('  (C)ancel'); WriteLn;
      WriteString('  (A)mend'); WriteLn;
      WriteString('  (E)xit '); WriteLn;
      WriteLn;
   REPEAT
      WriteString('selection? ');
      ReadChar(MenuCode); MenuCode:=CAP(MenuCode); SkipLine;
   UNTIL (MenuCode='I') OR (MenuCode='C') OR (MenuCode='A')
                        OR (MenuCode='E');
END menu;

PROCEDURE search(VAR head, last, current : pointer;
                 key : REAL; VAR NotFound : BOOLEAN);
(* search for the position of a key in the linked list *)
BEGIN
   NotFound:=TRUE;
   (* point at head of list with variables current and head *)
   current:=head;
   last:=current;
   WHILE (current # NIL) AND NotFound DO
      IF key < current^.time THEN
         RETURN;
      ELSIF key=current^.time THEN
         NotFound:=FALSE;
         RETURN;
      ELSE
         (* move to next node in list and continue search *)
         last:=current;
         current:=current^.link;
      END;
   END;
END search;

PROCEDURE insert(VAR head, last, current : pointer;
                 key:REAL; number, name, message:string);
(* insert a new node into the linked list *)
VAR temp : pointer;
BEGIN
   ALLOCATE(temp, SIZE(node));
   temp^.time:=key;
   temp^.number:=number;
   temp^.name:=name;
   temp^.message:=message;
   temp^.link:=current;
   IF last = current THEN
      head:=temp;
   ELSE
      last^.link:=temp;
   END;
END insert;


PROCEDURE delete(VAR head, last, current : pointer);
(* delete an existing node from the linked list *)
VAR
   temp : pointer;
BEGIN
   IF last = current THEN
      temp:=head;
      head:=head^.link;
      DEALLOCATE(temp, SIZE(node));
   ELSE
      last^.link:=current^.link;
      DEALLOCATE(current, SIZE(node));
   END;
END delete;

BEGIN
   head := NIL;
   menu(MenuCode);
   LOOP
      IF MenuCode=exit THEN EXIT;END;
      CASE MenuCode OF
      'I':InputTime(key);
         search(head, last, current, key, NotFound);
         IF NotFound THEN
            InputData(name, number, message);
            insert(head,last,current,key,number,name,message);
         ELSE
            WriteString('***warning time already in list***');
            WriteLn; END|
      'C':InputTime(key);
         search(head, last, current, key, NotFound);
         IF NotFound THEN
            WriteString('***warning time not found in list***');
            WriteLn;
         ELSE
            delete(head, last, current);
         END|
      'A':InputTime(key);
         search(head, last, current, key, NotFound);
         IF NotFound THEN
            WriteString('***warning time not found in list***');
            WriteLn;
         ELSE
            InputData(name, number, message);
            current^.name:=name;
            current^.number:=number;
            current^.message:=message;
         END;
      END;
      display(head);
      menu(MenuCode);
   END;
END C13Q5.
```

Chapter 14

```
1.
IMPLEMENTATION MODULE horologic;

IMPORT Lib;
IMPORT SYSTEM;
FROM STextIO IMPORT WriteString, WriteChar;
FROM SWholeIO IMPORT WriteCard;

PROCEDURE time_of_day(VAR hours, minutes, seconds : CARDINAL);
VAR
  r : SYSTEM.Registers;
BEGIN
  r.AH := 2CH;
  Lib.Dos(r);
  hours   := CARDINAL(r.CH);
  minutes := CARDINAL(r.CL);
  seconds := CARDINAL(r.DH);
END time_of_day;

PROCEDURE am() : BOOLEAN;
VAR
  hours, minutes, seconds : CARDINAL;
BEGIN
  time_of_day(hours, minutes, seconds);
  IF hours >= 12 THEN
    RETURN FALSE;
  ELSE
    RETURN TRUE;
  END;
END am;

PROCEDURE clock_24;
VAR
  hours, minutes, seconds : CARDINAL;
BEGIN
  time_of_day(hours, minutes, seconds);
  WriteCard(hours,2);
  WriteChar(':');
  WriteCard(minutes,2);
END clock_24;

PROCEDURE clock_12;
VAR
  hours, minutes, seconds : CARDINAL;
BEGIN
  time_of_day(hours, minutes, seconds);
  IF NOT am() AND (hours # 12) THEN
    hours := hours - 12;
  END;
  WriteCard(hours,2); WriteChar(':');
  WriteCard(minutes,2);
  IF am() THEN
    WriteString(' AM ');
  ELSE
    WriteString(' PM ');
  END;
END clock_12;

PROCEDURE elapsed_time() : LONGCARD;
VAR
  hours, minutes, seconds : CARDINAL;
BEGIN
  time_of_day(hours, minutes, seconds);
  RETURN (3600 * LONGCARD(hours))+
         (60 * LONGCARD(minutes))+LONGCARD(seconds);
END elapsed_time;

END horologic.

2.
MODULE C14Q2;
(* NOTE: since clock_24, clock_12, am and elapsed time all de-
pend upon time_of_day, there is no need to explicitly test
the procedure time_of_day *)

FROM horologic IMPORT clock_24, clock_12, am, elapsed_time;
FROM STextIO IMPORT WriteString, WriteLn;
FROM SRealIO IMPORT WriteFixed;

VAR
  h, m, s : CARDINAL;
BEGIN
  WriteString('24 hour clock ');  clock_24;  WriteLn;
  WriteString('12 hour clock ');  clock_12;  WriteLn;
  IF am() THEN
    WriteString('Good Morning');
  ELSE
    WriteString('Good Afternoon');
  END;
  WriteLn;
  WriteString('number of elapsed seconds since midnight ');
  WriteFixed(FLOAT(elapsed_time()),0,7);
END C14Q2.

3.
DEFINITION MODULE Random;

PROCEDURE RND():LONGREAL;
(* function to compute a pseudo-random number in the range
0.1 <= RND < 1.0, using a congruence method *)
```

```
PROCEDURE RANDOMIZE;
(* selects a new seed for the list of random numbers gener-
ated by RND *)

END Random.

IMPLEMENTATION MODULE Random;
FROM horologic IMPORT elapsed_time;
VAR
   seed : LONGINT;

PROCEDURE RND():LONGREAL;
CONST
   a=LONGINT(19);
   b=LONGINT(100000000);
VAR
   y : LONGINT;
   random_number : LONGREAL;
BEGIN
   y:=(a*seed) MOD b; seed := y;
   random_number := LONGREAL(ABS(y));
   REPEAT
      random_number := random_number / 10.0;
   UNTIL random_number < 1.0;
   RETURN random_number;
END RND;

PROCEDURE RANDOMIZE;
VAR
   index        : LONGCARD;
   flush_number : LONGREAL;
BEGIN
   FOR index := 0 TO elapsed_time() - 1 DO
      flush_number := RND();
   END;
END RANDOMIZE;
(* body of implementation module *)
BEGIN
   seed := 19;
END Random.

4.
MODULE C14Q4;
FROM STextIO IMPORT WriteLn, WriteString;
FROM SWholeIO IMPORT ReadCard, WriteCard;
FROM Random IMPORT RND, RANDOMIZE;
VAR
   trials        : CARDINAL;
   number        : CARDINAL;
   RandomNumber  : CARDINAL;
   StartPosition : CARDINAL;
```

```
PROCEDURE generate_numbers;
BEGIN
   FOR number:=1 TO 100 DO
      IF (number-1) MOD 20 = 0 THEN WriteLn; END;
      RandomNumber:=(TRUNC(1000.0*RND()) MOD 6)+1;
      WriteCard(RandomNumber,2);
   END;
   WriteLn;
END generate_numbers;

BEGIN
   RANDOMIZE;
   generate_numbers;
   RANDOMIZE;
   generate_numbers;
   RANDOMIZE;
   generate_numbers;
END C14Q4.

5.
IMPLEMENTATION MODULE CharClass;
PROCEDURE IsNumeric(ch : CHAR) : BOOLEAN;
BEGIN
   IF (ch >= 60C) AND (ch <= 71C) THEN
      RETURN TRUE;
   ELSE
      RETURN FALSE;
   END;
END IsNumeric;

PROCEDURE IsLetter(ch : CHAR) : BOOLEAN;
BEGIN
   IF ((ch >= 101C) AND (ch <= 132C)) OR
      ((ch >= 141C) AND (ch <= 172C)) THEN
      RETURN TRUE;
   ELSE
      RETURN FALSE;
   END;
END IsLetter;

PROCEDURE IsUpper(ch : CHAR) : BOOLEAN;
BEGIN
   IF (ch >= 101C) AND (ch <= 132C) THEN
      RETURN TRUE;
   ELSE
      RETURN FALSE;
   END;
END IsUpper;

PROCEDURE IsLower(ch : CHAR) : BOOLEAN;
BEGIN
   IF (ch >= 141C) AND (ch <= 172C) THEN
      RETURN TRUE;
```

```
    ELSE
      RETURN FALSE;
    END;
  END IsLower;

PROCEDURE IsControl(ch : CHAR) : BOOLEAN;
BEGIN
  IF (ch >= 0C) AND (ch <= 37C) THEN
    RETURN TRUE;
  ELSE
    RETURN FALSE;
  END;
END IsControl;

PROCEDURE IsWhiteSpace(ch : CHAR) : BOOLEAN;
BEGIN
  IF (ch = 40C) THEN
    RETURN TRUE;
  ELSE
    RETURN FALSE;
  END;
END IsWhiteSpace;
END CharClass.

6.
MODULE C14Q6;
FROM CharClass IMPORT IsNumeric, IsLetter, IsUpper, IsLower,
                      IsControl, IsWhiteSpace;
FROM STextIO IMPORT WriteString, ReadChar, WriteLn, SkipLine;
CONST
  space = 40C;
VAR
  character : CHAR;
BEGIN
  REPEAT
    WriteString('character? ');
    ReadChar(character); SkipLine;
    IF   IsNumeric(character)     THEN
         WriteString('numeric');
    ELSIF IsLetter(character)     THEN
         WriteString('letter - case ');
         IF IsUpper(character)    THEN
           WriteString('upper');
         ELSE
           WriteString('lower');
         END;
    ELSIF IsControl(character)    THEN
         WriteString('control');
    ELSIF IsWhiteSpace(character) THEN
         WriteString('white space');
    ELSE WriteString('cannot classify character');
    END;
```

```
      WriteLn;
    UNTIL character = space;
END C14Q6.

7.
DEFINITION MODULE triangle;

PROCEDURE Side1Angle2(SideA, AngleB, AngleC : REAL;
                      VAR SideB, SideC, AngleA : REAL);
PROCEDURE Side2Angle1(SideA, SideB, AngleC : REAL;
                      VAR SideC, AngleA, AngleB : REAL);
PROCEDURE Side3(SideA, SideB, SideC : REAL;
                VAR AngleA, AngleB, AngleC : REAL);
PROCEDURE Area(SideA, SideB, SideC : REAL;
               VAR area, perimeter : REAL);
PROCEDURE Circles(SideA, SideB, SideC : REAL;
                  VAR Circum, Inscribe : REAL);

END triangle.

IMPLEMENTATION MODULE triangle;
FROM RealMath IMPORT pi, sqrt, sin, cos, arctan;

PROCEDURE Side1Angle2(SideA, AngleB, AngleC : REAL;
                      VAR SideB, SideC, AngleA : REAL);
BEGIN
  AngleA := 180.0 - (AngleB + AngleC);
  SideB := SideA * sin(AngleB*pi/180.0)
                 / sin(AngleA*pi/180.0);
  SideC := SideA * sin(AngleC*pi/180.0)
                 / sin(AngleA*pi/180.0);
END Side1Angle2;

PROCEDURE Side2Angle1(SideA, SideB, AngleC : REAL;
                      VAR SideC, AngleA, AngleB : REAL);
VAR
  area : REAL;
BEGIN
  area  := 0.5*SideA*SideB*sin(AngleC*pi/180.0);
  SideC := sqrt((SideA*SideA) + (SideB*SideB)
             - 2.0*SideA*SideB*cos(AngleC*pi/180.0));
  AngleA:= (180.0/pi)*arctan(4.0*area/((SideB*SideB)
             + (SideC*SideC) - (SideA*SideA)));
  AngleB:= 180.0 - (AngleC + AngleA);
END Side2Angle1;

PROCEDURE Side3(SideA, SideB, SideC : REAL;
                VAR AngleA, AngleB, AngleC : REAL);
VAR
  area : REAL;
  s    : REAL; (* semi-perimeter *)
BEGIN
  s:=(SideA+SideB+SideC)/2.0;
```

```modula2
      area :=sqrt(s*(s-SideA)*(s-SideB)*(s-SideC)) ;
      AngleA:=(180.0/pi)
             *arctan(4.0*area/((SideB*SideB)+(SideC*SideC)
             -(SideA*SideA))) ;
      Side2Angle1(SideB, SideC, AngleA, SideA, AngleB, AngleC) ;
END Side3;

PROCEDURE Area(SideA, SideB, SideC : REAL;
               VAR area, perimeter : REAL) ;
VAR
   s : REAL;  (* semi-perimeter *)
BEGIN
   s:=(SideA+SideB+SideC)/2.0;
   area:=sqrt(s*(s-SideA)*(s-SideB)*(s-SideC)) ;
   perimeter := 2.0*s;
END Area;

PROCEDURE Circles(SideA, SideB, SideC : REAL;
                  VAR Circum, Inscribe : REAL);
VAR
   area, perimeter : REAL;
BEGIN
   Area(SideA, SideB, SideC, area, perimeter) ;
   Circum   := (SideA*SideB*SideC)/(4.0*area);
   Inscribe := area/(perimeter/2.0) ;
END Circles;
END triangle.

8.
MODULE C14Q8;
FROM STextIO IMPORT WriteLn, WriteString;
FROM SWholeIO IMPORT ReadCard;
FROM SRealIO IMPORT ReadReal, WriteFixed;
FROM triangle IMPORT Side1Angle2, Side2Angle1, Side3,
                     Area, Circles;

VAR
   SideA, SideB, SideC                :REAL;
   AngleA, AngleB, AngleC             :REAL;
   area, perimeter, Circum, Inscribe  :REAL;
   code                               :CARDINAL;

PROCEDURE report;
BEGIN
   WriteLn; WriteLn;
   WriteString('size of triangle');WriteLn;
   WriteString('sides:');WriteFixed(SideA,2,7);
   WriteFixed(SideB,2,7);
   WriteFixed(SideC,2,7); WriteLn;
   WriteString('angles:');WriteFixed(AngleA,0,6);
   WriteFixed(AngleB,0,6);
   WriteFixed(AngleC,0,6); WriteLn;
   WriteString('area:'); WriteFixed(area,1,6);
   WriteLn; WriteString('perimeter: ');
   WriteFixed(perimeter,1,6);      WriteLn;
   WriteString('radius of circumcircle: ');
   WriteFixed(Circum,1,6); WriteLn;
   WriteString('radius of inscribed circle: ');
   WriteFixed(Inscribe,1,6); WriteLn;
END report;

PROCEDURE menu(VAR code:CARDINAL) ;
BEGIN
   WriteString('input code for data available '); WriteLn;
   WriteString('1. one side and two angles'); WriteLn;
   WriteString('2. two sides and one included angle'); WriteLn;
   WriteString('3. three sides '); WriteLn;
   WriteString('0. no data '); WriteLn;
   ReadCard(code);
END menu;

BEGIN
   menu(code);
   WHILE code # 0 DO
     CASE code OF
     1: WriteString('input length of side ');
        ReadReal(SideA);
        WriteString('input first angle (degrees) ');
        ReadReal(AngleB);
        WriteString('input second angle (degrees) ');
        ReadReal(AngleC);
        Side1Angle2(SideA, AngleB, AngleC, SideB, SideC,
                    AngleA)|
     2: WriteString('input first length of side ');
        ReadReal(SideA);
        WriteString('input second length of side ');
        ReadReal(SideB);
        WriteString('input angle (degrees) ');
        ReadReal(AngleC);
        Side2Angle1(SideA, SideB, AngleC, SideC, AngleA,
                    AngleB)|
     3: WriteString('input first length of side ');
        ReadReal(SideA);
        WriteString('input second length of side ');
        ReadReal(SideB);
        WriteString('input third length of side ');
        ReadReal(SideC);
        Side3(SideA, SideB, SideC, AngleA, AngleB, AngleC)
     ELSE
        WriteString('*** error - illegal code ***'); WriteLn;
     END;
     Area(SideA, SideB, SideC, area, perimeter);
     Circles(SideA, SideB, SideC, Circum, Inscribe);
     report;
     menu(code);
   END;
END C14Q8.
```

Appendix I

Chapter 15

1. The definition and implementation modules for StackIO should be modified to include the function StackSize and changes to procedure push.

```
PROCEDURE StackSize(s:stack):CARDINAL;
VAR
  temp    : stack;
  counter : CARDINAL;

BEGIN
  counter := 0;
  temp := s;
  WHILE temp # NIL DO
    temp:=temp^.link;
    INC(counter);

  END;
  RETURN counter;
END StackSize;
```

The necessary modifications to procedure push follow.

```
PROCEDURE push(VAR s:stack; character:CHAR);
VAR
  temp:stack;

BEGIN
  (* MaxStack is a predefined limit on the maximum size of
     the stack *)
  IF StackSize(s) = MaxStack THEN
    WriteLn;
    WriteString('*** STACK OVERFLOW ***');
    WriteLn;
  ELSE
    (* coding same as push in text *)
  END;
END push;
```

2.

```
DEFINITION MODULE C15Q2;

TYPE FIFOq;
PROCEDURE initialise(VAR q:FIFOq);
PROCEDURE empty(q:FIFOq):BOOLEAN;
PROCEDURE PlaceInQueue(VAR q, rear:FIFOq;
         customer, arrival, service :CARDINAL;
         VAR NumberInQueue:CARDINAL);
PROCEDURE RemoveFromQueue(VAR q:FIFOq;
         VAR arrival, departure, service,
         NumberInQueue:CARDINAL;
         LastDeparture:CARDINAL);
```

```
PROCEDURE QueueDetails(VAR q:FIFOq; NumberInQueue:CARDINAL);
END C15Q2.

IMPLEMENTATION MODULE C15Q2;

FROM Storage IMPORT ALLOCATE, DEALLOCATE;
FROM STextIO IMPORT WriteString, WriteLn;
FROM SWholeIO IMPORT WriteCard;
TYPE
  FIFOq = POINTER TO node;
  node = RECORD
           CustomerNumber:CARDINAL;
           TimeOfArrival:CARDINAL;
           ServiceTime:CARDINAL;
           link:FIFOq;

         END;

PROCEDURE initialise(VAR q:FIFOq);
BEGIN
  q:=NIL;
END initialise;

PROCEDURE empty(q:FIFOq):BOOLEAN;
BEGIN
  IF q=NIL THEN
    RETURN TRUE;
  ELSE
    RETURN FALSE;
  END;
END empty;

PROCEDURE QueueDetails(VAR q:FIFOq; NumberInQueue:CARDINAL);
VAR current:FIFOq;
BEGIN
  WriteString('—————————————————');
  WriteLn;
  WriteString('size of queue => ');
  WriteCard(NumberInQueue,3);
  WriteLn;
  WriteString('members of queue are:'); WriteLn;
  current:=q;
  WHILE current # NIL DO
    WriteString('customer number  => '); WriteCard(current^.CustomerNumber,2); WriteLn;
    WriteString('time of arrival    => ');
    WriteCard(current^.TimeOfArrival,6); WriteLn;
    WriteString('time at check out => ');
    WriteCard(current^.ServiceTime,6); WriteLn;
    current:=current^.link;
    WriteLn;
  END;
  WriteString('—————————————————');
```

```
FROM Random IMPORT RND;
CONST  SampleSize=21;
VAR
   q, rear:FIFOq;
   arrival, departure, customer, service:CARDINAL;
   data:ARRAY[1..SampleSize], [1..2] OF CARDINAL;
   NextCustomer:CARDINAL;
   LastDeparture:CARDINAL;
   TimeElapsed : CARDINAL;
   NumberInQueue:CARDINAL;

PROCEDURE InterArrivalTime():CARDINAL;
VAR
   x:CARDINAL;
   y:REAL;
BEGIN
   x:=(TRUNC(1000.0*RND()) MOD 100)+1;
   IF    x>=97 THEN  y:=9.55;
   ELSIF x>=95 THEN  y:=8.55;
   ELSIF x>=93 THEN  y:=7.55;
   ELSIF x>=89 THEN  y:=6.55;
   ELSIF x>=85 THEN  y:=5.55;
   ELSIF x>=70 THEN  y:=4.55;
   ELSIF x>=50 THEN  y:=3.55;
   ELSIF x>=25 THEN  y:=2.55;
   ELSIF x>= 8 THEN  y:=1.55;
   ELSE  y:=0.55;
   END;
   RETURN TRUNC(y);
END InterArrivalTime;

PROCEDURE TimeAtCheckOut ():CARDINAL;
VAR
   x:CARDINAL;
   y:REAL;
BEGIN
   x:=(TRUNC(1000.0*RND()) MOD 100) +1;
   IF    x>=95 THEN  y:=4.75;
   ELSIF x>=90 THEN  y:=4.25;
   ELSIF x>=85 THEN  y:=3.75;
   ELSIF x>=75 THEN  y:=3.25;
   ELSIF x>=60 THEN  y:=2.75;
   ELSIF x>=40 THEN  y:=2.25;
   ELSIF x>=15 THEN  y:=1.75;
   ELSE  y:=1.25;
   END;
   RETURN TRUNC(y);
END TimeAtCheckOut;

PROCEDURE QueueAnalysis;
BEGIN
   NextCustomer:=customer+1;
```

```
END QueueDetails;
PROCEDURE PlaceInQueue(VAR q, rear:FIFOq;
                       customer, arrival, service:CARDINAL
                       VAR NumberInQueue:CARDINAL);
VAR
   temp : FIFOq;
BEGIN
  IF q=NIL THEN
    ALLOCATE(q, SIZE(node));
    q^.CustomerNumber:=customer;
    q^.TimeOfArrival:=arrival;
    q^.ServiceTime:=service;
    q^.link:=NIL;
    rear:=q;
    NumberInQueue:=NumberInQueue+1;
  ELSE
    IF customer > rear^.CustomerNumber THEN
      ALLOCATE(temp, SIZE(node));
      rear^.link:=temp;
      temp^.CustomerNumber:=customer;
      temp^.TimeOfArrival:=arrival;
      temp^.ServiceTime:=service;
      temp^.link:=NIL;
      rear:=temp;
      NumberInQueue:=NumberInQueue+1;

    END;

END PlaceInQueue;

PROCEDURE RemoveFromQueue(VAR q:FIFOq;
                VAR arrival, departure, service,
                NumberInQueue:CARDINAL;
                LastDeparture:CARDINAL);
VAR
   temp:FIFOq;
BEGIN
   temp:=q;
   arrival:=q^.TimeOfArrival;
   departure:=LastDeparture+q^.ServiceTime;
   q:=q^.link;
   DEALLOCATE(temp, SIZE(node));
   NumberInQueue:=NumberInQueue-1;
END RemoveFromQueue;
END C15Q2.

3.
MODULE C15Q3;
FROM C15Q2 IMPORT QueueDetails, PlaceInQueue,
       RemoveFromQueue, FIFOq,initialise, empty;
FROM STextIO IMPORT WriteString, WriteLn;
FROM SWholeIO IMPORT WriteCard;
```

419

```
    arrival:=arrival+data[NextCustomer,1];
    WHILE (arrival<departure)
      AND (NextCustomer < SampleSize) DO
      PlaceInqueue(q, rear, NextCustomer, arrival,
                   data[NextCustomer,2], NumberInQueue);
      NextCustomer:=NextCustomer+1;
      arrival:=arrival+data[NextCustomer,1];
    END;
END QueueAnalysis;

BEGIN
  initialise(q);
  NumberInQueue:=0;
  FOR customer:=1 TO SampleSize-1 DO
    data[customer,1]:=InterArrivalTime();
    data[customer,2]:=TimeAtCheckOut();
    WriteString('customer number       => ');
    WriteCard(customer,2);WriteLn;
    WriteString('inter arrival time => ');
    WriteCard(data[customer,1],3);WriteLn;
    WriteString('time at check out => ');
    WriteCard(data[customer,2],3);WriteLn;
    WriteLn;
  END;
  WriteLn;
  WriteString('————————— end of generated data —————————');
  WriteLn;

  arrival:=data[1,1];
  departure:=arrival+data[1,2];
  FOR customer:=1 TO SampleSize-1 DO
    WriteLn;
    WriteString('customer number         => ');
    WriteCard(customer,2);WriteLn;
    WriteString('arrival                 => ');
    WriteCard(arrival,4);WriteLn;
    WriteString('departure               => ');
    WriteCard(departure,4);WriteLn;
    WriteString('time elapsed            => ');
    WriteCard(departure-arrival,4);WriteLn;
    LastDeparture:=departure;
    QueueAnalysis;
    IF NOT empty(q) THEN
      QueueDetails(q, NumberInQueue);
      RemoveFromQueue(q, arrival, departure, service,
                      NumberInQueue, LastDeparture);
    ELSE
      departure:=arrival+data[NextCustomer,2];
    END;
  END;
END C15Q3.
```

```
4.
MODULE C15Q4;
FROM BinTreeIO IMPORT tree, initialise, attach, display;
FROM Random IMPORT RND;
FROM STextIO IMPORT WriteLn, WriteString;
FROM SWholeIO IMPORT WriteCard;
CONST
  SetSize=20;

VAR
  structure:tree;
  value:CARDINAL;
  success:BOOLEAN;
  count:CARDINAL;

BEGIN
  count:=0;
  initialise(structure);
  REPEAT
    value:=TRUNC(1000.0*RND()) MOD 100+1;
    IF count MOD 10 = 0 THEN
      WriteLn;
    END;
    WriteCard(value,5);
    attach(structure, value, success);
    IF success THEN
      count:=count+1;
    END;
  UNTIL count=SetSize;
  WriteLn; WriteLn;
  WriteString(
    'contents of tree - sorted into ascending order ');
  WriteLn;
  display(structure);
END C15Q4.

5.
MODULE C15Q5;
FROM LinkLst IMPORT list, search, insert, NewList;
FROM Stack IMPORT stack, initialise, push, pop;
FROM StreamFile IMPORT ChanId, Open, Close, read, OpenResults;
FROM IOResult IMPORT ReadResult, ReadResults;
FROM TextIO IMPORT ReadString;
FROM SRealIO IMPORT WriteFixed, ReadReal;
FROM StringType IMPORT string;
FROM STextIO IMPORT WriteString, WriteChar, WriteLn;
CONST
  null=0C;

VAR
  expression          : string;
  head,current,last:list;
  data             :ChanId;
  results          :OpenResults;
```

```
OK              :BOOLEAN;
(* length of reverse Polish string *)
size            :CARDINAL;

PROCEDURE evaluate(expression:ARRAY OF CHAR; size:CARDINAL);
(* routine to traverse the reverse Polish string and evaluate
the string according to the algorithm given in the question *)
VAR
index           :CARDINAL;
answer          :REAL;
s               :stack;
first, second:REAL;
symbol          :CHAR;
OperandValue :REAL;

BEGIN
initialise(s); index:=0;
FOR index:=0 TO size-1 DO
    symbol:=expression[index];
    IF (symbol='+') OR
       (symbol='-') OR
       (symbol='*') OR
       (symbol='/') THEN
        pop(s,first);
        pop(s,second);
        CASE symbol OF
        '+':answer:=second+first|
        '-':answer:=second-first|
        '*':answer:=second*first|
        '/':IF first # 0.0 THEN
                answer:=second/first;
            ELSE
                answer:=MAX(REAL);
            END;
        END;
        push(s,answer);
    ELSE
        search(head,last,current,symbol,OperandValue,OK);
        push(s,OperandValue);
    END;
END;
pop(s,answer);
WriteLn;
WriteString('evaluation of reverse Polish string ');
WriteString('using the operands given is ');
WriteFixed(answer,2,8); WriteLn; WriteLn;
END evaluate;

PROCEDURE AssignOperands(VAR expression:ARRAY OF CHAR;
                         VAR size:CARDINAL);
(* procedure to build a linked list containing the names of
the operands and their values *)
VAR
NextOperand:CHAR;
index:CARDINAL;
OperandValue:REAL;

BEGIN
WriteString('reverse Polish string is ');
WriteString(expression); WriteLn;
NewList(head);
index:=0;
WHILE expression[index] # null DO
    NextOperand:=expression[index];
    IF (NextOperand #'+') AND (NextOperand #'-')
       AND (NextOperand #'*') AND (NextOperand #'/') THEN
        search(head, last, current, NextOperand,
                OperandValue, OK);
        IF  OK THEN
            WriteString('input value of operand    ');
            WriteChar(NextOperand);
            WriteString('  '); ReadReal(OperandValue);
            insert(head, last, current, NextOperand,
                    OperandValue);
        END;
    END;
    index:=index+1;
END;
size:=index;
END AssignOperands;

BEGIN
Open(data, 'a:data2.txt', read, results);
IF results # opened THEN HALT; END;
ReadString(data,expression);
WHILE ReadResult(data) # endOfInput DO
    AssignOperands(expression, size);
    evaluate(expression, size);
    ReadString(data,expression);
END;
Close(data);
END C15Q5.

6 and 7 combined.
MODULE C15Q67;
(* Program to store a representation of a graph and find a
possible route given the names of the starting and finishing
points *)
FROM Storage IMPORT ALLOCATE, DEALLOCATE;
FROM TextIO IMPORT ReadChar;
FROM STextIO IMPORT WriteString, ReadString, WriteChar,
                    WriteLn, SkipLine;

FROM StackIO IMPORT stack, empty, initialise, push, pop;
FROM StreamFile IMPORT ChanId, Open, Close, read, OpenResults;
FROM IOResult IMPORT ReadResult, ReadResults;
FROM StringType IMPORT string;
```

Appendix I

```
IMPORT STextIO;
CONST
    eoln    =15C;
    FormFeed=12C;
    no      ='N';
    MaxEntry=100;
TYPE
    pointer = POINTER TO node;
    node    = RECORD
                place : CHAR;
                link  : pointer;
              END;
    tagged = RECORD
                place : CHAR;
                tag   : BOOLEAN;
             END;

VAR
    direction              : ARRAY[0..MaxEntry-1] OF pointer;
    visit                  : ARRAY[0..MaxEntry-1] OF tagged;
    DataFile               : ChanId;
    filename               : string;
    start, finish, reply   : CHAR;
    StackTemp, StackRoute  : stack;
    SizeOfArray            : CARDINAL;
    results                : OpenResults;

PROCEDURE BuildGraph(filename:string;
                     VAR SizeOfArray:CARDINAL);

(* Read a file of directions and place each direction in the
node of a linked list. The pointers to the head of each
linked list are stored in the array named direction *)

VAR
    character : CHAR;
    index     : CARDINAL;

PROCEDURE CreateList(VAR head:pointer);
(* create a single linked list *)
VAR
    last:pointer;

PROCEDURE CreateNode(VAR next:pointer);
BEGIN
    ReadChar(DataFile, character);
    IF character # eoln THEN
        ALLOCATE(next, SIZE(node));
        next^.place:=character;
        next^.link:=NIL;
    ELSE
        ReadChar(DataFile, character); (* read line feed *)
    END;
END CreateNode;
BEGIN
    CreateNode(head);
    last:=head;
    WHILE ((character # eoln) AND (character # FormFeed) AND
          (ReadResult(DataFile) # endOfInput)) DO
        CreateNode(last^.link);
        last:=last^.link;
    END;
END CreateList;

BEGIN
    Open(DataFile, filename, read, results);
    IF results # opened THEN HALT; END;
    index:=0;
    CreateList(direction[index]);
    WHILE ReadResult(DataFile) # endOfInput DO
        INC(index);
        CreateList(direction[index]);
        SizeOfArray:=index+1;
    END;
    Close(DataFile);

(* mark the position of each point on the graph to FALSE
   indicating that the point has not yet been visited *)
    FOR index:=0 TO SizeOfArray-1 DO
        visit[index].place:=direction[index]^.place;
        visit[index].tag:=FALSE;
    END;
END BuildGraph;

PROCEDURE search(VAR NextPlace:CHAR);
(* search for the next place in the graph to visit *)
VAR
    temp             :pointer;
    TempIndex, index : CARDINAL;
    character        : CHAR;

BEGIN
    FOR TempIndex:=0 TO SizeOfArray-1 DO
        IF NextPlace = direction[TempIndex]^.place THEN
            index:=TempIndex;
        END;
    END;
    IF direction[index]^.link # NIL THEN
        NextPlace:=direction[index]^.link^.place;
        temp:=direction[index]^.link;
        direction[index]^.link:=direction[index]^.link^.link;
        DEALLOCATE(temp, SIZE(node));
    END;
END search;
```

```
PROCEDURE BeenThere(NextPlace:CHAR; VAR Newindex:CARDINAL;
                    VAR visited :BOOLEAN);

(* This is a multi-purpose procedure. Given a value for the
NextPlace to visit it will return (a) the value of the index
associated with the NextPlace in the arrays named direction
and visit; (b) return whether a point on the graph has already
been visited *)

VAR
  TempIndex : CARDINAL;
BEGIN
  visited:=FALSE;
  FOR TempIndex:=0 TO SizeOfArray-1 DO
    IF (visit[TempIndex].place = NextPlace) THEN
      Newindex:=TempIndex;
      IF (visit[TempIndex].tag = TRUE) THEN
        visited:= TRUE;
      END;

    END;
  END;
END BeenThere;

PROCEDURE FindRoute(start, finish : CHAR);
(* Will find a route from start to finish if one exists. The
route chosen is NOT optimised *)

VAR
  NextPlace : CHAR;
  character : CHAR;
  Newindex  : CARDINAL;
  visited   : BOOLEAN;

BEGIN
  (* push the start on the stack and find the next point on
  the graph *)
  NextPlace:=start;
  BeenThere(NextPlace, Newindex, visited);
  IF NOT visited THEN
    visit[Newindex].tag :=TRUE;
  END;
  push(StackTemp, NextPlace);
  search(NextPlace);
  WHILE (finish # NextPlace) AND (NOT empty(StackTemp)) DO
    BeenThere(NextPlace, Newindex, visited);

    (* If new point on route tag it. Only push on to stack
    if it is not a dead-end, otherwise backtrack to the
    last point visited *)
    IF (NOT visited) THEN
      visit[Newindex].tag := TRUE;
      IF direction[Newindex]^.link # NIL THEN
        push(StackTemp, NextPlace);
      ELSE
        pop(StackTemp, NextPlace);
        push(StackTemp, NextPlace);
      END;

    * Have visited point before so it is necessary to
    backtrack to a previous point *)
    ELSE

      (* Have entered a loop so it is necessary to
      backtrack through all the points in the loop
      until an alternative
      route can be found *)

      IF direction[Newindex]^.link # NIL THEN
        REPEAT
          pop(StackTemp, character);
        UNTIL character = NextPlace;
        push(StackTemp, character);
      ELSE
        (* backtrack to previous point that will lead to
        an alternative route *)
        WHILE (direction[Newindex]^.link = NIL) AND
              (NOT empty(StackTemp)) DO
          pop(StackTemp, NextPlace);
          BeenThere(NextPlace, Newindex, visited);
          IF direction[Newindex]^.link # NIL THEN
            push(StackTemp, NextPlace);
          END;

        END;
      END;
    END;
    search(NextPlace);
  END;

  (* At end of route reverse order of contents of stack
  and output the result in the order from start to finish *)
  IF finish = NextPlace THEN
    push(StackTemp, NextPlace);
    WriteString('Route to take ');
    REPEAT
      pop(StackTemp, NextPlace);
      push(StackRoute, NextPlace);
    UNTIL empty(StackTemp);
    REPEAT
      pop(StackRoute, NextPlace);
      WriteChar(NextPlace);
    UNTIL empty(StackRoute);
    WriteLn;
  ELSE
    WriteString('Route cannot be taken');
    WriteLn;
  END;
END FindRoute;
```

```
BEGIN
  REPEAT
    initialise(StackTemp); initialise(StackRoute);
    WriteString('input name of graph ');
    ReadString(filename); SkipLine;
    REPEAT
      BuildGraph(filename, SizeOfArray);
      WriteString('input start of route ');
      STextIO.ReadChar(start); SkipLine;
      WriteString('input finish of route ');
      STextIO.ReadChar(finish);
      SkipLine;
      FindRoute(start, finish);
      WriteLn;
      WriteString('do you want another route? y/n ');
      STextIO.ReadChar(reply); SkipLine; reply:=CAP(reply);
    UNTIL reply = no;
    WriteString('do you want another graph? y/n ');
    STextIO.ReadChar(reply); SkipLine; reply:=CAP(reply);
  UNTIL reply = no;
END C15Q67.
```

Chapter 16.

```
1.
MODULE C16Q1;
IMPORT Storage;
FROM SYSTEM IMPORT TSIZE, ADDRESS;
FROM COROUTINES IMPORT NEWCOROUTINE, TRANSFER, COROUTINE;
FROM StreamFile IMPORT ChanId, Open, Close, read, write,
                       OpenResults;

FROM IOResult IMPORT ReadResult, ReadResults;
FROM TextIO IMPORT ReadString, WriteString, WriteChar,
                   WriteLn;
FROM WholeIO IMPORT WriteCard;
FROM StringType IMPORT string;
FROM Strings IMPORT Length;
IMPORT STextIO;

CONST
  work_space_size = 4096;
  max_string      = 50;
  space           = 40C;
  null            = 0C;
TYPE
  line = RECORD
    line_number : CARDINAL;
    stream      : string;
  END;

VAR
  work_space1, work_space2, work_space3 : ADDRESS;
  main, processA, processB, processC    : COROUTINE;
  character                             : CHAR;
  data, new_file                        : ChanId;
  results                               : OpenResults;
  output                                : line;
  line_count, char_count, index         : CARDINAL;
  data_string                           : string;

PROCEDURE A;
BEGIN
  Open (data, "a:datafl1.txt", read, results);
  IF results # opened THEN HALT; END;
  Open (new_file, "a:datfl2.txt", write, results);
  IF results # opened THEN HALT; END;
  ReadString(data, data_string);
  WHILE ReadResult(data) # endOfInput DO
    STextIO.WriteString(data_string);
    STextIO.WriteLn;
    index := 0;
    character := data_string[0];
    WHILE index # Length(data_string) DO
      TRANSFER(processA, processB);
      INC(index);
      character := data_string[index];
    END;
    ReadString(data, data_string);
  END;
  (* flush remainder of data string *)
  char_count := 50;
  TRANSFER(processA, processB);
  Close(data); Close(new_file);
  TRANSFER(processA, main);
END A;

PROCEDURE B;
VAR temp : CARDINAL;
BEGIN
  line_count := 0; char_count := 0;
  LOOP
    FOR temp:=0 TO max_string - 1 DO
      output.stream[temp] := space;
    END;
    REPEAT
      output.stream[char_count] := character;
      INC(char_count);
      TRANSFER(processB, processA);
    UNTIL char_count = 50;
    INC(line_count);
    output.stream[char_count + 1] := null;
    TRANSFER(processB, processC);
    char_count := 0;
  END;
END B;
```

```
PROCEDURE C;
BEGIN
  LOOP
    WriteCard(new_file, line_count, 3);
    WriteChar(new_file, space);
    WriteString(new_file, output.stream);
    WriteLn(new_file);
    TRANSFER(processC, processB);
  END;
END C;

(* main program *)
BEGIN
  Storage.ALLOCATE(work_space1, work_space_size);
  Storage.ALLOCATE(work_space2, work_space_size);
  Storage.ALLOCATE(work_space3, work_space_size);
  NEWCOROUTINE(A, work_space1,TSIZE(work_space1), processA);
  NEWCOROUTINE(B, work_space2,TSIZE(work_space2), processB);
  NEWCOROUTINE(C, work_space3,TSIZE(work_space3), processC);
  TRANSFER(main, processA);
END C16Q1.

2.
MODULE c16q2;
IMPORT Storage;
FROM SYSTEM IMPORT TSIZE, ADDRESS;
FROM COROUTINES IMPORT COROUTINE, NEWCOROUTINE, IOTRANSFER,
                        ATTACH, TRANSFER;

FROM SWholeIO IMPORT WriteCard;
IMPORT Lib;
IMPORT SYSTEM;
IMPORT Window;

CONST
  work_space_size = 2048;

VAR
  handler, main                 : COROUTINE;
  work_space                    : ADDRESS;
  digit_64, digit_8, digit_1    : CARDINAL;
  r                             : SYSTEM.Registers;

PROCEDURE display_number;
BEGIN
  Window.Clear;
  WriteCard(digit_64,1);
  WriteCard(digit_8, 1);
  WriteCard(digit_1, 1);
END display_number;

PROCEDURE interrupt_handler;
BEGIN
  ATTACH(60H);
  LOOP
    IOTRANSFER(handler, main);
    IF digit_1 = 7 THEN
      INC(digit_8);
      IF digit_8 = 8 THEN
        digit_8  := digit_8 MOD 8;
        digit_64 := (digit_64 +1) MOD 8;
      END;
    END;
    digit_1 := (digit_1 + 1) MOD 8;
    display_number;
  END;
END interrupt_handler;

BEGIN
  Storage.ALLOCATE(work_space, work_space_size);
  NEWCOROUTINE(interrupt_handler, work_space,
               TSIZE(work_space), handler);

  TRANSFER(main, handler);

  digit_64 := 0;
  digit_8  := 0;
  digit_1  := 0;
  display_number;
  LOOP
    Lib.Delay(250);
    Lib.Intr(r,60H);
  END;
END c16q2.

3.
MODULE C16Q3;
FROM Concurrent IMPORT CreateProcess, StartScheduler, Wait,
                        Signal,Initialise, CONDITION, EndProcess;

IMPORT Window;
IMPORT STextIO;
IMPORT SWholeIO;
IMPORT Lib;
FROM StreamFile IMPORT ChanId, Open, Close, read, write,
                        OpenResults;

FROM IOResult IMPORT ReadResult, ReadResults;
FROM TextIO IMPORT ReadString;
FROM StringType IMPORT string;
FROM Strings IMPORT Length;
CONST

  window_1 = Window.WinDef(
               0,0,79,11,Window.White, Window.Black,
               TRUE,TRUE,TRUE,Window.SingleFrame,
               Window.White, Window.Black);
```

Appendix I

```
window_2 = Window.WinDef(
          0,12,79,24,Window.White, Window.White, Window.Black,
          TRUE,TRUE,FALSE,TRUE,Window.SingleFrame,
          Window.White, Window.Black);

CONST
    work_space_size = 2048;
    max_string      = 50;
    space           = 40C;
    null            = 0C;
TYPE
    line = RECORD
           line_number : CARDINAL;
           stream      : string;
    END;
VAR
    data        : ChanId;
    results     : OpenResults;
    output      : line;
    line_count  : CARDINAL;
    data_string : string;
    w1, w2      : Window.WinType;
    transfer    : CONDITION;

PROCEDURE A;
BEGIN
    line_count := 0;
    Open_(data, "a:datafl1.txt", read, results);
    IF results # opened THEN HALT; END;
    ReadString(data, data_string);
    WHILE ReadResult(data) # endOfInput DO
        Window.Use(w1);
        STextIO.WriteString(data_string);
        STextIO.WriteLn;
        INC(line_count);
        output.stream := data_string;
        output.stream[Length(data_string)+1] := null;
        Lib.Delay(100);
        Wait(transfer);
        ReadString(data, data_string);
    END;
    Close(data);
    EndProcess;
END A;

PROCEDURE B;
BEGIN
    LOOP
        IF ReadResult(data) = endOfInput THEN EndProcess; END;
        Window.Use(w2);
        SWholeIO.WriteCard(line_count, 3);
        STextIO.WriteChar(space);
        STextIO.WriteString(output.stream);
        STextIO.WriteLn;
        Lib.Delay(100);
        Signal(transfer);
    END;
END B;

BEGIN
    (* open windows *)
    w1 := Window.Open(window_1);
    w2 := Window.Open(window_2);

    (* title each window *)
    Window.SetTitle(w1, ' file ', Window.CenterUpperTitle);
    Window.SetTitle(w2, ' lines ', Window.CenterUpperTitle);
    CreateProcess(A);
    CreateProcess(B);
    Initialise(transfer);
    StartScheduler;
    (* close windows *)
    Window.Close(w1);
    Window.Close(w2);
END C16Q3.

4.
IMPLEMENTATION MODULE Semaphores;

FROM Concurrent IMPORT CONDITION, Initialise, Wait, Signal,
                       Awaited;

TYPE
    SEMAPHORE = POINTER TO sem_queue;
    sem_queue = RECORD
                counter     : CARDINAL;
                sem_pointer : CONDITION;
    END;

PROCEDURE Create(VAR s:SEMAPHORE; initialCount : CARDINAL);
BEGIN
    s^.counter := initialCount;
    Initialise(s^.sem_pointer);
END Create;

PROCEDURE Claim(s:SEMAPHORE);
BEGIN
    IF s^.counter > 0 THEN
        DEC(s^.counter);
    ELSE
        Wait(s^.sem_pointer);
    END;
END Claim;
```

```
PROCEDURE Release(s:SEMAPHORE);
BEGIN
  IF Awaited(s^.sem_pointer) THEN
    Signal(s^.sem_pointer);
  ELSE
    INC(s^.counter);
  END;
END Release;

PROCEDURE CondClaim(s:SEMAPHORE):BOOLEAN;
BEGIN
  IF s^.counter = 0 THEN
    RETURN FALSE;
  ELSE
    DEC(s^.counter);
    RETURN TRUE;
  END;
END CondClaim;

END Semaphores.

5.
MODULE C16Q5;
FROM Concurrent IMPORT CreateProcess, StartScheduler,
                       EndProcess;
FROM Semaphores IMPORT SEMAPHORE, Create, Claim, Release;
IMPORT Random;
IMPORT SWholeIO;
IMPORT Window;
IMPORT Lib;
IMPORT SysClock;
CONST
  time_slice = 1000;  (* units hundredths of a second *)
  buffer_size = 10;

  window_1 = Window.WinDef
    ( 0,0,39,15,Window.White, Window.Black,
      TRUE,TRUE,FALSE,TRUE,Window.SingleFrame,
      Window.White, Window.Black);

  window_2 = Window.WinDef
    ( 40,0,79,15,Window.White, Window.Black,
      TRUE,TRUE,FALSE,TRUE,Window.SingleFrame,
      Window.White, Window.Black );

VAR
  buffer       : ARRAY[1..buffer_size] OF CARDINAL;
  full         : SEMAPHORE;
  w1, w2       : Window.WinType;
  start_time   : LONGCARD;

PROCEDURE elapsed_time():LONGCARD;
VAR
  info : SysClock.DateTime;
BEGIN
  SysClock.GetClock(info);
  RETURN 100 * ((3600 * LONGCARD(info.hour))
    + (60 * LONGCARD(info.minute))+ LONGCARD(info.second))
    + LONGCARD(info.fractions);
END elapsed_time;

PROCEDURE put_into;
VAR
  in : CARDINAL;
BEGIN
  in := 1;
  LOOP
    Claim(full);
    Window.Use(w1);
    buffer[in]:=TRUNC(10000.0*Random.RND()) MOD 100 + 1;
    SWholeIO.WriteCard(buffer[in],4);
    in := in MOD buffer_size + 1;
    Lib.Delay(250);
  END;
END put_into;

PROCEDURE take_from;
VAR out : CARDINAL;
BEGIN
  start_time := elapsed_time();
  out := 1;
  LOOP
    Window.Use(w2);
    SWholeIO.WriteCard(buffer[out],4);
    out := out MOD buffer_size + 1;
    IF elapsed_time() - start_time > time_slice THEN
      EXIT; END;
    Release(full);
  END;
  EndProcess;
END take_from;

BEGIN
  (* open windows *)
  w1 := Window.Open(window_1);
  w2 := Window.Open(window_2);
  (* title each window *)
  Window.SetTitle(w1, 'put_into', Window.CenterUpperTitle);
  Window.SetTitle(w2, 'take_from', Window.CenterUpperTitle);
  CreateProcess(put_into);
  CreateProcess(take_from);
  Create(full, buffer_size);
  StartScheduler;
  (* close windows *)
  Window.Close(w1);
  Window.Close(w2);
END C16Q5.
```

Modula-2 Syntax

1. Programs, Program Modules and Separate Modules

1.1 Programs and Compilation Modules

compilation module ::= program module | definition module | implementation module

1.2 Program Module

program module ::=   MODULE module identifier [priority] ';'
                     import lists, module block, module identifier '.'
module identifier ::=   identifier
identifier ::=   letter | underscore {alphanumeric | underscore}
priority ::=   '[' constant expression ']'

1.3 Definition Module

definition module ::=   DEFINITION MODULE module identifier ';'
                        import lists, definitions END module identifier '.'

1.4 Implementation Module

implementation module ::= IMPLEMENTATION MODULE module identifier
                          '[' priority ']' ';'
                          import lists, module block, module identifier '.'

1.5 Import Lists

import lists ::= {import list}

1.5.1 Import List

import list ::= simple import | unqualified import

1.5.2 Simple Import

simple import ::=   IMPORT identifier list ';'
identifier list ::=   identifier {',' identifier}

1.5.3 Unqualified Import

unqualified import ::= FROM module identifier IMPORT identifier list ';'

1.6 Export List

export list ::= unqualified export | qualified export

1.6.1 Unqualified Export

unqualified export ::= EXPORT identifier list ';'

1.6.2 Qualified Export

qualified export ::= EXPORT QUALIFIED identifier list ';'

2. Definitions and Declarations

2.1 Qualified identifier

qualified identifier ::=   {module identifier '.'} identifier

2.2 Definitions

definitions ::=   {definition}
definition ::=   CONST {constant declaration ';'} |
                 TYPE {type definition ';'} |
                 VAR {variable declaration ';'} |
                 procedure heading ';'
procedure heading ::=   proper procedure heading | function procedure heading

2.2.1 Type Definitions

type definition ::=   type declaration | opaque type definition
opaque type definition ::=   identifier

2.2.2 Proper Procedure Heading

proper procedure heading ::=
                     PROCEDURE procedure identifier [formal parameters]
formal parameters ::=   '(' [formal parameter list] ')'
formal parameter list ::=   formal parameter {';' formal parameter}

2.2.3 Function Procedure Heading

function procedure heading ::=
PROCEDURE procedure identifier, formal parameters ':' function result type
function result type ::=   type identifier

2.2.4 Formal Parameters

formal parameter ::=   value parameter specification |
                       variable parameter specification

2.2.4.1 Value Parameters

value parameter specification ::= identifier list ':' formal type

2.2.4.2 Variable Parameters

variable parameter specification ::= **VAR** identifier list ':' formal type

2.3 Declarations

declarations ::= {declaration}
declaration ::= **CONST** {constant declaration ';'} |
                 TYPE {type declaration ';'} |
                 VAR {variable declaration ';'} |
                 procedure declaration ';'
                 local module declaration ';'

2.4 Constant Declarations

constant declaration ::= identifier '=' constant expression

2.5 Type Declarations

type declaration ::=   identifier '=' type denoter

2.6 Variable Declaration

variable declaration ::=   identifier list ':' type denoter

2.7 Procedure Declaration

procedure declaration ::=   proper procedure declaration |
                            function procedure declaration

2.8 Proper Procedure Declaration

proper procedure declaration ::=   proper procedure heading ';' **FORWARD** |
                                   (proper procedure block, procedure identifier)

procedure identifier ::=   identifier

2.8.1 Function Procedure Declaration

function procedure declaration ::=   function procedure heading ';' **FORWARD** |
                                     (function procedure block, procedure identifier)

note: *parenthesis ( ) implies a grouping of the productions*

2.9 Local Module Declaration

local module declaration ::=   **MODULE** module identifier [priority] ';'
                               import lists [export list] module block,
                               module identifier ';'

3. Types

3.1 Type Denoters and Ordinal Type Denoters

type denoter ::=   type identifier | new type
ordinal type denoter ::=   ordinal type identifier |new ordinal type
ordinal type identifier ::= type identifier

3.2 Type Identifiers

type identifier ::= qualified identifier
ordinal type identifier ::= type identifier

3.3 New Types

new type ::=   new ordinal type | set type | pointer type |
                   procedure type | array type | record type
new ordinal type ::= enumeration type | subrange type

3.3.1 Enumeration Types

enumeration type ::=   '(' identifier list ')'

3.3.2 Subrange Types

subrange type ::=   [range type] '[' constant expression ' .. ' constant expression ']'
range type ::=   ordinal type identifier

3.3.3 Set Types

set type ::=   **SET OF** base type
base type ::=   ordinal type denoter

Modula-2 Syntax

3.3.4 Pointer Types

pointer type ::=   **POINTER TO** bound type
bound type ::=   type denoter

3.3.5 Procedure Types

procedure type ::=   proper procedure type | function procedure type
proper procedure type ::=   **PROCEDURE** ['(' [formal parameter type list] ')']
function procedure type ::=   **PROCEDURE** '(' [formal parameter type list] ')'
    ':' function result type

function result type ::=   type identifier
formal parameter type list ::=   formal parameter type {';' formal parameter type}
formal parameter type ::=   variable formal type | value formal type
variable formal type ::=   **VAR** formal type
value formal type ::=   formal type

3.3.6 Formal Types

formal type ::=   type identifier | open array formal type
open array formal type ::=   **ARRAY OF** {**ARRAY OF**} type identifier

3.3.7 Array Types

array type ::=   **ARRAY** index type {',' index type } **OF** component type
index type ::=   ordinal type denoter
component type ::= type denoter

3.3.8 Record Types

record type ::=   **RECORD** field list **END**
field list ::=   fields {';' fields }
fields ::=   [fixed fields | variant fields]
fixed fields ::=   identifier list ':' field type
field type ::=   type denoter
variant fields ::=   **CASE** [tag identifier] ':' tag type **OF** variant list **END**
tag identifier ::=   identifier
tag type ::=   ordinal type identifier
variant list ::=   variant {'|' variant } [variant else part]
variant else part ::= **ELSE** field list
variant ::=   [variant label list ':' field list]
variant label list ::= variant label {';' variant label }
variant label ::=   constant expression ['..' constant expression]

4. Blocks

4.1 Proper Procedure Block

proper procedure block ::= declarations [procedure body] **END**
procedure body ::=   **BEGIN** block body

4.2 Function Procedure Block

function procedure block ::= declarations, function body, **END**
function body ::= **BEGIN** block body

4.3 Module Block

module block ::=   declarations [module body] **END**
module body ::=   **BEGIN** block body
block body ::=   statement sequence

5. Statements

statement ::=   empty statement | assignment statement | procedure call |
    return statement | with statement | if statement |
    case statement | while statement | repeat statement |
    loop statement | exit statement | for statement

5.1 Statement Sequence

statement sequence ::= statement {';' statement }

5.2 Empty Statements

empty statement ::=

5.3 Assignment Statements

assignment statement ::= variable designator, ':=', expression

5.4 Procedure Calls

procedure call ::= procedure designator [actual parameter]
procedure designator ::= value designator

5.5 Return Statements

return statement ::= simple return statement | function return statement

5.5.1 Simple return statements

simple return statement ::= **RETURN**

5.5.2 Function Return Statements

function return statement ::= **RETURN** expression

5.6 With Statements

with statement ::= **WITH** record designator **DO** statement sequence **END**

record designator ::= variable designator | value designator

5.7 If Statements

if statement ::=   guarded statements [if else part] **END**

guarded statements ::= **IF** Boolean expression **THEN** statement sequence

    {**ELSIF** Boolean expression **THEN** statement sequence }

if else part ::=   **ELSE** statement sequence

Boolean expression ::= expression

5.8 Case Statements

case statement ::=   **CASE** case selector **OF** case list **END**

case selector ::=   ordinal expression

case list ::=   case alternative {'|' case alternative } [case else part]

case else part ::=   **ELSE** statement sequence

5.8.1 Case Alternatives

case alternative ::= [case label list ':' statement sequence]

case label list ::=   case label {',' case label }

case label ::=   constant expression ['..' constant expression]

5.9 While Statements

while statement ::= **WHILE** Boolean expression **DO** statement sequence **END**

5.10 Repeat Statements

repeat statement ::= **REPEAT** statement sequence **UNTIL** Boolean expression

5.11 Loop Statements

loop statement ::= **LOOP** statement sequence **END**

5.12 Exit Statement

exit statement ::= **EXIT**

5.13 For Statements

for statement ::=   **FOR** control variable identifier ':=' initial value **TO**

    final value [**BY** step size] **DO** statement sequence **END**

control variable identifier ::=   identifier

initial value ::=   ordinal expression

final value ::=   ordinal expression

step size ::=   constant expression

6. Variable Designators

variable designator ::= entire designator | indexed designator | selected designator |

    dereferenced designator

6.1 Entire Designators

entire designator ::= qualified identifier

6.2 Indexed Designators

indexed designator ::=   array variable designator '[' index expression

    { ',' index expression } ']'

array variable designator ::=   variable designator

index expression ::=   ordinal expression

6.3 Selected Designators

selected designator ::=   record variable designator '.' field identifier

record variable designator ::=   variable designator

field identifier ::=   identifier

6.4 Dereferenced Designators

dereferenced designator ::=   pointer variable designator, '^'

pointer variable designator ::= variable designator

7. Expressions

expression ::=   simple expression [relational operator, simple expression]

Modula-2 Syntax

Modula-2 Syntax

simple expression ::= [sign] term {term operator, term}

term ::= factor {factor operator, factor}

factor ::= '(' expression ')' | logical negation operator, factor | value designator | function call | value constructor | constant literal

ordinal expresion ::= expression

7.1 Infix Expressions

relational operator ::= '=' | '<>' | '#' | '<' | '>' | '<=' | '>=' | 'IN'

term operator ::= '+' | '-' |

factor operator ::= '*' | '/' | 'DIV' | 'MOD'

7.2 Value Designators

value designator ::= entire value | indexed value | selected value | dereferenced value

7.2.1 Entire Values

entire value ::= qualified identifier

7.2.2 Indexed Values

indexed value ::= array value '[' index expression { ',' index expression } ']'

array value ::= value designator

7.2.3 Selected Values

selected value ::= record value '.' field identifier

record value ::= value designator

7.2.4 Dereferenced Values

dereferenced value ::= pointer value, '^'

pointer value ::= value designator

7.3 Function Calls

function call ::= function designator, actual parameters

function designator ::= value designator

8. Parameters

8.1 Actual Parameters

actual parameters = '(' [actual parameter list ')'

actual parameter list ::= actual parameter [',' actual parameter}

actual parameter ::= variable designator | expression | type parameter

8.2 Type parameters

type parameter ::= type identifier

9. Atomic items

9.1 Constant Literals

constant literal ::= numeric literal | string literal | pointer literal

9.1.1 Numeric Literals

numeric literal ::= whole number literal | real literal

9.1.1.1 Whole Number literals

whole number literal ::= decimal number | octal number | hexadecimal number

decimal number ::= digit {digit}

digit ::= '0' | '1' | '2' | '3' | '4' | '5' | '6' | '7' | '8' | '9'

octal number ::= octal digit {octal digit} 'B'

octal digit ::= '0' | '1' | '2' | '3' | '4' | '5' | '6' | '7'

hexadecimal number ::= digit {hex digit} 'H'

hex digit ::= '0' | '1' | '2' | '3' | '4' | '5' | '6' | '7' | '8' | '9' | 'A' | 'B' | 'C' | 'D' | 'E' | 'F'

9.1.1.2 Real Literals

real literal ::= digit {digit} '.' {digit} [scale factor]

scale factor ::= 'E' [sign] digit {digit}

9.1.2 String Literals

string literal ::= quoted string | quoted character | character number literal

```
quoted string ::=          '' {character} '''' | '''' {character} ''''
quoted character ::=       '' character '''' | '''' character ''''
character number literal ::= octal digit {octal digit} 'C'
```

9.1.2.1 Characters

```
character ::=              graphic character | format effector | space
graphic character ::=      alphanumeric | punctuation character |
                           implementation defined graphic

alphanumeric ::=           letter | digit
letter ::=                 'A'|'B'|'C'|'D'|'E'|'F'|'G'|'H'|'I'|'J'|'K'|'L'|'M'|'N'|'O'|'P'|
                           'Q'|'R'|'S'|'T'|'U'|'V'|'W'|'X'|'Y'|'Z'|
                           'a'|'b'|'c'|'d'|'e'|'f'|'g'|'h'|'i'|'j'|'k'|'l'|'m'|'n'|'o'|'p'|'q'|'r'|'s'|
                           't'|'u'|'v'|'w'|'x'|'y'|'z'

implementation defined graphic ::= implementation-defined character
punctuation character ::=  implementation-defined punctuation character
format effector ::=        implementation-defined format effector
```

9.1.3 Pointer Literals

```
pointer literal ::= NIL
```

9.2 Separators

```
separator ::=              white space | comment
white space ::=            space | newline | white space control
space ::=                  ' '
new line ::=               implementation-defined character sequence
white space control ::=    implementation-defined character sequence
comment ::=                '(*' comment body '*)'
comment body ::=           {character | separator}
```

Modula-2 Syntax

433

```
DEFINITION MODULE COROUTINES;
(* facilities for coroutines and the handling of interrupts *)

IMPORT SYSTEM;

TYPE
    COROUTINE;
    (* values of this type are created dynamically by
       NEWCOROUTINE and identify the coroutine in subsequent
       operations *)

PROCEDURE NEWCOROUTINE (procBody      : PROC;
                        workspace     : SYSTEM.ADDRESS;
                        size          : CARDINAL;
                        VAR cr        : COROUTINE);

(* creates a new coroutine whose body is given by procBody,
   and returns the identity of the coroutine in cr; workspace is
   a pointer to the work space allocated to the coroutine; size
   specifies the size of this workspace in terms of SYSTEM.LOC *)

PROCEDURE TRANSFER (VAR from : COROUTINE; to : COROUTINE);
(* returns the identity of the calling coroutine in from, and
   transfers control to the coroutine specified by to *)

PROCEDURE IOTRANSFER (VAR from : COROUTINE; to : COROUTINE);
(* returns the identity of the calling coroutine in from and
   transfers control to the coroutine specified by to; on occur-
   rence of an interrupt, associated with the caller, control is
   transferred back to the caller, and the identity of the inter-
   rupted coroutine is returned in from. The calling coroutine
   must be associated with a source of interrupts *)

PROCEDURE ATTACH (source : CARDINAL);
(* associates the specified source of interrupts with the
   calling coroutine *)

PROCEDURE DETACH (source : CARDINAL);
(* dissociates the specified source of interrupts from the
   calling coroutine *)

PROCEDURE IsATTACHED (source : CARDINAL) : BOOLEAN;
(* returns TRUE if and only if the specified source of inter-
   rupts is currently
   associated with a coroutine, otherwise returns FALSE *)

PROCEDURE HANDLER (source : CARDINAL) : COROUTINE;
(* returns the coroutine, if any, that is associated with the
   source of interrupts; the result is undefined if
```

```
DEFINITION MODULE ChanConsts;
(*
Common types and values for channel open requests and results
*)

TYPE
    ChanFlags =        (
                            readFlag,
                            writeFlag,
                            oldFlag
                        );

FlagSet = SET OF ChanFlags;

(* Singleton values of FlagSet, to allow for example,
   read + write *)

CONST
    read    = FlagSet{readFlag};
    write   = FlagSet{writeFlag};
    old     = FlagSet{oldFlag};

(* Possible results of open requests *)

TYPE
    OpenResults =      (
                            opened,
                            wrongFlags,
                            otherProblem
                        );

END ChanConsts.
```

IsATTACHED(source) = FALSE *)

PROCEDURE CURRENT() : COROUTINE;
(* returns the identity of the calling coroutine *)

END COROUTINES.

DEFINITION MODULE IOChan;

TYPE
    ChanId;

END IOChan.

DEFINITION MODULE IOConsts;

(* Type and constant for input modules *)

TYPE
    ReadResults =   (
                            notKnown,
                            allRight,
                            endOfInput
                        );

END IOConsts.

DEFINITION MODULE IOResult;

(* Read result for specified channel *)

IMPORT IOConsts, IOChan;

TYPE
    ReadResults = IOConsts.ReadResults;

PROCEDURE ReadResult(cid : IOChan.ChanId) :ReadResults;
(* Returns the result for the last read operation on the
channel cid *)

END IOResult.

```
DEFINITION MODULE RealIO;
(*
Input and output of real numbers in decimal text form over
specified channels
*)

IMPORT IOChan;

TYPE
    ChanId = IOChan.ChanId;

PROCEDURE ReadReal(cid : ChanId; VAR real:REAL);
(* Skips leading spaces, and removes any remaining characters
from cid that forms part of the signed fixed or floating
point number.The value of this number is assigned to real.
*)

PROCEDURE WriteFloat(cid : ChanId; real:REAL;
                sigFigs:CARDINAL; width:CARDINAL);

(* Writes the value of real to cid in floating-point text
form, with sigFigs significant figures, in a field of the
given minimum width.
*)

PROCEDURE WriteFixed(cid : ChanId; real:REAL; place:INTEGER;
                width:CARDINAL);

(* Writes the value of real to cid in fixed-point text form,
rounded to the given place relative to the decimal point, in
a field of the given minimum width.
*)

END RealIO.
```

```
DEFINITION MODULE RealMath;
(*
Mathematical functions for the type REAL
*)

CONST
    pi = 3.141593;
    exp1 = 2.718282;

PROCEDURE sqrt(x:REAL):REAL;
(* Returns the positive square root of x *)

PROCEDURE exp(x:REAL):REAL;
(* Returns the exponential of x *)

PROCEDURE ln(x:REAL):REAL;
(* Returns the natural logarithm of x *)

(* The angle in all trigonometric functions is measured in
radians *)

PROCEDURE sin(x:REAL):REAL;
(* Returns the sine of x *)

PROCEDURE cos(x:REAL):REAL;
(* Returns the cosine of x *)

PROCEDURE tan(x:REAL):REAL;
(* Returns the tangent of x *)

PROCEDURE arcsin(x:REAL):REAL;
(* Returns the arcsine of x *)

PROCEDURE arccos(x:REAL):REAL;
(* Returns the arccosine of x *)

PROCEDURE arctan(x:REAL):REAL;
(* Returns the arctangent of x *)

PROCEDURE power(base, exponent:REAL):REAL;
(* Returns the value of the number base raised to the power
exponent *)

END RealMath.
```

DEFINITION MODULE SRealIO;

(*
Input and output of real numbers in decimal text form over the
default channels for keyboard input and screen output
*)

PROCEDURE ReadReal(VAR real:REAL);

(* Skips leading spaces, and removes any remaining characters
from the default input channel that forms part of the signed
fixed or floating point number. The value of this number is
assigned to real.
*)

PROCEDURE WriteFloat(real:REAL; sigFigs:CARDINAL;
                     width:CARDINAL);

(* Writes the value of real to the default output channel in
floating-point text form, with sigFigs significant figures,
in a field of the given minimum width.
*)

PROCEDURE WriteFixed(real:REAL; place:INTEGER;
                     width:CARDINAL);

(* Writes the value of real to the default output channel in
fixed-point text form, rounded to the given place relative to
the decimal point, in a field of the given minimum width.
*)

END SRealIO.

DEFINITION MODULE STextIO;

(* Input and output of characters and string types over default channels *)

(* The following procedures do not read past line marks *)

PROCEDURE ReadChar(VAR ch:CHAR);

(* If possible, removes a character from the default input
stream, and assigns the corresponding value to ch.
*)

PROCEDURE ReadString(VAR s:ARRAY OF CHAR);

(* Removes only those characters from the default input
stream before the next line mark that can be accommodated in
s as a string value, and copies them to s.
*)

(* The following procedure reads past the next line mark *)

PROCEDURE SkipLine;

(* Removes successive items from the default input stream up
to and including the next line mark or until the end of input
is reached.
*)

(* Output procedures *)

PROCEDURE WriteChar(ch:CHAR);

(* Writes the value of ch to the default output stream. *)

PROCEDURE WriteLn;

(* Writes a line mark to the default output stream. *)

PROCEDURE WriteString(s:ARRAY OF CHAR);

(* Writes the string value of s to the default output stream.
*)

END STextIO.

Appendix III

DEFINITION MODULE StreamFile;
(* Independent sequential data streams *)

IMPORT IOChan, ChanConsts;

TYPE
```
    ChanId      = IOChan.ChanId;
    FlagSet     = ChanConsts.FlagSet;
    OpenResults = ChanConsts.OpenResults;
```

(* Accepted singleton values of FlagSet *)

```
CONST
    read    = FlagSet{ChanConsts.readFlag};
    write   = FlagSet{ChanConsts.writeFlag};
    old     = FlagSet{ChanConsts.oldFlag};
```

PROCEDURE Open (VAR cid : ChanId; name : ARRAY OF CHAR;
               flags : FlagSet; VAR res : OpenResults);

(*
Attempts to obtain and open a channel connected to a sequential stream of the given name. The read flag implies old
(file exists). If successful, assigns to cid the identity of
the opened channel, and assigns the value opened to res.*)

PROCEDURE Close (VAR cid : ChanId);
(*
Closes the channel
*)

END StreamFile.

DEFINITION MODULE StringType;
IMPORT IO;

TYPE
    string = ARRAY[0..IO.MaxRdLength - 1] OF CHAR;

END StringType.

DEFINITION MODULE Strings;
(* Facilities for manipulating strings *)

PROCEDURE Length(stringVal:ARRAY OF CHAR):CARDINAL;
(* returns the length of stringVal *)

PROCEDURE Assign(source:ARRAY OF CHAR;
                 VAR destination:ARRAY OF CHAR);
(* copies source to destination *)

PROCEDURE Append(source:ARRAY OF CHAR;
                 VAR destination:ARRAY OF CHAR);
(* appends source to destination *)

PROCEDURE Concat(source1, source2:ARRAY OF CHAR;
                 VAR destination:ARRAY OF CHAR);
(* concatenates source2 onto source1 and copy the result into
destination *)

TYPE
    CompareResults = (less, equal, greater);

PROCEDURE Compare(stringVal1,
                  stringVal2:ARRAY OF CHAR):CompareResults;

(* Returns less, equal or greater according as stringVal1 is
lexically less than, equal to, or greater than stringVal2 *)

PROCEDURE Equal(stringVal1,
                stringVal2:ARRAY OF CHAR):BOOLEAN;
(* Returns Strngs.Compare(stringVal1, stringVal2)
=Strings.equal *)

PROCEDURE Capitalize(VAR stringVar : ARRAY OF CHAR);
(* Applies the function CAP to each character of the string
value in stringVar *)

END Strings.

```
DEFINITION MODULE SysClock;
(*
facilities for accessing a system clock that records the date
and time of day *)

CONST
    maxSecondParts = 100;

TYPE
    Month    =  [1..12];
    Day      =  [1..31];
    Hour     =  [0..23];
    Min      =  [0..59];
    Sec      =  [0..59];
    Fraction =  [0..maxSecondParts];
    UTCDiff  =  [-780..720];

    DateTime = RECORD
                 year      : CARDINAL;
                 month     : Month;
                 day       : Day;
                 hour      : Hour;
                 minute    : Min;
                 second    : Sec;
                 fractions : Fraction;
                 zone      : UTCDiff;
               END;

(* fractional parts of a second *)

(* Time zone Differential Factor which is the numberof min-
utes to add to local time to obtain UTC *)
                                summerTimeFlag : BOOLEAN;

(* Interpretation of flag depends on local usage *)
               END;

PROCEDURE CanGetClock() : BOOLEAN;
(* tests if a system clock can be read *)

PROCEDURE CanSetClock() : BOOLEAN;
(* tests if a system clock can be set *)

PROCEDURE IsValidDateTime(userData : DateTime) : BOOLEAN;
(* tests if the values of userData represent a valid date and
time *)

PROCEDURE GetClock(VAR userData : DateTime);
(* if possible, assigns system date and time of day to
userData *)

PROCEDURE SetClock(userData : DateTime);
(* if possible, sets the system clock to the values of
userData *)

END SysClock.
```

```
DEFINITION MODULE SWholeIO;

(* Input and output of whole numbers in decimal text form
over the default channels of keyboard input and screen output
*)

PROCEDURE ReadInt(VAR int:INTEGER);
(* Skips leading spaces, and removes any remaining characters
from the default input channel that form part of a signed
whole number. The value of this number is assigned to int.
*)

PROCEDURE WriteInt(int:INTEGER; width:CARDINAL);
(* Writes the value of int to the default output channel in
text form, in a field of the given minimum width.
*)

PROCEDURE ReadCard(VAR card:CARDINAL);
(* Skips leading spaces, and removes any remaining characters
from the default input channel that form part of an unsigned
whole number. The value of this number is assigned to card.
*)

PROCEDURE WriteCard(card:CARDINAL; width:CARDINAL);
(* Writes the value of card to the default output channel in
text form, in a field of the given minimum width.
*)

END SWholeIO.
```

Appendix III

```
DEFINITION MODULE _SYSTEM;

IMPORT SYSTEM; (* from TopSpeed Modula-2 *)

CONST TSIZE ::= SIZE;

TYPE
  LOC     = SYSTEM.BYTE;
  ADDRESS = POINTER TO LOC;

END _SYSTEM.
```

```
DEFINITION MODULE TextIO;
(* Input and output of characters and string types over speci-
fied channels *)

(* The following procedures do not read past line marks *)

IMPORT IOChan;
TYPE
  ChanId = IOChan.ChanId;

PROCEDURE ReadChar(cid:ChanId; VAR ch:CHAR);
(* If possible, removes a character from the input stream
cid, and assigns the corresponding value to ch. The read re-
sult is set to the value allRight, endOfLine,
or endOfInput.
*)

PROCEDURE ReadString(cid:ChanId; VAR s:ARRAY OF CHAR);
(* Removes only those characters from the input stream cid be-
fore the next line mark that can be accommodated in s as a
string value, and copies them to s. The read result is set to
the value allRight, endOfLine,
or endOfInput.
*)

(* The following procedure reads past the next line mark *)

PROCEDURE SkipLine(cid:ChanId);
(* Removes successive items from the input stream cid up to
and including the next line mark or until the end of input is
reached. The read result is set to the value
allRight, or endOfInput.
*)

(* Output procedures *)

PROCEDURE WriteChar(cid:ChanId; ch:CHAR);
(* Writes the value of ch to the output stream cid. *)

PROCEDURE WriteLn(cid:ChanId);
(* Writes a line mark to the output stream cid. *)

PROCEDURE WriteString(cid:ChanId; s:ARRAY OF CHAR);
(* Writes the string value of s to the output stream cid. *)

END TextIO.
```

```
DEFINITION MODULE WholeIO;
(*
Input and output of whole numbers in decimal text form over
specified channels
*)

IMPORT IOChan;

TYPE
    ChanId = IOChan.ChanId;

PROCEDURE ReadInt(cid : ChanId; VAR int:INTEGER);
(* Skips leading spaces, and removes any remaining characters
from cid that form part of a signed whole number. The value
of this number is assigned to int.
*)

PROCEDURE WriteInt(cid : ChanId; int:INTEGER; width:CARDINAL);
(* Writes the value of int to the default output channel in
text form, in a field of the given minimum width.
*)

PROCEDURE ReadCard(cid : ChanId; VAR card:CARDINAL);
(* Skips leading spaces, and removes any remaining characters
from the default input channel that form part of an unsigned
whole number. The value of this number is assigned to card.
*)

PROCEDURE WriteCard(cid : ChanId; card:CARDINAL;
                    width:CARDINAL);
(* Writes the value of card to the default output channel in
text form, in a field of the given minimum width.
*)

END WholeIO.
```

```
IMPLEMENTATION MODULE ChanConsts;
END ChanConsts.

IMPLEMENTATION MODULE COROUTINES;

IMPORT Storage;
IMPORT SYSTEM;
IMPORT STextIO;

TYPE
    COROUTINE = POINTER TO ADDRESS;
    pointer   = POINTER TO node;

    node = RECORD
               id                : COROUTINE;
               interrupt_flag    : BOOLEAN;
               interrupt_source  : CARDINAL;
               link              : pointer;
           END;

VAR
    coroutine_list    : pointer;
    temp_coroutine    : pointer;
    new_coroutine     : pointer;
    current_coroutine : COROUTINE;
    main              : COROUTINE;
    main_found        : BOOLEAN;
    coroutine_found   : BOOLEAN;

PROCEDURE find_interrupt_source(from : COROUTINE;
                VAR source : CARDINAL) : BOOLEAN;

(* given a coroutine find the interrupt source that has been
attached to it; if successful return TRUE, otherwise return
FALSE *)

BEGIN
    temp_coroutine := coroutine_list;
    WHILE temp_coroutine # NIL DO
        IF (temp_coroutine^.id = from) AND
           (temp_coroutine^.interrupt_flag) THEN
            source := temp_coroutine^.interrupt_source;
            RETURN TRUE;
        END;
        temp_coroutine := temp_coroutine^.link;
    END;
    RETURN FALSE;
END find_interrupt_source;

PROCEDURE IsATTACHED(source : CARDINAL) : BOOLEAN;
BEGIN
    temp_coroutine := coroutine_list;
```

```
    WHILE temp_coroutine # NIL DO
        IF (temp_coroutine^.interrupt_source = source) AND
           (temp_coroutine^.interrupt_flag) THEN
            RETURN TRUE;
        END;
        temp_coroutine := temp_coroutine^.link;
    END;
    RETURN FALSE;
END IsATTACHED;

PROCEDURE HANDLER(source : CARDINAL) : COROUTINE;
BEGIN
    IF IsATTACHED(source) THEN
        RETURN temp_coroutine^.id.
    END;
END HANDLER;

PROCEDURE NEWCOROUTINE (body             : PROC;
                        workspace        : SYSTEM.ADDRESS;
                        size             : CARDINAL;
                        VAR cr           : COROUTINE);

VAR
    new_coroutine : pointer;

BEGIN
    SYSTEM.NEWPROCESS(body, ADDRESS(workspace), size, cr);
    Storage.ALLOCATE(new_coroutine, SIZE(node));
    new_coroutine^.id              := cr;
    new_coroutine^.interrupt_flag  := FALSE;
    new_coroutine^.link            := coroutine_list;
    coroutine_list                 := new_coroutine;
END NEWCOROUTINE;

PROCEDURE CURRENT() : COROUTINE;
BEGIN
    RETURN current_coroutine;
END CURRENT;

PROCEDURE ATTACH (source : CARDINAL);
BEGIN
    temp_coroutine := coroutine_list;
    WHILE temp_coroutine # NIL DO
        IF temp_coroutine^.id = CURRENT() THEN
            WITH temp_coroutine^ DO
                interrupt_source := source;
                interrupt_flag := TRUE;
                RETURN;
            END;
        END;
        temp_coroutine := temp_coroutine^.link;
    END;
END ATTACH;
```

```
PROCEDURE DETACH(source : CARDINAL);
BEGIN
  temp_coroutine := coroutine_list;
  WHILE temp_coroutine # NIL DO
    IF (temp_coroutine^.id = CURRENT())
      AND (temp_coroutine^.interrupt_flag) THEN
        temp_coroutine^.interrupt_flag := FALSE;
    END;
    temp_coroutine := temp_coroutine^.link;
  END;
END DETACH;

PROCEDURE TRANSFER (VAR from : COROUTINE; to : COROUTINE);
VAR
  main_node : pointer;
BEGIN
  (* search for main coroutine in linked list *)
  temp_coroutine := coroutine_list;
  coroutine_found := FALSE;
  WHILE NOT main_found AND (temp_coroutine # NIL) DO
    IF temp_coroutine^.id = to THEN
      coroutine_found := TRUE;
    END;
    main_node := temp_coroutine;
    temp_coroutine := temp_coroutine^.link;
  END;

  (* if main found then assign true identity of main *)
  IF coroutine_found THEN
    coroutine_found := FALSE;
  ELSE
    IF NOT main_found THEN
      main_found := TRUE;
      main_node^.id := to;
    END;
  END;

  current_coroutine := to;
  SYSTEM.TRANSFER(from,to);
END TRANSFER;

PROCEDURE IOTRANSFER (VAR from : COROUTINE; to : COROUTINE);
VAR
  interrupt_vector : CARDINAL;
BEGIN
  IF find_interrupt_source(from, interrupt_vector) THEN
    current_coroutine := to;
    SYSTEM.IOTRANSFER(from, to, interrupt_vector);
    RETURN;
  ELSE
    STextIO.WriteString('FATAL ERROR - CALLING COROUTINE
                         NOT ATTACHED'+
                        ' TO SOURCE OF INTERRUPT');
    HALT;
  END;
END IOTRANSFER;

BEGIN
  coroutine_list := NIL;
  current_coroutine := main;
  main_found := FALSE;
  coroutine_found := FALSE;

  (* store initial node to represent main routine *)
  Storage.ALLOCATE(new_coroutine, SIZE(node));
  new_coroutine^.id            := main;
  new_coroutine^.interrupt_flag := FALSE;
  new_coroutine^.link          := coroutine_list;
  coroutine_list := new_coroutine;
END COROUTINES.

IMPLEMENTATION MODULE IOChan;
IMPORT FIO;

TYPE ChanId = POINTER TO FIO.File;

BEGIN
  FIO.IOcheck := FALSE;
END IOChan.

IMPLEMENTATION MODULE IOConsts;
END IOConsts.

IMPLEMENTATION MODULE IOResult;

FROM STextIO IMPORT WriteString, WriteLn;
IMPORT FIO;

PROCEDURE ReadResult(cid:IOChan.ChanId):ReadResults;
VAR
  ErrorCode : CARDINAL;
BEGIN
  ErrorCode:=FIO.IOresult();
  IF (ErrorCode = 0) AND NOT FIO.EOF THEN
    RETURN IOConsts.allRight;
  ELSIF FIO.EOF = TRUE THEN
    RETURN IOConsts.endOfInput;
  ELSIF ErrorCode > 0 THEN
    RETURN IOConsts.notKnown;
```

```
  END;
END ReadResult;

END IOResult.


IMPLEMENTATION MODULE RealIO;

IMPORT FIO; IMPORT IO;
IMPORT Str;
IMPORT StringType;

PROCEDURE ReadReal(cid : ChanId; VAR real:REAL);
BEGIN
  real:=FIO.RdReal(FIO.File(cid));
END ReadReal;

PROCEDURE WriteFloat(cid : ChanId; real:REAL;
                     sigFigs:CARDINAL; width:CARDINAL);
BEGIN
  FIO.WrReal(FIO.File(cid), real, sigFigs, width);
END WriteFloat;

PROCEDURE WriteFixed(cid : ChanId; real:REAL;
                     place:INTEGER; width:CARDINAL);
VAR
  number : StringType.string;
  flag   : BOOLEAN;
BEGIN
  Str.FixRealToStr(LONGREAL(real), CARDINAL(place),
                   number, flag);
  FIO.WrStrAdj(FIO.File(cid), number, width);
END WriteFixed;

BEGIN
  FIO.Eng:=FALSE;
END RealIO.


IMPLEMENTATION MODULE RealMath;

IMPORT MATHLIB;

PROCEDURE sqrt(x:REAL):REAL;
BEGIN
  RETURN REAL(MATHLIB.Sqrt(LONGREAL(x)));
END sqrt;

PROCEDURE exp(x:REAL):REAL;
BEGIN
  RETURN REAL(MATHLIB.Exp(LONGREAL(x)));
END exp;

PROCEDURE ln(x:REAL):REAL;
BEGIN
  RETURN REAL(MATHLIB.Log(LONGREAL(x)));
END ln;

PROCEDURE sin(x:REAL):REAL;
BEGIN
  RETURN REAL(MATHLIB.Sin(LONGREAL(x)));
END sin;

PROCEDURE cos(x:REAL):REAL;
BEGIN
  RETURN REAL(MATHLIB.Cos(LONGREAL(x)));
END cos;

PROCEDURE tan(x:REAL):REAL;
BEGIN
  RETURN REAL(MATHLIB.Tan(LONGREAL(x)));
END tan;

PROCEDURE arcsin(x:REAL):REAL;
BEGIN
  RETURN REAL(MATHLIB.ASin(LONGREAL(x)));
END arcsin;

PROCEDURE arccos(x:REAL):REAL;
BEGIN
  RETURN REAL(MATHLIB.ACos(LONGREAL(x)));
END arccos;

PROCEDURE arctan(x:REAL):REAL;
BEGIN
  RETURN REAL(MATHLIB.ATan(LONGREAL(x)));
END arctan;

PROCEDURE power(base, exponent:REAL):REAL;
BEGIN
  RETURN REAL(MATHLIB.Pow(LONGREAL(base),
                          LONGREAL(exponent)));
END power;

END RealMath.


IMPLEMENTATION MODULE SRealIO;
IMPORT IO;
IMPORT Str; IMPORT StringType;

PROCEDURE ReadReal(VAR real:REAL);
BEGIN
  real:=IO.RdReal();
END ReadReal;
```

```
PROCEDURE WriteFloat(real:REAL; sigFigs:CARDINAL;
                     width:CARDINAL);
BEGIN
  IO.WrReal(real, sigFigs, width);
END WriteFloat;

PROCEDURE WriteFixed(real:REAL; place:INTEGER;
                     width:CARDINAL);
VAR
  number : StringType.string;
  flag   : BOOLEAN;
BEGIN
  Str.FixRealToStr(LONGREAL(real), CARDINAL(place),
                   number, flag);
  IO.WrStrAdj(number, width);
END WriteFixed;

BEGIN
  IO.Prompt:=FALSE;
  IO.RdLnOnWr:=FALSE;
  IO.Eng:=FALSE;
END SRealIO.

IMPLEMENTATION MODULE STextIO;
IMPORT IO;

PROCEDURE ReadChar(VAR ch:CHAR);
BEGIN
  ch:=IO.RdChar();
END ReadChar;

PROCEDURE ReadString(VAR s:ARRAY OF CHAR);
BEGIN
  IO.RdStr(s);
END ReadString;

PROCEDURE SkipLine;
BEGIN
  IO.RdLn;
END SkipLine;

PROCEDURE WriteChar(ch:CHAR);
BEGIN
  IO.WrChar(ch);
END WriteChar;

PROCEDURE WriteLn;
BEGIN
  IO.WrLn;
END WriteLn;

PROCEDURE WriteString(s:ARRAY OF CHAR);
BEGIN
  IO.WrStr(s);
END WriteString;

BEGIN
  IO.Prompt := FALSE;
  IO.RdLnOnWr := FALSE;
END STextIO.

IMPLEMENTATION MODULE StreamFile;
IMPORT FIO;

PROCEDURE Open (VAR cid : ChanId; name : ARRAY OF CHAR;
                flags : FlagSet; VAR res : OpenResults);
VAR
  io_result : CARDINAL;

BEGIN
  FIO.IOcheck := FALSE;
  IF (flags = read) OR (flags = old) OR (flags = read+old)
  THEN
    cid := ChanId(FIO.Open(name));
  ELSIF flags = write THEN
    cid := ChanId(FIO.Create(name));
  ELSIF flags = write+old THEN
    cid := ChanId(FIO.Open(name));
  ELSE
    res := ChanConsts.wrongFlags;
  END;

  io_result := FIO.IOresult();
  IF io_result = 0 THEN
    res := ChanConsts.opened;
  ELSE
    res := ChanConsts.otherProblem;
  END;
END Open;

PROCEDURE Close(VAR cid : ChanId);
BEGIN
  FIO.Close(FIO.File(cid));
END Close;

END StreamFile.

IMPLEMENTATION MODULE StringType.
END StringType.
```

```
IMPLEMENTATION MODULE Strings;
IMPORT Str;

PROCEDURE Length(stringVal:ARRAY OF CHAR):CARDINAL;
BEGIN
    RETURN Str.Length(stringVal);
END Length;

PROCEDURE Assign(source:ARRAY OF CHAR;
                 VAR destination:ARRAY OF CHAR);
BEGIN
    Str.Copy(destination, source);
END Assign;

PROCEDURE Append(source:ARRAY OF CHAR;
                 VAR destination:ARRAY OF CHAR);
BEGIN
    Str.Append(destination, source);
END Append;

PROCEDURE Concat(source1, source2:ARRAY OF CHAR;
                 VAR destination:ARRAY OF CHAR);
BEGIN
    Str.Concat(destination, source1, source2);
END Concat;

PROCEDURE Compare(stringVal1,
                  stringVal2:ARRAY OF CHAR):CompareResults;
VAR
    result : INTEGER;
BEGIN
    result := Str.Compare(stringVal1, stringVal2);
    IF result < 0 THEN
        RETURN less;
    ELSE
        IF result = 0 THEN
            RETURN equal;
        ELSE
            RETURN greater;
        END;
    END;
END Compare;

PROCEDURE Equal(stringVal1, stringVal2:ARRAY OF CHAR):BOOLEAN;
BEGIN
    IF Compare(stringVal1, stringVal2) = equal THEN
        RETURN TRUE;
    ELSE
        RETURN FALSE;
    END;
END Equal;
```

```
PROCEDURE Capitalize(VAR stringVar:ARRAY OF CHAR);
BEGIN
    Str.Caps(stringVar);
END Capitalize;

END Strings.

IMPLEMENTATION MODULE SWholeIO;

IMPORT IO;

PROCEDURE ReadInt(VAR int:INTEGER);
BEGIN
    int:=IO.RdInt();
END ReadInt;

PROCEDURE WriteInt(int:INTEGER; width:CARDINAL);
BEGIN
    IO.WrInt(int, width);
END WriteInt;

PROCEDURE ReadCard(VAR card:CARDINAL);
BEGIN
    card:=IO.RdCard();
END ReadCard;

PROCEDURE WriteCard(card:CARDINAL; width:CARDINAL);
BEGIN
    IO.WrCard(card, width);
END WriteCard;

BEGIN
    IO.Prompt:=FALSE;
    IO.RdLnOnWr:=FALSE;
END SWholeIO.

IMPLEMENTATION MODULE SysClock;

IMPORT Lib;
IMPORT SYSTEM;

VAR
    r : SYSTEM.Registers;

PROCEDURE CanGetClock() : BOOLEAN;
BEGIN
    RETURN TRUE;
END CanGetClock;
```

```
PROCEDURE CanSetClock() : BOOLEAN;
BEGIN
    RETURN TRUE;
END CanSetClock;

PROCEDURE IsValidDateTime(userData : DateTime) : BOOLEAN;
VAR
    days_in_month : CARDINAL;

BEGIN
    WITH userData DO

        (* validate date *)

        CASE month OF
        2               :  IF year MOD 4 = 0 THEN
                              days_in_month := 29;
                           ELSE
                              days_in_month := 28;
                           END |
        4,6,9,11        :  days_in_month := 30 |
        1,3,5,7,8,10,12 :  days_in_month := 31 ;
        ELSE
              RETURN FALSE;
        END;

        IF   (month < 1) OR (month > 12) OR
             (day   < 1) OR (day   > days_in_month) THEN
              RETURN FALSE;
        END;

        (* validate time *)
        IF   (hour < 0)       OR (hour > 23) OR
             (minute < 0)     OR (minute > 59) OR
             (second < 0)     OR (second > 59) OR
             (fractions < 0)  OR
             (fractions > maxSecondParts) THEN
              RETURN FALSE;
        END;

    END;

    RETURN TRUE;

END IsValidDateTime;

PROCEDURE GetClock(VAR userData : DateTime);
VAR
    YY                              : CARDINAL;
    MM, DD, Hrs, Mins, Secs, Hsecs : SHORTCARD;

BEGIN
    r.AH := 2AH;
    Lib.Dos(r);
```

```
    YY := r.CX;
    MM := r.DH;
    DD := r.DL;

    r.AH := 2CH;
    Lib.Dos(r);
    Hrs   := r.CH;
    Mins  := r.CL;
    Secs  := r.DH;
    Hsecs := r.DL;

    WITH userData DO
        year           := YY;
        month          := CARDINAL(MM);
        day            := CARDINAL(DD);
        hour           := CARDINAL(Hrs);
        minute         := CARDINAL(Mins);
        second         := CARDINAL(Secs);
        fractions      := CARDINAL(Hsecs);
        zone           := 0;       (* zone value for England *)
        summerTimeFlag := FALSE;   (* assume Winter *)
    END;

END GetClock;

PROCEDURE SetClock(userData : DateTime);
BEGIN
    WITH userData DO
        r.CX := year;
        r.DH := SHORTCARD(month);
        r.DL := SHORTCARD(day);
        r.AH := 2BH;
        Lib.Dos(r);

        r.CH := SHORTCARD(hour);
        r.CL := SHORTCARD(minute);
        r.DH := SHORTCARD(second);
        r.DL := SHORTCARD(fractions);
        r.AH := 2DH;
        Lib.Dos(r);

    END;
END SetClock;

END SysClock.

IMPLEMENTATION MODULE _SYSTEM;
END _SYSTEM.
```

Appendix IV

```
IMPLEMENTATION MODULE TextIO;
IMPORT FIO; IMPORT IO;

PROCEDURE ReadChar(cid:ChanId; VAR ch:CHAR);
BEGIN
   ch:=FIO.RdChar(FIO.File(cid));
END ReadChar;

PROCEDURE ReadString(cid:ChanId; VAR s:ARRAY OF CHAR);
BEGIN
   FIO.RdStr(FIO.File(cid),s);
END ReadString;

PROCEDURE SkipLine(cid:ChanId);
VAR
  line : ARRAY[0..IO.MaxRdLength - 1] OF CHAR;

BEGIN
   ReadString(cid, line);
END SkipLine;

PROCEDURE WriteChar(cid:ChanId; ch:CHAR);
BEGIN
   FIO.WrChar(FIO.File(cid),ch);
END WriteChar;

PROCEDURE WriteLn(cid:ChanId);
BEGIN
   FIO.WrLn(FIO.File(cid));
END WriteLn;

PROCEDURE WriteString(cid:ChanId; s:ARRAY OF CHAR);
BEGIN
   FIO.WrStr(FIO.File(cid),s);
END WriteString;

END TextIO.


IMPLEMENTATION MODULE WholeIO;

IMPORT FIO;

PROCEDURE ReadInt(cid : ChanId; VAR int:INTEGER);
BEGIN
   int:=FIO.RdInt(FIO.File(cid));
END ReadInt;

PROCEDURE WriteInt(cid : ChanId; int:INTEGER; width:CARDINAL);
BEGIN
   FIO.WrInt(FIO.File(cid), int, width);
END WriteInt;

PROCEDURE ReadCard(cid : ChanId; VAR card:CARDINAL);
BEGIN
   card:=FIO.RdCard(FIO.File(cid));
END ReadCard;

PROCEDURE WriteCard(cid : ChanId; card:CARDINAL; width:CARDI-
NAL);
BEGIN
   FIO.WrCard(FIO.File(cid), card, width);
END WriteCard;

END WholeIO.
```

Appendix V

code	character	code	character	code	character
000	NUL	043	+	086	V
001	SOH	044	,	087	W
002	STX	045	-	088	X
003	ETX	046	.	089	Y
004	EOT	047	/	090	Z
005	ENQ	048	0	091	[
006	ACK	049	1	092	\
007	BEL	050	2	093	]
008	BS	051	3	094	^
009	HT	052	4	095	_
010	LF	053	5	096	`
011	VT	054	6	097	a
012	FF	055	7	098	b
013	CR	056	8	099	c
014	SO	057	9	100	d
015	SI	058	:	101	e
016	DLE	059	;	102	f
017	DC1	060	<	103	g
018	DC2	061	=	104	h
019	DC3	062	>	105	i
020	DC4	063	?	106	j
021	NAK	064	@	107	k
022	SYN	065	A	108	l
023	ETB	066	B	109	m
024	CAN	067	C	110	n
025	EM	068	D	111	o
026	SUB	069	E	112	p
027	ESC	070	F	113	q
028	FS	071	G	114	r
029	GS	072	H	115	s
030	RS	073	I	116	t
031	US	074	J	117	u
032	space	075	K	118	v
033	!	076	L	119	w
034	"	077	M	120	x
035	#	078	N	121	y
036	$	079	O	122	z
037	%	080	P	123	{
038	&	081	Q	124	|
039	'	082	R	125	}
040	(	083	S	126	~
041	)	084	T	127	del
042	*	085	U		

	0C	1C	2C	3C	4C	5C	6C	7C
000C	NUL	SOH	STX	ETX	EOT	ENQ	ACK	BEL
010C	BS	HT	LF	VT	FF	CR	SO	SI
020C	DLE	DC1	DC2	DC3	DC4	NAK	SYN	ETB
030C	CAN	EM	SUB	ESC	FS	GS	RS	US
040C	space	!	"	#	$	%	&	'
050C	(	)	*	+	,	-	.	/
060C	0	1	2	3	4	5	6	7
070C	8	9	:	;	<	=	>	?
100C	@	A	B	C	D	E	F	G
110C	H	I	J	K	L	M	N	O
120C	P	Q	R	S	T	U	V	W
130C	X	Y	Z	[	\	]	^	_
140C	`	a	b	c	d	e	f	g
150C	h	i	j	k	l	m	n	o
160C	p	q	r	s	t	u	v	w
170C	x	y	z	{	|	}	~	DEL

The corresponding ASCII code, in octal, can be found by locating the required character in the table, for example Z, and summing the corresponding row and column values (130C + 2C) = 132. Note 132 (base 8) is the same as 90 (base 10).

Bibliography

British Standards Institute, Leicester University,
Andrews, D.J, Cornelius, B.J, Henry, R.B, Sutcliffe,R, Ward, D.P, Woodman, M
Information technology - Programming Languages - Modula-2; 2nd Committee Draft Standard:
CD 10514 ; Document ISO/IEC JTC1/SC22/WG13 D181 December 1992

Helman, P & Veroff, R
Intermediate Problem Solving and Data Structures - Walls and Mirrors, Benjamin Cummings 1986

Holmes, B.J
Modula-2 Programming (first edition), DP Publications 1989
Holmes, B.J
Introductory Pascal, DP Publications 1993

Jensen & Partners International
TopSpeed Modula-2 Language and Reference 1991

King, K.N
TopSpeed Modula-2 Language Tutorial 1991

Koffman, E.B
Problem Solving and Structured programming in Modula-2, Addison-Wesley 1988

Pomberger, G
Software Engineering in Modula-2, Prentice-Hall 1984

Sale, A
Modula-2 Discipline and Design, Addison-Wesley 1986

Stubbs, D.F & Webre, N.W
Data Structures with Abstract Data Types and Pascal, Brooks/Cole 1985

Welsh, J & Elder, J
Introduction to Modula-2, Prentice-Hall 1987

Wirth, N
Programming in Modula-2, Springer-Verlag 1985

Index